1970

S0-AYE-934

Loeb Classical Monographs

ROMANS ON THE BAY OF NAPLES · *A Social and Cultural Study of the Villas and Their Owners from 150 B.C. to A.D. 400* · JOHN H. D'ARMS

Harvard University Press · Cambridge Massachusetts · 1970

PARENTIBUS OPTIMIS

PREFACE

It was the practice of ancient geographers and historians, when moved to write of Roman Campania, to separate discussion of the inland towns from their accounts of the cities of the coast. Of the maritime cities common to the lists of Strabo and the Elder Pliny—for they are generally agreed to comprise the canonical register [1]—Cumae, Dicaearchia (Roman Puteoli), and Neapolis were pre-eminent in antiquity and fame. There Romans first encountered Greek civilization directly, in cities set along an indented shoreline amid volcanic craters, sulphurous soil, and mineral springs. This portion of the coast, say both Polybius and Strabo, was known familiarly as the "Crater"; [2] it was the gulf which, bounded on the northwest by Cape Misenum, and on the south by Cape Athenaeum, forms the Bay of Naples. Around the "Crater" were the *Campi Phlegraei* of forbidding aspect, associated in myth and legend with gigantomachy, the workshops of Vulcan, and the dark approaches to the infernal regions. [3] But by Cicero's day the coast glittered with luxurious villas of the Roman upper classes; he calls the region *cratera illum delicatum*—"the Bay of Luxury." [4] In Augustan times Strabo concluded his account of the "Crater" with the observation that an unbroken succession of houses and

[1] Volturnum, Liternum, Cumae, Misenum, Baiae, Dicaearchia, Neapolis, Herculaneum, Pompeii, Stabiae, and Surrentum: Strab. 5.4.4 (C 243); Pliny *NH* 3.61–2; cf. Polyb. 3.91.4. See further, H. Nissen, *Italische Landeskunde* II (Berlin 1902), 717–752.

[2] Strab. 5.4.3 (C 242): μέχρι Μισηνοῦ, κἀκεῖθεν ἄλλος κόλπος πολὺ μείζων τοῦ προτέρου, καλοῦσι δ' αὐτὸν Κρατῆρα, ἀπὸ τοῦ Μισηνοῦ μέχρι τοῦ Ἀθηναίου . . . Πολύβιος δ' ἐμφαίνει δύο ἔθνη νομίζων ταῦτα· Ὀπικοὺς γάρ φησι καὶ Αὔσονας οἰκεῖν τὴν χώραν ταύτην περὶ τὸν Κρατῆρα.

[3] Polyb. 3.91.7; Strab. 5.4.5 (C 244); Prop. 1.20.9; Virg. *Aen.* 6, *passim*; Diod. Sic. 4.21.5–7; Sil. Ital. 12.133–146.

[4] *Att.* 2.8.2.

vegetation from Misenum to Athenaeum presented the aspect of a single city.[5] Under the later principate the pattern remained the same: the Roman Emperors added prodigally to already lavish palaces at Baiae and on the Campanian islands; Symmachus owned six villas on the Campanian coast. By the end of the Republic, through the Antonine Age, and again during the fourth century, the Bay of Naples served as the preferred setting for the pleasure villas of the Roman aristocracy, a center of fashion and of cultivated ease. The following pages attempt to trace the stages of this development.

This is above all a social and cultural study: an attempt to identify the Romans who owned coastal properties in Campania and to account, as fully as the evidence permits, for their activities while in retreat. And since the Bay of Naples is the geographical focus of these chapters, close attention is paid throughout both to the contacts between Roman proprietors and resident Campanians, and to the social character—and Greek traditions—of the local towns. The Republican chapters of the present work are a much revised version of a doctoral thesis presented to the Department of the Classics, Harvard University, in the spring of 1965. I have subsequently extended the chronological limits to include the imperial evidence of the first four centuries, in the belief that the historical phenomenon which forms the subject of this study must be considered in its entirety rather than in one or more isolated phases. Here, although the villas and the leisure of Emperors and of private citizens remain steadily in focus, I have thought it important to include some discussion of the acts of policy by which Augustus and his successors bound the Bay of Naples more closely to Rome, and I have tried to view the phenomenon of Campanian *peregrinatio* within the wider context of known historical developments. On the other hand, the reader will find the geographical scope more severely restricted: following the practice of the ancients, who distinguished between the luxurious *villae maritimae* of the "Crater" and Campania's productive inland

[5] Strab. 5.4.8 (C 247).

estates, I have not considered, except when relevant to my main themes, the evidence from the Campanian cities inland, nor, except when the owners can be shown to have been prominent Romans, the many villas and farms in the environs of Pompeii or the splendid houses on the south front of Herculaneum: it has been thought superfluous to include material which is already easily accessible in the well-known studies by Della Corte, Day, and Rostovtzeff.

Excavations of the ancient Campanian sites in this century have gone forward, with dramatic results, under the direction of the late Amedeo Maiuri, Superintendent of Antiquities for Campania, and since Maiuri's death in 1963, his successor A. De Franciscis has capably assumed the immense responsibilities imposed by one of the world's richest archaeological zones. Yet save for several important discoveries in the districts of Herculaneum, Pompeii, and Stabiae, architectural remains contribute disappointingly little of direct relevance to our knowledge of the Campanian *villae maritimae* and their owners because those villas lay either along the ancient coastline (now under water), or within the coastal towns (where life, and building, have continued uninterruptedly from ancient times), or finally in volcanic territory (where subsequent eruptions have buried them beyond recovery). Thus the principal evidence for this study lies in the testimony of the ancient literary sources, and in inscriptions. The former has never been systematically exploited, although K. J. Beloch made an important start in his justly famous *Campanien* (1890), O. E. Schmidt contributed an excellent monograph on Cicero's villas in 1899, and C. Dubois included some additions in an Appendix of his *Pouzzoles Antique* (1907). The great bulk of the epigraphical evidence was published by T. Mommsen in the two parts of the tenth volume of the *Corpus Inscriptionum Latinarum* (Berlin 1883), where the material has been assembled, arranged, and elucidated in the magisterial fashion characteristic of that greatest of modern Roman historians. But many new inscriptions have come to light since Mommsen's day; other stones are now known to belong to towns other than those to which Mommsen had originally assigned them; and the material is constantly increasing. Further, in an inquiry such as the present, the evidence from inscriptions can often serve as a control over the casual statements of the literary authorities; and the combination of epigraphical and literary materials, often discussed only in isolation by earlier scholars, on some occasions yields fruitful results.

A number of scholars have generously assisted me at various stages of my research. I am deeply obliged to Professor Herbert Bloch, my supervisor at Harvard University, to whose great learning and valuable counsel the thesis owed much, and for whose continued interest and encouragement I am very grateful. M. W. Frederiksen of Worcester College, Oxford, read, criticized and discussed with me both the thesis and an early draft of the imperial chapters, and his enviable command of both the ancient sources and the modern literature has enabled me to make innumerable improvements—though he is in no way responsible for whatever errors and infelicities remain. Among others who have aided me in matters of substance I should like particularly to mention J. P. V. D. Balsdon, G. W. Bowersock, T. V. Buttrey, E. S. Gruen, M. Hammond, F. Rakob, Sir Ronald Syme, and T. P. Wiseman. In Naples, Professor A. De Franciscis has courteously and promptly responded to my requests for permission to inspect monuments and inscriptions, conversation with Professor E. Lepore illuminated certain historical problems, and Dr. W. Johannowsky and Dr. G. Buchner have discussed topographical points with me, always to my profit. At the American Academy in Rome, the Director, Professor Frank E. Brown, and Dr. Ernest Nash of the Fototeca Unione, have graciously encouraged me to draw upon their archaeological knowledge and expertise, and Signora Longobardi and the Library staff were consistently helpful and efficient.

In Michigan, the former chairman of the Department of Classical Studies, Gerald F. Else, provided unfailing support and encouragement; and a grant from Michigan's Horace H. Rackham

School of Graduate Studies greatly facilitated the completion of my research. It is through the kind offices of Wendell Clausen that the present work, after having been accepted for publication by the Harvard University Press, appears in the series of Loeb Classical Monographs. Finally, my thanks are due to the editors of the *American Journal of Philology* and the *Classical Quarterly*, for permitting me to reproduce in revised form materials first published in those periodicals.

Ann Arbor   J.H.D.
April 1969

CONTENTS

ILLUSTRATIONS

12. Villa del Capo di Sorrento. Roman masonry at the landing place, with view N across the Bay.
Courtesy of E. Nash, Fototeca Unione, American Academy in Rome.

13. *Villa maritima* on the Bay of Naples. Part of wall decoration of a house in Stabiae. Museo Nazionale, Naples (photo Alinari, Rome).

14. Group of buildings of a *villa maritima*, with terracing and steps to the sea. Wall painting from *tablinum* of the House of M. Lucretius Fronto, Pompeii.
Courtesy of E. Nash, Fototeca Unione, American Academy in Rome.

15. A. *Villa maritima* on the Bay of Naples with curved portico in two stories. Part of wall decoration from a house in Stabiae.
Courtesy of German Archaeological Institute, Rome.

B. *Villa maritima* on the Bay of Naples; construction of three stories with artificial terracing. Wall decoration from the same Stabian house.
Courtesy of German Archaeological Institute, Rome.

MAPS

ABBREVIATIONS

ABBREVIATIONS *Attention is called to the following abbreviations of the titles of books, articles, and periodicals cited frequently in the notes:*

AE	*L'Année épigraphique.*
AJA	*American Journal of Archaeology.*
AJP	*American Journal of Philology.*
Beloch, *Campanien*²	K. J. Beloch, *Campanien: Geschichte und Topographie des antiken Neapel und seiner Umgebung* (Second Edition, 1890).
Broughton, *MRR*	T. R. S. Broughton, *Magistrates of the Roman Republic* (1951).
BCH	*Bulletin de correspondence hellénique.*
CAH	*Cambridge Ancient History.*
Camp. Rom. I	*Campania Romana: Studi e materiali editi a cura della sezione Campana degli Studi Romani*, vol. 1 (1938).
Cichorius, *Röm. Stud.*	C. Cichorius, *Römische Studien* (1922).
CIL	*Corpus Inscriptionum Latinarum.*
CQ	*Classical Quarterly.*
CR	*Classical Review.*
Della Corte, *CeA*³	M. Della Corte, *Case ed Abitanti di Pompei* (Third Edition, ed. P. Soprano, 1965).
Drumann-Groebe	W. Drumann and P. Groebe, *Geschichte Roms* (Second Edition, vols. 1-6, 1899-1929).
Dubois, *PA*	C. Dubois, *Pouzzoles Antique* (Bibliothèque des Écoles Françaises d'Athènes et de Rome, fasc. 98, 1907).
Eph. Epigr.	*Ephemeris Epigraphica.*
Frank, *ESAR*	T. Frank, *Economic Survey of Ancient Rome.*
Frederiksen, *Rep. Cap.*	M. W. Frederiksen, "Republican Capua: a Social and Economic Study," *Papers of the British School at Rome* N.S. 14 (1959), 80-130.
Günther, *Pausilypon*	R. T. Günther, *Pausilypon, The Imperial Villa near Naples* (1913).
Hirschfeld, *GRK*	O. Hirschfeld, "Der Grundbesitz der Römischen Kaiser in den ersten drei Jahrhunderten," *Klio* 2 (1902), 45-72; 284-315.

How	W. W. How, *Cicero, Select Letters* (1926).
HTR	*Harvard Theological Review.*
IG	*Inscriptiones Graecae.*
ILS	Dessau, *Inscriptiones Latinae Selectae.*
JRS	*Journal of Roman Studies.*
MAAR	*Memoirs of the American Academy in Rome.*
Maiuri, *Campi Flegrèi*	A. Maiuri, *I Campi Flegrèi* (Itinerari dei musei e monumenti d'Italia, no. 32), Fourth Edition (1963).
Not. d. Sc.	*Notizie degli Scavi di Antichità.*
PBSR	*Papers of the British School at Rome.*
PdP	*Parola del Passato.*
PIR	*Prosopographia Imperii Romani* (*PIR²* refers to available volumes of the Second Edition).
RAAN	*Rendiconti dell'Accademia di Archeologia, Lettere e Belle Arti di Napoli.*
RE	Pauly-Wissowa-Kroll, *Real-Encyclopädie der klassischen Altertumswissenschaft.*
Röm. Mitt.	*Mitteilungen des Deutschen Archäologischen Instituts, Römische Abteilung.*
Rostovtzeff, *SEHRE²*	M. Rostovtzeff, *Social and Economic History of the Roman Empire* (Second Edition, ed. P. M. Fraser [1957]).
Sartori, *Problemi*	F. Sartori, *Problemi di Storia Costituzionale Italiota* (1953).
Schmidt	O. E. Schmidt, "Ciceros Villen," *Neue Jahrbücher für das klassische Altertum* (1899), 328–355; 466–497.
SB	D. R. Shackleton Bailey, *Cicero's Letters to Atticus,* vols. 1–2 (1965); 3–4 (1968); 5–6 (1967).
SIG	Dittenberger, *Sylloge Inscriptionum Graecarum* (Third Edition).
Syme, *RR*	R. Syme, *The Roman Revolution* (1939).
Syme, *Tacitus*	R. Syme, *Tacitus* (1958).
TAPA	*Transactions of the American Philological Association.*

Taylor, *Voting Districts* L. R. Taylor, *The Voting Districts of the Roman Republic* (Papers and Monographs of the American Academy in Rome, 20 [1960]).

TLL *Thesaurus Linguae Latinae*

T&P R. Y. Tyrrell and L. C. Purser, *The Correspondence of Cicero*, vol. 1 (Third Edition, 1904); 2–6 (Second Edition, 1906–1933); 7 (index, 1901).

ROMANS ON THE BAY OF NAPLES

ONE · *The First Coastal Villas—The Second Century* B.C.

Livy states that P. Cornelius Scipio Africanus Maior, accused of bribery in 184, refused to stand trial and retired to his place at Liternum on the Campanian coast; his accusers dared not drag him, though a private citizen, *e villa sua* and there he lived out the remainder of his life without longing for the capital.[1] This is the first distinguished Roman known to have owned a country villa. We are not informed when it was built, but Livy's words clearly imply that the villa was in the possession of Scipio at the time of his accusation, an implication which Cicero supports when he remarks that love of solitude prompted Scipio to make a practice of withdrawing at regular intervals from the city's throngs.[2]

It has been suggested that Scipio acquired the property when the state sold part of the *ager Campanus* in 205 B.C. to raise money for the war with Hannibal.[3] The villa would then presumably have been built sometime after the battle of Zama. This suggestion is attractive. The Romans approved in 197 and established in 194 a colony of three hundred families at Liternum, one of a group of five such colonies *in ora maritima*.[4] The purpose of these seaboard colonies was mainly defensive: to protect ports and nearby coastline from the depredations of enemy fleets, and, particularly after the Hannibalic wars, of pirates.[5] Now Seneca, who visted the villa of

[1] Livy 38.52.1 (*in Literninum concessit*); cf. 38.52.7, 53.8. For the date and details of the accusation see H. H. Scullard, *Roman Politics 220–150 B.C.* (Oxford 1951), 290–303.

[2] Cic. *Off.* 3.2: *otium sibi sumebat aliquando et e coetu hominum frequentiaque interdum tamquam in portum se in solitudinem recipiebat*...The imperfect tense indicates recurrent action.

3. Frank, *ESAR* I, 208. Cf. Livy 28.46.4–5: ... *agri Campani regionem a fossa Graeca ad mare versam vendere* ...

[4] Livy 32.29.3; for the date 197 B.C. see Broughton, *MRR* I, 334, "special commissions"; 34.45.2 (194 B.C.). The other colonies were at Volturnum, Puteoli, Salernum, and Buxentum.

[5] E. T. Salmon, *Phoenix* 9 (1955), 63–75.

Scipio and describes it in detail, stresses the fortified character of its walls and towers,[6] while, in an anecdote of Valerius Maximus, Scipio is reputedly paid a visit *in Liternina villa* by captains of pirate bands, against whom he barricaded his doors until they announced that they had come not as enemies but as admirers.[7] The fortified towers and bands of roving pirates seem more appropriate to a period in the early 190's when Scipio's was an isolated estate before the foundation of the colony, than after it, when the presence of so many fellow citizens would presumably have lessened the need for fortifications and discouraged *praedones* from approaching.[8] But this evidence can hardly be pressed, for the possibility remains that Scipio built after 194 in an area somewhat isolated from that of the colony.

Association with the name of Scipio lent a luster to Liternum which this bleak community later rarely achieved. Valerius Maximus calls it *ignobilis vicus*,[9] and the town's epithet in Silius Italicus is *stagnosum*; Livy too, who had seen the tomb of Scipio, speaks of the dreary swamps of Liternum.[10] In contrast, the sulphurous waters near Cumae, whose acropolis breaks the flat

[6] Sen. *Ep.* 86.4: *Vidi villam exstructam lapide quadrato, murum circumdatum silvae, turres quoque in propugnaculum villae utrimque subrectas, cisternam aedificiis ac viridibus subditam quae sufficere in usum vel exercitus posset* . . .

[7] Val. Max. 2.10.2: *Ad eundem Africanum in Liternina villa se continentem conplures praedonum duces videndum eodem tempore forte confluxerunt. Quos cum ad vim faciendam venire existimasset, praesidium domesticorum in tecto conlocavit, eratque in his repellendis et animo et apparatu occupatus. Quod ut praedones animadverterunt, dimissis militibus abiectisque armis ianuae adpropinquant et clara voce nuntiant Scipioni non vitae eius hostes sed virtutis admiratores venisse conspectum* . . .

[8] Seneca (*Ep.* 86.10) mentions the pleasure it gave him to wash in the bath at Scipio's villa "where Cato as aedile had washed, or Fabius Maximus, or one of the Cornelii (had washed)." Cato was aedile in 199 B.C., and Fabius died in 203 B.C. (cf. Scullard, *Roman Politics*, 112; 78). If Seneca meant that these Romans had actually been in Scipio's villa, the passage might serve to establish a *terminus ante quem* for the building's construction. But the next sentence shows that Seneca was not thinking of a particular visit; he says that all aediles in the old days bore the responsibility for testing bath water. His aim was thus to elucidate the early functions of aediles, not to name persons who had in fact visited the villa.

[9] Val. Max. 5.3.2.

[10] Sil. Ital. 6.653-4 (cf. Ovid *Met.* 15.714); Livy 22.16.4. Livy had seen the tomb: *monumentoque statua superimposita fuit, quam tempestate disiectam nuper vidimus ipsi* (38.56.3). On Liternum generally see Beloch, *Campanien*², 377–379; A. Maiuri, *Passeggiate Campane* (Florence 1950), 57–62.

Campanian coastline some four miles south of Liternum, appear to
have attracted ailing Romans by the first quarter of the second
century B.C. In 176, not long after the death of Scipio, his cousin
Cn. Cornelius Scipio Hispallus, consul for the year, had a fall
which led to infection; Livy says that he set out for the *Aquae
Cumanae*, but the disease grew worse and he died at Cumae.[11] The
Aquae Cumanae are mentioned only here; undoubtedly sulphurous
springs, they may have stood in the region of Baiae which, together with the remainder of the peninsula south and west of lakes
Avernus and Lucrinus, was normally designated as Cumaean
territory in early times.[12]

It is not impossible that Hispallus had a villa in the area, but
Livy does not say so, and there is good reason to suppose Hispallus
to have been hospitably received within the town itself. Other
evidence attests the cordiality of relations between Cumae and
Rome in this period. Livy states that in 180 the Cumaeans, at
their own request, were permitted to substitute Latin for Oscan as
the town's official language and, more interestingly, that the
praecones of Cumae were permitted to use Latin.[13] It is in the
highest degree likely that economic motives formed the basis of
Cumae's request to Rome:[14] with the foundation of the Roman
colonies at Volturnum, Liternum and Puteoli in 194,[15] a new influx of Latin speakers had come to rely permanently upon Campanian markets and the *praecones* of Cumae would have wanted
their full share of the new business. The substitution of Latin for
Oscan at Cumae in 180 thus testifies to the increasing presence of
Romans in the area, and since Livy appears to have felt no need to

[11] Livy 41.16.3–4: *parte membrorum captus ad Aquas Cumanas profectus ingravescente
morbo Cumis decessit.* For the relationship of Hispallus and Africanus see Scullard, *Roman
Politics,* 309.

[12] On the topography of the Bacoli peninsula in antiquity, see R. F. Paget, *JRS*
58 (1968), 163–164.

[13] Livy 40.42.13: *Cumanis eo anno petentibus permissum, ut publice Latine loquerentur,
et praeconibus Latine loquendi ius esset.*

[14] Livy may even have found a reference in his source to the economic fact that the
praecones were officially permitted to employ Latin, and expanded that fact, to the greater
glory of Rome, into a statement that the entire town was eager for the privilege.

[15] See above, n. 4.

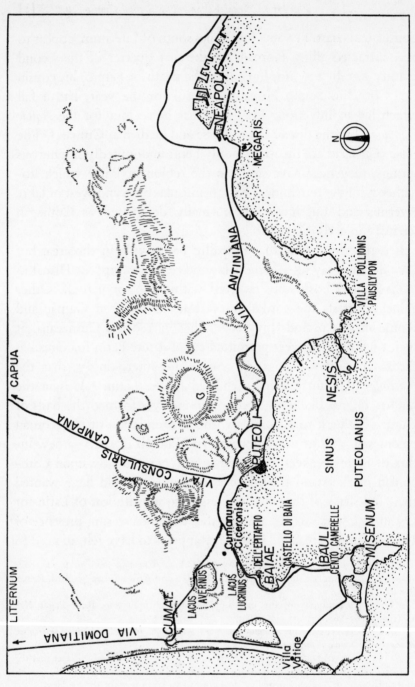

1. *The Phlegraean Fields in Roman Times.*

explain what or where the *Aquae Cumanae* were, he too implies that
a consul's visit in 176 was no unusual occurrence.

During this same period there are brief notices in the sources of
other coastal estates, both north and south of Campania, belonging
to distinguished Romans. Three years before the visit of Hispallus
to the *Aquae Cumanae* Livy records that M. Aemilius Lepidus,
censor and *pontifex maximus*, was chosen *princeps senatus* and constructed a mole at Tarracina; but his efforts lacked public appro-
bation because Lepidus owned property in the area and had used
public funds for work which should have been done at his own
expense.[16] We know no further details about these *praedia* themselves, nor where they lay in relation to the mole; therefore we
are unable to determine whether Lepidus employed state funds to
make improvements in his property. But since *praedium* regularly
implies a dwelling house as well as land, it is a likely hypothesis
that Lepidus spent some time in residence on the coast of Latium
before his death in 153/152 B.C.

Actual ownership of property is also probable in the case of L.
Aemilius Paullus Macedonicus, who celebrated his triumph over
king Perseus in 167 and was elected censor in 164. Plutarch states
that after performing most of the duties of the latter office, Paullus
fell ill and sailed to the city of Velia in Lucania. There he spent
much time in country places by the sea,[17] only returning to Rome
shortly before his death in 160. It is not clear from Plutarch's
narrative exactly when Paullus reached Velia, or who owned the
seaside places. On the other hand, both Polybius and Plutarch
record the size of the estate of Paullus at the time of his death, and
though it seemed surprisingly small to both of them (three hundred and seventy thousand drachmas[18]), the family has been
ranked along with that of the considerably more opulent Scipio

[16] Livy 40.51.2: *Lepidus molem ad Tarracinam, ingratum opus, quod praedia habebat ibi
privatamque publicae rei impensam inseruerat.*
[17] Plut.*Aem.Paull.*39.1: ἐπεὶ δὲ πεισθεὶς ὑπὸ τῶν ἰατρῶν ἔπλευσεν εἰς Ἐλέαν
τῆς Ἰταλίας καὶ διέτριβεν αὐτόθι πλείω χρόνον ἐν παραλίοις ἀγροῖς καὶ πολλὴν
ἡσυχίαν ἔχουσιν . . .
[18] Plut. *Aem. Paull.* 39.5; cf. Polyb. 31.28.3.

Africanus Maior as among the wealthiest of the time.[19] Means could have constituted no serious obstacle to Paullus' ownership of the seaside property at Velia. Furthermore, Plutarch implies that Paullus would not have returned to Rome from Velia had not the people clamored for him, and shows that Paullus had been away for the better part of three years.[20] The planned and lengthy retreat at distant Velia suggests that Paullus did not impose on citizens' hospitality but rather owned the seaside estate.

We are somewhat better informed about the owners of seaside villas in the next generation. According to a fragment of Cicero's *De Fato* preserved by Macrobius, P. Cornelius Scipio Aemilianus Africanus Numantinus, *cos.* 147, the second son of Aemilius Paullus and adopted by Publius, elder son of P. Cornelius Scipio Africanus Maior, had at some unspecified date a house located *ad Lavernium.*[21] The place is mentioned only here and in a letter of Cicero's where the context makes clear that it was near Formiae, nearly equidistant from Tarracina and Volturnum, the coast town on the river which marked the northern border of the *ager Campanus.*[22] Cicero's *De Re Publica* is set in the *horti Scipionis* in 129 B.C., the year of Scipio's death, but these pleasure gardens, the earliest attested at Rome, were inside the city.[23] Scipio's celebrated friendship with Gaius Laelius Sapiens (*cos.* 140 B.C.) flourished in their respective villas; Laelius too had an estate at Formiae where he entertained his famous friend,[24] and that either he or Scipio owned a villa at Lavinium (= Laurentum) south of Ostia on the coast of Latium, may be inferred from a passage in the *De Oratore* in which Scipio and Laelius are pictured *ad Caietam* [the

[19] Frank, *ESAR* I, 209.
[20] Plut. *Aem. Paull.* 39.1–2.
[21] Macrob. *Sat.* 3.16.4 (= Cic. *Fat.* fr. 5): *Nam cum esset apud se ad Lavernium Scipio unaque Pontius . . .*
[22] Cic. *Att.* 7.8.4 (T&P 299; SB 131); cf. Tyrrell and Purser *ad loc.*
[23] Cic. *Amic.* 25; *Rep.* 1.14; cf. P. Grimal, *Jardins Romains*, Bibliothèque des Écoles Françaises d'Athènes et de Rome, fasc. 155 (Paris 1943), 107.
[24] Laelius older than Scipio: Cic. *Rep.* 1.18; cf. *Rep.* 1.61 (Scipio is speaking): *Quia animum adverti nuper, cum essemus in Formiano, te familiae valde interdicere, ut uni dicto audiens esset.* This passage seems to show that Laelius kept a resident staff of servants at this villa; it is our only explicit information on this subject for the second century B.C.

headland near Formiae] *et ad Laurentum.*²⁵ Again, a passage preserved by Donatus from the life of Terence records another villa in the *ager Albanus*, the property of either Scipio or Laelius.²⁶

The same source shows that Laelius, possibly native to the Campanian region, was the owner of the first attested villa at Puteoli; here he is alleged to have written lines of Terence's *Heautontimoroumenos* which he later recited with some satisfaction to his wife.²⁷ Since according to the *didascalia* this play was performed in Rome in 163 B.C., the reference places Laelius in a villa at Puteoli at about this time; and he must have been in his middle to late twenties because he was somewhat older than his friend Scipio, who was born in 185–184.²⁸

Laelius outlived Scipio, whose *laudatio* he composed in 129; how long the *Puteolanum* remained in his possession is not known. But it is appropriate that the first mention of a villa at Puteoli should fall in the same period as the first testimony to the town's importance as a port and distinction as a city. Polybius, who may well have disembarked at Puteoli from Greece after the Third Macedonian War in 168 and soon after became the inseparable companion of Laelius' friend Scipio, says that the Campanian coast contained "the most famous and most beautiful cities in Italy,"

---

²⁵ Cic. *De Or.* 2.22 (Crassus is speaking): *Otium autem quod dicis esse, assentior; verum otii fructus est, non contentio animi, sed relaxatio. Saepe ex socero meo audivi, cum is diceret socerum suum Laelium semper fere cum Scipione solitum rusticari eosque incredibiliter repuerascere esse solitos, cum rus ex urbe tamquam e vinculis evolavissent. Non audeo dicere de talibus viris, sed tamen ita solet narrare Scaevola, conchas eos et umbilicos ad Caietam et ad Laurentum legere consuesse, et ad omnem animi remissionem ludumque descendere . . .* Laurentum was the later site of the famous villa of the younger Pliny: cf. Pliny *Ep.* 2.17.

²⁶ *Vita Terenti* 1 (verses of Porcius): *Dum Africani vocem divinam inhiat avidis auribus, /dum ad Philum se cenitare et Laelium pulchrum putat, /dum in Albanum crebro rapitur ob florem aetatis suae . . .*

²⁷ *Vita Terenti* 3: *Nepos auctore certo comperisse se ait, C. Laelium quondam in Puteolano Kal. Martiis admonitum ab uxore temperius ut discumberet petisse ab ea ne interpellaret, seroque tandem ingressum triclinium dixisse, non saepe in scribendo magis sibi successisse; deinde . . . pronuntiasse versus qui sunt in "Heautontimorumeno" . . .* Laelii are attested in Pompeii from an early age; and it has been plausibly argued that the *gens Laelia* came originally from the sea-faring upper classes of Campania: M. L. Gordon, "The *Ordo* of Pompeii", *JRS* 17 (1927), 172; and see further Münzer, "Laelius", *RE* 12 (1924), 400 (no. 2), 404 (no. 3).

²⁸ Cic. *Rep.* 1.18.

and names Cumae, Puteoli, and Neapolis.[29] The Campanian satirist Lucilius, born at Suessa Aurunca probably in 180,[30] himself a close friend of Scipio and Laelius, and apparently an honorary citizen of Neapolis at the time of his death at the end of the century,[31] calls Puteoli a second Delos.[32] The verse which contains this reference cannot be dated with exactness, but Delos became a free port after Rome's defeat of Perseus in the third Macedonian War, and the names of Campanian and South Italian Greek traders, attested in Delian inscriptions in the early 150's, recur with increasing frequency after the fall of Carthage and Corinth.[33] Lucilius' comparison of Puteoli with Delos, therefore, would well fit both ports in the late 140's or even earlier. And since Polybius and Lucilius certainly knew both Puteoli and Laelius, they may have actually visited Laelius' villa at Puteoli.

Finally, Cornelia, the second daughter of P. Cornelius Scipio Africanus Maior, wife of Ti. Sempronius Gracchus and mother of the Gracchi, owned a villa at Misenum, on the northwest corner of the Bay of Naples. The flat headland which forms the promontory of Misenum together with the surrounding hills subsequently became a choice location for the seaside villas of the Roman aristocracy; and the villa of Cornelia, a member of a distinguished family with earlier connections along the Campanian coast, is the first of which we hear. Plutarch states that after the death of Gaius Gracchus in 121 B.C. Cornelia kept on living at the place called Misenum, making no change in her accustomed way of

---

[29] Polyb. 3.91.3-4: περιέχουσι δὲ καὶ τὰς ἐπιφανεστάτας καὶ καλλίστας πόλεις τῆς Ἰταλίας ἐν αὐτοῖς. τὴν μὲν γὰρ παραλίαν αὐτῶν Σενουεσανοὶ καὶ Δικαιαρχῖται νέμονται, πρὸς δὲ τούτοις Νεαπολῖται . . .

[30] E. H. Warmington, *Remains of Old Latin* III (London 1958), 9. Cf. C. Cichorius, *Untersuchungen zu Lucilius* (Berlin 1908), 8.

[31] Suet. ed. Roth (Teubner 1904), 295, 10–12: *C. Lucilius saturarum scriptor Neapoli moritur ac publico funere effertur.* . . .

[32] Lucilius, in *ROL* III, 38 (= Paulus, ex Fest. 88.4): *inde Dicarchitum populos Delumque minorem.*

[33] J. Hatzfeld, "Les Italiens résidant à Délos", *BCH* 36 (1912), 102–104; cf. the same author's *Les Trafiquants Italiens dans l'Orient Hellénique* (Paris 1919), 179; Frank, *ESAR* I, 274–275; and see now A. J. N. Wilson, *Emigration from Italy in the Republican Age of Rome* (Manchester 1966), 113–118.

life.[34] Misenum could well have been her chief residence from 154, the year in which her husband died; and the same inference can be drawn from a passage in Valerius Maximus, which records Cornelia's entertainment of a Campanian woman in the days when Tiberius and Gaius Gracchus were still school boys.[35] Tiberius very probably there met his subsequent adviser, the philosopher Blossius of Cumae.[36]

These are the earliest Roman coastal estates, in Campania and elsewhere, recorded in the literary sources. What were the functions of such villas? Of course, there exists no archaeological evidence for any of these properties. But it has generally been assumed that, like the inland farms (*villae rusticae*) of Cato at Casinum and Venafrum, these early seaside properties too were essentially productive.[37] Ancient evidence corroborates this view only in the case of the earliest villa, that of Scipio Africanus Maior who, it pleased the younger Seneca to think, wore out his body by working the soil himself in the good old Roman way.[38] But this is our lone piece of evidence, and it may be asked how long the seaside properties of the second century continued to have complements of productive lands. Tenney Frank himself included the villas of Scipio Aemilianus and Laelius at Formiae within the period 150–80 B.C., among luxury seaside villas (*villae urbanae*, *villae maritimae*) "which are seldom connected with productive estates."[39] Certainly by the first decade of the first century, as will be seen, it is *delectatio* and *amoenitas*, rather than *fructus*, which

---

[34] Plut. *Gaius Gracch.* 19.1-2: αὕτη [*sc.* ἡ Κορνηλία] δὲ περὶ τοὺς καλουμένους Μισηνοὺς διέτριβεν, οὐδὲν μεταλλάξασα τῆς συνήθους διαίτης. ἦν δὲ πολύφιλος καὶ διὰ φιλοξενίαν εὐτράπεζος, ἀεὶ μὲν Ἑλλήνων καὶ φιλολόγων περὶ αὐτὴν ὄντων, ἁπάντων δὲ τῶν βασιλέων καὶ δεχομένων παρ' αὐτῆς δῶρα καὶ πεμπόντων.

[35] Val. Max. 4.4.1.

[36] Plut. *Tib. Gracch.* 8.4–5; 17.4; 20.3–4. Blossius of Cumae was a Campanian, not a Greek: D. R. Dudley, *JRS* 31 (1941), 94–96; Frederiksen, *Rep. Cap.* 117.

[37] Frank, *ESAR* I, 208–209, followed by Grimal, *Jardins Romains*, 24.

[38] Sen. *Ep.* 86.5: ... *abluebat corpus laboribus rusticis fessum. Exercebat enim opere se, terramque (ut mos fuit priscis) ipse subigebat.*

[39] Frank, *ESAR* I, 295.

concerned the wealthy owners of *villae maritimae*: the exceedingly
luxurious estate of Marius at Misenum, built probably in the early
nineties,[40] is the first attested example of the type of Campanian
coastal villa abundantly documented in the works of Cicero and
Varro, depicted in wall paintings recovered from Pompeii and
Stabiae, and defined by late jurists as designed to give pleasure
alone.[41] But to what date in the second century may one with
justification ascribe the origins of such villas since without additional evidence it would be misleading to classify mid-second
century estates at Formiae with luxurious coastal retreats which
are first documented explicitly half a century later?

There is in fact good evidence to show that as early as 164 B.C.,
about the time of our first reference to a villa at Puteoli, domestic
architecture was becoming more ostentatious and elaborate. M.
Porcius Cato, not surprisingly, was critical of others' luxury in
building. Although none of his strictures are to be found in the
De Agri Cultura, in the censor's speech *De Sumptu Suo* of 164 B.C.,
he is said to have boasted that up to his seventieth year his country
places were unornamented and rough, and that no dwelling which
he owned was ever costly.[42] The clear implication of this remark is
that the villas of others could not be so described. Another excerpt,
from Cato's speech opposing second consulships at Rome delivered in or soon after 152 B.C., is still more revealing:

> ... dicere possum, quibus villae atque aedes aedificatae atque
> expolitae maximo opere citro atque ebore atque pavimentis
> Poenicis sient.[43]

The sentence is tantalizing because incomplete, but it is perfectly
clear that the owners of *villae expolitae* are being singled out for

[40] Plut. *Mar.* 34.2; see below, Chapter 2, p. 23.

[41] *Digesta* 50.16.198: *"urbana praedia"* omnia aedificia accipimus, non solum ea quae sunt
in oppidis, sed et si forte stabula sunt vel alia meritoria in villis et in vicis, vel si praetoria
voluptati tantum deservientia. ...

[42] H. Malcovati, *Oratorum Romanorum Fragmenta*[2] (Turin 1955), M. Porcius Cato fr.
174, p. 71 (= Aul. Gell. 13.24.1): ... villas suas inexcultas et rudes ne tectorio quidem prae-
litas fuisse dicit [sc. M. Cato].

[43] *Ibid.*, fr. 185, p. 75 (= Festus, p. 282, 4).

censure. Implicit in both these passages is the earliest record of strong protest against the rise of *luxuria* in building, a protest which became a commonplace by the time of Cicero.

To Gellius we owe the preservation of a fragment of another speech of 140 B.C. in which Scipio Aemilianus makes an admiring reference to country houses very handsomely adorned (*villae expolitissimae*).[44] One scholar has recently called attention to the significance of this passage for dating the earliest Roman luxury villas;[45] and taken together with the fragments of Cato's speeches quoted above, the argument acquires a more compelling force. For by the middle of the first century B.C. the adjective *expolitus* (or simply *politus*) has become a conventional epithet, often pejorative, for a private villa built on a sumptuous scale. Varro, for example, deplores his generation's cupidity by saying that everyone competes to have the biggest and most elaborate villa possible (*villam urbanam quam maximam ac politissimam*).[46] But the adjective clearly has something of the same force in the excerpts from the speeches cited above, where its use bears witness to the rise of ostentation in private building by the middle of the second century B.C.

There are no explicit links between these passages and the seaside estates of Scipio Aemilianus, Laelius, and Cornelia; we are not informed that any of their own villas were *expolitae*. Yet in the first place we know these families to have been among the wealthiest of their generation, and therefore best equipped to indulge a taste for elaborate private villas.[47] Furthermore, it will be

---

[44] Malcovati, *ORF²*, P. Cornelius Scipio Aemilianus Africanus, fr. 20, p. 129 (= Aul. Gell. 2.20.6).

[45] D. Mustilli, "La villa pseudourbana ercolanese", *RAAN* N.S. 31 (1956), 90. On early Roman luxury villas in general, cf. A. Boëthius, *The Golden House of Nero* (Ann Arbor 1960), 96–99.

[46] Varro *Rust.* 1.13.7; cf. Cic. *QFr.* 3.1.6 (T&P 148): *urbanam expolitionem.*

[47] Polybius, (31.28; cf. Frank *ESAR* I, 209) says that Scipio Aemilianus renounced the inheritance of half of the estate of his father—60 talents—in order that his brother Fabius might possess a fortune equal to his own; in *Vita Terenti* I, Scipio and Laelius are called two of the wealthiest men of the time; and Cornelia brought a dowry of 50 talents to her marriage with Tiberius Sempronius Gracchus (Polyb. 31.27; cf. Frank, *ESAR* I, 209).

2

remembered that Scipio and Laelius are the first Romans known to have owned more than one coastal villa: both had estates at Formiae, Laelius one at Puteoli, and one of the pair still another at Lavinium, in addition to the *Albanum* further inland. In this respect they may have anticipated an established practice of the first century. It will be seen how common it became for the well-to-do Roman to possess several villas, at least one of which was by the sea; and as villas became increasingly numerous and luxurious, the interest in the productivity of some of the estates declined: some villas were owned to give profit, others merely pleasure. The *villa maritima* on the Campanian coast came to have high value as real estate, but no appreciable agricultural worth; this fact is strikingly illustrated by a passage in the *De Lege Agraria* of 63 B.C. in which Cicero says that people are eager to buy farms in the *ager Campanus* in order to finance their lavish coastal establishments at Cumae and at Puteoli.[48] The notices, therefore, which prove that Scipio Aemilianus and Laelius owned estates at various points on the coast of Latium and Campania may well be early signs that the villas themselves were undergoing change, and beginning to function not merely as sources of profit but also as seats of pleasure.

A last and related consideration further supports the view that the coastal estates of Scipio Aemilianus, Laelius, and Cornelia were the prototypes of the *villa maritima* of the late Republic. Descriptions and anecdotes in the ancient sources reveal that like the villas themselves, villa life had also altered appreciably by the latter half of the second century, when it attained a high level of culture and sophistication. A Roman possessed a villa in his capacity of *privatus*; it was the fixed seat in which to pass periods of leisure time when free of the press of business or public life at Rome. Thus, in the third book of the *De Officiis*, Cicero's fullest discussion of *otium*, he was doubtless thinking of the villa at Liternum when he

---

[48] Cic. *Leg. Agr.* 2.78: *neque istorum pecuniis quicquam aliud deesse video nisi eius modi fundos quorum subsidio familiarum magnitudines et Cumanorum ac Puteolanorum praediorum sumptus sustentare possint.*

says that Scipio Africanus Maior, to rest from public duties (*negotia*), *otium sibi sumebat aliquando*.[49] Scipio is the first Roman whose *otium* is connected with a villa, and the first known to have attached high value and importance to his private life.[50] But his was no luxurious ease. Cicero goes on to approve the statement of Africanus, quoted by Cato, that he was never less idle than when at leisure, for it showed that *otium* and *solitudo*, the two conditions which prompt others to laziness (*languor*), served only to spur Scipio on: his thoughts were *in otio de negotiis*.[51]

In the following generation, Roman *otium* had come to include a wider range of activities. Vivid vignettes in both Cicero and Horace suggest that for Scipio and Laelius *otium* meant fleeing the city at regular intervals to resume the harmless follies of boyhood; they gathered shells along the seashore and, flinging off all restraint, indulged in carefree sport and relaxation.[52] These diversions prompted a different definition of leisure in the *De Oratore*: *verum otii fructus est, non contentio animi, sed relaxatio*;[53] and since Cicero is careful to make his speaker cite contemporary evidence for the pastimes of Scipio and Laelius, he manifestly was not simply transferring to an earlier generation the notions of *otium* current in his own day. Mental relaxation could also include more intellectual pursuits; indeed, cultural entertainments are so much a part of the villa life of Scipio and Laelius that without them we should not know of the villas at all. The *Puteolanum* of Laelius is mentioned because the owner was writing Terentian verses there; we owe our reference to the villa of Scipio at Lavernium to an anecdote about a dinner at which the philosopher Pontius, Scipio's guest, made a memorable remark; nor would we know of the *horti Scipionis* had Cicero not chosen them as the dramatic setting

[49] See above, n. 2.
[50] Cf. W. Fowler, *Social Life at Rome in the Age of Cicero* (New York 1909), 247–248.
[51] Cic. *Off.* 3.1–2; and cf. Sen. *Ep.* 86.5; 51.11: *Literni honestius Scipio quam Bais exulabat: ruina eius non est tam molliter collocanda.*
[52] Cic. *De Or.* 2.22, quoted above in n. 25; Hor. *Serm.* 2.1.71–74: *Quin ubi se a vulgo et scaena in secreta remorant / virtus Scipiadae et mitis sapientia Laeli, / nugari cum illo et discincti ludere donec / decoqueretur holus soliti.*
[53] See above, n. 25.

of the discussion in *De Re Publica*.[54] Even the estate of Cornelia at Misenum interested Plutarch primarily for the cultivated life its mistress lived there: she set a good table in order to be hospitable; Greeks and literary people were in constant attendance; and she exchanged gifts with all the reigning kings.[55]

Philosophers, literary figures, good dinners, serious discussions, poetry—all have become standard features of villa life in the time of Scipio Aemilianus, Laelius, and Cornelia, contrasting sharply with the hardy activities of Scipio Africanus Maior when at leisure at Liternum. And though it is difficult to gauge exactly the part played by Greek influences in the increased sophistication of Roman *otium*, contacts with Greeks and receptivity to Greek culture were clearly factors of paramount importance. The tastes of Aemilius Paullus were conspicuously Hellenic: during the Macedonian War, mainland Greece had marvelled at his humanity and nicety of tact;[56] Plutarch states that the Greek library of Perseus was the only part of the spoils which Paullus appropriated for his own use;[57] after his return to Rome he showed great kindness to Polybius.[58] When he fell ill in 164, it was at Greek Velia that he passed his time in quiet seaside places (Velia, where the survival of Greek institutions late into the Roman period is attested by inscriptions, by the nature of her alliance with Rome, and by Cicero's remark that even in his day priestesses for the cult of Ceres at Rome were chosen from among the maidens of Neapolis and Velia[59]). The doctors who, Plutarch says, urged Paullus to retire to Velia may well have been Greeks themselves.

[54] Puteolanum: see above, n. 27; Lavernium: Cic. *Fat.* fr. 5; *horti Scipionis*: Cic. *Amic.* 25; *Rep.* 1.14.

[55] See above, n. 34.

[56] Plut. *Aem. Paullus* 28.4. On Roman Hellenism in this period see P. Grimal, *Le Siècle des Scipions* (Paris 1953), 127–163.

[57] Plut. *Aem. Paullus* 28.6.

[58] Polyb. 31.22.1–7. Pliny (*NH* 35.135) says that the Athenian Metrodorus, a painter and a philosopher, also became a part of Paullus' household.

[59] Inscriptions of Velia: P. C. Sestieri, *Fasti Archeologici* 4 (1951), no. 1861; *foedus*: Polyb. 1.20.14 with Livy 26.39.5; priestesses of Ceres: Cic. *Balb.* 55. See further F. Sartori, *Problemi*, 105–107, and the collection of sources by D. Musti, in *PdP* fasc. 108–110 (1966), 318–335.

The evidence for the philhellenism of Scipio Aemilianus is well known. Friendship between Polybius and Scipio began with a loan of some books and conversations about them;[60] the two became inseparable and hunted together—Aemilius Paullus had introduced his son to this royal Greek habit in Macedonia.[61] This famous friendship between the young Scipio, who seemed *otiosus* to his more energetic compatriots,[62] and Polybius, who confesses that Roman domination relieved the Greeks of ambition and gave men of action like himself leisure for study and inquiry,[63] marks the first in a series of similar relationships between learned Greeks and aristocratic Roman patrons. Terence could also claim the patronage of both Scipio and Laelius; in the prologue to the *Adelphoe* he referred to his patrons as "men whose timely help everyone has used without shame in war, in leisure, in business."[64] Finally Greeks, as at Cornelia's villa at Misenum, could enliven the leisure hours of their distinguished patrons, but again, as at Misenum, might also supervise the education of their patrons' sons. Polybius is said to have been critical of Roman educational practices, possibly because Roman education in his day was the choice of individual families and not, as in Greek cities, a matter of collective policy.[65] Private Roman villas, rather than public Greek stoas, served as schools as well as seats for philosophical discussions.[66] It is almost certainly right, therefore, to connect the villa at Misenum with Cicero's statement that Tiberius Gracchus was from boyhood taught Greek literature and always had tutors imported from Greece, among whom was Diophanes of Mitylene.[67]

[60] Polyb. 31.23.4.
[61] *Ibid.*, 31.29.1–9.
[62] Polyb. 31.23.11 (Scipio speaking): δοκῶ γὰρ εἶναι πᾶσιν ἡσύχιός τις καὶ νωθρός, ὡς ἀκούω, καὶ πολὺ κεχωρισμένος τῆς Ρωμαϊκῆς αἱρέσεως καὶ πράξεως, ὅτι κρίσεις οὐχ αἱροῦμαι λέγειν.
[63] Polyb. 3.59.3–5.
[64] Ter. *Ad.* prologue 20: . . . *in bello, in otio, in negotio.*
[65] Cic. (*Rep.* 4.3) says that Roman education was the thing *in qua una Polybius, noster hospes, nostrorum institutorum neglegentiam accusat.* Cf. F. Walbank, *Commentary on Polybius* I (Oxford 1957), 145 (on *Polyb.* 6.81.10); J. P. Mahaffy, *The Greek World under Roman Sway* (London 1890), 81.
[66] Grimal, *Le Siècle des Scipions*, 145.
[67] Cic. *Brut.* 104.

The cumulative force of this evidence—allusions in speeches of 164, 152, and 140 B.C. to increased luxury in private building; proof that Scipio Aemilianus and Laelius each owned more than one coastal villa; and a changing, more Hellenized view of the diversions deemed appropriate for periods of leisure—appreciably strengthens the hypothesis that the first Roman luxury villas were beginning to appear along the coast of Campania by the middle of the second century B.C. The limitations of our evidence preclude greater precision in dating and architectural detail. But it may be noticed, first, that these general findings are in close chronological accord with some of the excavated private construction at Pompeii, where many of the largest and finest houses—including the "house of Pansa," the "house of Sallustius," and the "house of the Faun"—are to be dated to the middle of the second century B.C.[68] The further evidence that some of these dwellings were superimposed on foundations of still older houses provides striking testimony to the rapid increase of wealth during this period.[69] Frederiksen's recent study of Republican Capua confirms there what had already been suspected from the findings at Pompeii: Campanian cities in general profited greatly from the expansion of Roman power in the second century B.C.[70] Increasingly elaborate building by illustrious Romans on the Campanian coast was thus complemented, as in any case was to have been expected, by a corresponding prosperity in the local towns.

Second, and more obvious, this first testimony to the *otium*, comfortable and civilized, of the upper-class Roman begins in the period immediately following the traditional date of the introduction to Rome of the wealth, booty, slaves and luxury which villas and their pleasures presuppose. Polybius assigned the first extravagance at Rome to the period immediately after Paullus' defeat of Perseus at Pydna in 168 B.C.; he cited as causes both Rome's confidence in her own power after the Macedonian Wars,

[68] Cf. Frank, *ESAR* I, 288.
[69] *Ibid.*, 288.
[70] Frederiksen, *Rep. Cap.*, 124.

and the transfer of Greek riches to the city.[71] Velleius Paterculus held that the first Scipio (Africanus) opened the way for world power, the second (Aemilianus) for *luxuria*; in the days of the latter Scipio *a negotiis in otium conversa civitas*.[72] Works of art, sculptors, delicacies, cooks, jewels, pleasure gardens and villas followed in due course. But these luxuries are largely important as the material signs of a transformation of upper class customs,[73] a social change into which the civilized leisure and coastal villas of Scipio Aemilianus, Laelius, and Cornelia provide some insights.

As has been seen, the evidence for coastal villas of the second century, not unlike the geographical locations of the villas themselves, is scattered. In the next century, the sources of information are more substantial and reveal that Cumae, Misenum, Bauli, Baiae, Puteoli, and Neapolis were the towns where the *villae maritimae* came to crowd the shoreline. The ensuing pages will address themselves to the following questions: which members of the Roman aristocracy owned such villas, in what ways did they acquire them, what were the social details of villa life, and what, finally, can be said of the relations, social, political and economic, between owners of villas and inhabitants of the Campanian towns?

[71] Polyb. 31.25.6–8.
[72] Vell. Pat. 2.1.1–2.
[73] Cf. Grimal, *Le Siècle des Scipions*, 141.

TWO · Coastal Campania During the Period of Marius and Sulla

In other parts of coastal and central Italy, increased wealth fostered the building of new villas and elaborate renovations in older houses toward the end of the second century B.C. Publius Rutilius Rufus (*cos.* 105 B.C.), the much younger contemporary and friend of Scipio Aemilianus, under whom he served at Numantia, had an estate at Formiae, apparently complete with vineyards. Whether it was already built when acquired is unknown; but that Rufus lost it when exiled in 92 we learn from a passage deploring such human vicissitudes in the *De Natura Deorum*.[1] Again, the family estate of Cicero at Arpinum, the imaginary setting of the *De Legibus*, was elegantly renovated by Cicero's father, probably not long after 106 B.C.[2] On the Campanian coast the early nineties appear to have seen the first marked increase in the building of private villas—an increase which the ancient sources associate with the resourceful enterprise of a certain C. Sergius Orata. The notices concerning this remarkable figure are regrettably brief, but all accounts stress that Orata was an acute and fortunate speculator, a type new to the Rome of his day and indeed infrequent throughout antiquity.[3]

There is further agreement that the Lucrine Lake, near Baiae, was the source of his profits. Here the present aspect of the terrain is a poor guide to its appearance in antiquity: radical alterations in topography began in 37 B.C. with Agrippa's construction of the

---

[1] Cic. *Nat. D.* 3.86; the dramatic date was 77–6, by which time Rufus was in exile. Cf. Frank, *ESAR* I, 295.

[2] Cic. *Leg.* 2.3; Grimal, *Jardins Romains*, 108.

[3] Münzer, "C. Sergius Orata," *RE* 2 A (1923), 1713–1714, no. 33. See also A. Maiuri, *Passeggiate Campane* (Florence 1950), 29. Maiuri supposes Orata to have been of Campanian, even Puteolan, origin.

Portus Iulius, which linked Lake Avernus with the Lucrine Lake and the latter with the sea; they culminated in 1538 with the volcanic eruption of Monte Nuovo, which destroyed the medieval village of Tripergole and reduced the Lucrine Lake to approximately its present size.[4] Before the activities of Orata, however, *Lacus Lucrinus* appears to have been a large and untapped natural resource. The elder Pliny says that in the time of Licinius Crassus the orator and before the Social War, Orata was the first to use the lake to breed and supply oysters *nec gulae causa, sed avaritiae*; Pliny also ascribes to him the invention and installation of unusual baths in villas which he subsequently sold.[5] Valerius Maximus also believed that Orata's baths and ponds were the first in Italy and comments further on his dealings in real estate:

Aedificiis etiam spatiosis et excelsis deserta ad id tempus ora Lucrini Lacus pressit, quo recentiore usu conchyliorum frueretur.[6]

The implication of these accounts is clear: Orata did not produce his oyster beds, baths or lake houses for personal use exclusively, nor for the benefit of resident Campanians—for these are all luxury goods, not staples. His intended market must have been the wealthy Romans who were beginning to want pleasure villas on the coast.[7] Orata was the first Campanian speculator to cater to the leisure of the great grandees; he prospered. Thus he earned his modest place in Roman social history.

---

[4] *Portus Iulius*: Strabo 5.4.5 (C 244); Cass. Dio 48.50.1–4; Virg. G. 2.161–164; cf. Beloch, *Campanien*[2], 170. Monte Nuovo: Beloch, *Campanien*[2], 172–174; Nissen, *Italische Landeskunde* I (Berlin 1883), 267–268: Maiuri, *Campi Flegrèi*, 60–61.

[5] Pliny *NH* 9.168: *Ostrearum vivaria primus omnium Sergius Orata invenit in Baiano aetate L. Crassi oratoris, ante Marsicum bellum, nec gulae causa sed avaritiae, magna vectigalia tali ex ingenio suo percipiens, ut qui primus pensiles invenerit balnea, ita mangonicatas villas subinde vendendo. Is primus optimum saporem ostreis Lucrinis adiudicavit. . . .*

[6] Val. Max. 9.1.1. *Pensiles* are properly openings in the floor which admitted hot air; see e.g. H. Stuart Jones, *Companion to Roman History* (Oxford 1912), 118; J. W. Duff, *CAH* IX, 794.

[7] Cf. Maiuri, *Passegg. Camp.*, 31: "Il lido di Baia era a quel tempo deserto"; but cf. *Campi Flegrèi*, 61, where Maiuri states that the oyster farm obtained immediate success, and Frank, *ESAR* I, 290: "Orata . . . when Baiae became a fashionable summer resort . . . raised oysters . . . at the Lucrine lake for the epicures."

We are unfortunately not told to what extent Sergius Orata simply satisfied existent demand for his products, and to what extent he created that demand. But further details of his affairs are preserved in accounts of a trial in 91 B.C. at Rome in which Orata figured prominently. According to Cicero, Sergius Orata had sold to M. Marius Gratidianus a house which he repurchased a few years later. But by then the house had become subject to an encumbrance; this Gratidianus neglected to mention. A legal dispute ensued. Gratidianus was defended by M. Antonius, Orata by L. Licinius Crassus.[8] In the somewhat less lucid account of Valerius Maximus, the dispute was between Orata and Considius, a publican, apparently the official overseer of fishing rights at the Lucrine Lake.[9] Münzer has plausibly reconciled these two accounts and argued that they stem from a single trial,[10] all the details of which need not detain us here. That the house sold to Gratidianus stood on the Lucrine Lake is Münzer's conjecture, but a highly probable one because both Pliny and Valerius Maximus explicitly connect Orata's activities with the lake. One is therefore prompted to ask whether the house was bought for pleasure or as an investment. Cicero and Valerius Maximus do not call the property a villa but rather *aedes* and *aedificia* respectively; Gratidianus might therefore have hoped to sell it at a profit as the demands for coastal properties increased, or even to have used it in connection with fishing activities at the lake. But the probability that he was a sojourner, rather than an investor in the area is greater still: neither his origins nor his career connect him with the mercantile interests of Campania; on the other hand, we know that his famous uncle C. Marius owned two luxury villas, at Misenum and Baiae, probably by the mid-nineties, and that Gratidianus was a strong partisan of Marius.[11] Thus it seems likely that the two

8 Cic. *De Or.* 1.178; *Off.* 3.67. For the date, cf. E. Malcovati, *ORF*², 234 and 253.
9 Val. Max. 9.1.1.
10 Münzer (see above, n. 3), 1713–1714.
11 Münzer, *RE* 14 (1930), 1825–1826, no. 42; Ed. Meyer, *Kleine Schriften* I², 415; on C. Marius' villas see below, pp. 23–28. It may be that two inscriptions bearing identical texts, and certainly originating from the territory of Baiae, indicate an official connection between Gratidianus and the Bay of Naples during his first praetorship, tentatively

kinsmen bought pleasure villas in the same region at about the same time; why that of Gratidianus was later sold cannot be satisfactorily determined.

Münzer implies that Cicero's ownership of villas near the Lucrine Lake in later years accounts for his interest in the trial of Sergius Orata.[12] It has not been generally noticed in this connection that M. Antonius and perhaps also L. Licinius Crassus, who provided legal counsel in the case, themselves owned villas in the area. M. Antonius the orator (*cos.* 99, *censor* 97 B.C.) was one of the speakers in Cicero's *De Oratore* whose dramatic date was 91; he once refers to books which he read carefully *ad Misenum*, since there was scarcely time at Rome.[13] That this is certainly a reference to a villa at Misenum is supported by three grounds: first by the fact that the phrase *ad Misenum* is regular Ciceronian usage to indicate not the territory of Misenum but a villa there;[14] second by the purport of the entire phrase—Antonius is too busy at Rome for books, but at leisure in his villa at Misenum has ample time; third, and decisively, by good evidence that both the son and grandson of Antonius had villas at Misenum[15]—

---

placed by Broughton (*MRR* II, 57) in 85 B.C.; they read M. *Marius M(arci) F(ilius) Pr(aetor) d(e) S(enatus) S(ententia)*. See *CIL* X, 4651, and especially *Not. d. Sc.* (1930), 547, where the editor, Mingazzini, notes that the stones demarcated local boundaries, and assigns them to the Sullan period on the basis of the letter forms. (For an epigraphical parallel from Ostia see *Not. d. Sc.* [1910], 233; with R. Meiggs, *Roman Ostia* [Oxford 1960], 32.) But there remains the possibility that this Marius was a local, rather than a Roman, magistrate.

[12] Münzer, *RE* 2 A (1923), 1714.

[13] Cic. *De Or.* 2.60: *sic, cum istos libros ad Misenum (nam Romae vix licet) studiosius legerim*. Beloch, *Campanien²*, 199, followed by Dubois, *PA*, 362.

[14] Cf. Cic. *Att.* 10.8.10 (T&P 392; SB 199), on which see also How II, 373; *Phil* 2.48; 2.73; see below, Catalogue I, no. 7.

[15] That M. Antonius Creticus (*praetor* 75) inherited the villa at Misenum upon his father's death in 87 follows

1) from Cicero's statement (*Phil.* 2.48; cf. 2.73) that Antonius the triumvir's only true possession was a part of Misenum; this implies that it was part of his inheritance; and it is far more plausible to assume that the estates of Creticus and the orator were identical than to suppose them to have been different villas in the same small area;

2) from a passage of the *De Lege Manilia*. As an example of the outrage committed by pirates against the Roman name, Cicero alludes to a theft from Misenum of the children of one *qui cum praedonibus antea ibi bellum gesserat* (*Leg. Man.* 33). The phrase is not without ambiguity, for both the consul of 99 and his son fought the pirates (for details,

Cicero even implies that the estate of the triumvir was part of his patrimony.[16] When Antonius acquired the estate cannot be determined; if the early nineties were, as seems surely indicated, a period of concentrated building on the Campanian littoral, he may have built the villa early in that decade.

More circumstantial is the evidence for the villa of L. Licinius Crassus (cos. 95, censor 92), whose location has been generally attributed to Baiae.[17] The wealth and luxurious tastes of Crassus indirectly strengthen the supposition that he owned a villa; it is certain that he owned fish ponds and numbered Campanians among his friends.[18] But this is the extent of the evidence, for the passage from Pliny usually considered an unequivocal allusion to Crassus' villa near Baiae refers more probably instead to an estate belonging to a proprietor of imperial date.[19]

see Klebs, "Antonius," RE I [1894], nos. 28 and 29); but as Beloch rightly saw (Campanien², 199; as against RE I [1894], 2591, lines 9–11 [no. 28; cf. no. 109]), Cicero must be alluding to Creticus rather than to his father, for he implies that the kidnapping occurred only a short time before the speech in 66. Further corroboration comes from Plutarch, who cites pirates' violence to the praetors Sextilius and Belli(e)nus (Broughton gives their year of office as 68: MRR II, 138) and their kidnapping of "a daughter of Antonius, who had triumphed" as examples of the gross indignities which immediately preceded conferral of extraordinary imperium upon Pompey in 67 (Plut. Pomp. 24.6; cf. Appian Mith. 93). Thus, chronology requires the outrage at Misenum to have occurred around 68; and the abused Antonia must be the daughter of Creticus (who is mentioned elsewhere as having married P. Vatinius), not a daughter of the orator (of whom no female offspring are known), even though Creticus is not elsewhere said to have triumphed, whereas the orator's triumph is well attested. Since we lack the Fasti for these years, Plutarch may well have stated the facts correctly; in any case, confusion of the two Antonii, whose careers bore such patent similarities, would be a perfectly understandable error. The villa at Misenum, probably built by the orator, passed to Creticus in 87 and to his son, the triumvir, after 71 (see below, Catalogue I, no. 3).

16 Cic. Leg. Man. 33 (M. Antonius Creticus, praetor 75); Phil. 2.48; 2.73; Att. 15.1a.2 (T &P 730; SB 378) (M. Antonius the triumvir). See further Catalogue I, no. 3).

17 Beloch, Campanien², 185–186 (and not, as listed in Beloch's index and by Dubois [PA, 362, n. 3], 175).

18 Wealth: Pliny NH 33.147; cf. 34.14; 36.7. Ponds: Macrob. Sat. 3.15.4. Campanian friends: according to Cicero (Brut. 160), Lucilius mentioned that Crassus, as tribune in 107 B.C., was a dinner guest at the house of Granius the praeco, almost certainly a native of Puteoli (cf. Dubois, PA, 49).

19 Pliny NH 31.5: vaporant et in mari ipso quae Licinii Crassi fuere. But Pliny regularly refers to the consul of 95 B.C. as L. Crassus orator (cf. NH 17.1–6; 36.7; 33.147; 34.14; 9.168), or simply Crassus orator (35.25); this Licinius Crassus will therefore be a different man (despite D'Arms in AJP 88 [1967], 201). For his identity see below, Catalogue II, no. 23.

Of course, proof of ownership of villas at Misenum and Baiae is not required to explain the participation of Antonius and Crassus in the trial of Sergius Orata; the two men were the most famous lawyers and orators of their day. Yet a case involving Lucrine real estate might seem somewhat unworthy of the talents of such distinguished advocates, did we not know at least one of them to own property on the Campanian coast. Villa ownership may provide at least some clarification of their lively interest in a local dispute.

Thus the *novus homo* C. Marius could number certain members of the Roman political elite among his neighbors when visiting his famous villa at Misenum, the first coastal estate whose appointments are explicitly described as luxurious. There are brief references to the house in Seneca, the Elder Pliny and Plutarch. We learn from Seneca that Marius built (*extruxit*) the villa, and on a height (*in summis iugis montium*); of the location he says vaguely, *in regione Baiana*, because the subject of the epistle is the depravity of Baiae, and Seneca only refers to the early villas in the area in order to contrast their military character with the luxuries of the imperial resort.[20] For this reason, his remark that the houses of the Republican commanders (Marius, Pompey, and Caesar) were more like military camps than villas is best taken figuratively, not literally.

Pliny locates the site of Marius' villa more precisely *in Misenensi*.[21] From Plutarch's somewhat fuller account comes a first indication of date and a different impression of architectural character. He states that after the Social War, when Sulpicius proposed Marius and others Sulla for command in the Mithridatic War (88 B.C.), the detractors of Marius urged him to look after his failing health and to go to the warm baths at Baiae.[22] For at Misenum, Plutarch continues, Marius owned a very costly villa

[20] Sen. *Ep.* 51.11.
[21] Pliny *NH* 18.32: *Novissime villam in Misenensi posuit C. Marius septies consul, sed peritia castra metientis*; cf. M. Fiévez, *Latomus* 9 (1950), 381–382.
[22] Plut. *Mar.* 34.2: . . . τῶν δὲ Σύλλαν καλούντων καὶ τὸν Μάριον ἐπὶ θερμὰ κελευόντων εἰς βαίας βαδίζειν καὶ τὸ σῶμα θεραπεύειν . . .

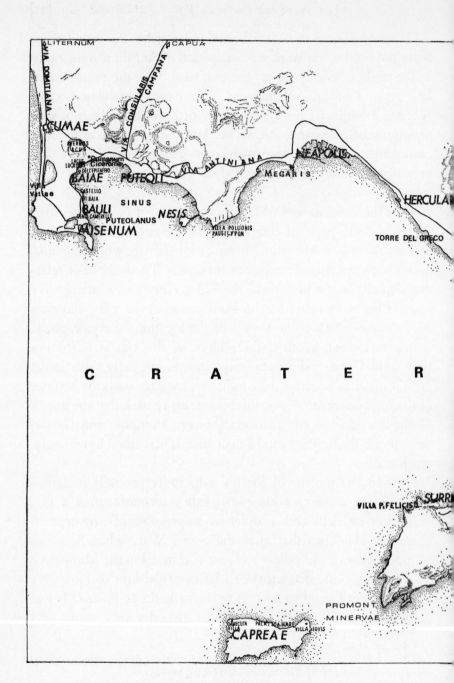

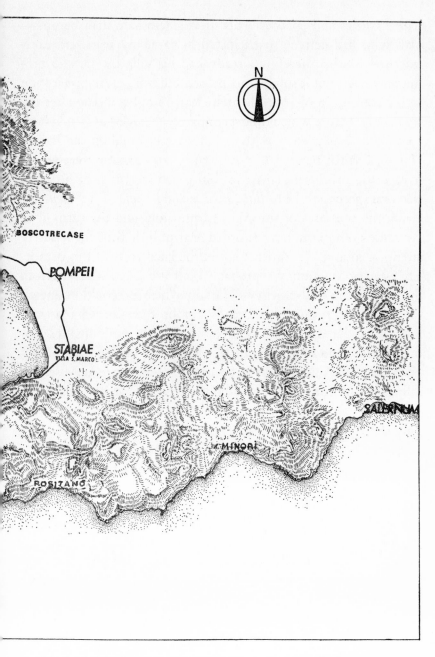

N

BOSCOTRECASE

POMPEII

STABIAE
VILLA S. MARCO

MINORI

POSITANO

SALERNUM

2. *The Bay of Naples in Roman Times.*   *Scale: 1:235,000*

with luxuries and appointments more effeminate than became a man who had actively participated in so many wars and campaigns.[23] Marius therefore already had his villa by 88, and presumably had built it some years before, but not before his election to the consulship of 107: Plutarch clearly implies a date after the consulship, before which time it is unlikely that Marius would have commanded sufficient wealth or influence to build on the Bay of Naples; further, possession of so luxurious a coastal retreat would have made mockery of Marius' bitter denunciation, in his post-electoral speech, of the *mollitia, luxuria* and *ignavia* of the *nobiles*;[24] again, the pressures of subsequent campaigns and the turmoil of domestic politics can have afforded Marius little time for leisurely attention to a villa's construction in the later years of this decade. The estate at Misenum was probably built after Marius' return from the east in the mid-nineties—years in which he could count on some support from noble friends, for he then forged marriage links with the Crassi and Scaevolae, and M. Antonius (*cos.* 99) defended the old Marian legate M'. Aquillius.[25] Indeed, it is highly probable that Antonius' own possession of an estate at Misenum influenced Marius' decision to build there, and as has been seen, Marius' nephew Gratidianus bought a house on the Lucrine Lake only shortly thereafter.

From a Ciceronian allusion in a letter to Atticus, a fragment of a partially preserved oration, and an exegesis of this fragment by the Bobiensian scholiast, it appears that Marius owned a second Campanian villa nearer Baiae. In the *oratio in Clodium et Curionem*, delivered (but not published) in 61, Cicero denounced both Clodius, for profanation of the mysteries of the *Bona Dea*, and his patron C. Scribonius Curio (*cos.* 76), who spoke on Clodius' behalf.[26] To Atticus Cicero had previously boasted of his skill at

---

[23] *Ibid.*: καὶ γὰρ ἦν περὶ Μισηνοὺς τῷ Μαρίῳ πολυτελὴς οἰκία, τρυφὰς ἔχουσα καὶ διαίτας θηλυτέρας ἢ κατ' ἄνδρα πολέμων τοσούτων καὶ στρατειῶν αὐτουργόν.
[24] Sall. *Iug.* 85.35–43.
[25] See Badian, *Historia* 6 (1957), 329; and *Foreign Clientelae* (Oxford 1958), 212, n. 5.
[26] *Att.* 3.12.2 (SB 57) with SB's comments, *ad loc.* (II, 148).

senatorial repartee. Clodius had charged him with having been at Baiae, and had sneeringly inquired what a man from Arpinum would want with hot baths. Cicero replied that Clodius should put the same question to his patron Curio, who had coveted the waters belonging to another Arpinate.[27] That Curio not merely coveted those waters but actually acquired them later is proved by a fragment of the *Oratio in Clodium et Curionem* in which Cicero remarks that Curio had been to Baiae and indeed still owned the waters which had formerly been the delight of a man from Arpinum.[28] And that the "man from Arpinum" in both those passages designates Marius receives direct corroboration from the Bobiensian scholiast.[29]

But since Baiae is very near Misenum, and since references in the sources to the locations of Republican villas are rarely precise, may not the notices from Seneca, Pliny, Plutarch, and Cicero denote a single villa of Marius on the Campanian coast? The decisive objection to this hypothesis is provided by Plutarch, who appends to his description of Marius' villa at Misenum the statement that the property was bought by Cornelia for seventy five thousand drachmas and not long afterwards by L. (Licinius) Lucullus for more than thirty times this sum.[30] He does not mention C. Scribonius Curio, nor can Curio have possessed the villa for a short time before its sale to Cornelia: aside from the fact that Plutarch mentions no such transaction, the clear implication of his narrative is that Cornelia's ownership directly followed that of Marius, who died in 86; furthermore the passage of the *Oratio in Clodium et Curionem* cited above shows that Curio still owned

---

[27] *Att.* 1.16.10 (SB 16): *Surgit pulchellus puer, obicit mihi me ad Baias fuisse. falsum, sed tamen 'quid? hoc simile est' inquam 'quasi in operto dicas fuisse?' 'quid' inquit 'homini Arpinati cum aquis calidis?' 'narra' inquam 'patrono tuo, qui Arpinatis aquas concupivit' (nosti enim Marianas)*.

[28] *Clod. et Cur.* fr. 20 (edd. Klotz–Schoell, VIII 447): *nec enim respexit illum ipsum patronum libidinis suae non modo apud Baias esse, verum eas ipsas aquas habere, quae gustu tamen [Boot: rustici atque] Arpinatis fuissent*.

[29] T. Stangl, *Ciceronis Orationum Scholiastae* II (Leipzig 1912), 89: *C. Curionem qui de proscribtione Syllana fundum emerat in Campania; qui C. Marii nuper fuerat, et ipsius Arpinatis*.

[30] Plut. *Mar.* 34.2.

Marius' villa in 61 B.C. Thus it is clear that there existed two Campanian villas belonging to Marius, one at Misenum, the other at Baiae; they are to be differentiated by their subsequent owners, Cornelia (followed by Lucullus) and C. Scribonius Curio.[31]

When and how did Curio and Cornelia come to acquire the villas of Marius? The answers are suggested by career and genealogy respectively and are instructive of one way in which villas were acquired throughout the last half century of Republican revolution. Before the consulship, the career of C. Scribonius Curio is closely linked with that of Sulla,[32] whereas Cornelia was Sulla's daughter.[33] And the implications of Curio's career and Cornelia's genealogy are clear; two pieces of Marius' property on

[31] E. Gabba (*Athenaeum* N.S. 29[1951], 256–272), followed by T. F. Carney (*A Biography of C. Marius*, 23–24; *Greece and Rome* N.S. 8 [1961], 102) has argued that Campania was a center of Marian influence; Badian has protested (see his analysis in *Historia* 6 [1957], 344) and has called for new arguments (*JRS* 52 [1962], 209). Meanwhile Marius' second Campanian villa has gone unnoticed (but cf. Frank, *ESAR* I, 295). It would be surprising if the owner of two Campanian villas situated in close proximity could not claim some contacts and friends among the local inhabitants. But if (as was suggested above) Marius followed Antonius in placing his villa at Misenum, his "Campanian following" cannot have been large before the mid-nineties. It may be further observed that although Carney produces no evidence for his assertion (*Greece and Rome* N.S. 8 [1961], 105) that Marius owned another villa at Minturnae, the slave of a C. Marius, surely the consul, is epigraphically attested there among the *magistri* of local cults; and Johnson long ago interpreted the evidence to mean that Marius had a villa in the district (J. Johnson, *Excavations at Minturnae* II, pt. 1 [Rome 1933], 63, no. 64).

[32] For Curio's early career see Münzer, *RE* 2 A (1921), 862–863, no. 10: a consistent optimate, he opposed Saturninus in 100 B.C., was tribune in 90, and then left for the east where he served as a Sullan lieutenant in Greece and Asia Minor, besieging Athens along with Sulla in 85 and returning to fight at Sulla's side in the civil wars of 83.

[33] Plutarch states that Sulla had a daughter by his first marriage in early youth with Ilia; he does not supply this daughter's name (Plut. *Sull.* 6.16). But we know that Q. Pompeius Rufus, Sulla's consular colleague of 88, had a son and grandson with the same name (Livy *Epit.* 77); Asconius shows that the latter, tribune in 52, was also the grandson of Sulla by Sulla's daughter (Ascon. *Mil.* 28), whose name is supplied in an anecdote of Valerius Maximus: Cornelia (Val. Max. 4.2.7). Thus, although Plutarch neglects the genealogy of the Cornelia who acquired the villa at Misenum, the buyer has been regularly, and reasonably, identified with Sulla's daughter of the same name (cf. Beloch, *Campanien*², 198; Münzer, *RE* 4 [1900], 1596, no. 412; Frank, *ESAR* I, 295). Her age, distinction, and wealth all support this identification. Further, Cornelia's subsequent sale of the villa to Lucullus for more than thirty times the purchase price helps to confirm some independent evidence (Val. Max. 4.2.7) that in matters of real estate Sulla's daughter was avaricious. For her son's later activities at Bauli, see Catalogue I, no. 33.

the Campanian coast fell into the hands of a supporter and daughter, respectively, of Sulla. Now the Bobiensian scholiast states unequivocally that Curio bought the estate of Marius during the Sullan proscriptions (of 82–81 B.C.),[34] and there can be no doubt that this was also the occasion of Cornelia's purchase at Misenum because systematic confiscations of goods—the first attested at Rome on such a mammoth scale[35]—were intimately bound up with Sulla's destruction of his political enemies. Plutarch says Sulla seized and sold the property of those whom he had put to death, considering it the spoil of war.[36] Pleasure villas clearly comprised a proportion of such property: a certain Quintus Aurelius is alleged to have read his name on the public list of those proscribed and to have exclaimed that his villa at Alba was proscribing him.[37] In this way, according to Pliny, Sulla died the richest man in Rome.[38] We know, furthermore, that the friends and supporters of the dictator now reaped enormous benefits from their political allegiance. Sulla seems to have attended auctions in person and ordered the auctioneers to sell particularly lavish estates at low prices to his friends.[39] Some of these friends can be named. The actions of M. Crassus during these years were consonant with the meaning of his *cognomen*, *Dives*; Plutarch says he never tired of buying up confiscated estates and in Bruttium he is reported to have proscribed a man without Sulla's orders merely to get his property.[40] Men like Q. Caecilius Metellus Pius (*cos.* 80), Servilius Vatia Isauricus, L. Licinius Lucullus and Cn. Pompeius must also have prospered. Sullan largesse also extended to the lower orders, especially to such trusted freedmen as the sinister L. Cornelius Chrysogonus, who at "public" auction bought for

---

[34] Stangl, *Cic. Orat. Schol.* II, 89: *C. Curionem qui de proscribtione Syllana fundum emerat in Campania; qui C. Marii nuper fuerat, et ipsius Arpinatis.* Cf. Frank, *ESAR* I, 299.
[35] M. Fuhrmann, "*publicatio bonorum*" *RE* 23 (1959), 2491–2492.
[36] Plut. *Crass.* 2.3.
[37] Plut. *Sull.* 31.5.
[38] Pliny *NH* 33.134.
[39] Plut. *Lysander and Sulla* 3.3.
[40] Plut. *Crass.* 6.6; cf. Pliny *NH* 33.134.

2,000 sesterces the property of Sextus Roscius of Ameria—property assessed at 6,000,000 sesterces.[41]

Plutarch states that some men lost luxurious houses, others warm baths, still others pleasure gardens.[42] Such choice possessions, it would be only natural to suppose, were seized with alacrity along the Campanian coast.[43] The connections of Curio and Cornelia with Sulla have been demonstrated; that villas belonging to Marius would have been among the first to be seized scarcely requires demonstration. One may therefore accept with confidence the statement of the Bobiensian scholiast that Curio bought Marius' estate in the Sullan proscriptions, and propose a similar date and similar circumstances for Cornelia's purchase at Misenum. One may also supplement Plurarch's explanation of the enormous disparity in the sums paid by Cornelia and Lucullus for the villa. Plutarch believed that the immensely high price which Lucullus paid reflected the rapid growth of luxury in Rome.[44] Yet, as we have seen, mere friends of Sulla could well expect to spend low sums for a confiscated estate. Cornelia, therefore, is certain to have bought the villa of Marius at a price that was as exceptionally low as that paid by Lucullus was high.

L. Cornelius Sulla, at the close of his career, chose coastal Campania as the scene of his retirement; he died in his villa in 78 but his body was returned to Rome for burial. Ancient authorities apparently, modern certainly, are in disagreement as to the site of the estate. Valerius Maximus, our earliest source, describes a dispute at Puteoli between Sulla and Granius, a local magistrate of prominence, and says that Sulla's resultant apoplectic rage caused his death.[45] The substance of this anecdote acquires in-

---

[41] Cic. Rosc. Amer. 6.

[42] Plut. Sull. 31.5.

[43] In Leg. Agr. (2.81) Cicero expressly denies that Sulla, for all his indiscriminate largesse, dared to give away any part of the Ager Campanus. See below, p. 34 (with n. 63) for Sulla's Campanian colonies. The territory of the coastal towns was not regarded as part of the Ager; cf. Leg. Agr. 2.78, and Strabo's separate discussion (5.4.3; cited above, Preface n. 2) of the towns which formed the "Crater."

[44] Plut. Mar. 34.2.

[45] Val. Max. 9.3.8.

creased versimilitude by its reappearance in Plutarch, who adds the detail that Sulla summoned Granius to his room and ordered the magistrate strangled by his servants.[46] Both authors thus regard Puteoli as the scene of this incident, although neither refers to Sulla's villa; a passage from the fourth century *De Viris Illustribus* contains the only explicit reference to Puteoli as the site of Sulla's retirement.[47]

On the other hand, Appian says that Sulla put down power in Rome and retired to his private estate at Cumae;[48] and since he is the only author to mention a villa it is curious that most modern scholars have located the estate at Puteoli,[49] where Sulla may have gone merely to do business with Granius. Nor need Appian's phrase "ἐς Κύμην" imply that Sulla's villa was as far distant from Puteoli as the Roman *municipium* of Cumae. It will be seen that Cicero's villa, regularly called Cumanum in his correspondence, was situated to the east of the Lucrine Lake, in the area presently occupied by Monte Nuovo. This area, only 1.5 miles from the harbor, apparently marked the western boundary of Puteoli until well after Appian's time.[50] If the villa of Sulla, therefore, stood somewhere in this extensive eastern district of Cumae, its location would be entirely consistent with Appian's phrase "ἐς Κύμην." And there is in fact some reason to believe that its site was near that of Cicero's villa, for Cicero wrote to Atticus from the *Cumanum* in 55 to say that he was there devouring the library of Faustus.[51] This is our only reference to a villa belonging to Faustus Cornelius Sulla, the son of the dictator. He has been presumed to have inherited the estate from his father, along with the library

---

[46] Plut. *Sull.* 37.3.
[47] *De Vir. Ill.* 75.12.
[48] App. *BCiv.* 1.104.
[49] Beloch, *Campanien*², 142; Drumann-Groebe II, 422; Frank, *ESAR* I, 295 (where Frank names Puteoli, but cites only Appian); M. W. Frederiksen, "Puteoli," *RE* 23 (1959), 2050; R. Annecchino, *Storia di Pozzuoli* (Pozzuoli 1960), 81. But some scholars have followed Appian: A. Sogliano, *Pompei nel suo Sviluppo Storico* (Rome 1937), 9; Rostagni, *PdP* fasc. 25–27 (1952), 347.
[50] Frederiksen, *RE* 23 (1959), 2053.
[51] Cic. *Att.* 4.10.1 (T&P 121; SB 84); see below, Catalogue I, no. 11.

which Sulla brought back from the East.[52] If so, the villa may have
been in Cumaean territory. But Cicero's loose terminology does
not exclude Puteoli as a possible site; the precise location of the
villa of Sulla must continue to remain conjectural.[53]

The few indications of Sulla's preferred activities during his
residence in Campania, and of his relations with the local towns,
fail to support Plutarch's view that he did not cease to transact the
public business,[54] and suggest instead that his break with Roman
politics was complete. If, as Appian expressly states, Sulla refused
the consulship for 79, his retirement is probably to be dated to late
in 80,[55] and no later than early 79; Plutarch says Sulla looked on

[52] Plut. *Sull.* 26.1.

[53] In the fullest recent discussion of the site of the villa of Sulla, that of G. Della Valle,
"La villa sillana ed augustea Pausilypon," *Camp. Rom.* I, 207–267, the author rejects
most of the ancient testimony (on which see below, Catalogue II, no. 44, P. Vedius
Pollio) and proposes that the villa was at Posillipo, the headland which protrudes into
the Bay of Naples southwest of the city, thus forming a natural boundary between
Neapolis and the towns set along the western coast. Della Valle dismisses the reference
to Cumae on the grounds that, as a Greek himself, Appian would have been prone to
associate Sulla's retirement with a Greek city of ancient fame (p. 212); he conjectures
that the ancient tunnel commonly known as the "Grotta di Seiano" but earlier, probably, as "Grotta di Sillano" was in fact constructed by Sulla to connect Puteoli with his
villa at Pausilypon (pp. 220–223; esp. 223); he finds support for this conjecture in the
presence at the villa site of a theater and odeon (pp. 228–231), apparatus inappropriately
sophisticated, he feels, for P. Vedius Pollio, the Augustan *eques*, to whom ownership
and construction of the villa are generally ascribed (p. 230). This series of imaginative
hypotheses cannot be accepted. In the first place, the testimony of Appian is too summarily
dismissed. Greek bias cannot have induced him to name Cumae instead of Puteoli as
the site of Sulla's retreat, for Puteoli is named eight times in the *Civil Wars*, designated
always by her Greek name Δικαιάρχεια and would certainly have been so designated in
the above passage if Appian had believed Sulla to have retired there. Second, the archaeological evidence conclusively reveals that the "Grotta di Seiano" cannot belong to the
Sullan era (see W. Johannowsky, *RAAN* N.S. 27 [1952], 135) and that the theater and
odeon were not built before the age of Augustus (Günther, *Pausilypon* pp. 31, 47).
Finally, Della Valle holds not merely that Sulla built at Posillipo, but that his construction was on a mammoth scale. But could such a monumental house of pleasure, engineered by so conspicuous a personality, completely escape the notice of all ancient historians
and biographers? Did Sulla leave so few traces on Posillipo that Appian could believe
Cumae, and Plutarch Puteoli, to have been the scene of the dictator's last days? Could
Dio ascribe ownership of the villa to an Augustan *eques* but ignore L. Cornelius Sulla?
None of these possibilities seems even remotely likely; the conjectures of Della Valle
are unacceptable. On the imperial villa see below, Chapter 4, pp. 76–77, 111–112.

[54] Plut. *Sull.* 37.2.

[55] App. *BCiv.* 1.104.

during the elections for 78 "ὥσπερ ἰδιώτης," and that he subsequently rebuked Pompey for his efforts to secure the victory of Lepidus, statements which clearly imply that Sulla was in retirement before the canvassing for those elections began.[56] He died early in 78; Campania thus cannot have been his principal base for much more than a year, and during much of that time Sulla must have been busy with his memoirs (what Cicero later called *fructus otii*[57]), for they amounted to 22 books, and he was at work on the last only two days before his death.[58] The library from Athens (above, note 52) was apparently in the villa during Cicero's day; it would have been a suitable part of Sulla's furnishings. Appian says that the dictator used his leisure to hunt and enjoyed the sea; this proved, he continues, that Sulla had had his fill of wars, of power, and of Rome, and at the end fell completely in love with country life.[59]

Appian also stressed Sulla's isolation, ἐρημία. But there are many signs that Sulla's retirement bore little resemblance to that of Scipio Africanus Maior at Liternum: he did not lack for company, nor were his social contacts restricted to members of his own class. We are told that a trusted freedman, Cornelius Epicadus (a Greek, and subsequently a great favorite also of Faustus Sulla), finished the last book of Sulla's autobiography.[60] It may therefore be assumed that Epicadus formed part of Sulla's Campanian entourage. Plutarch names others: Roscius the comedian, Sorex the mime, and Metrobius the impersonator of women;[61] they are not explicitly linked by Plutarch with Sulla's retirement, but

---

[56] Plut. *Sull.* 34.3–5 (cf. Plut. *Pomp.* 15). For the date of Sulla's renunciation of dictatorship see E. Gabba, *Appiano-Bellorum Civilium Liber Primus* (Florence 1958), on *BCiv.* 1.103, and the references *ad loc.* (pp. 282–283); add Cic. *Rosc. Amer.* 139, on which see Badian, *Historia* 11 (1962), 230–231, which strongly supports the view that Sulla was dictator in 81, consul in 80, and *privatus* in 79.

[57] E.g., *Fam.* 7.1.1; but the phrase is commonplace.

[58] Plut. *Sull.* 37.1.

[59] App. *BCiv.* 1.104, with Gabba (see above, n. 56), 286 *ad loc.*

[60] Suet. *Gramm.* 12.

[61] Plut. *Sull.* 36.1; cf. Münzer, "Norbanus," *RE* 17 (1936), 935; on a later Norbanus Sorex at Pompeii, see below, Chapter 5, n. 169. Cf. A. Rostagni, *PdP* fasc. 25–27 (1952), 347.

neither is there explicit mention that Sulla's coastal villa near Cumae was the scene of that retirement. It is even possible that they owned Campanian villas near that of Sulla, for during the proscriptions the complaint was frequently voiced that Sulla bestowed riches and property on handsome women, musicians, mimes, as well as the lowest freedmen.[62] Modern studies, further, have tended to stress the proximity of Sulla's villa to the colonies of his veterans located in Campania certainly at Urbana, Nola, and Pompeii— possibly also at Suessula and Abella.[63] But, in the first place, sixteen such colonies are attested, scattered throughout central and South Italy; Sulla could scarcely have retired anywhere without having some of his former soldiers in settlements nearby. Second, there is no evidence that Sulla maintained contacts with any of the Campanian colonies or their inhabitants while in retreat; he apparently confined his movements to the coastal towns of Puteoli, Cumae, and Neapolis, fashionable watering places with Greek traditions, where no Sullan colonial foundations are attested. It may have given the dictator some satisfaction to know that colonies of his veterans were comfortably near; but local pleasures, not the nearness of the colonies, seem to have been Sulla's primary motive for seeking out the Campanian coast: a remark of Sallust's tends also to support this view.[64]

Sulla had notable associates close by. Cornelia and Curio had villas, as previously shown, at Misenum and Baiae. P. Servilius Vatia (*cos.* 79) a Sullan supporter, may now have built the Cumaean villa in which, half a century later, his unambitious grandson idled.[65] Another relative, Publius Sulla, later a client of Cicero, was co-founder of the Sullan colony at Pompeii, and acquired

[62] Plut. *Sull.* 33.2.
[63] App. *BCiv.* 1.104, with Gabba (see above, n. 56), *ad loc.*, 271; 1.96 (= Gabba, 260). For the full list and a discussion of Sulla's colonies cf. Gabba, *Athenaeum* N.S. 29 (1951), 270–272; but the list has been scrutinized and pared by Badian, *Historia* 6 (1957), 346–347, who argues convincingly that Sulla's Campanian colonization was "very limited."
[64] Sall. *Jug.* 95.3.
[65] See below, Catalogue II, no. 39.

a bad name during the Sullan proscriptions.[66] He probably bought or built a house at Neapolis during these years, for Cicero shows that this Sulla was certainly living at Neapolis by 64 B.C.[67] and mentions in a later letter a *domum Sullanam* at Neapolis which he himself considered buying.[68] It is a safe conjecture that this house belonged to Cicero's former client; and although it cannot be conclusively demonstrated that he had established residence by 79 B.C., there is good precedent for such a practice: C. Scribonius Curio, it will be recalled, acquired the villa of Marius during the proscriptions and owned it still in 61 B.C.

This small group of relatives, distinguished friends, entertainers, and freedmen must not be presumed to exhaust the list of Sulla's companions in Campania, yet it is of itself sufficient to show that Appian's oversimplified description of the dictator in rustic isolation must be partially revised. What, finally, were Sulla's relations with the local towns? Here the evidence, though meager, tends to support Appian's view that Sulla broke sharply with public life when he retired to Campania—when Plutarch explicitly denies that Sulla stopped transacting the public business, the example which he gives is precisely local; he says that at Puteoli, Sulla intervened to reconcile opposing political factions and revised the laws of city government.[69] Constitutional historians are not in agreement as to the political components of these Puteolan factions. Probably the dispute reflected grievances of new citizens against inadequate provisions of the earlier duumviral constitution;[70] but whatever the nature of the strife, Sulla's intervention is entirely consistent with his retirement from Roman politics, and, for all we know, the municipal government at Puteoli may have invited and welcomed the mediation of their immensely influential new

---

[66] Cic. *Sull.* 62; *Off.* 2.29. See also Syme, *RR*, 66. For the Roman element in Sulla's colony, see Gordon, "The *Ordo* of Pompeii," *JRS* 17 (1927), 168–169.

[67] Cic. *Sull.* 53.

[68] Cic. *Fam.* 9.15.5; see below, Catalogue I, no. 12.

[69] Plut. *Sull.* 37.3: . . . τοὺς ἐν Δικαιαρχείᾳ στασιάζοντας διαλλάξας νόμον ἔγραψεν αὐτοῖς καθ᾽ ὃν πολιτεύσονται . . .

[70] Frederiksen, *RE* 23 (1959), 2040–2041, *q.v.* also for a summary of other views; Gabba, *Athenaeum* N.S. 32 (1954), 284–289.

neighbor in their local dispute. Next, the cause of Sulla's altercation with Granius, according to Plutarch, was the magistrate's failure to make a promised payment to the treasury; Valerius Maximus adds that the money was to be used for rebuilding the *Capitolium*.[71] Even if true (and the testimony of the anecdotist is hardly unimpeachable), it is improbable that Sulla regularly concerned himself with such matters. In general these accounts of Sulla's political interference at Puteoli seem unduly sensational because our sources neglect to state that Sulla was living in his Campanian villa at the time; as a local resident he could hardly avoid occasional dealings in local affairs.

Of Sulla at Neapolis, finally, we hear less. Appian says that the Neapolitans suffered much at the hands of Sulla's supporters during the civil wars of 82[72]—no very reliable guide to Sulla's subsequent relations with the town. Already in this period foreign Greeks were finding the Hellenic way of life (διαγωγή) at Neapolis especially congenial: the polymath Poseidonius knew the city, and Iaia, a lady painter from Cyzicus, worked both in Rome and in Neapolis.[73] Roman aristocrats were also in the habit of visiting Neapolis, the city nearest Rome that had a thoroughly Greek flavor: Cicero once observed that the sons of Roman senators walked the streets there dressed in Greek garb; there even L. Cornelius Sulla wore the chlamys.[74] There is no indication of a particular occasion; Sulla may regularly have affected such a practice. In any case, he would not thereby have meant to indicate frivolity or contempt; the gesture is better interpreted as showing Sulla's willingness, when in a Greek city, to adopt Greek ways.

The Antonii, possibly Crassus, Marius and his nephew, Sulla,

---

[71] Plut. *Sull.* 37.3; Val. Max. 9.3.8: *Granius . . . pecuniam a decurionibus ad refectionem Capitolii promissam cunctantius daret.*

[72] App. *BCiv.* 1.89. The economic consequences ·of Sulla's harshness appear to have been disastrous for Neapolis, whose maritime primacy passed rapidly to Puteoli: see E. Lepore, "Per la storia economico-sociale di Neapolis," *PdP* fasc. 25–27 (1952), 318–319.

[73] Poseidonius: Athenaeus 9.401; Iaia: Pliny *NH* 35.147.

[74] Cic. *Rab. Post.* 26. The text is partially corrupt, but *Neapoli* followed by *viderunt chlamydatum illum L. Sullam* is sound.

Cornelia, Curio, and P. Sulla comprise the list of notable Romans known to have owned villas or houses in Campanian coastal towns during the first decades of the first century B.C. This list is brief, but we have seen signs that it was actually much longer.[75] In the nineties, the Lucrine enterprises of Sergius Orata must have prospered, for they attracted notice; wealthy owners of villas near Baiae must have formed the clientele, because oysters are not easily exported. The sneering suggestion that Marius should repair to Baiae in 88, and Marius' choice of Misenum as a villa site, imply that for the upper classes the area had already acquired distinctive allure. During the Sullan proscriptions, the numerous attested instances of loss of property, together with evidence that fortunate profiteers accumulated enormous sums, show how many and how choice must have been the estates then ripe for seizing; and not all the property, as has been seen, consisted of farms and city houses. The research, finally, of archaeologists and architectural historians shows that although coastal Campania may have been a favorite region for villas, prosperity was general and other sites were not neglected.[76]

The year 74 B.C. marks an important stage in the history of Roman sojourning on the Bay of Naples. Cicero had been quaestor at Lilybaeum in the preceding year. Upon his return from his province, as he relates in a famous passage in the *Pro Plancio*, he disembarked at Puteoli, just at the spring season, when the area swarmed with upper class visitors from Rome. To his great amazement, and deeper discomfiture, he found that his accomplishments in Sicily, highly esteemed by himself, were unknown at Puteoli; he thenceforth pretended to be a part of the crowd come

[75] In this connection it is perhaps significant that the *Histories* of Q. Lutatius Catulus (*cos.* 102) contain the first attested application of the word *amoenitas* to the cities on the Bay of Naples. Cf. H. Peter, *Historicorum Romanorum Reliquiae*² I (Leipzig 1914), 192–193 (fr. 7); and see further below, Chapter 3, pp. 46–48.

[76] G. Lugli, *Forma Italiae, Regio* I, vol. 1, pt. 1 (Rome 1926), 102–103, no. 58 (a Sullan cryptoporticus at Tarracina); cf. Grimal, *Jardins Romains*, 109; M. E. Blake, *Ancient Roman Construction in Italy from the Prehistoric Period to Augustus* (Washington, D.C. 1947), 234, 245; A. Böethius, *The Golden House of Nero* (Ann Arbor 1960), 96; Rostovtzeff, *SEHRE*², 551, n. 26.

to take the waters.[77] This is not only excellent indication of the enticements of the Campanian coast to regular, seasonal retreat; it further shows that these enticements have extended to an entire class, composed of Romans of sufficiently high social and economic status. The foregoing pages have attempted to mark the stages by which this development occurred.

[77] Cic. *Planc.* 65: . . . *decedens e provincia, Puteolos forte venissem, cum plurimi et lautissimi in iis locis solent esse* . . . For *lautus,* "splendid," "elegant," see, e.g., Cic. *Fam.* 9.16.8; cf. *lautitia, Fam.* 9.16.8; *Fam.* 9.20.1.

THREE · *The Last Years of the Republic*

Introduction

The riches of Cn. Pompeius Magnus surpassed even those of M. Licinius Crassus Dives, generally supposed to have been the wealthiest Roman of his day. Pompey's property, which included great estates at Cumae, Alba, Formiae, and *in agro Falerno*, brought fifty million denarii, only a fraction of its true worth, when auctioned by his enemies.[1] Few contemporaries, to be sure, could boast of such vast wealth; it has been estimated that no more than six men in Cicero's day possessed the annual income of four million sesterces which Crassus thought the minimum sum required to make a person wealthy.[2] Yet like Pompey, large numbers of his fellow senators and Roman knights amassed in these years estates of prodigious size, luxury, and magnificence; also like Pompey, they could fear that owing to the Civil War those estates might never reach intended heirs. The contrast of unprecedented wealth and luxury with chronic political uncertainty characterizes the last years of the Roman Republic. In this chapter my aim is to illustrate both conditions as they are reflected by ownership of villas on the Campanian coast; that is, to describe villa life on the Bay of Naples within the context of the political strife which came to dominate the period. A somewhat different methodological procedure has been adopted in the following pages and requires a word of explanation. Owing to the relative abundance of the literary testimony for the Ciceronian

[1] Crassus: Pliny *NH* 33.134; Plut. *Crass.* 2; Frank, *ESAR* I, 393. Pompey: Cass. Dio 48.36.5 on which cf. Frank, 393: "This is the largest property reported for any Roman of the Republic." On Pompey's villas see Catalogue I, no. 31 (Cumae); Drumann-Groebe IV², 542.

[2] Frank, *ESAR* I, 393.

age, and to the obvious impracticability of a strictly chronological treatment, I have here, in the interests of clarity, categorized the evidence in topical form and have presented the most important subjects in a series of eight separately titled but logically related sections.

Luxuria *and the Bay of Naples*

Pliny says that inside Rome the house of Lepidus was the finest in 78 B.C.; thirty-five years later a hundred houses had surpassed it.[3] But to denouncers of *luxuria* in the Ciceronian age it was the villas—in the suburbs, in the country, and especially at the seaside—which furnished congenial material. *Aedificare* now first acquires a pejorative sense. Nepos says of Atticus: *nemo illo minus fuit emax, minus aedificator*, for he owned *nullam suburbanam aut maritimam sumptuosam villam.*[4] In a famous passage in Lucretius, restlessness moves a rich man to hasten from Rome to his country villa, boredom sends him back again;[5] Sallust cites houses and villas raised to the size of cities as signs of the *luxuria* rampant during the days of Catiline;[6] in the philosophical works Cicero records his disapproval of showy villas and their plush appurtenances;[7] Varro deplores the ostentation of modern villas the building of which has been a national disaster, and promises better profits with farms modelled on the *diligentia* of the ancients.[8]

In the Bay of Naples—*cratera illum delicatum*[9]—the villas and

[3] Pliny *NH* 36.109.

[4] Nep. *Att.* 14.3; and, for a convenient summary of the other literary evidence, cf. J. E. B. Mayor, *Juvenal*[3] II (1881), 300 (on 14.86).

[5] Lucr. 3.1060–1067.

[6] Sall. *Cat.* 12.3: *operae pretium est, cum domos atque villas cognoveris in urbium modum exaedificatas . . .*

[7] Cic. *Leg.* 2.1: *. . . magnificasque villas et pavimenta marmorea et laqueata tecta contemno . . .*; cf. *Paradoxa Stoic.* 5(38): *. . . quorum in villa ac domo nihil splendidum nihil ornatum . . .*

[8] Varro *Rust.* 1.13.7: *Nunc contra villam urbanam quam maximam ac politissimam habeant dant operam ac cum Metelli ac Luculli villis pessimo publico aedificatis certant*; 1.13.6: '*Fructuosior*' *inquit* '*est certe fundus propter aedificia, si potius ad anticorum diligentiam quam ad horum luxuriam derigas aedificationem.*'

[9] *Att.* 2.8.2. (T&P 35; SB 28): *putas praetermittendum nobis esse hoc tempore Cratera illum delicatum* (April 59); see above, Preface, vii.

fishponds of an opulent few served as paradigms of the luxury of the age. At Naples, Lucullus spent more to tunnel through a mountain and admit sea water than to build his villa, thereby earning the sobriquet *Xerxes togatus*.[10] Who, asks Varro rhetorically, does not know about the fishponds of Philippus, Hortensius, and the Luculli?[11] In 60 B.C. letters of Cicero's contain repeated and contemptuous references to the *piscinarii*, the noble owners of fishponds, who worried only when their bearded mullets refused to eat from their hands and neglected the business of state; Macrobius identified these *nobiles principes* with Lucullus, Philippus, and Hortensius—at their villas at Naples, Cumae, and Bauli were the most famous of such ponds.[12] Those of M. Lucullus were also in Campania but less sedulously cared for; Hortensius disdained them because they lacked suitable tidal basins and Lucullus' fish thus lived in stagnant waters.[13] Among men so eminent, all senators with pretensions to culture and sophistication, conscious of the stigma attached by their class to forms of income not based on agriculture, and never harassed by economic need, pisciculture seems to have been only an expensive affectation, a Roman adoption of a diversion first indulged by Hellenistic kings.[14] Around these Campanian ponds, the fish, and their famous owners there

[10] Pliny *NH* 9.170; Vell. Pat. 2.33.4: *Lucullus . . . profusae huius in aedificiis convicti busque et apparatibus luxuriae primus auctor fuit*; cf. Catalogue I, no. 22b.

[11] Varro *Rust.* 3.3.10: *Quis enim propter nobilitates ignorat piscinas Philippi, Hortensi, Lucullorum?*

[12] *Att.* 1.18.6 (T&P 24; SB 18); 1.19.6 (T&P 25; SB 19); 1.20.3 (T&P 26; SB 20); 2.1.7 (T&P 27; SB 21): *. . . nostri autem principes digito se caelum putent attingere si mulli barbati in piscinis sint qui ad manum accedant, alia autem neglegant . . .* Macrob. *Sat.* 3.15.6: *nobilissimi principes Lucullus, Philippus, et Hortensius, quos Cicero piscinarios appellabat.* See Catalogue I, no. 22, no. 28, no. 17.

[13] Varro *Rust.* 3.17.8; Catalogue I, no. 42.

[14] On Hellenistic precedents, cf. Plato *Polit.* 264 c; Arist. *Hist. An.* 8.2.592 a; K. Schneider, "Piscina," *RE* 20 (1950), 1783–1785. Fishponds a costly, aristocratic affectation: Varro *Rust.* 3.17.2: *illae autem maritimae piscinae nobilium, quibus Neptunus ut aquam et piscis ministrat, magis ad oculos pertinent, quam ad vesicam, et potius marsippium domini exinaniunt, quam implent. Primum enim aedificantur magno . . . tertio aluntur magno.* Too little heed is paid to this fundamental passage by T. Corcoran, *Class. Bull.* (1959), 37–39, 43, who stresses the profitable aspects of pisciculture without sufficient regard for the social status of the ponds' owners. Cf. Syme, *RR*, 22–23; and for early imperial ponds, see below, Chapter 5, p. 135.

grew up a host of anecdotes ranging from the merely improbable to the patently absurd. The fish were pets, were decorated with jewels, had famous names; men wept when they died. Hortensius appears to have been particularly susceptible to such inordinate grief: Varro says that he could not bear to eat the fish nurtured so tenderly in his ponds at Bauli, but regularly sent to Puteoli to supply his table.[15]

Baiae

If luxury villas on the Bay of Naples were thus subject to general censure, Baiae was particularly notorious, a curiosity among Roman towns. At neighboring Cumae, Puteoli, and Neapolis, city origins were linked with the age of Greek colonization, and local traditions and institutions—Greek, Oscan, and Roman— flourished apart from the visits of vacationers from Rome. In contrast Baiae figured nowhere in early Roman history; she is first mentioned in a line of Hellenistic poetry which offers an aetiological explanation of her name; an inscription shows that she never possessed local magistrates or independent territory, but comprised part of the administrative district of Cumae.[16] And yet, when first mentioned frequently in the works of first-century authors, Baiae is already famous as a city of hot sulphur baths and seaside allurements, catering alike, as Strabo later observed, to the ailments of the sick and the pleasures of the sound.[17] Thus no Roman *municipium* but rather a collection of villas set around and above a glittering bay, Baiae was Rome's first resort. Here it gave pleasure to build and then extend villas into the sea itself by means

[15] Varro *Rust.* 3.17.5. For other absurdities *ibid.*, 3.17, *passim*; Pliny *NH* 9.171; Cic. *Par. Stoic.* 5(38); Drumann-Groebe III², 100.

[16] Baiae first mentioned: Lycophron *Alexandra*, 695; not an independent municipality: Mommsen, *CIL* X, p. 351; Beloch, *Campanien*², 186–187, no. 227, a decree of the *decuriones* of Cumae, 289 A.D. For the archaeological evidence, including architectural remains datable to the sixth century B.C., see below, Chapter 4, pp. 109–110.

[17] Strab. 5.4.5 (C 244); cf. Cass. Dio. 48.51.2. On Baiae see especially Friedländer, *Sittengeschichte Roms*⁹ I (Leipzig 1919), 405–408; Beloch, *Campanien*², 180–189; Schmatz, *Baiae, das erste Luxusbad der Romer* (Regensburg 1905–1906); Maiuri, *Campi Flegrèi*, 66–86.

of supporting piers. Sallust first mentions and condemns this practice without specifying the exact locale, but he was clearly thinking of Baiae, which Horace, decrying human folly, later associates with this habit and whence Vergil drew material for an expressive simile: the giant limbs of Bitias fell in a heap, like the collapse of a huge stone pier on the shore of Baiae.[18]

It is no matter for surprise that in this city of pleasure luxury was condemned from the start, nor was it the only vice attested. Varro devoted one of the *Menippean Satires* to Baiae; the single surviving line well illustrates both the character of the whole and the reputation of the town: *quod non solum innubae fiunt communes, sed etiam veteres repuerascunt et multi pueri puellascunt.*[19] It has already been seen that during the trial of Clodius in 61 B.C., when charged with having been to Baiae, Cicero was prompt to sidestep and then return the accusation.[20] And five years later, in an unforgettable list of dissolute practices in the *Pro Caelio*—orgies, flirtations, Baiae, beach parties, dinner parties, drinking parties, musical entertainments and concerts, boating picnics[21]—the mere mention of Baiae contributed effectively to the impression of Clodia's immorality which Cicero was striving to establish.

Proprietors

These castigations of Campanian *luxuria* and Baian immorality are proof that the "villa-habit," as it has been named,[22] had seized the collective fancy of upper-class Romans of the late Republic; a practice must be widespread before it can become a commonplace of social criticism. At the beginning of this century, Günther was able to detect the remains of numerous Roman villas

[18] Sall. *Cat.* 20.11: ... *quas profundant in extruendo mari* ...; cf. 13.1: *maria constrata esse.* Hor. *Carm.* 3.1.33–46; 3.24.4; and before all *Carm.* 2.18.17–22. Virg. *Aen.* 9.710–718: *Talis in Euboico Baiarum litore quondam / saxea pila cadit, magnis quam molibus ante . constructam ponto iaciunt, sic illa ruinam / prona trahit penitusque vadis inlisa recumbit* ...

[19] Varro (ed. Buecheler), *Sat. Menipp.* fr. 44.

[20] Cic., *Or. in Clod. et Cur.* fr. 20 (edd. Klotz-Schoell, VIII 447); see above, Chapter 2, p. 27.

[21] Cic. *Cael.* 35.

[22] Duff, *CAH* IX, 793.

3

along the submerged ancient shoreline of the Naples Bay and thereby to give some indication of the popularity of the practice.[23] But the works of Cicero are a still better guide. He owned three villas on the Bay of Naples, and even before he acquired his *Cumanum* in 56, he knew the northern district of the bay intimately enough to include a detailed topographical description in one of his speeches.[24] Many of his letters were composed in the course of leisurely stays in his *Pompeianum*, *Cumanum* or *Puteolanum* and contain local allusions. His correspondents, furthermore, included both Campanian residents and Romans visiting the seaside resorts. His letters thus comprise a unique guide to the meaning of *otium* as applied to villa life in the coastal Campania of his day: more than forty Romans, among them the most prominent political personalities of the Ciceronian age, can be shown to have owned villas or private houses along the Campanian coast. This substantial body of evidence has been arranged in catalogue form and is presented as the first part of the appendix. The catalogue is alphabetically designed for purposes of more convenient reference, and is intended to be consulted in conjunction with the more general account of Campanian *villeggiatura* which follows in this chapter; to this end frequent cross references have been supplied.

Just as Cicero's letters are by far the most important source for the compilation of the catalogue, so also in the discussion his testimony, and his personality, occupy the foreground. From his references to the owners of coastal Campanian villas and from his

[23] Günther, *Pausilypon*, 145: "No spot on the Italian littoral, extensive as that littoral is, lends itself to the development of the peculiar style of marine architecture (employed by wealthy Romans in their villas) . . . so well as this short strip of Campania that lies between Misenum and Pausilypon. The requisites are: an almost tideless sea, comparative shelter, a relatively narrow foreshore backed by the cliffs of a soft volcanic rock, easy to quarry, hardening in use: these conditions obtaining, we have a line of such magnificent watering-places, Misenum, Baiae, Puteoli, Pausilypon, as did not exist elsewhere, though no doubt there may have been isolated instances of sumptuous palaces built out into the sea, as at Formia or Antium."

[24] *Att.* 1.13.5 (T &P 19; SB 13): τοποθεσίαν *quam postulas Miseni et Puteolorum includam orationi meae.* The speech referred to may be the *Oratio Metellina* delivered at the beginning of 62 (cf. SB I, 305, *ad loc.*); the relevance of the *topothesia* to the speech remains obscure.

frequent allusions elsewhere to their enticements—topographical, architectural, social, and even gastronomic—it is possible to comprehend the more attractive aspects of the practice so fervently condemned by the castigators of *luxuria* cited above, and thereby to place those unfriendly judgments in more realistic perspective. Cicero could distinguish between a villa which was *philosopha* (tastefully, but not sumptuously, appointed) and those which exhibited insane extravagance.[25] It is extremely doubtful whether any one of his own estates, which he variously calls *voluptarias possessiones, villulas, praediola, maritima, ocellos Italiae*,[26] was excessively luxurious: Plutarch expressly denies that they were,[27] and we are told that in his *Cumanum* Cicero was hard pressed to find room for the retinue of Caesar which Philippus appears to have accommodated easily in his lavish villa nearby.[28] The coming and going from Rome to country houses, of which Lucretius was so scornful, Cicero called *peregrinatio* (the seasonal visiting of one's villas in the country and by the sea),[29] and for him and the majority of his equally distinguished contemporaries—wealthy, but with fortunes more modest than those of Lucullus and Hortensius, Pompey and Caesar, Crassus, and Metellus—such visits were the source of keen and innocent pleasure.

The Setting: Amoenitas

The location of *piscinae* reveals a predilection for setting villas at the sea's very edge. High hills were another preferred site. The villa of Julius Caesar near Baiae, according to Tacitus, looked forth

---

[25] QFr. 3.1.5 (T&P 148): *quamquam ea villa quae nunc est tamquam philosopha videtur esse, quae obiurget ceterarum villarum insaniam* (Quintus' villa at Arcanum).

[26] Att. 12.25.1 (T&P 561; SB 264); 8.9.3 (T&P 340; SB 188); 16.3.4 (T&P 773; SB 413); Fam. 2.16.2 (T&P 394); Att. 16.6.2 (T&P 775; SB 414).

[27] Plut. Cic. 8.2: καὶ περὶ Νέαν πόλιν ἦν ἀγρὸς καὶ περὶ Πομπηΐους ἕτερος, οὐ μεγάλοι . . . Cicero in fact had no property at Neapolis; cf. Catalogue I, no. 43.

[28] Att. 13.52.1 (T&P 679; SB 353).

[29] Att. 16.3.4 (T&P 773; SB 413): . . . *quodque temporis in praediolis nostris et belle aedificatis et satis amoenis consumi potuit in peregrinatione consumimus.* Cf. Fam. 2.12.2 (T&P 263); Att. 2.4.3 (T&P 31; SB 24); Att. 2.6.1 (T&P 33; SB 26); Att. 6.2.2 (T&P 256; SB 116). For imperial developments, see below, Chapter 5, pp. 118, 133.

from its height onto the bay beneath,[30] which recalls Seneca's description of the promontories where the estates of Marius and Pompey were also constructed. A good view of the sea was a main desideratum. At Pompeii Cicero's sedentary friend M. Marius had cut a window into one room and obtained a panorama of the entire bay.[31] In the villa of Hortensius at Bauli, Cicero turned the conversation to sense perception and suddenly exclaimed *o praeclarum prospectum*; from his seat in the colonnade he could see the *Cumanum* of Catulus and had a good view of Puteoli, but says he could not make out his *Pompeianum* though nothing intervened to block his vision.[32] The orator's *Cumanum* overlooked both the Lucrine Lake and the sea, into which he considered hurling, in a discouraged moment, the *De Re Publica*.[33] Replying to a question of Atticus, in 44 shortly after he had acquired his *Puteolanum*, Cicero professes not to know whether he more enjoys hills and a view or walks along the seashore.[34] It is generally believed that the hills of Cicero's native Arpinum are here contrasted with the shores at Puteoli.[35] But it would have been odd for so constant and topical a correspondent as Atticus to ask whether Cicero preferred Arpinum to the Campanian coast where he had owned property for more than a decade. The *tumuli* here refer to the hills near Cumae; Atticus is asking which of Cicero's neighbouring villas, the *Cumanum* or *Puteolanum*, the old or the new, gave him more pleasure.[36]

The sites of the *villae maritimae* are clues to their distinctive

[30] Tac. *Ann.* 14.9.3: . . . *villam Caesaris dictatoris quae subiectos sinus editissima prospectat.* The evidence for the architectural character of these hillside villas is discussed in detail by F. Noack and K. Lehmann-Hartleben, *Baugeschichtliche Untersuchungen am Stradtrand von Pompeji* (Berlin and Leipzig 1936), 202–217.

[31] *Fam.* 7.1.1 (T &P 127); Catalogue I, no. 29.

[32] *Acad. Pr.* 2.80; Catalogue I, no. 17.

[33] *QFr.* 2.12.1 (T &P 139): . . . *in illud ipsum mare deiciemus quod spectantes scribimus* . . . Catalogue I, no. 43b.

[34] *Att.* 14.13.1 (T &P 718; SB 367): . . . *quaeris, idque etiam me ipsum nescire arbitraris, utrum magis tumulis prospectuque an ambulatione ἀλιτενεῖ delecter. Est mehercule, ut dicis, utriusque loci tanta amoenitas ut dubitem utra anteponenda sit.*

[35] Schmidt, 485 and n. 2.

[36] Cf. SB *ad loc.* (VI, 226): "Do you prefer your new acquisition on the Bay to what you had already?" That was Atticus' question.

allure: *amoenitas*. Unlike the adjectives *iucundus, suavis*, or *dulcis, amoenus* is properly applied only to things affecting the sense of sight; and as Servius further explains, *amoena sunt loca solius voluptatis plena . . . unde nullus fructus exsolvitur*.[37] In the *De Finibus*, Cicero includes a *locus amoenus* in a list of pleasures intrinsically delightful.[38] Something *amoenum* is thus that which is intrinsically lovely to look upon, from the contemplation of which nothing but pleasure can be sought or gained. Used indifferently from earliest Latin Literature to describe both the works of nature and the works of man,[39] *amoenus* is particularly appropriate to a landscape (*rus, locus*) or seascape (*litus, ora*) which is smooth and gentle, not rugged or harsh (as Quintilian explains, *litus amoenum non infestos scopulos habet*)[40] or to Roman pleasure villas, which were indeed works of man *unde nullus fructus exsolvitur*,[41] and were expressly designed to take full visual advantage of natural surroundings.

The *villa maritima*, both attractive in its own right and set amid the beauties of an indented shoreline, is thus *amoena* on two counts, and in Cicero's correspondence is regularly so described. Cicero once expresses his regret that, in the midst of the right season for *peregrinatio*, he is not amusing himself *in praediolis nostris . . . satis amoenis*;[42] caught up in the bustle of Rome he envies Marius at Pompeii *in ista amoenitate paene solum relictum*;[43] *nihil amoenius*, he once writes, than his house at Antium;[44] such was the *amoenitas* of both *Cumanum* and *Puteolanum* that he found it impossible to choose between them.[45] To Atticus he once says, "you thought when you wrote me that I was *in actis nostris*".[46] The unusual word

[37] Servius, *ad Aen.* 5.734.
[38] Cic. *Fin.* 2.107.
[39] *TLL* I, 1962–1964 (*amoenus*); 1960–1961 (*amoenitas*). I have not seen G. Schönbeck, *Der Locus Amoenus von Homer bis Horaz* (Cologne 1962).
[40] Quint. *Decl.* 388, ed. Ritter (Teubner 1884), p. 437, ll. 24–25.
[41] Cf. the expression of the *Digesta* 50.16.198 (cited above, Chapter 1, n. 41): "*Urbana praedia*" *omnia aedificia accipimus, non solum ea, quae sunt in oppidis, sed et si forte stabula sunt . . . vel si praetoria voluptati tantum deservientia . . .*
[42] *Att.* 16.3.4 (T &P 773; SB 413).
[43] *Fam.* 7.1.1 (T &P 127).
[44] *Att.* 4.8.1 (T &P 112; SB 79).
[45] *Att.* 14.13.1 (T &P 718; SB 367).
[46] *Att.* 14.8.1 (T &P 710; SB 362).

acta, -ae is a transliteration of Greek ἀκτή,[47] and a comment of Servius helps to fix the meaning: *acta* at *Aeneid* 5.613 is explained as *secreta et amoena litorum*, and the glosses add *loca secreta circa mare, id est . . . voluptaria. In actis nostris* is thus "in one of my pleasure houses by the sea (*villae maritimae*)."

Social Life

Scipio Africanus Maior valued the quiet isolation of his villa at Liternum. Among Cicero's notable contemporaries a sojourn in Campania—where *peregrinatio* was seasonal, villas closely packed together, and their owners all Roman senators or wealthy *equites*—was usually the occasion for resuming, in a more attractive setting, the social life of the city: Cicero wrote to Atticus in 51 *habuimus in Cumano quasi pusillam Romam; tanta erat in iis locis multitudo.*[48] Springtime remained the preferred period of the year. A passage from the *Oratio in Clodium et Curionem* of 61 shows that April brought crowds of pleasure seekers to Baiae;[49] more than once in the *Pro Caelio* Cicero mentions that *Baiarum illa celebritas* was witness to Clodia's decadent misdeeds.[50] Twelve years later the fashion was the same; from his *Puteolanum* in April of 44, Cicero informs Atticus that the crowds were huge and destined to become still larger.[51] This apparent springtime migration from Rome to Campania, attested first in 74 B.C.,[52] was only indirectly the result of climatic conditions; more significant is the coincidence of these visits with the Roman senate's spring recess (*senatus*

---

[47] Cf. SB, *ad loc.* (VI, 219); and, for the same sense, see *Anth. Pal.* 5.39.5–6: καὶ γράφε πρός με, εἰς ποίην ἀκτὴν εὐφροσυνῶν γέγονας; Plut. *Quaest. conviv.* 4.2.8 (= 668 B): τί δ' οἱ πολλοὶ βούλονται . . . ὅταν ἡδέως γενέσθαι παρακαλοῦντες ἀλλήλους λέγωσι, 'σήμερον ἀκτάσωμεν' (where ἀκτάζειν = "to enjoy oneself, in a place at the seaside").

[48] *Att.* 5.2.2 (T &P 185; SB 95).

[49] Cic. *Or. in Clod. et Cur.* fr. 20 (quoted above, Chapter 2, n. 28), with the comment of the Bobiensian Scholiast *ad loc.* (Stangl, *Cic. Orat. Schol.* II, 88): *Consuetudo erat multis ineunte verno ad aquarum, quae sunt in Campania, velut fomenta salubria convenire.*

[50] E.g., *Cael.* 47, 49.

[51] *Att.* 14.9.2 (T &P 712; SB 363).

[52] See above, Chapter 2, p. 37.

discessus) to which there are three allusions in Cicero's correspondence and which appears to have begun regularly in the
beginning of April, extending into May.[53] Only then could a
senator enjoy a connected holiday of any length; consequently at
other times of the year, and even during the scorching summer
months through which senators and *iudices* continued to toil in
Rome, it was to the more accessible suburban villas that prominent
Romans repaired for shorter visits. Doubtless, too, the hills in
summer were considerably cooler than the coast. There were
opportunities for brief sojourns at other times, and of course those
who remained outside political life or those whose active careers
had ended, could arrange *peregrinationes* to suit their pleasure. The
autumn was another popular period on the Bay of Naples, and
unseasonal visits are attested; Cicero was once in Cumae in late
November, and again in December the following year.[54] Dolabella was settled in his villa at Baiae, and apparently comfortable,
in December of 45, but Cicero's remark that sky and land were then
foregoing their usual evil effects suggests that in the winter Baiae
was ordinarily avoided.[55]

In full season social life was brisk. We hear of few inns, and since
we know that Cicero owned little lodges (*deversoria*) located at
points along the *Via Appia*, which enabled him to break his
journeys between Rome and his villas,[56] it may be presumed that
vacationers had their own estates or stayed with friends. Proprietors often spent several days at the villas of near neighbors:
Pompey was a guest at Cicero's *Cumanum* in April of 53; Curio
passed some days there in 49; in 46, Cicero wrote to Varro at

[53] *Fam.* 3.9.2 (T&P 249); *Att.* 12.40.3 (T&P 584; SB 281, with SB's comments *ad loc.*
[V, 332]); *Att.* 14.5.2 (T&P 707; SB 359).
[54] *Fam.* 9.23 (T&P 504), and 7.4 (T&P 503): November 46; *Att.* 13.52 (T&P 679;
SB 353): December 45.
[55] *Fam.* 9.12.1 (T&P 680).
[56] Cicero owned *deversoria* at Anagnia on the Latin Road between Tusculum and
Arpinum, *Att.* 16.8.1 (T&P 797; SB 418); Lanuvium, *Att.* 12.44.3 (T&P 590; SB 285);
Sinuessa, *Att.* 14.8.1 (T&P 710; SB 362); and perhaps at Frusino, *Att.* 11.4.1 (T&P 413;
SB 215). See further J. Carcopino, *Cicero: Secrets of his Correspondence* (London 1951),
51–53; *Att.* 11.5.2 (T&P 414; SB 216).

Cumae asking that the bath be made ready for his imminent visit.[57] Caesar was staying with Octavian's stepfather Philippus in Puteoli in 45, along with a retinue of two thousand men, when Cicero gave dinner to the dictator.[58] It was normal for Cicero to forewarn L. Papirius Paetus and M. Marius, who chose to reside permanently in Campania, of his own intended visits, respectively, to Naples and Pompeii; Paetus could then alert his cook, whose cheese and sardine dishes Cicero particularly fancied.[59] Marius was of frail health and in April of 55 Cicero hesitated to subject him to the discomforts of his *Cumanum*, then only partially built; he therefore made arrangements to put Marius up at the nearby villa of Anicius.[60] A host might or might not himself be present during a guest's stay. In the spring of 44 Cicero placed his *Cumanum* and its resident staff of *vilici* and *procuratores* at the disposal of Atticus' wife Pilia,[61] and repaired to his *Pompeianum* and *Puteolanum*, pausing to look in again on Pilia during his return north to Rome. Quintus Cornificius once used Cicero's *deversorium* at Sinuessa and seems to have been jokingly impolite about its lack of comforts.[62] To spurn proferred hospitality could give offense; when Brutus refused Cicero's offer of the use of the *Cumanum* in 45, it seemed to Cicero that he could not have behaved less graciously.[63]

Shorter visits crowded the daily schedule. A proprietor seems rarely to have dined alone. In 43 word reached Cicero in Rome that Paetus had ceased going out to dinner; he urged his friend not

[57] Pompey: *Fam.* 16.10.2 (T&P 926); Curio: *Att.* 10.7.3 (T&P 388; SB 198); Cicero to Varro: *Fam.* 9.5.3 (T&P 463).

[58] *Att.* 13.52.1 (T&P 679; SB 353).

[59] *Fam.* 9.23 (T&P 504); 7.4 (T&P 503); Paetus' cook: *Att.* 14.16.1 (T&P 721; SB 370); cf. *Fam.* 9.16.7 (T&P 472).

[60] *QFr.* 2.8.3 (T&P 123): Catalogue I, no. 1.

[61] *Att.* 14.15.4 (T&P 720; SB 369); *Att.* 14.16.1 (T&P 721; SB 370). As SB observes (VI 232, *ad loc.*), the plurals are noteworthy; he suggests that the *miniscula villa* (*Att.* 14.13.5 [T&P 718; SB 367]) had a separate *vilicus*. On the resident staff of slaves (*vilici*) and freedmen (*procuratores*) cf. above, Chapter 1, n. 24; confirmed for the Ciceronian age by *Att.* 7.7.3 (T&P 298; SB 130); Ascon. *Mil.* (ed. Clark) 30. For imperial bailiffs see below, Chapter 4, pp. 112–113.

[62] *Fam.* 12.20 (T&P 930).

[63] *Att.* 12.36.2 (T&P 578; SB 275): *cogitanti enim mihi nihil tam videtur potuisse facere rustice.*

to deprive himself of such a source of pleasure, advised him to attend and give dinner parties once spring arrived and thereby to cultivate the society of good, agreeable, and affectionate friends: nothing is more satisfying or contributes more *ad beate vivendum*.[64] *Salutatio*, the customary social call, was a detail of propriety not neglected even in the country. Cicero was gratified in 51 by a visit from Hortensius, pleased in 49 that young Hortensius had turned out of his way to salute Terentia at Cumae, mildly irritated by a client's failure to appear at the *salutatio*, and not surprised in 44 that Balbus should have called on Octavius in Naples and himself at Cumae later the same day.[65] Nor were such calls the extent of one's social obligations: Cicero and Pilia once chanced to meet at the same funeral in the *municipium* of Cumae, where Cn. Lucceius was burying his mother.[66]

There remained time for sojourners to enjoy the pleasures peculiar to the region. Some were gastronomic. Cicero admits to feeding on Puteolan and Lucrine commodities;[67] these must be the oysters and other shellfish whose continuing availability had been assured by the enterprise of Sergius Orata a generation earlier.[68] Cicero would have us believe that these delicacies were absent from Piso's table, and thus implies that they added *lautitia* and *elegantia* to a meal.[69] When Marius came from Pompeii to the *Cumanum*, he and Cicero took advantage of the climate and scenery by going for rides in a litter.[70] This was apparently a standard diversion; Antony's ill-bred mistress created a singular spectacle when she left Misenum by litter, ceremoniously attended

[64] *Fam.* 9.24.2–3 (T &P 820); cf. Cic. *Sen.* 45.

[65] Hortensius: *Att.* 5.2.2 (T &P 185; SB 95); young Hortensius: *Att.* 10.16.5 (T &P 402; SB 208); 'Rufio's' absence from the *salutatio*: *Att.* 5.2.2 (T &P 185; SB 95); Balbus: *Att.* 14.10.3 (T &P 713; SB 364).

[66] *Att.* 15.1a.1 (T &P 731; SB 378). "Lucceius" is SB's convincing emendation (VI, 244, *ad loc.*) of the puzzling "Lucullus" of the MSS.

[67] *Att.* 4.10.1 (T &P 121; SB 84) (SB's translation).

[68] See above, Chapter 2, p. 19.

[69] *Pis.* 67: *Nihil apud hunc (sc. Pisonem) lautum, nihil elegans, nihil exquisitum . . . exstructa mensa non conchyliis aut piscibus, sed multa carne subrancida.*

[70] *QFr.* 2.8.2 (T &P 123); *Fam.* 7.1.5 (T &P 127, to Marius): *. . . ut facis, ut nostras villas obire et mecum simul lecticula concursare possis.*

by lictors.[71] Musical concerts (*symphoniae*) could be heard, and small pleasure boats hired, at Baiae.[72] The entire length of the *Via Herculanea*, which ran from Baiae to Puteoli, passing between Lake Lucrinus and the sea, offered a host of pleasures to the sojourner.[73]

More perhaps for Cicero than for other Roman grandees, a major portion of social life in Campania consisted of strengthening contacts with *homines municipales*, eminent persons in the local towns. As the second *novus homo* from Arpinum to have attained political distinction at Rome, Cicero was ever mindful that he had worked hard for the privileges which accrued automatically to the *nobiles*; that, as his brother said of him in 64, his was the equestrian order; and that patronage among the *municipia*, if bestowed with discrimination, could be a source of private profit as well as of prestige.[74] Puteoli was Republican Rome's chief seaport. Here, where vacation gaiety mingled with the daily bustle of export and import traffic, M. Cluvius and C. Vestorius were the closest of Cicero's important friends. They were financiers whose interests ranged over a wide field and included the higher forms of trade (*mercatura*) condoned and even commended by Cicero in an instructive passage in the De Officiis.[75] In 51, five Carian towns had outstanding debts to Cluvius. Cicero wrote warmly on his behalf to Q. Minucius Thermus, then governor of Asia, and noted that Cn. Pompeius appeared more anxious about the repayment of the money than was Cluvius himself[76]—it may

---

[71] *Att.* 10.10.5 (T &P 395; SB 201), from Cumae; cf. *Phil.* 2.58.

[72] *Cael.* 35 with the comments of R. G. Austin (*Pro Caelio*[3], Oxford 1960) *ad loc.*, p. 96; Sen. *Ep.* 51.4; *ibid.* 12; Juv. 12.80; Suet. *Nero* 27.3.

[73] Cic. *Leg. Agr.* 2.14: *illa via vendibilis Herculanea multarum deliciarum et magnae pecuniae*—whence it follows that the land was the property of the state. See further Beloch, *Campanien*[2], 172–173. Portions of this roadway, due largely to the effects of bradyseism, are today more than 18 feet under water: see R. F. Paget, *JRS* 58 (1968), 154.

[74] Cic. *Verr.* 2.5.180 (*nobiles*). For Cicero's ties with the Campanian *municipium* of Atella, cf. *Fam.* 13.7.1.

[75] *Off.* 1.150–151: *Mercatura autem, si tenuis est, sordida putanda est; sin magna et copiosa, multa undique apportans multisque sine vanitate impertiens, non est admodum vituperanda, atque etiam, si satiata quaestu vel contenta potius, ut saepe ex alto in portum, ex ipso portu se in agros possessionesque contulit, videtur iure optimo posse laudari.*

[76] *Fam.* 13.56.1–3 (T &P 231). The towns were Mylasa, Alabanda, Heraclea, Bargylia

be that Pompey was the chief creditor, pressing his claims through Cluvius of Puteoli. In any case, the extent of Cluvius' gratitude for this and doubtless similar services fully emerges from letters written in 45; when Cluvius died, part of the inheritance fell to Cicero, whose co-heirs included Caesar and Hordeonius, apparently a member of another commercial family of Puteoli.[77]

In seeing to the legal intricacies of the inheritance, Cicero, who managed to buy out the other heirs, found Vestorius to be re-markably efficient and obliging.[78] The property consisted in part of shops, two of which were so dilapidated as to require the atten-tions of an architect in the spring of 44. But the shrewdness of Vestorius again intervened, this time to turn loss into profit. And the profit was considerable. Cicero boasts that from Cluvius' legacy he cleared 80,000 sesterces the first year and hoped that the annual income was then in the process of increasing by 20,000 sesterces.[79] Apart from the rented shops which were let out to produce this income, Cicero kept for his own pleasure the *horti Cluviani* on the seashore; these became his *Puteolanum*.[80] Relation-ships such as those with Cluvius and Vestorius well show how Cicero combined pleasure with profit in Campania; indeed, together with the scenery, they gave *peregrinatio* in these parts a genuinely local flavor.[81]

and Caunus. Alabanda had a reputation in antiquity for its cut gems and glass (Pliny *NH* 37.92; cf. Strab. 14.2.25–26 [C 660]), and at Puteoli glass ware was sold and exported in great quantities; vases, decorated with views of the harbor seem often to have been bought as souvenirs (see below, Chapter 4, p. 109). Cluvius and Vestorius (the latter the inventor of the color *caeruleum*, Vitr. *De arch.* 7.11.1; Dubois, *PA*, 127–128) may well have included manufacture and sale of glass among their varied economic interests.

[77] On the inheritance see *Att.* 13.48.1 (T&P 656; SB 345); 13.37.4 (T&P 657; SB 340); 13.45.2 (T&P 662; SB 337); 13.46.3 (T&P 663; SB 338); 13.47.1 (T&P 664; SB 339); 13.50.2 (T&P 667; SB 348). On Hordeonius see below, n. 82.

[78] *Att.* 13.45.3 (T&P 662; SB 337): *Equidem, si ex omnibus esset eligendum, nec dili-gentiorem nec officiosiorem nec nostri studiosiorem facile delegissem Vestorio . . .*

[79] *Att.* 13.46.3 (T&P 663; SB 338); 14.9.1 (T&P 712; SB 363); 14.10.3 (T&P 713; SB 364).

[80] See Catalogue I, no. 43c.

[81] On Cluvius and Vestorius of Puteoli see further Dubois, *PA*, 51–52; Münzer, *RE* 4 (1900), 120–121 (no. 6); Gundel, *RE* 8 A (1958), 1789–1790. On the Campanian flavor of *peregrinatio* see Catalogue I, no. 29 (M. Marius of Pompeii), and no. 30 (L. Papirius Paetus of Neapolis).

The Campanian letters fairly teem with allusions to other *Puteolani*: C. Andronicus, P. Asicius, C. Avianius, Brinnius, Hordeonius, Cn. Lucceius, C. Sempronius Rufus;[82] most of

---

[82] (1) C. Andronicus: *Att.* 5.15.3 (T &P 207; SB 108): ... *sed dabam (sc. epistulam) familiari homini ac domestico, C. Andronico Puteolano; Fam.* 16.14.1 (T &P 924).

(2) P. Asicius: *QFr.* 2.8.2 (T &P 123): Cicero borrowed a litter—which had once belonged to king Ptolemy—from Asicius, to ride from Neapolis to Baiae; Asicius seems to have been implicated in the murder of Egyptian ambassadors, probably at Puteoli (a very shadowy affair: Cic. *Cael.* 23–24; cf. Tac. *Dial.* 21; Austin, *Pro Caelio*[3] [Oxford 1960], 75, on 23.6); he is thus almost certainly a local man. A "Ti. Asicius Ti. f." appears as one of the Campanian *magistri* in 105 B.C. (Frederiksen, *Rep. Cap.*, 127, no. 10; cf. p. 119).

(3) C. Avianius: *Acad. Pr.* 2.80: Cicero can see Puteoli from Hortensius' villa, but can't make out Gaius Avianius, strolling through the colonnade of Neptune. From *Fam.* 13.75.1–2 (T &P 178), it may be inferred that he was engaged in the corn trade, the major part of which passed through Puteoli. His *cognomen* was Flaccus (*Fam.* 13.79 [T &P 526], where his sons are introduced to Aulus Allienus, proconsul of Sicily); C. Avianius Philoxenus (*Fam.* 13.35.1 [T &P 687]) took his name from Flaccus, which proves him too a local man. The Avianii "étaient une grande famille locale" (Dubois, *PA*, 46).

(4) Brinnius: in 45 Cicero was named among the heirs of Brinnius' estate, which lay somewhere in the region of Puteoli (*Att.* 13.50.2 [T &P 667; SB 348]; cf. *Att.* 13.12.4; 13.13.4); Frederiksen notes that the name, though rare, occurs in inscriptions from Puteoli (*CIL* X, 1987, 2174–2176; *Rep. Cap.* p. 121; cf. p. 122: "at Puteoli, the Celtic name Brinnius attests an early immigrant"); he was very likely a *Puteolanus*.

(5) Hordeonius: mentioned among the heirs of Cluvius in 45 (*Att.* 13.46.3 [T &P 663; SB 338]) and therefore almost certainly a native of Puteoli, though the family was ultimately of Capuan extraction (Frederiksen, *Rep. Cap.* pp. 116, 119). A "T. Hordeonius Secundus Valentinus" was one of the *decuriones* at Puteoli in 196 A.D. (Dubois, *PA*, 49).

(6) Cn. Lucceius Puteolanus: see Catalogue I, no. 24.

(7) C. Sempronius Rufus: *Att.* 5.2.2 (T &P 185; SB 95). He is associated with Vestorius (cf. *Att.* 14.14.2: "Rufio Vestorianus") and very probably a local man; at least, his estates and business appear to have been at Puteoli. Cf. *Att.* 6.2.10 (T &P 256; SB 116); *CIL* X, 3776 for a "L. Sempronius L. f.," one of the Campanian magistri in 108 B.C.

(8) Precianus the jurist, who left Cicero some property, again near Neapolis (*Att.* 6.9.2 [T &P 282; SB 123]; cf. *ILS* 946 and *CIL* X, 5678; *Fam.* 7.8.2).

(9) N. Caeparius: *Fam.* 9.23 (T &P 504) proves him an acquaintance of Paetus of Neapolis and suggests that he was a Campanian.

(10) Plotius *unguentarius*, probably of Puteoli (*Att.* 13.46.3 [T &P 663; SB 338]); for the name at Capua cf. *Rep. Cap.*, 111.

(11) C. Caecius (*Att.* 9.11.1 [T &P 367; SB 178]; cf. 9.13.7) apprised Cicero, at Formiae, of Lentulus Spinther's movements at Puteoli: presumably, therefore, he was a *Puteolanus*.

(12) Haterius. He was apparently a friend of Paetus at Neapolis (*Fam.* 9.18.3 [T &P 473]) and relative (father? cf. *PIR*[2] H 24) of Q. Haterius (*cos. suff.* 5 B.C.), the *novus homo* whose family Tacitus explicitly designates as senatorial, *Ann.* 4.61.1; see further Münzer, *RE* 7 (1912), 2513, no. 1, and especially Syme, *Tacitus*, 323. The *nomen* is attested later in Herculaneum: G. Pugliese Carratelli, *PdP* 3 (1948), 183.

whom were linked with Cicero in local business matters the exact nature of which is rarely explained. One service concerned real estate; a local man then as now could buy buildings for considerably less than a mere visitor would be forced to pay.[83] Nor was Cicero the only great villa owner to exploit his local contacts. Hortensius had helpful friends, and owned property, at Puteoli.[84] In the same city L. Manlius Torquatus may have considered purchasing private granaries, while at Herculaneum L. Marcius Philippus consented to assume the chief magistracy; the aged senator C. Rabirius, a proprietor in Neapolis, adopted his prosperous nephew, whose ships put in at Puteoli.[85]

Cultural Life

Once, after dining at Vestorius' house, Cicero declared that worthy Campanian to be as much at sea in a philosophical argument as he was at home with his account books.[86] Local tradesmen and financiers must have had little to do with the more sophisticated aspects of Cicero's leisure. Culture in first century Rome remained an aristocratic prerogative; hence it was to the neighboring aristocrats and their learned Greek clients that Cicero resorted for philosophical discussion, that fusion of social and intellectual pleasure which had long enlivened the leisure of the upper classes in villas in Campania and elsewhere. In the earlier edition of the *Academica*, the setting of the first conversation was the *Cumanum* of Catulus; on the next day the scene shifted to Hortensius' villa at Bauli; in the later edition, whose dramatic date was close to the actual time of composition in 45, Varro played host to the participants in his *Cumanum* near the Lucrine Lake. The discussions

---

[83] *Att.* 10.5.3 (T &P 384; SB 196).
[84] See Catalogue I, no. 17.
[85] Torquatus: Cic. *Fin* (ed. Reid) 2.84. But the text makes clear that Torquatus did not then own the granaries: cf. Dubois, *PA*, 112, n. 1. Philippus: Catalogue I, no. 28. Rabirius: Catalogue I, no. 35.
[86] *Att.* 14.12.3 (T &P 715; SB 366): . . . *apud Vestorium, hominem remotum a dialecticis, in arithmeticis satis exercitatum.* But *arithmetica* was a branch of culture: SB VI, 225 *ad loc.*

in *De Finibus* I and II, and in *De Fato* took place respectively in Cicero's own *Cumanum* and *Puteolanum*.[87]

All these conversations are avowedly fictitious. But their Campanian setting has a better claim to authenticity, since the Bay of Naples was a flourishing intellectual center in Cicero's day. In the first place, it was sought out and inhabited by philosophers of foreign extraction. Staseas, a Greek Peripatetic and long time house guest of his patron M. Pupius Piso Frugi Calpurnianus, resided at Neapolis.[88] M. Pompilius Andronicus, Suetonius informs us, was a Syrian by birth, a Roman resident at the same time as Gnipho the teacher of Caesar, and a grammarian by profession. His devotion to the sect of Epicurus made him seem indolent, unfit to conduct a school. He moved to Cumae where he lived at leisure and composed numerous works.[89] The Academic Dio, a native of Alexandria, spent time in Neapolis, where he taught and dined with Paetus.[90] Nearby were still greater luminaries. L. Manlius Torquatus, spokesman for Epicureanism in the *De Finibus*, there promises to consult more skilful expounders of these doctrines, Philodemus and Siro, whom Cicero here calls *familiares nostros . . . cum optimos viros tum homines doctissimos*, and mentions elsewhere in a Campanian context.[91] That the towns of Herculaneum and Neapolis, respectively, were the principal Italian bases of these famous Epicureans has long been argued and is now coming to be more generally accepted. Philodemus lived and worked at Herculaneum in the lavish villa which was almost certainly the

[87] *Academica*: see J. S. Reid's edition (London 1885), introduction, 41–48; *De Finibus*: *Fin.* 1.14; *De Fato*: see Catalogue I, no. 43 b, c.

[88] Cic. *Fin.* 5.8, and 5.75; cf. Hobein, *RE* 3 A (1929), 2153–2154.

[89] Suet. *Gram.* 8: *M. Pompilius Andronicus, natione Syrus, studio Epicureae sectae desidiosior in professione grammatica habebatur minusque idoneus ad tuendam scholam. Itaque cum se in urbe non solum Antonio Gniphoni, sed ceteris etiam deterioribus postponi videret, Cumas transiit ibique in otio vixit et multa composuit.*

[90] *Fam.* 9.26.1 (T &P 479); cf. *Acad. Pr.* 2.12.

[91] *Fin.* 2.119; *Acad. Pr.* 2.106 (the setting is Hortensius' villa at Bauli): *. . . et omnia meminit Siron Epicuri dogmata*; *Fam.* 6.11.2 (T &P 622): *Vestorius, noster familiaris, ad me scripsit te mihi maximas gratias agere. Haec praedicatio tua mihi valde grata est eaque te uti facile patior cum apud alios, tum mehercule apud Sironem, nostrum amicum*; the mention of Vestorius is sufficient indication that coastal Campania is the setting.

property of his patron L. Calpurnius Piso Caesoninus (*cos.* 58), father-in-law of Caesar.[92] Philodemus' fellow Epicurean, Siro, whose fame derives from the tradition, at least as old as Servius, that Virgil was his pupil, has variously been supposed to have taught at Rome and at Naples;[93] but all Ciceronian references to Siro point to his residence in Campania,[94] and a papyrus fragment which connects Philodemus with Herculaneum also links Siro with Neapolis.[95]

This already compelling evidence for Herculaneum and Neapolis as Epicurean centers may be increased still further. From Piso's patronage of Philodemus, Cicero's evident familiarity with both philosophers, and a reference in another Herculaneum papyrus fragment to "conversations held at Neapolis and Baiae,"[96] one might reasonably expect that among contemporary Roman aristocrats with proven sympathies for Epicurean doctrine, some had villas or lived permanently in Campania. Here caution is required: when wealthy and sophisticated consulars such as Piso befriended learned Greeks, such friendships are no necessary proof of the patron's philosophical convictions; they are better interpreted as a mark of aristocratic culture, of which philhellenic sentiments formed the central core. Although Greeks such as Antiochus, Theophanes, Archias, Diodotus and Philodemus graced the leisure of their respective patrons, *otium* claimed only limited

---

[92] See Catalogue I, no. 5.

[93] See Catalogue II, no. 45. Siro and Virgil in Naples: T. Frank, *Vergil* (New York 1922), 47–48; A. Rostagni, *Vergilio Minore*² (Rome 1961), 174, n. 15.

[94] Frank, *Vergil*, 48, n. 1 (where one should correct "Vestorius is a Neapolitan" to ". . . a Puteolan."

[95] *Pap. Herc.* 312, col. I, 4: ἐδ]όκει δ' ἐπ[ανελθεῖν] μεθ' ἡμῶν εἰς [τὴν Νεά]πολιν πρὸς τὸν [ἡμέτερο]ν Σίρωνα [κ]αὶ τὸν [περὶ αὐτ]ὸν ἐκεῖ διαίτη[σιν καὶ φι]λοσόφους ἐνεργ[ῆσαι συλλα]λίας Ἡρκλ[ανέωι τε συχνό]τε[ρον παρενδιατρῖψαι]. Cf. R. Philippson, "Philodemos," *RE* 19 (1938), 2445 (no. 5); W. Croenert, *Kolotes und Menedemos, Studien zur Paleographie und Papyruskunde* (Leipzig 1906), 126. See further Rostagni (above, n. 93), 175, n. 20: he there speaks of "un nuovo accurato esame e della collazione . . . fatta per me da Vittorio De Falco. Vi sono elementi congetturali; ma in ispecie il nome di Sirone, ΣΙΡΩΝΑ, e la lezione ΝΕΑ]ΠΟΛΙΝ (di cui si riesce a distinguere in parte anche lo A) non lasciano dubbio."

[96] "τὸ πρῶτον τῶν ἐν Νεαπόλει καὶ βαίαις διαλόγων." Philodemus, Περὶ τοῦ καθ' Ὅμηρον ἀγαθοῦ βασιλέως, col. 25.15; cf. R. Philippson (above, n. 95), 2447.

portions of the statesman's time; the phrase *Graeculus otiosus* reveals Roman contempt and disparagement of too much learning and too much leisure.[97] Diodotus long lived at Cicero's house, but Cicero was no Stoic. Papirius Paetus lived a life of leisure, and many of his views may be classified as Epicurean; however, these facts afford no proof that he was a committed disciple of Epicurus.[98] Yet it is nonetheless true that the number of Romans who had Epicurean interests and owned Campanian villas is significantly large. It has not been generally observed that M. Fabius Gallus, whose Epicurean views can be clearly deduced from two letters of Cicero, owned a farm at Herculaneum.[99] Trebianus was a friend of Siro; the same source reveals that he sojourned and perhaps lived permanently near Puteoli.[100] L. Manlius Torquatus, Vibius Pansa, and A. Hirtius, to whom Cicero dedicated the *De Fato*, had villas near Cicero's *Cumanum*.[101] Cassius Longinus, who embraced Epicureanism in 46, may have owned a house in Naples,[102] where L. Papirius Paetus certainly had an estate.[103]

[97] Antiochus and Lucullus: Cic. *Acad. Pr.* 2.4; Theophanes of Mytilene and Cn. Pompeius: Cic. *Arch.* 24 (Greeks accompanied great generals to the wars); Archias: *Arch. passim*; cf. *Att.* 1.16.15 (T &P 22; SB 16): Archias had composed a Greek poem on the exploits of the Luculli. Diodotus: *Att.* 2.20.6 (T &P 47; SB 40) (on Diodotus' death and legacy to Cicero, 59 B.C.); *Fam.* 9.4.1 (T &P 466); *Fam.* 13.16.4 (T &P 544): *Nam domi meae cum Diodoto Stoico, homine meo iudicio eruditissimo* . . . Philodemus and Piso: Cic. *Pis.* 67–72. Still useful, on learned Greeks and aristocratic patrons, is J. P. Mahaffy, *The Greek World under Roman Sway* (London 1890), chap. 6. *Graeculus otiosus*: Cic *Sest.* 110; cf. Plut. *Cic.* 5.2: ταῦτα δὴ τὰ ʿΡωμαίων τοῖς βαναυσοτάτοις πρόχειρα καὶ συνήθη ῥήματα, Γραικὸς καὶ σχολαστικὸς ἀκούων. See further W. Kroll, "Die Kultur der Ciceronischen Zeit," *Das Erbe der Alten* 22 (Lepizig 1933), 5–6.

[98] E. Zeller, *The Stoics, Epicureans, and Sceptics* (London 1892), 414, n. 3. Paetus' philosopher friends included Dio, an Academic from Alexandria (see above, n. 90).

[99] See Catalogue I, no. 14.

[100] *Fam.* 6.11.2 (T &P 622): the mention of Vestorius ties the letter to the area of Puteoli.

[101] Torquatus: Cic. *Fin.* 2.107, cf. Catalogue I, no. 27; Pansa: Catalogue I, no. 44; Hirtius: Catalogue I, no. 16.

[102] Cassius' Epicureanism: *Fam.* 15.16 (T &P 531); 19 (T &P 542); Plut. *Brut.* 37; see further, for Cassius' and other Epicureans' role in contemporary politics, the important discussion by A. Momigliano, *JRS* 31 (1941), 151–157. Villa at Neapolis: *Att.* 16.3.6 (T &P 773; SB 413): *Brutus erat in Neside etiam nunc, Neapoli Cassius.* But though it is possible that Cassius owned property there, he had arrived at Neapolis in July of 44 with a fleet bound for Syria (*Att.* 16.4.4 [T &P 771; SB 411]; 16.2.4 [T &P 772; SB 412]), and hence may simply have put in at the harbor at Neapolis for a few days.

[103] Catalogue I, no. 30.

To judge by Philodemus' closeness to Piso, the splendor of the "villa dei papiri," and several of Philodemus' extant epigrams, he does not appear to have endured undue asceticism in his pursuit of ἀταραξία.[104] But Philodemus had the good fortune to be house philosopher to Piso, a position from which a Greek doubtless derived as much profit as his patron did prestige. Siro's economic position seems not to have been so enviable,[105] and Pompilius Andronicus lived in poverty at Cumae, which suggests that he lacked patronage. Even so, he preferred Cumae and poverty to plying the grammarian's trade in Rome; nor is it difficult to imagine why foreign Epicureans found the Bay of Naples so congenial a setting for the *hortulus*. The essence of the attraction lay in the ancient Greek institutions in cities such as Cumae and especially Neapolis, where *otium* carried none of the opprobrium attached to it at Rome, but was instead woven deep into the way of daily life. Since the fourth century, when war with Rome resulted in a *foedus aequum* for Neapolis, the Greek language, cults, magistracies, and social institutions had enjoyed so unbroken a continuity that in 90 B.C., as Cicero says in the *Pro Balbo*, the Neapolitans could prefer the freedom guaranteed them by their ancient treaty to becoming Roman citizens.[106] Enticed by Neapolis' leisurely Greek ways, Romans as in Sulla's day came for visits, wore Greek dress *voluptatis causa*, and favored their delicate health, lingering until *negotium* or *officium* called them back to the capital. Some, like L. Papirius Paetus, lacked political ambition, had intellectual interests, and became permanent residents. Pace and spirit of Neapolitan life in this period are best captured by Cicero, who states that P. Sulla fled Rome in Neapolis, a city

[104] Approximately thirty of Philodemus' epigrams have survived in the *Greek Anthology*; together with Cicero's innuendos (*Pis.* 68–72) they are the only real evidence for Philodemus' style of life, and since many of the themes are clearly conventional, the evidence is not easy to assess. For an excellent summary, see R. G. M. Nisbet, *Cicero: In Pisonem* (Oxford 1961), 183–186.

[105] His house at Neapolis was extremely modest; see Catalogue II, no. 45.

[106] *Foedus Neapolitanum*: Livy 8.26.6, on which see G. Pugliese-Carratelli, *PdP* fasc. 25–27 (1952), 261–262. 90 B.C.: Cic. *Balb.* 21: *in quo magna contentio Heracliensium et Neapolitanorum fuit, cum magna pars in iis civitatibus foederis sui libertatem civitati anteerrent.* On Greek institutions see Chapter 5, pp. 142–143.

suited more for soothing men's passions than for rekindling the animosities of men in trouble.[107] The busy pursuits at Neapolis—philosophy, poetry—were the pursuits of leisure; the quiet doctrines of Epicurus were thus here thoroughly at home.

The Bay of Naples claimed residents with literary, as well as philosophical talent. In 46 Cicero informed Paetus that the *Atellanae* were becoming a thing of the past: the mimes were all the rage.[108] Decimus Laberius, Roman *eques* and exemplar of *aspera libertas* during Caesar's reign, was the first to give literary form to the farces; he died in Puteoli in 43.[109] That fact alone need not necessarily imply Campanian residence, but some of the surviving titles of Laberius' theatrical productions point directly to the Bay of Naples: *Piscator, Aquae Caldae,* and—decisively—*Lacus Avernus.*[110] And Campanian actors, as well as playwrights, enjoyed a certain measure of renown. Greek Neapolis included among her population large numbers of dramatic *technitae,* whose services Brutus, as *praetor,* sought energetically to secure for the games in 44.[111]

Amid such pleasant surroundings and varied diversions, Cicero managed regularly to give over part of his free time to literary composition, and in the midst of *peregrinatio* speaks almost as though under a kind of moral obligation to produce some *opus* or *fructum otii.*[112] From Marius, alone with his books and the

[107] Cic. *Rab. Post.* 26–27; Neapolis the home of the infirm: see Catalogue I, no. 20; *otiosa Neapolis*: see below, Chapter 5, p. 143. Cic. *Sull.* 17: *Hic contra ita quievit ut eo tempore omni Neapoli fuerit, ubi neque homines fuisse putantur huius adfines suspicionis et locus est ipse non tam ad inflammandos calamitosorum animos quam ad consolandos accommodatus.*

[108] *Fam.* 9.16.7.

[109] See W. Kroll, "Laberius" *RE* 12 (1924), 246–248 (no. 3). *Aspera libertas*: Macrob. *Sat.* 2.7.2. Puteoli: Suet. (ed. Roth), p. 295, 20–21: *Laberius mimorum scriptor decimo mense post C. Caesaris interitum Puteolis moritur.*

[110] O. Ribbeck, *Comicorum Romanorum Fragmenta* (Leipzig 1898), 339–353. For other Laberii in Puteoli, see below, Catalogue II, on no. 7 (C. Bruttius Praesens).

[111] Plut. *Brut.* 21.5; the abilities of the actor Canutius were especially prized. Cf. Cic. *Arch.* 10.

[112] *Att.* 2.4.3 (T &P 31; SB 24): *curabo ut huius peregrinationis aliquod tibi opus exstet.* Cf. *Att.* 2.6.1 (T &P 33; SB 26): *Quod tibi superioribus litteris promiseram, fore ut opus exstaret huius peregrinationis, nihil iam magno opere confirmo. Sic enim sum complexus otium ut ab eo divelli non queam.*

scenery at Pompeii, Cicero demanded similar fruits of leisure.[113]
De Re Publica was written in the *Cumanum* in 54, and Cicero was
at work on the *De Officiis* ten years later at Puteoli: *exstabit opera
peregrinationis huius*.[114] Scarcely a recluse, Cicero rarely objects to
the crowds in these fashionable parts; quite apart from its physical
attractions the social bustle of the coast was a major source of his
pleasure there, one reason why *in maritimis facillime sum*.[115] When
crowds oppress him, various reasons must be distinguished: there
is the longtime proprietor's resentment of interlopers, a genuine
wish for privacy brought on by personal misfortune,[116] and finally,
the want of quiet in which to work. For the sake of the *De
Officiis*, he meant to leave Puteoli for Pompeii in 44: interrupters
were less of a nuisance there.[117]

Villas and Civil War

Such then were the varied delights of *peregrinatio* on the Bay of
Naples. It remains to discuss the hazards. Before Pompey cleared
the seas in 67, depredations of pirates were a regular vexation to
owners of coastal properties: Plutarch says that the pirates would
disembark at points along the Italic coast and plunder the neighboring villas; both Cicero and Plutarch mention the indignity
to which a daughter of Antonius Creticus was subjected at the
family villa at Misenum.[118] But civil war presented peculiar
difficulties to the men of Rome's governing class. For most,
neutrality was impossible, while a wrong choice of champion
would involve harassment and downright danger. "How I wish,"
Cicero exclaimed in 49, "I had asked Caesar for what I hear
Philippus has got"; the boon was immunity, for himself and for

[113] *Fam.* 7.1.1 (T &P 127): *modo ut tibi constiterit fructus oti tui . . .*
[114] *De Re Publica: QFr.* 2.12.1 (T &P 139) (54 B.C.); *De Officiis: Att.* 15.13a.6 (T &P 795; SB 417).
[115] *Fam.* 2.16.2 (T &P 394).
[116] *Att.* 14.16.1 (T &P 721; SB 370) (interlopers); cf. 14.9.2 (T &P 712; SB 363); *Att.* 12.40.3 (T &P 584; SB 281) (from Astura, after death of Tullia in 45).
[117] *Att.* 15.13a.6 (T &P 795; SB 417); cf. 15.16b (T &P 747; SB 392).
[118] Plut. *Pomp.* 24.6; Cic. *Leg. Man.* 33 (cited above, Chapter 2, n. 15).

his goods.[119] The letters from 50 B.C. and afterwards well reflect the uncertainties of the times, and show that social life in Campania was much affected: Cicero feared that he had seen the last of his *villules*.[120]

Pompey was in Neapolis in the spring of 50, by which time the ominous indications of a rift in the coalition with Caesar had become too many to ignore. There he talked with Atticus; the conversation gratified Cicero, but he was worried about Pompey's health.[121] Worry increased when Pompey was attacked in Neapolis by a serious illness, but he recovered; Cicero says that garlanded Neapolitans, *Puteolani*, and all the local townsmen joined in public thanksgiving.[122] Plutarch adds that on the motion of the demarch Praxagoras the Neapolitans had offered sacrifices for Pompey's recovery, their neighbors had followed suit, and the prayers then went the round of South Italian cities, buttressing Pompey's confidence for the ensuing war.[123] *Ineptum sane negotium et Graeculum*, was Cicero's comment in the *Tusculans*,[124] because, as we learn from a letter written shortly before Pompey sailed from Brundisium in March of 49, the same country towns which had addressed pieties to Pompey a few months earlier had now heard reports of Caesar's clemency at Corfinium, and were offering him genuine prayers, as though to a god.[125] Caesar, however, was not unduly impressed by this display. In April he sent Curio to make a public speech in Puteoli,[126] where Caesar had close connections with the business classes: A. Granius Puteolanus, *eques Romanus*, was among the casualties from Caesar's

---

[119] See Catalogue I, no. 28.

[120] *Att.* 8.9.3 (T&P 340; SB 188).

[121] *Att.* 7.2.5 (T&P 293; SB 125): *sermo Pompei Neapolitanus*. Pompey's weak health: *Fam.* 8.13.2 (T&P 271); *Att.* 8.2.3 (T&P 332; SB 152).

[122] Cic. *Tusc.* 1.86: *Pompeio, nostro familiari, cum graviter aegrotaret Neapoli, melius est factum. Coronati Neapolitani fuerunt, nimirum etiam Puteolani, volgo ex oppidis publice gratulabantur* ...

[123] Plut. *Pomp.* 57; cf. Juvenal 10.283–285; Vell. Pat. 2.48.2.

[124] *Tusc.* 1.86.

[125] *Att.* 8.16.1 (T&P 352; SB 166): ... *quo modo autem se venditant Caesari! Municipia vero deum, nec simulant, ut cum de illo aegroto vota faciebant*; cf. 9.5.3 (T&P 359; SB 171).

[126] *Att.* 10.4.8 (T&P 382; SB 195): *cucurritque Puteolos ut ibi contionaretur*.

side at Dyrrachium.[127] Three weeks later, at Cumae, Cicero reports that Antony from his villa at Misenum had sent a letter summoning leading men from the local councils to a conference; when they arrived, he rudely lingered late in bed and finally sent away, unconsulted, the representatives from Neapolis and Cumae because, Cicero explains, Caesar was particularly angry with those towns.[128] Although the exact cause of Caesar's wrath is not known, it seems clear that he was intent upon securing official proclamations of loyalty from the Campanian coastal towns.

Cicero abandoned any hope of honest neutrality or negotiation after his interview with Caesar in late March, 49. From April until the end of May he was in his *Cumanum*. Why? In a letter to Caelius Rufus, who was on his way to join Caesar in Spain, he says that he was simply enjoying springtime in his villas; groundless, he insists, was the widespread suspicion that he intended to flee Italy by ship.[129] But that letter was meant for Caesar's eyes; with Atticus Cicero was more candid. Earlier, when he had considered retiring to some safe and solitary spot like Malta or Egypt, Puteoli was the obvious port of embarkation.[130] Now, despite his family's entreaties that he await the outcome of the war in Spain, he was resolved to join Pompey in Greece, and was at Cumae awaiting weather good enough for a quick retreat.[131] Others were at nearby villas for similar reasons. Lentulus Spinther, one of the Pompeians to surrender at Corfinium and to be dismissed unharmed by Caesar, fled to Puteoli, where Cicero's servants discovered him only with difficulty: he was hiding, terrified and indecisive, in his villa.[132] While L. Domitius Ahenobarbus was capitulating at Corfinium, his wife Porcia sought refuge at Naples, where her

[127] Caesar, *BCiv.* 3.71; cf. Dubois, *PA*, 49.

[128] *Att.* 10.13.1 (T&P 399; SB 205). Cf. E. Lepore, *PdP* fasc. 25–27 (1952), 320.

[129] *Fam.* 2.16.2 (T&P 394): *Quod autem in maritimis facillime sum, moveo non nullis suspicionem velle me navigare; quod tamen fortasse non nollem, si possem ad otium; nam ad bellum quidem qui convenit?*

[130] *Att.* 9.19.3 (T&P 377; SB 189): . . . *infero navigabimus et, si Puteolis erit difficile, Crotonem petemus* . . . *In Aegyptum nos abdemus*; cf. *Att.* 10.4.10 (T&P 382; SB 195); Malta: *Att.* 10.7.1 (T&P 388; SB 198); *Att.* 10.8.10 (T&P 392; SB 199).

[131] *Att.* 10.6.1 (T&P 386; SB 197).

[132] See Catalogue I, no. 10.

family had property and connections;[133] and L. Marcius Philippus, allowed by Caesar to live where he liked and to take no part in the war, retired to Neapolis.[134] Postumia and her son waited safely at their estate at Cumae while Cicero tried to persuade her hesitant husband, Servius Sulpicius Rufus, to join them.[135] When Servius arrived, Cicero decided not to divulge the fact that he too planned to flee: for though Servius eventually joined Pompey and fought at Pharsalus, he was timid in 49,[136] though not so timid as C. Claudius Marcellus (*cos.* 50), then at his villa at Liternum. That man had betrayed Cicero's travel plans to Antony in order to put his own cowardice in a better light.[137] While his ship was being provisioned, Cicero visited his villa at Pompeii, but he left before daylight of the next day because he had learned upon his arrival that the three cohorts stationed at Pompeii were eager to put the town under his protection. What good were three cohorts?[138] His last advice to Terentia before he sailed in June was to make use of the villas farthest away from men at arms.[139] In sharp contrast to earlier periods of *peregrinatio*, there was nothing placid or leisurely about the spring of 49.

Cicero does not appear to have revisited his Campanian villas until 46. He had returned to Italy, disconsolate and embittered, in October 48, about a month after Pharsalus, and had remained at Brundisium until Caesar arrived at Tarentum in September 47 and gave him leave to live where he liked. But his position and his hold on his property remained most precarious, for Caesar's supporters regarded him as a defeated enemy, Pompey's as a traitor to the cause.[140] He confided to Varro, also a Pompeian pardoned by Caesar, that he longed to leave Rome, longed to

[133] See Catalogue I, no. 13.
[134] See Catalogue I, no. 28.
[135] See Catalogue I, no. 40.
[136] *Att.* 10.14.1 (T &P 400; SB 206): *numquam vidi hominem perturbatiorem metu . . .*
[137] *Att.* 10.15.2 (T &P 401; SB 207).
[138] *Att.* 10.16.4 (T &P 402; SB 208).
[139] *Fam.* 14.7.3 (T &P 405): *. . . deinde, si tibi videbitur, villis iis utere, quae longissime aberunt a militibus.*
[140] *Fam.* 9.2.2 (T &P 461) (to Varro): *qui enim victoria se efferunt, quasi victos nos intuentur, qui autem victos nostros moleste ferunt, nos dolent vivere.*

avoid seeing and hearing what was being done there. The temptation was resisted. Whoever saw him would think him to be either frightened or making for a ship.[141] Consequently, when the crowds flocked to Baiae in the spring of 46, Varro and Cicero were not among them: it would be more to their joint credit, says Cicero, to be thought to have come to that neighborhood to weep rather than to swim.[142] Not even the *Tusculanum* was entirely safe: in August territory nearby was being measured for allotments of land to veterans; Cicero comments, *fruor dum licet: opto ut semper liceat*.[143] He only once considered buying a house and moving permanently to Neapolis: in this same summer, when the obvious ineffectuality of his political position at Rome had become almost too much for his *amour propre*. For, as he complains to Paetus, Caesar sent *senatus consulta* bearing Cicero's name to confer royalty on remote potentates in Armenia and Syria, although Cicero knew nothing of either the decrees or their beneficiaries. Consequently, he would move from Rome, where his political influence was negligible, to Neapolis, where life was openly apolitical.[144] But Paetus was not sanguine about his friend's proposal, and during these months his own philosophic calm had been ruffled by threatened confiscations and losses sustained as creditor under one of Caesar's laws concerning debts.[145]

After Caesar's assassination, Cicero's letters from Puteoli in the spring and late summer continue to reveal his concern for the safety of his person and his possessions. As he leaves to join Brutus

---

[141] *Fam.* 9.2.3 (T &P 461): *putabam qui obviam mihi venisset, ut cuique commodum esset suspicaturum . . .* 'Hic aut metuit et ea re fugit aut aliquid cogitat et habet navem paratam.'

[142] *Ibid.,* 5: *te vero nolo, nisi ipse rumor iam raucus erit factus, ad Baias venire; erit enim nobis honestius, etiam cum hinc discesserimus, videri venisse in illa loca ploratum potius quam natatum.* (April of 46, the most popular month at Baiae—see above, n. 53).

[143] *Fam.* 9.17.2 (T &P 480).

[144] *Fam.* 9.15.3 (T &P 481): *quod autem altera epistula purgas te non dissuasorem mihi emptionis Neapolitanae fuisse sed auctorem moderationis . . .* 9.15.4: *an minus multa senatus consulta futura putas, si ego sim Neapoli?* (to Paetus, late summer 46).

[145] *Fam.* 9.16.7 (T &P 472); 9.17.1 (T &P 480), with How (II, 397) *ad loc.*; 20.1 (T &P 475); cf. Frederiksen, *Rep. Cap.*, 121, n. 224 (where the date should be corrected to 46 B.C.). See further Frederiksen, "Caesar, Cicero and the Problem of Debt," *JRS* 56 (1966), 135–141.

in Greece in late spring he complains that he is missing the perfect season for *peregrinatio* among his villas;[146] but he envies Trebatius for his estates at Velia; to own a place of refuge (*perfugium*) in a safe and distant spot where the townsmen are one's friends seemed a most desirable thing in those times of crisis.[147] Back in Puteoli in November, with Octavian urging him to come to Rome, Cicero considered fleeing instead to Arpinum—there was at least some sense of security about that place.[148]

Cicero's prolonged hesitation as to whom to support may have been unusual, but the letters leave little doubt that in his concern for his property he voiced a grievance common among members of his class. The most persistent threat to proprietors during the civil wars between Pompey and Caesar, and again after 44 during the struggle between the tyrannicides and the triumvirs, was that their villas would become part of the spoils of war. As early as the spring of 49, Cicero was distressed by the Pompeians. He knew them for an indebted and rapacious lot, nothing but Sullas, talking of nothing but proscriptions.[149] He was similarly gloomy about the fate of *voluptariae possessiones* and reminded Atticus that although prices might be down owing to scarceness of ready money, pleasure villas seemed scheduled for destruction in the war.[150] Had Pompey's side been victorious, choice villas would certainly have been among the rewards expected by his supporters; we have Cicero's explicit testimony that L. Lentulus Crus (*cos.* 49)

---

[146] *Att.* 16.3.4 (T &P 773; SB 413): *relinquimus enim pacem ut ad bellum revertamur, quodque temporis in praediolis nostris et belle aedificatis et satis amoenis consumi potuit in peregrinatione consumimus* (from Pompeii, July 44).

[147] *Fam.* 7.20.2 (T &P 774).

[148] *Att.* 16.8.2 (T &P 797; SB 418).

[149] *Att.* 9.11.3 (T &P 367; SB 178): *sermones minacis, inimicos optimatium, municipiorum hostis, meras proscriptiones, meros Sullas;* cf. *ibid.,* 4; *Fam.* 6.6.6 (T &P 488); *Fam.* 7.3.2 (T &P 464). Caesar's supporters disturbed Cicero still more: *Att.* 10.8.2 (T &P 392; SB 199): *nam caedem video si vicerit et impetum in privatorum pecunias et exsulum reditum et tabulas novas et turpissimorum honores . . .*

[150] *Att.* 9.9.4 (T &P 364; SB 176): (Atticus had a chance to buy at Lanuvium) *sed nunc omnia ista iacere puto propter nummorum caritatem . . . Quamquam mihi ista omnia iam addicta vastitati videntur.*

had promised himself the town house of Hortensius, the gardens of Caesar, and Caesar's villa at Baiae as his share of the spoils.[151]

In the end, the Pompeians were defeated, and it was Caesar who organized confiscations upon his return from the east in 47. Among his supporters and friends, some are known to have received properties on the Bay of Naples. Cicero says that Servilia, the mother of M. Junius Brutus and, according to Plutarch, the mistress of Caesar, acquired the Neapolitan villa of Pontius.[152] Of this Pontius little is known; though the name is common in Campania from Samnite days his identification with the friend of Cicero is far from certain.[153] But it has been plausibly suggested that he was a Pompeian deprived of his Neapolitan villa, which Servilia coveted.[154] Cornelius Balbus was another profiteer: Cicero informs us that Pompey had once given him a plot of land on which to build pleasure gardens, and Balbus owed his citizenship to the good offices of Theophanes.[155] Nevertheless Balbus supported Caesar. And he does not appear to have had his villa at Puteoli until 46, when Cicero says that Caesar's other friends were feasting lavishly, at Balbus aedificat: τί γὰρ αὐτῷ μέλει;[156] Dolabella had a villa at Baiae, first mentioned in De-

---

[151] Att. 11.6.6 (T &P 418; SB 217): L. vero Lentulus Hortensi domum sibi et Caesaris hortos et Baias desponderat.

[152] Att. 14.21.3 (T &P 728; SB 375): Ponti Neapolitanum a matre tyrannoctoni possideri! On Caesar's confiscations see Cass. Dio 42.51.2; Cic. Phil. 2.64; Syme, RR, 76–77; Frank, ESAR I, 398. Obscure veterans of Caesar were among the profiteers: cf. Att. 14.10.2 (T &P 713; SB 364). Servilia the mistress of Caesar: Plut. Brut. 5.2; Cato Minor 24.2; acquired property from Caesar: Suet. Iul. 50.2; cf. Catalogue I, no. 38.

[153] L. Pontius Aquila was a friend and host of Cicero (Att. 5.2.1 [T &P 185; SB 95]; 7.3.12 [T &P 294; SB 126]) and owned a farm or villa in the country of the Hirpini at Trebula (cf. Mommsen in CIL X, p. 442; SB III, 191). C. Pontius the Samnite general won the battle of the Caudine Forks in 321 (Cic. Off. 2.75); M. Pontius M. l. Sal. occurs among the Campanian magistri (ILS 6303; Frederiksen, Rep. Cap., 129 no. 20). Cf. Catalogue I, no. 34.

[154] Drumann-Groebe III[2], 639 (where it is mentioned that Pontius was pardoned by Caesar); cf. How II, 492 on Att. 14.21.3; SB VI, 241, ad loc.

[155] Att. 9.13.8 (T &P 371; SB 180): et illud infimum caput ipsius Balbi optimi, cui Gnaeus noster locum ubi hortos aedificaret dedit . . . (March, 49). Balbus and Theophanes: Balb. 57; cf. How II, 211, on Fam. 7.5.2; Syme, RR, 77; see further Catalogue I, no. 8.

[156] Att. 12.2.2 (T &P 459; SB 238).

cember of 45.[157] Before the civil wars, at the time of his marriage to Tullia, he was a notorious rake and hard-pressed for money.[158] Rewarded for his services to Caesar with the consulship in 44, he also acquired Pompey's Alban villa and estate at Formiae.[159] There is thus every likelihood that the villa at Baiae was another confiscated estate, perhaps Pompey's own *Cumanum*. And though we have no explicit testimony, it is a reasonable hypothesis that the Campanian villas of many committed Pompeians—Lentulus Spinther, Faustus Sulla, L. Lucceius, C. Lucilius Hirrus—passed into the hands of Caesar's supporters between 47 and 44.

After Caesar's assassination Cicero represents Antony as encouraging his supporters to hope for spoils from three geographical sectors—houses at Rome, villas in the suburbs, and properties at the spas of Baiae and Puteoli.[160] Octavian, Antony, and Lepidus next instituted the proscriptions which the dictator had so studiously avoided. The lists were published, Appian says, after Mutina and included 1) men suspected because of their power; 2) the personal enemies of the triumvirs; 3) rich men—for money was required to carry on the war; 4) people who had handsome villas or city residences.[161] Again, the evidence for Campania is not abundant, in part because there was more property available than could find buyers; as Dio shows, most people lacked gold and silver, and the rest dared not reveal by buying that they had money, lest they should lose that too.[162] But in two instances where mere chance has preserved the names of later owners of Campanian *villae maritimae*, those names may be important clues to the circumstances in which the estates were acquired.

First, Pliny notes that Hortensius was passionately attached to a fish in his ponds at Bauli and adds that in the same villa, Antonia

[157] See Catalogue I, no. 9.
[158] Cic. *Phil.* 11.9–10; *Fam.* 3.12.2 (T &P 275); 3.10.4–5 (T &P 261).
[159] *Phil.* 13.11; *Att.* 15.13a.5 (T &P 795; SB 417).
[160] Cic. *Phil.* 8.9.
[161] App. *BCiv.* 4.5; cf. Syme, *RR*, 187–201.
[162] Cass. Dio 47.17.3.

the wife of Drusus put gold rings on her favorite *murena*.[163] The young Hortensius inherited his father's villa when the orator died in 50 B.C.[164] His subsequent career was less than creditable: after joining Caesar at the outbreak of civil war, he later supported Brutus; he was executed by M. Antonius after Philippi in revenge for his ordering the death of C. Antonius.[165] Antony and Octavianus, it is scarcely fanciful to suppose, would have had equally strong claims on Hortensius' property, including the villa at Bauli. Antonia, the wife of Drusus, was Antony's daughter by Octavia, born in 36 and only five years old at the time of her father's death in the east.[166] She was thus too young to have received the villa from her father; in any case, after Antony became a public enemy, it would have fallen to Octavian and have formed part, later, of the imperial domain. The villa probably came to Antonia through her mother Octavia, Augustus' sister, who could naturally expect sympathy and support from her brother after her divorce by Antony in 32. Young Hortensius' property at Bauli was certainly confiscated by the triumvirs after Philippi.

Second, the proscriptions claimed only one consular victim: M. Tullius Cicero. He was an extremely wealthy man. His country villas and the splendid town house were ripe for appropriation,[167] and we know that the latter fell to the Antonian noble, L. Marcius Censorinus.[168] But what became of the *Cumanum*? Pliny states that a short time after the death of Cicero the new owner was C. Antistius Vetus.[169] Something is known of his career. After Pharsalus, the Pompeian Q. Caecilius Bassus maintained himself and his army for three years at Apamea; Vetus was sent by Caesar

163 Pliny *NH* 9.172: *apud Baulos in parte Baiana piscinam habuit Hortensius orator, in qua murenam adeo dilexit, ut exanimatam flesse credatur. In eadem villa Antonia Drusi murenae quam diligebat inaures addidit, cuius propter famam nonnulli Baulos videre concupiverunt.* On the location of this villa see Catalogue I, no. 17.
164 See Catalogue I, no. 18.
165 Cic. *Phil.* 10.26; *Phil.* 10.13: Plut. *Brut.* 28.1.
166 Cf. Groebe, *RE* 1 (1894) 2640, no. 114.
167 Syme, *RR*, 195.
168 Vell. Pat. 2.14.3.
169 Pliny *NH* 31.6; and see Catalogue I, no. 43b.

to attack him.[170] But in 44, like others, he switched sides and joined the liberators; legate to Octavian in 34, suffect consul in 30, and later a legate in Spain, he can be included among the nobles who survived the Republic by joining Antony and Octavian.[171] Thus, though it cannot be conclusively proved that the prudence of Vetus' politics was handsomely rewarded by the present of Cicero's villa, those politics were certainly no obstacle.

Leisure and Politics

As early as the days of Scipio Africanus Maior and his daughter Cornelia, Campanian villas had functioned not merely as pleasure houses, but as havens away from the city, where the dissatisfactions of politics or disappointed ambitions might be forgotten, and private grief indulged. There are parallel examples in the Ciceronian age: P. Sulla found Neapolis a safe refuge from danger and suspicion during the days of Catiline;[172] Hortensius' concern for his fishponds at Bauli seems to have increased after Cicero replaced him as first orator in Rome; Lucullus waited long—too long—for his triumph in 63, and it was as a host and epicure that he was known in his last years.[173]

It is Cicero himself who best illustrates the changing attitude towards leisure which was ushered in by Caesar's reign. For Cicero, a man's *otium* was simply time free from political duties, *negotia* and *officia*.[174] It is a neutral word, which takes its particular sense from its context: *otium* may be put to fruitful use, or may be abused. If abused, it is *molestum* (as for Catullus), linked (as in the *Pro Sestio*) with *voluptas*, and breeds *luxuriam, inertiam, desidiam*: *otium Graecum* has distinctly derogatory implications.[175] Alter-

---

[170] *Att.* 14.9.3 (T &P 712; SB 363); Cass. Dio 47.27.2.

[171] Syme, *RR*, 206. His career: *PIR*[2] A 770; Broughton, *MRR* II, 342; cf. Catalogue I, no. 2.

[172] Cic. *Sull.* 53; cf. Catalogue I, no. 12.

[173] Syme, *RR*, 23; cf. Catalogue I, nos. 17, 22.

[174] Cf. Kroll (above, n. 97), 5–6; E. Bernert, 'Otium,' *Wurzburger Jahrbucher* 4 (1949–1950), 89–99; J.P.V.D. Balsdon, "*Auctoritas, Dignitas, Otium*," *CQ.* N.S. 10 (1960), 47.

[175] Cat. 51.13: *Otium, Catulle, tibi molestumst* (on which see E. Fraenkel, *Horace* [Oxford 1957], 212–213); Cic. *Sest.* 138: *nam, si qui voluptatibus ducuntur . . . patiantur*

natively, *otium* may be *honestum*: such was the *otium* of a whole class of men, the wealthy *equites* (Atticus, Marius of Pompeii, Paetus of Neapolis) who had turned their backs on political life, preferring, in Sallust's phrase, *otium cum libertate* to *labori cum honoribus*.[176]

Both Sallust and Cicero, whose leisure was given over largely to their literary pursuits, regarded such *otium* as the very opposite of disreputable. It was *honestissimum*.[177] But for Cicero, priorities were clearly defined: his fullest energies were devoted to service of the state; his writings were but *vacatio quaedam publici muneris*.[178] Under Caesar's dictatorship, he was finally deprived of all real political power and influence—the *negotia* and *officia* which, even though his *auctoritas* had diminished considerably by the time of his return from exile in 57, still then used regularly to curtail his vacations and draw him back to Rome—and was left only with the *studia* of his leisure hours. They seemed to him but sorry compensation. In a letter to Varro in 46, Cicero says that learned men are wrong to regard intellectual pursuits as preferable to public affairs.[179] When in his *Puteolanum* in 44 working on the *De Officiis*, the last of his philosophical works, Cicero candidly remarks to Atticus: *nos hic φιλοσοφοῦμεν* (*quid enim aliud?*).[180] The opening chapters of the third book of the same work are Cicero's fullest

---

virorum fortium labore se otio suo perfrui. Cf. Cic. *Brut.* 2.8; Sall. *Cat.* 4.1: *non fuit consilium socordia atque desidia bonum otium conterere.* Plutarch *Comp. Luc. & Cim.* 1.3 has instructive comments on the proper and improper uses of σχολή; cf. Bernert (see above, n. 174), 93–94. *Otium Graecum*: Cic. *Or.* 108; cf. Sall. *Ep.* 9.3; and see above, n. 97.

[176] Sall. *Hist.* 1.55.9 m: *illa quies et otium cum libertate quae multi probi potius quam laborem cum honoribus capessebant.* Cf. Cic. *Clu.* 153; Kroll (see above, n. 97), 5; *Att.* 1.17.5 (T &P 23; SB 17): . . . *neque ego inter me atque te quicquam interesse umquam duxi praeter voluntatem institutae vitae, quod me ambitio quaedam ad honorum studium, te autem alia minime reprehendenda ratio ad honestum otium duxit.*

[177] Sall. *Jug.* 4.4; cf. Sall. *Cat.* 4.1; Cic. *Fam.* 7.33.2 (T &P 474); *Fam.* 4.4.4 (T &P 495); *Off.* 2.4; *Acad. Post.* 1.11: . . . *doloris medicinam a philosophia peto et otii oblectationem hanc honestissimam iudico.* As precedent for the view that distinguished men ought to be held accountable for their use of leisure no less than for their public actions, there was the famous pronouncement of an earlier *novus homo*, in the preface to his *Origines*; see H. Peter, *Historicorum Romanorum Reliquiae*[2] I, p. 43, fr. 2 (M. Porcius Cato).

[178] *Fam.* 9.6.5 (T &P 470); cf. *Fam.* 9.2.5 (T &P 461).

[179] *Fam.* 9.6.5 (T &P 470).

[180] *Att.* 15.13 a.6 (T &P 795; SB 417).

discussion of *otium*, and still more revealing. They contain the praise of Scipio Africanus Maior cited in the first chapter of this study; Cicero proceeds to contrast the leisure of Africanus with his own. He makes perfectly clear that he continues with his writing only in order not to be thought completely idle, in order to forget the troubles of the state which he would prefer to be serving, in order to make more bearable "the leisure which has been forced upon me by want of public business, not by my own desire for repose."[181] His literary pursuits thus always remained to Cicero merely *studia leviora*. Whereas once they had been the decorative adjuncts to a life principally devoted to service of the state, by the end they had become a *pis aller*, as was *otium* itself, to full political engagement longed for but no longer attainable. It is not that Cicero's leisure became *inhonestum*; rather, his attitude towards *otium* changed because, under the dictatorship, he had more of it than he could bear.[182]

Cicero's experience was of course not analogous to that of his much younger contemporaries, for he was sixty-two years old in 44, with clear memories of the earlier Republic. There is some evidence, however, that by imperial times Cicero's reactions to his final days of *otium* had become one standard response to leisure among men of senatorial status. That is a subject for a later chapter.

---

[181] *Off.* 3.1–4.
[182] Cf. C. Wirszubski, "Cicero's *cum dignitate otium*: a Reconsideration," *JRS* 44 (1954), 13: The difference between Scipio Africanus and Cicero "lies principally in the former's political situation and not in the content of his *otium*."

FOUR · *The Emperors and Campania*

Augustus

The emperor Augustus possessed estates near Rome at Lanuvium, Praeneste, and Tibur. But Suetonius states that he took no pleasure in luxurious palaces, having conceived a special liking for the seaside places and islands of Campania.[1] As early as 29 B.C. the island of Capreae had caught his fancy. Acquiring it from the Neapolitans, to whom Aenaria (Ischia) was given in compensation, he regarded it, says Strabo, as his personal property and arranged for buildings to be constructed there.[2] Instead of costly statues and paintings the emperor favored terraces and groves for his villas, where also antique curiosities were on display: the immense bones of mammoth sea creatures and wild beasts, and the weapons of the heroes.[3]

The exact location of the Augustan buildings remains uncertain. Tacitus refers in a famous passage (*Ann.* 4.67.5) to twelve imperial villas on Capreae in Tiberius' time. It was to the rediscovery and cataloguing of these that archaeologists from Bourbon days had largely dedicated their efforts; a complete register, including several highly dubious entries, was published in 1834.[4] Excavations in this

---

[1] Suet. *Aug.* 72.2: *Ex secessibus praecipue frequentavit maritima insulasque Campaniae aut proxima urbi oppida, Lanuvium, Praeneste, Tibur, ubi etiam in porticibus Herculis templi persaepe ius dixit. Ampla et operosa praetoria gravabatur.* Cf. Hirschfeld, *GRK*, 533–534.

[2] Strab. 5.4.9 (C 248): Νεαπολῖται δὲ καὶ ταύτην (*sc.* Καπρέας) κατέσχον, πολέμῳ δὲ ἀποβαλόντες τὰς Πιθηκούσσας ἀπέλαβον πάλιν, δόντος αὐτοῖς Καίσαρος τοῦ Σεβαστοῦ, τὰς δὲ Καπρέας ἴδιον ποιησαμένου κτῆμα καὶ κατοικοδομήσαντος. Suet. *Aug.* 92.2; for the date, Cass. Dio 52.43.2. On the imperial administration of Capreae, see Sartori, *Problemi*, 28–29.

[3] Suet. *Aug.* 72.3.

[4] R. Mangoni, *Ricerche topografiche ed archeologiche sull' isola di Capri* (Naples 1834). Mangoni drew heavily upon the work of G. Feola, whose *Rapporto sullo stato dei ruderi augusteo-tiberiani nell'isola di Capri* was communicated to the director of Neapolitan

century under the direction of A. Maiuri have securely established the existence of at least three vast imperial complexes; the *Villa Iovis*, which commands the heights of the north eastern promontory of Capreae; the villa at the Torre Damecuta, which stands on the northwestern headland below Monte Solaro; and "Palazzo a Mare," situated along the north shore of the island on a low headland some 800 meters to the west of the modern "Marina Grande." Maiuri was confident that "Palazzo a Mare" (Plate 1) was Augustus' principal residence when on the island. He argues that the proximity of the villa to the ancient harbor, its accessibility to the island's ancient municipal center, and the rectangular simplicity of the villa's plan (which allowed for open terraces [*ambulationes*] and gardens) well suit Suetonius' description of Augustan Capreae and of the emperor's architectural predilections.[5] Maiuri cannot be said to have proved his case. No inscriptions have survived; depredations and looting at the site began between 1786 and 1790 during the Austrian Hadrawa's notorious explorations ("nefasti scavi" to Maiuri), and the area suffered further damage early in the nineteenth century when the English and French leveled much of the villa to fortify the buildings on the eastern side; to none of the meager existing remains is an Augustan date able to be assigned with certainty.[6]

A passage from Suetonius testifies both to Augustus' abiding interest in his island and to its Greek character. Shortly before his death the emperor passed at Capreae four days dedicated to leisure and its attendant entertainments.[7] He had Romans don the pallium, Greeks the toga, and was a regular spectator at the

antiquities in 1830, but actually first published by I. Cerio sixty-four years later: Maiuri, *Atti del III Cong. Naz. di Studi Romani* I (1933), 158. Cf. Beloch, *Campanien*[2], 278–292.

[5] A. Maiuri, "La villa augustea di 'Palazzo a Mare' a Capri," *Camp. Rom.* I, 115–141: especially 131–132. Cf. the same scholar's *Capri, Instituto Poligrafico dello Stato* (Rome 1958), 70. Cf. below, n. 10.

[6] *Camp. Rom.* I, 123. Maiuri thus introduces the discussion of the villa's vicissitudes: "'Palazzo a Mare' ha avuto forse il più tragico e il più doloroso destino di tutte le altre ville romane capresi."

[7] Suet. *Aug.* 98.1: *tunc Campaniae ora proximisque insulis circuitis Caprearum quoque secessui quadriduum impendit remississimo ad otium et ad omnem comitatem animo.*

exercises of the Greek ephebes, who *ex vetere instituto* were represented in good numbers on the island. Augustus even gave and attended a banquet in honor of those youths, taking pains to ensure that they should find the imperial presence no impediment to their merriment, but quite the reverse.[8] The emperor gathered round him Moorish and Syrian youths, delighting in their good looks and aimless loquacity.[9] One Moorish favorite, Masgabas, was buried on Capreae. The emperor could see his tomb from his *triclinium*, as he once observed in spontaneous Greek trimeters to a party of dinner guests.[10]

Literary and epigraphical evidence compels the conclusion that a large imperial estate was maintained by Augustus also at Surrentum. Agrippa Postumus, owing to his contumacious disposition, was sent to Surrentum not long after his adoption by Augustus, probably in A.D. 6, when the youth was in his eighteenth year.[11] When Mommsen published the inscriptions from Surrentum, he was impressed by the large numbers of epitaphs bearing the names and often listing the functions of slaves and freedmen of the

---

[8] Suet. *Aug.* 98.3. Capri's former dependence upon Neapolis (see above, n. 2) certifies that the island was Greek in character.

[9] Suet. *Aug.* 83.

[10] Suet. *Aug.* 98.4: *Vicinam Capreis insulam Apragopolim appellabat a desidia secedentium illuc e comitatu suo. Sed ex dilectis unum, Masgaban nomine, quasi conditorem insulae κτίστην vocare consueverat. Huius Masgabae ante annum defuncti tumulum cum e triclinio animadvertisset magna turba multisque luminibus frequentari, versum compositum ex tempore clare pronuntiavit* . . . Masgabas' name signals his Moorish origin (cf. Livy 45.13.12)—this much at least can be said with certainty about a passage fraught with difficulties. The chief problem is topographical: where is the island near to Capri and visible from Augustus' dining room? No such island exists today; scholars have therefore either strained the sense of *insulam* or been inclined to emend Suetonius' text. Della Corte and Maiuri understand *insula* as = *pagus, vicus,* and suppose that the area here alluded to is either the inhabited center of ancient Capri (Della Corte in *Atti della Accad. di Arch. Lettere ed Arti di Napoli,* N.S. 13 [1933–1934], 69), or Anacapri (Maiuri, *ibid.,* 211–213). More recently Motzo has argued for the identification of Apragopolis with the Punta di Tragara, and the Faraglioni on the southeastern side of the island, suggesting that remains of the Augustan villa be sought in the vicinity of the modern Marina Piccola (B. R. Motzo, "Augusto in Capri, Masgaba, Apragopoli," *Annali delle Facolta di Lett. di Cagliari,* 27 [1957], 363). But given the present state of the evidence, a verdict of *non liquet* seems inescapable. For the name Mazgaba in a graffito from Pompeii, cf. *CIL* IV, 1917 and the discussion of Della Corte, *Atti* . . . *Napoli,* N.S. 13 (1933–1934), 78.

[11] Suet. *Aug.* 65.1: *Agrippam brevi ob ingenium sordidum ac ferox abdicavit seposuitque Surrentum.* For the date cf. *PIR*[2] I 214; and cf. Catalogue II, no. 20.

4

imperial house;[12] but unlike Beloch, who had already interpreted the evidence to mean that an imperial villa had been situated in the Sorrentine territory,[13] Mommsen supposed that Surrentum merely served as the burial place for slaves and freedmen attached to the emperor's estates on Capreae.[14] But the provenience of the inscriptions tells heavily against this view.[15] Furthermore in 1928 twenty-four additional sepulchral epitaphs were published, all recovered from the Surrentine locality of Sottomonte and corresponding exactly to the earlier type; none exhibits the slightest trace of a connection with Capreae.[16] The slaves and freedmen therefore must have been employed on a local imperial estate in Augustan times; the latest datable epitaph belongs to the reign of the emperor Claudius.[17] Thereafter silence surrounds both the town and the estate.

Augustus acquired additional property on the Bay of Naples by bequest. When P. Vedius Pollio, the *eques* of libertine stock, died in 15 B.C., Augustus was one of his chief beneficiaries, inheriting the villa near Naples called Pausilypon. The euphemistic name masked the grotesque proclivities of its owner, who, when a slave once dropped and shattered a costly goblet, would have fed his flesh to the *murenae* in his fish ponds, had not the emperor interceded. Pollio's will stipulated that Augustus construct some glorious public monument to commemorate his memory. The instructions were ignored. The emperor razed Pollio's house in Rome, but must have decided to accept the villa,[18] which subsequently passed

---

[12] *CIL* X, 691–713.

[13] Beloch, *Campanien*[2], 254.

[14] Mommsen, *CIL* X, p. 76: *familiae imperatoriae partem ibi constitisse ostendunt tituli 691–713, nisi forte constitit Capreis magis quam Surrenti, sed hoc loco sepulturam habuit.*

[15] So also Hirschfeld, *GRK*, 539; and Della Corte, *Atti del IV Cong. Naz. di Studi Romani* II (1938), 301.

[16] P. Mingazzini in *Not. d. Sc.* (1928), 205–213. These inscriptions are discussed below, pp. 113–114.

[17] *CIL* X, 696: *Charito Ti. Claudi. Caesaris Augusti Topiarius* .See in general on the imperial estate, P. Mingazzini and F. Pfister, *Forma Italiae, Regio I*, vol. 2, *Surrentum* (Florence 1946), 9–11.

[18] Cass. Dio 54.23.1–6; and see Catalogue II, no. 44 (P. Vedius Pollio).

to his imperial successors: this is quite clear from inscriptions which have been recovered at the site.[19]

The vicinity of Baiae must have boasted at least one imperial palace during Augustan times: the villa of Caesar doubtless passed to his adopted son; and it has been seen that the villa of Hortensius at Bauli was probably in the hands of Octavia, the emperor's sister, by the early 20's B.C.[20] On that estate, it is fair to assume, her son Marcellus languished and died in 23.[21] Augustus' daughter Julia was residing in one of the imperial villas at Baiae when L. Vinicius chose to call. That visit elicited from Augustus a sharp letter of reproof.[22] Vinicius' social credentials were unexceptionable; Baiae was notorious.[23] Augustus will not have relished an association of his name with those alluring shores, and it may be significant that despite numerous literary references to Augustus' activities in the towns of Campania, his presence in Baiae is not once attested.

Not every imperial villa served the ends of pleasure. Augustus established a grim precedent when he exiled Julia to Pandateria in 2 B.C.[24] Relegation to the Campanian islands became a punishment regularly inflicted upon disaffected members of the Julio-Claudian families. Pandateria (Ventotene) lay thirty-six kilometers to the west of Aenaria (Ischia); Pontia (Ponza) some forty kilometers northwest of Pandateria. On both islands the traces of vast

---

[19] See below, pp. 111–112.

[20] A building in the vicinity could be identified as *villa Caesaris dictatoris* in Tacitus' day (*Ann.* 14.9.3, describing events of 59); cf. Catalogue I, no. 19 (C. Julius Caesar). Villa of Hortensius: Catalogue I, no. 17 (Q. Hortensius Hortalus). Subsequent ownership by Octavia: above, Chapter 3, pp. 68–69.

[21] Propertius 3.18.1–16; cf. Servius on *Aen.* 6.861.

[22] Suet. *Aug.* 64.2: *extraneorum quidem coetu adeo prohibuit, ut L. Vinicio, claro decoroque iuveni, scripserit quondam parum modeste fecisse eum, quod filiam suam Baias salutatum venisset.*

[23] "Augustus disapproved of (L. Vinicius') assiduities towards Julia." So Syme (*RR*, 375, n. 3), citing the passage quoted in the preceding note. But as Syme indicates, L. Vinicius was son of the consul of 33 B.C. and himself attained a suffect consulship in 5 B.C.; and after Agrippa's death Augustus, as is well known, looked even to the *equites* for prospective husbands for Julia: Tac. *Ann.* 4.39.5; Suet. *Aug.* 63.2. Perhaps the disrepute of Baiae (on which see below, Chapter 5, pp. 119–120) rather than the unsuitability of L. Vinicius lay behind the emperor's displeasure in this instance.

[24] Tac. *Ann.* 1.53.1; Suet. *Aug.* 65.1–3.

imperial villas have been detected. The villa on Pandateria contained paintings of the "third style," and can be dated, on these and other criteria, to the Augustan age: it included an odeon and small stadium among its elaborate appointments.[25] Its counterpart on Pontia, probably of Tiberian date, was still more magnificent; the total area comprised more than 40,000 square meters.[26] In 29 Tiberius commanded that the widow of Germanicus be dispatched to Pandateria, her son to Pontia; Agrippina and Nero ended their lives by starvation in their respective luxurious prisons.[27] Gaius banished his sisters to Pontia; Octavia was confined on Pandateria by Nero in 62.[28] Here literary documentation ceases, but the few surviving inscriptions from Pontia attest the presence of imperial freedmen until well into the second century.[29] The epitaph of a certain Metrobius, *Augusti libertus*, has survived from Pandateria, and is of more than routine interest: Metrobius claims, in elegiacs, that he long presided over the island, *providaque in melius iussa dedit populo*.[30] It appears that, like Capreae, Pandateria and perhaps also Pontia were incorporated by the first emperor into the imperial domain.[31] But the villas on those islands can scarcely have been centers of conviviality.

Finally, it was in a villa in Campania inherited from his father that the emperor died. Augustus left Capreae after his four-day sojourn in 14 and despite severe physical discomfort accompanied Tiberius (bound for Illyricum) as far as Beneventum. When his illness became aggravated during his return, he stopped to convalesce at Nola. Neither Suetonius nor Dio mentions that the villa

[25] L. Jacono, *Atti del III Cong. Naz. di Studi Romani* I (1933), 318–324, with plate 46.

[26] L. Jacono, *Not. d. Sc.* (1926), 219–232;——*Camp. Rom.* I, 145–162; esp. 146–147. For Hyacinthus, a slave of Julia Augusta, at Ponza, see *Not. d. Sc.* (1926), 222; for the date, after A.D. 14, see J. B. Ward Perkins, *PBSR* N.S. 14 (1959), 154, n. 4.

[27] Suet. *Tib.* 53 (Agrippina); *Tib.* 54.2 (Nero).

[28] Cass. Dio 59.22.8 (sisters of Gaius); Tac. *Ann.* 14.63–64 (Octavia).

[29] *CIL* X, 6773: *M. Ulpi Phaedimi Aug. L.*; cf. 6775.

[30] *CIL* X, 6785 (= Buecheler, *Carmina Latina Epigraphica*, 1189), lines 5–6, and cf. Mommsen's note *ad loc.* (p. 678). The subscript names the two consuls L. Arr[?un]tius and T. Flavius Bassus; probably, therefore, the second century, as Degrassi suggests (*Fasti Consulares*, 113), but not certainly, as Sartori asserts (*Problemi*, 59).

[31] Cf. Sartori, *Problemi*, 58–60; Beloch, *Campanien*[2], 210–211. But Ponza's villa may have been built under Tiberius: see above, n. 26.

which there housed the emperor was part of his *patrocinium*, but that must have been the case: Suetonius notices that Augustus died in the same house as his father Octavius.[32]

The Augustan villas at Capreae, Surrentum, Pausilypon, Baiae, and Nola lend abundant support to Suetonius' assertion that it was among the seaside places of Campania that the first emperor of Rome sought respite from the grave affairs of state. But those villas and that relaxation must be viewed within the larger context of Augustus' other Campanian activities, lest their actual significance be misgauged. Augustan innovations and adjustments in Campanian cities embraced the economic, military, social and cultural spheres; his policies did much to shape the future pattern of Campanian institutions. Yet collectively these Augustan influences have passed largely unnoticed by historians of Rome, and the most important thus require some discussion here.

The huge Serino aqueduct, *Aqua Augusta*, was perhaps Augustus' single most spectacular Campanian benefaction. Originating at the falls of Acquaro some ten kilometers south east of Abellinum, it extended at its greatest length for more than 96 kilometers; an inscription, commemorating repairs carried out in the fourth century, lists in order of importance the towns which the waters then supplied: Puteoli, Neapolis, Nola, Atella, Cumae, Acerrae, Baiae, and Misenum; before 79 A.D. it also served Pompeii.[33] Just when the extensions to Puteoli and Misenum were completed cannot be precisely gauged—it may have been Claudius who first brought the Serino waters as far as Misenum—but much of the

---

[32] Vell. Pat. 2.123; Tac. *Ann.* 1.9.1; Suet. *Aug.* 100.1; Cass. Dio 56.29.2. The house subsequently became hallowed ground: Cass. Dio 56.45.3; cf. Tac. *Ann.* 4.57.1. A scholiast asserts that the famous cold water cure of Augustus by M. Antonius Musa occurred at Atella *in domo Caesaris* (Ps. Acron, on Hor. *Epist.* 1.15.3); that Campanian property is not elsewhere attested. The *cognomen* Musa appears also in four graffiti on the walls of the celebrated "Villa dei Misteri" at Pompeii (see Chapter 5, n. 153). Arguing from these, from other graffiti, and from the statue of Livia discovered in the villa, Della Corte reasoned that the estate was once the property of Augustus and passed subsequently to his imperial successors (Della Corte, *CeA*[3], 420–429, on the "Villa Iuliana"). Although the case rests entirely upon circumstantial evidence, Della Corte's hypothesis is both plausible and attractive.

[33] I. Sgobbo, *Not. d. Sc.* (1938), 75–97; and note further the observations of Frederiksen, *RE* 23 (1959), 2057.

construction, indisputably, was completed during the triumviral period,[34] when Octavian was not yet Augustus and when the policies by which he might win the allegiance of the towns of Italy must have been a major preoccupation. It is surely in this political light that his construction of the mammoth Campanian aqueduct (as well as that of the *Aqua Iulia* at Capua[35]) is to be interpreted.

At Cumae, on the lower terrace of the Greek acropolis, stood a famous temple of Apollo.[36] Greek builders, characteristically adapting construction to the natural alignment of the terrain, had provided the edifice with north–south orientation. During the reign of Augustus the temple was reoriented on an east–west axis, and an ornamental pronaos, clearly visible from the Roman forum of the *municipium* below, was added on the eastern side, at the very edge of the bluff.[37] It is not known whether the imperial or local treasury supplied the money for these alterations, but it is tempting to connect the realignment of the temple with the prominent role assigned to Apollo by the victor at Actium—a prominence which is conspicuous in the 8th book of the *Aeneid* and even more pronounced in the 6th, where Aeneas visits the temple of Apollo at Cumae within moments after his fleet reached Italian shores.[38]

Before the Augustan age, Misenum is mentioned primarily as a favored site for coastal villas. Under Augustus the town became the headquarters of the western imperial navy, lending its name to the fleet which for four centuries was charged with the protection of the Italian coast.[39] It has been estimated that in the time of

---

[34] Maiuri, "Virgilio e Nola," *Quaderni di Studi Romani* 4 (1939), 7–9; Maiuri argues from archaeological as well as literary evidence.

[35] Cass. Dio 49.14.5.

[36] Beloch, *Campanien*[2], 160–161; Maiuri, *Campi Flegrèi*, 117–121.

[37] Maiuri, *Campi Flegrèi*, 119–120.

[38] Virg. *Aen.* 8.704–728; 6.9–44. Augustus had friends at Cumae: observe C. Cupiennius Libo, Hor. *Serm.* 1.2.35–36, with the comment of Porphyry, *ad loc.* The testimony of the scholiast has often been impugned, most recently by N. Rudd (*The Satires of Horace*, Cambridge [1966], 143, 145); but there are signs that Porphyry may have known whereof he spoke. Cupiennii recur in the inscriptions of Cumae: see A. Degrassi, *Scritti Vari di Antichità* I (Rome 1962), 473–475. See further J. D'Arms, "Canidia and Campania," *Philologus* 111 (1967), 141–145.

[39] Tac. *Ann.* 4.5.1; Suet. *Aug.* 49.1; Beloch, *Campanien*[2], 190–200; C. Starr, *Roman*

Nero the squadrons at Misenum numbered more than ten thousand sailors, who were recruited—as their epitaphs reveal—largely from among the economically backward regions of the Empire: Egypt, Thrace, and parts of the Greek East.[40] Contracting marriage ties with either compatriots or local women and settling their families in the nearby towns, the foreign members of the *classis Misenensis* became consumers in large numbers of local and imported merchandise, and contributed an additional cosmopolitan element to the already polyglot character of much of the population on the Bay of Naples.

It is not known precisely when the *Portus Iulius*, the Lucrine naval base engineered by Agrippa for the wars with Sextus Pompey, was abandoned in favor of the new headquarters at Misenum.[41] But Augustus' choice of a permanent Campanian base for the imperial navy should occasion no surprise; the explanation lies in the proximity of Misenum to Puteoli, which became, as a direct result of the policy and foresight of Augustus, the single city in Italy most vital to the imperial economy. Imperial Rome imported annually one hundred and fifty thousand tons of Egyptian corn.[42] The creation of a special imperial department responsible for the *annona* (grain supply) was among the most important and durable of the innovations of Augustus, who, soon after the annexation of Egypt, provided also for the corn to be conveyed by special fleet from Alexandria to the harbor of Puteoli.[43] There a mammoth new breakwater was constructed, its wonders commemorated in Greek elegiac verses by a contemporary poet from Byzantium; new granaries were built to

---

Imperial Navy[2] (Cambridge 1960), 13–16. For the immense cistern (the *piscina mirabilis*) which supplied fresh water for the fleet, see Maiuri, *Campi Flegrèi*, 91–93; its capacity was 12,600 cubic meters; the masonry, in good reticulate, tufa, and brick, is certainly of early Julio-Claudian date.

[40] Numbers: Starr, *Roman Imperial Navy*[2], 16–17; recruitment: *ibid.*, 74–80; esp. 75, the valuable table of sailors' origins, based upon epigraphical sources. A few new texts were presented and analyzed by L. F. Fitzhardinge, *JRS* 41 (1951), 17–21.

[41] Both date and pretext are discussed below, Chapter 5, pp. 136–137.

[42] Aur. Vict. *Caes.* 1.6 (twenty million *modii*).

[43] Frederiksen, *RE* 23 (1959), 2043.

store the immense quantities of corn, to the general profit of local contractors.[44] Nor were foreign imports confined to corn. When once Augustus sailed past the port of Puteoli he was hailed and praised by Alexandrian merchants who had just put into harbor; it was because of him, they shouted, that they made their living and sailed the seas, enjoying both freedom and fortune. The emperor, well pleased, responded with a revealing gesture: distributing gold pieces to all the members of his company, he directed them to buy none but Alexandrian wares.[45] Traders from the Orient thus found a market for their various merchandise in Augustan Puteoli. The arrangement was reciprocal. Inscriptions disclose the names of affluent contemporary *Puteolani* who were greatly influential in the markets of the East. Lucius and Gaius Calpurnius, members of a local commercial family of the first importance, were honored in an inscription from Puteoli by "traders who do business in Alexandria, Asia, and Syria."[46] It was only natural that Augustus, stimulator and guarantor of all this international commerce and local prosperity, should receive a temple at Puteoli; natural, too, that the donor should be a man with strong personal reasons for gratitude to the emperor: in fact, L. Calpurnius.[47]

A portion of Augustus' territorial transactions with the city of Neapolis has already been mentioned. The Elder Pliny supplies the information that from 36 B.C. Octavian annually paid to that

[44] Breakwater: *CIL* X, 1640–1641 (*opus pilarum*); Lehmann-Hartleben, *Klio*, Beiheft 14, 163; Dubois, *PA*, 249–268. Antiphilus of Byzantium: *Anth. Gr.* 7.379; cf. 9.708. Granaries: Frederiksen, *RE* 23 (1959), 2043.

[45] Suet. *Aug.* 98.2: *Forte Puteolanum sinum praetervehenti vectores nautaeque de navi Alexandrina, quae tantum quod appulerat, candidati coronatique et tura libantes fausta omina et eximias laudes congesserant: per illum se vivere, per illum navigare, libertate atque fortunis per illum frui. Qua re admodum exhilaratus quadragenos aureos comitibus divisit iusque iurandum et cautionem exegit a singulis, non alio datam summam quam in emptionem Alexandrinarum mercium absumpturos.* Alexandrian prosperity was in fact intimately linked with Puteoli in this age: Strab. 17.1.7 (C 793).

[46] *CIL* X, 1797; on the Calpurnii see further Dubois, *PA* 46–47; and Rostovtzeff *SEHRE*[2], 562, n. 18; the family gave its name to a *vicus* in Puteoli (*CIL* X, 1631). As did the Vestorii (*ibid.*, 1631); that family too did brisk business in the east: Pliny *NH* 33.162; on which cf. Frederiksen, *RE* 23 (1959), 2048.

[47] *CIL* X, 1613.

city 200,000 sesterces *e fisco suo* for the *Collis Leucogaeus*, a range of hills important for their sulphur deposits, which lay between Neapolis and Puteoli.[48] The beneficiary of these negotiations was Octavian's enlarged colony at Capua, which now acquired the mining rights to the hills together with other fresh sources of revenue, among them lands near Cnossus in Crete.[49] There is no indication that the Neapolitans chafed under these imperial encroachments: on the contrary, they had cause to be grateful for imperial subventions after damage sustained during earthquakes and fire; Neapolis instituted sacred quinquennial games, *Italica Romaea Sebasta Isolympia*, in Augustus' honor in A.D. 2.[50] That Neapolis should have been the single Campanian city to establish Greek games, Dio opined, was to be explained by her citizens' unswerving devotion to life in accordance with Greek ways. Throughout the first century, as is revealed by inscriptions recording the victories of contestants, the *Sebasta*, with their musical and gymnastic contests, rivaled in prestige all but the four great games of Greece and the *Actia*. A cultural compliment paid Augustus by the most thoroughly Greek of Italian cities, the games flourished at least until the middle of the third century.[51] Augustus himself, despite ill-health, made a special effort to attend their performance in Neapolis shortly before his death in 14.[52]

The foregoing survey aims at illustration, not completeness. Its primary purpose has been to indicate the variety, scope, and durability of the Campanian projects and policies of Augustus, and thereby to suggest that the emperor's yearning for seaside

[48] Pliny *NH* 18.114. On the use of the word *fiscus* in connection with the emperor's ownership or lease of landed property, see F. Millar, "The Fiscus in the First Two Centuries," *JRS* 53 (1963), 30 (where Pliny's figure appears as 20,000 sesterces); cf. the modifications proposed by P. A. Brunt, *JRS* 56 (1966), 75–91. *Montes Leucogaei*: Beloch, *Campanien*[2], 25–26; Frederiksen, *RE* 23 (1959), 2054.

[49] Pliny *NH* 18.114; Vell. Pat. 2.81; cf. Cass. Dio 49.14.5.

[50] Cass. Dio 55.10.9; for the correct date (Dio erroneously assigned the foundation of the games to 2 B.C.) see R. M. Geer, "The Greek Games at Naples," *TAPA* 66 (1935), 216.

[51] Geer, "Greek Games," 214 (citing *IG* III, 129); G. W. Bowersock, *Augustus and the Greek World* (Oxford 1965), 83–84; and see below, Chapter 5, p. 143.

[52] Vell. Pat. 2.123.1; Suet. *Aug.* 98.5; Cass. Dio 56.29.2.

recreation can be no more than a partial explanation for his visits to his villas on the Bay of Naples. Those days will often have been crowded with official appointments, dedications, administrative burdens. For the would-be *optimi status auctor*[53] there was much that required personal supervision—in Campania as at Rome.

Augustus set all manner of precedents for his imperial successors. It is only reasonable to expect, therefore, that in Campania as at Rome those successors tended to conceive and execute policy along Augustan lines. Although the local activities of later *principes* unfortunately are not so clearly documented, the evidence is nonetheless sufficient to suggest an important distinction. An emperor's presence on the Bay of Naples, his local administrative actions, his public works and his benefactions, should not be construed as expressions of his personal liking for the Campanian towns. They were also, as with Augustus, acts of imperial policy.

Tiberius

Modicus privatis aedificationibus—such, Tacitus explicitly asserts, was Tiberius. In his thriftiness he recalled the men of the early days of the Republic, and he discouraged all but his closest friends from bequeathing to the emperor a portion of their estates.[54] Yet properties accrued: those acquired by Augustus passed inevitably to his successor; other estates were seized. In fact, construction and repairs of imperial estates and public buildings were far from negligible under Tiberius. A quantity of tiles stamped with the name *Augusta* have turned up in Capri, Stabia, Naples, and Pozzuoli, inviting the conclusion that Livia—and therefore the imperial house—owned local brickworks.[55] That indicates a high

53 Suet. *Aug.* 28.2.
54 Tac. *Ann.* 6.45.2; 3.52.2 (*princeps antiquae parsimoniae*); 2.48.2: *neque hereditatem cuiusquam adiit nisi cum amicitia meruisset: ignotos et aliis infensos eoque principem nuncupantes procul arcebat.* Cf. R. S. Rogers, "The Roman Emperors as Heirs and Legatees," *TAPA* 78 (1947), 140–158.
55 L. Jacono, *Not. d. Sc.* (1926), 230, n. 5. For the same tile at Ponza, see above, n. 26; for other examples, cf. *CIL* X, 8042, 60 (Capreae, Stabiae, Neapolis); Paribeni, *Not. d. Sc.* (1902), 630 (Puteoli).

degree of building activity in Tiberian Campania, and suggests also the closeness of imperial supervision and control.

"The first crime of the new reign was the murder of Agrippa Postumus." At his death Agrippa's handsome villa at Boscotrecase near Pompeii, which he had not seen since his banishment to Planasia six years before, became the property of Rome's second *princeps*; a passage of Dio suggests that the villa may even have been appropriated by Augustus in A.D. 8 when, at Agrippa's exile, his property entered the category of *bona damnatorum*. Certainly the villa comprised a part of the imperial domain in later years, administered by a freedman of the emperor Claudius.[56] It was very possibly during a period of residence here that Claudius' son Drusus met death by a freakish accident in 20.[57]

The resorts on the northwestern shores of the Bay of Naples were not neglected. Suetonius remarks that Tiberius had received in Sicily certain presents from the sister of Sextus Pompey, and that these mementos could still be seen displayed at Baiae in the biographer's day;[58] they were doubtless contributed to the imperial collection by Tiberius himself, and housed at an imperial villa at Baiae also during his reign. When Octavia died in 11 B.C., Augustus delivered one funeral oration, Drusus, her son-in-law, another.[59] Drusus had married Antonia; after her mother's death the imperial villa at Bauli seems to have been placed at Antonia's disposal, and she doubtless presided there until she died in 37. According to the Elder Pliny, there were curiosities in Antonia's fishponds.[60] But their mistress was known also for her intellectual diversions. Antonia patronized two cultivated Greeks, who may

[56] On all this, see Catalogue II, no. 46 (M. Vipsanius Agrippa); no. 20 (Agrippa Iulius Caesar). For appropriation by the "fiscus" of *bona damnatorum*, cf. P. A. Brunt, "The 'Fiscus' and its Development," *JRS* 56 (1966), 81.

[57] Suet. *Claud.* 27.1: *Drusum Pompeis impuberem* [Roth; *Pompeis puberem*, Lipsius; *Pompeium puberem, MSS*] *amisit, piro per lusum in sublime iactato et hiatu oris excepto strangulatum.* For the date, cf. *PIR*² C 856.

[58] Suet. *Tib.* 6.3: *munera, quibus a Pompeia Sex. Pompei sorore in Sicilia donatus est, chlamys et fibula, item bullae aureae, durant ostendunturque adhuc Baiis.*

[59] Cass. Dio 54.35.5; *PIR* O 45.

[60] Pliny *NH* 9.172 (quoted above, Chapter 3, n. 163).

well have enjoyed her hospitality in Campania.[61] And she was politically alert in 31, as a grateful Tiberius, on nearby Capreae, could testify.[62] Near Bauli at Misenum the famous villa of C. Marius—the subsequent owners, as has been seen, were persons of consequence in the late Republic—also came into Tiberius' possession; Phaedrus, Tacitus, and Suetonius are in agreement that this estate was the scene of the emperor's death.[63]

To some observers in 31, it seemed that Sejanus was the true ruler of the Roman world, Tiberius master only of an island.[64] Departing from Rome for Campania in 26, and pausing to dedicate temples to Jupiter in Capua and to Augustus at Nola, Tiberius thence withdrew to reside permanently on Capreae; he did not once thereafter re-enter Rome.[65] The *causa abscessus* was to be found in Sejanus' intrigues: on that there was consensus among the ancient literary authorities, and Tacitus also was persuaded.[66] He represents Sejanus as having catalogued for Tiberius the tedious annoyances of residence at Rome and urged instead the delights of quiet and scenic isolation.[67] Yet even after the fall of Sejanus Tiberius lingered on Capreae, implanting in Tacitus some doubts as to the truth of the received opinion and suggesting other possible interpretations. First, the seclusion of Capreae enabled Tiberius to indulge at last his latent proclivities for cruelty and lust.[68] Although

61 Thallus and Honestus: Cichorius, *Röm. Stud.*, 356–358; 363–365; cf. *PIR*[2] A 885.

62 Cass. Dio 65.14.1–2; Josephus *AJ* 18.181–182.

63 See above, Chapter 2, pp. 23–27; Catalogue I, no. 22a (L. Licinius Lucullus); Phaedr. 2.5: *Caesar Tiberius . . . in Misenensem villam suam quae monte summo imposita Luculli manu . . .* Tac. *Ann.* 6.50.2; Suet. *Tib.* 73.1.

64 Cass. Dio 58.5.1: . . . ὥστε συνελόντι εἰπεῖν αὐτὸν (sc. Σεϊανόν) μὲν αὐτοκράτορα τὸν δὲ Τιβέριον νησίαρχόν τινα εἶναι δοκεῖν . . .

65 Tac. *Ann.* 4.57.1; Capreae: 4.67.1; Tiberius never re-entered Rome, but sometimes approached the city: Tac. *Ann.* 4.74.4; 6.39.2; 6.50.2. Tiberius had withdrawn still earlier to Campania and had stayed away a year, offering poor health as a pretext (in 21: Tac. *Ann.* 3.31.2; 3.64.1).

66 Tac. *Ann.* 4.57.2: *causam abscessus quamquam secutus plurimos auctorum ad Seiani artes rettuli . . .*

67 *Ann.* 4.41.1: *huc (sc. Seianus) flexit, ut Tiberium ad vitam procul Roma amoenis locis degendam impelleret. Ibid., 41.3: igitur paulatim negotia urbis, populi adcursus, multitudinem adfluentium increpat, extollens laudibus quietem et solitudinem, quis abesse taedia et offensiones ac praecipua rerum maxime agitari.*

68 Tacitus' doubts: *Ann.* 4.57.2; and cf. Syme, *Tacitus*, 402. Saevitia ac libido: *Ann.* 4.57.2.

Tiberius could be both cruel and vindictive, this explanation, favored also by Suetonius,[69] can be summarily rejected. The theme is a late motif in Tacitus; had it been the commonplace which Tacitus implies, it could not fail to have been taken up by Seneca, whose silence is compelling evidence against it.[70] Observe, further, that the persons selected to accompany Tiberius to his island retreat were men most singularly ill-suited for partnership in debauchery and secret vice: M. Cocceius Nerva, a senator with deep knowledge of the complexities of law, the *eques* Curtius Rufus, and learned Greeks to lighten cares with conversation, Thrasyllus, the astrologer, chief among them.[71] Other persons who are known to have been entertained by Tiberius at Capreae inspire no more confidence in the view that the island was, under Tiberius, a center of degeneracy: a *vir consularis* who wrote *Annales*; Asinius Gallus, the septuagenarian consular; Sulpicius Galba, to whom Tiberius disclosed imperial destiny.[72] The future emperor Gaius, then in his nineteenth year, was called by Tiberius to Capreae in 29. The *princeps* found his youthful excesses most distressing.[73]

Tacitus duly listed and considered other motives, including the possibility that Tiberius' earlier retirement to Rhodes had accustomed him to unsociability and secret pleasures.[74] This statement—divested, however, of its derogatory implications—surely contains the clue to Tiberius' fascination for Capreae. That earlier retirement was voluntary and lasted for eight years; it revealed a temperamental disposition to look to solitude for solace in times of crisis.[75] At Rhodes, as later at Capreae, Tiberius found con-

[69] Suet. *Tib.* 42.1.

[70] Syme, *Tacitus*, 422, n. 7; cf. *ibid.*, 695.

[71] Tac. *Ann.* 4.58.1; 6.21.1–5 (Thrasyllus). M. Cocceius Nerva may have had Campanian connections: Catalogue II, no. 15 (L. Cocceius Nerva).

[72] *Vir consularis*: Suet. *Tib.* 61.6; perhaps Servilius Nonianus, Syme, *Tacitus*, 277. Asinius Gallus: Cass. Dio 58.3.3; cf. Syme, *Tacitus*, 423. Sulpicius Galba: Tac. *Ann.* 6.20.2.

[73] Suet. *Gaius* 10–11. Aulus Vitellius, too, was there (Suet. *Vit.* 3.2): *pueritiam primamque adulescentiam Capreis egit inter Tiberiana scorta . . .*

[74] Tac. *Ann.* 4.57.3 (very likely a marginal insertion by the author: Syme, *Tacitus*, 695).

[75] Suet. *Tib.* 10–13; cf. F. Marsh, *The Reign of Tiberius* (Oxford 1931), 37. And the essay "Tiberius" by Norman Douglas (in *Siren Land* [London 1911]) may still be profitably consulted.

genial both isolation and the presence of learned Greeks; it was there that he first encountered the astrologer whose ministrations proved indispensable.[76] Thrasyllus returned to Rome with the future emperor in A.D. 2. Both men had ample opportunity to sample the attractions of Capreae during Augustan times; they were certainly there as part of the company of Augustus shortly before his death in 14;[77] Augustus will have impressed upon his successor the commercial importance of the Bay of Naples. Twelve years later Tiberius was wearied by fatigue and dissatisfaction. A diversity of motives may have influenced his decision to withdraw: Drusus was dead; the ways of Livia were vexatious; he may even have feared for his safety at Rome. Above all, Tiberius had never relished the discharge of public business and had always been devoted to liberal studies in both languages. Retirement to Capreae in old age brought at last the leisure for attention to matters of substance: literature, contemplation, and the music of the Sirens.[78] But the motives of so complex a personality were certain to be impugned by such writers as Suetonius; as Euripides had observed, he who absents himself from the public gaze cannot but be thought to be bent upon evil.[79]

According to the usual interpretation of a Tacitean phrase, Tiberius settled upon Capreae in twelve different villas with diverse names.[80] The numeral twelve has induced most scholars to accept an old emendation of the better MSS of Suetonius and to conclude that the villa Iovis was chief among the island estates of Tiberius, while the remaining villas are presumed to have

[76] Suet. Tib. 11 (Tiberius' Greek tastes); ibid., 14.4 (Thrasyllus); cf. Bowersock, Augustus and the Greek World, 77, 133–134.

[77] Suet. Aug. 98.4. On Thrasyllus' connections and descendants, see Cichorius, Röm. Stud., 390–398.

[78] For Tiberius' interests, Tac. Ann. 4.41.3 (quoted above, n. 67) is of the first importance; cf. Suet. Tib. 70: artes liberales utriusque generis studiosissime coluit . . .

[79] Eur. Medea, 215–221.

[80] Tac. Ann. 4.67.5 (mentioned above, p. 73): sed tum Tiberius duodecim villarum nominibus et molibus insederat. Maiuri proposes to read numinibus, which, however, has no manuscript support, and does not so expressively balance molibus: Atene e Roma N.S. 1 (1956), 35–36.

derived their names from the other divinities of the pantheon.[81] Already after explorations in the eighteenth century the title of *villa Iovis* had been claimed for the mass of ruins near the pharos on the extreme northeastern heights of Capri. G. Feola conducted a brief investigation of the upper quarters of the remains in 1827; Beloch and Weichardt contributed, respectively, a precise description and elaborate architectural drawings; but it remained for Maiuri to carry out, between 1932 and 1935, the systematic excavations to which the site owes its present appearance.[82] The villa (Plates 2–3) was by far the largest of the ancient buildings on Capreae; massive and inaccessible, it answers perfectly to the Elder Pliny's reference to the *arx Tiberii* on the island; the windy heights and isolation were congenial to Tiberius, just as Augustus had favored a location close to the island's harbor—center of communications—and to the social amenities of the town.[83] Maiuri's well-known and accessible publications of the villa render superfluous extensive discussion here; it may be remarked, however, that this vast imperial complex was constructed upon volcanic rock along heights which varied between 297 and 334 meters above sea level, and comprised a total area of more than 30,000 square meters. Four immense cisterns (Plate 3b) occupy the nucleus of the villa, and reveal that in the architect's plans the provision of an adequate supply of water took first place.[84] A small number of local inscriptions contribute somewhat to our knowledge of Capreae in Tiberius' days: two marble columns, bearing the legend *d(omus) Cae(saris)*, appear to have adorned the

---

[81] Suet. *Tib.* 65.2: *per novem proximos menses non egressus est villa quae vocatur Ionis* (*Iovis:* Roth). Cf. Hirschfeld, *GRK*, 534, n. 2; and Maiuri's article (see above, n. 80).

[82] On the excavations of Feola, see above, n. 4. Cf. Beloch, *Campanien*², 289–290; C. Weichardt, *Das Schloss des Tiberius und andere Römerbauten auf Capri* (Leipzig 1900); Hirschfeld *GRK,* 534; A. Maiuri, "Il palazzo di Tiberio detto 'villa Iovis 'a Capri," *Atti del III Cong. Naz. di Studi Romani* I (1933), 156–171; A. Maiuri, *Capri,* Istituto Poligrafico dello Stato (Rome 1958). But the detailed publication of the excavations, alluded to by Maiuri (p. 160) in the article cited above has not yet appeared.

[83] *Arx Tiberii:* Pliny *NH* 3.82; cf. Maiuri, *Camp. Rom.* I, 122.

[84] Maiuri, *Atti del III Cong. Naz. di Studi Romani* I (1933), 161–162. The plan is reproduced below, Plate 2.

imperial palaces; a freedwoman of Julia Augusta, a *verna Caprensis*, is attested.[85]

Gaius

Born at Antium, as Suetonius established by diligent research, the emperor Gaius retained his affection for that place, preferring it to all his other villas.[86] But those were numerous because Gaius was an enthusiastic builder.[87] In coastal Campania he was remembered for architectural extravagances, works of demolition as well as of construction. During the first months of his reign he ordered the destruction of an imperial villa at Herculaneum where his mother Agrippina had passed a part of her imprisonment under Tiberius; the younger Seneca had seen the property and pronounced it most attractive.[88] The imperial estates on the Bay of Naples, according to Philo, were both plentiful and expensively appointed; Gaius constructed Liburnian galleys equipped with all manner of luxuries and, amid songs and choruses, passed from one to another of his villas during a prolonged sojourn in Campania in the summer of 40. Pompeii may have been included in this itinerary: Lollia Saturnina, the sister of Gaius' third wife Lollia Paulina, belonged to a Pompeian family; herein may lie a clue to Gaius' attentions to that city.[89]

In the previous year, 39, a spectacular exhibition in the Bay of Baiae satisfied the emperor that he had put the god of the sea to

---

[85] *CIL* X, 6808; *CIL* VI, 8958. See further *CIL* VI, 8409; Hirschfeld, *GRK*, 534, n. 2.

[86] Suet. *Gaius* 8.

[87] Suet. *Gaius* 37.2: *In extructionibus praetoriorum atque villarum omni ratione posthabita nihil tam efficere concupiscebat quam quod posse effici negaretur.* On Gaius' buildings and public works, see J. P. V. D. Balsdon, *The Emperor Gaius* (Oxford 1934), 173–178.

[88] Sen. *De ira* 3.21.5: *C. enim Caesar villam in Herculanensi pulcherrimam, quia mater sua aliquando in illa custodita erat, diruit fecitque eius per hoc notabilem fortunam; stantem enim praenavigabamus, nunc causa dirutae quaeritur.* Cf. K. Scott, "Notes on the Destruction of Two Roman Villas," *AJP* 60 (1939), 459–462.

[89] Gaius' estates in the Bay of Naples: Philo, *Leg. ad Gaium* 29.185–186; the luxurious sojourn: Suet. *Gaius* 37.2. For the year see Balsdon (above, n. 87), p. 96, n. 1 and p. 135. Lollia Saturnina, sister of Lollia Paulina: Groag, "Lollia Saturnina," *RE* 13 (1927), 1395, no. 31. Lollii at Pompeii: Gordon, *JRS* 17 (1927), 172. Gaius twice became honorary *duumvir* at Pompeii, in 34 and again in 40: *CIL* X, 901, 904. On Gaius at Baiae, see below, p. 102 and n. 144.

flight and that the feats of engineering achieved by Darius and Xerxes at the Hellespont were fit only for derision.[90] From a point near the modern "cento camerelle" at Bacoli,[91] a double row of merchant vessels was anchored and extended for 26 *stadia* across the bay to Puteoli; the ships supported a wooden roadway heaped with earth. The emperor arrayed himself in full military regalia, stationed infantry and cavalry behind him, and mounted his horse. The ceremonies began: dashing out onto the bridge at the western end, Gaius charged fiercely across into Puteoli. Suetonius and Dio present conflicting accounts as to the exact number of subsequent crossings;[92] they are in agreement that the spectacle of the second day surpassed the first. Gaius then renounced his charger in favor of a chariot, and crossed the bridge at the head of a long procession which included the boy Darius (a royal Parthian hostage), a crowd of the emperor's friends in Gallic vehicles, and the entire Praetorian Guard. An imperial harangue, delivered from a platform erected near the center of the bridge, seems to have marked the formal conclusion of the ceremonies, but banqueting and heavy drinking continued well into the night. The crowds from the seaside towns witnessed the aquatic revelry as in a theater: lights were positioned along the bridge, torches on the hills of the crescent shaped bay. Gaius had transformed night into day, just as he had changed sea into land.

In the view of Suetonius, Gaius was attempting to disprove by so elaborate a pageant an oracular utterance of Thrasyllus' which had stipulated that Gaius could no more become emperor of Rome than ride a horse across the Bay of Baiae.[93] To Josephus, Gaius seemed simply to wish to improve upon travel by trireme, which

[90] Cass. Dio 59.17.11. The account which follows in the text is based upon Cass. Dio 59.17.1–11, and Suet. *Gaius* 19. Cf. Balsdon (see above, n. 87), 51–54.

[91] For Gaius' starting point, see Maiuri, *Atti della Reale Accademia d'Italia, Rendiconti,* 7th ser. II (1941), 257–258.

[92] Suetonius (*Gaius* 19.2) states that the emperor journeyed back and forth for two successive days; Cass. Dio (59.17.5) asserts that Gaius passed a day in Puteoli after his crossing from Bauli, as though resting from battle.

[93] Suet. *Gaius* 19.3.

he found a tiresome conveyance.[94] More recently attention has been rightly called to the prominence of the Parthian hostages in ancient descriptions of Gaius' crossings of his bridge,[95] and it has been suggested that the spanning of the Bay of Baiae was a gesture designed to impress the Parthians with Roman military might.[96] There is much to recommend this view; yet Gaius was capable of presenting the display for its own sake: he had a passion for *spectacula*.[97] But if the motives of the emperor were variously explained by the ancient authorities, there was consensus as to the economic consequences: the bridge required so great an outlay of ships and money that a severe famine resulted in Rome.[98] Their objection on economic grounds is misplaced, as closer scrutiny of the relevant passages of Seneca and Dio has now conclusively revealed.[99]

Claudius

On March 15, 46, Claudius published the famous edict on the enfranchisement of the Anauni; the word went out from the *praetorium* at Baiae where the emperor was residing at the time.[100] There also a favorite freedman appears to have owned property; he lent his name to the *Aquae Posidianae*, hot water springs re-

[94] Josephus *AJ* 19.5.

[95] Suet. *Gaius* 19.2: *per hunc pontem ultro citro commeavit biduo continenti . . . prae se ferens Dareum puerum ex Parthorum obsidibus . . .* Cass. Dio 59.17.5: καὶ ἄλλα τε αὐτῷ πολλὰ ὡς καὶ λάφυρα συνηκολούθησε, καὶ Δαρεῖος, ἀνὴρ Ἀρσακίδης, ἐν τοῖς ὁμηρεύουσι τότε τῶν Πάρθων ὤν.

[96] Balsdon (see above, n. 87), 53–54. Cf. *ibid.*, 52: "That the building of the bridge was not a mere irrational caprice can be assumed safely from the fact that our authorities are at pains to give reasons for its construction and, especially, from its mention by Suetonius among the acts of the *princeps*, not among those of the 'monster.'" The second argument is compelling.

[97] He even put on shows in foreign lands: Suet. *Gaius* 20.

[98] Cass. Dio 59.17.2; Sen. *Dial.* 10.18.5.

[99] Balsdon (see above, n. 87, 189–190) rightly observes that the famine to which Dio alludes appears in his narrative for the year 42 instead of 39; the number of improbabilities in Seneca's account is sufficient to call into question its entire historicity.

[100] *CIL* V, 5050 (= *ILS* 206): *M. Iunio Silano, Q. Sulpicio Camerino cos. idibus Martis, Bais in praetorio, edictum Ti. Claudi Caesaris Augusti Germanici propositum fuit id quod infra scriptum est.*

markable for their concentrated heat.[101] Posides, in fact, was notorious in the capital as an *aedificator*, and it has been plausibly suggested that he owned another villa on the southern coast of the Sorrentine peninsula, whence the modern place name Positano.[102] Certainly the stretch of coast line between Salerno and Amalfi became popular with the emperors from Claudian times: that is evident from the numerous sepulchral inscriptions of *Augusti liberti*, none earlier than the reign of Claudius, which have been recovered from the area, and which clearly imply the existence of an imperial villa, very possibly constructed by Claudius, somewhere on the Sorrentine peninsula's southern coast.[103] Polybius *Aug. lib.*, almost certainly the well-known *ab studiis* to Claudius, was the recipient of a handsome epigraphical tribute from his friend Perelia Gemella, a free born woman; the stone was found less than two miles from Cumae and suggests that Polybius also may have acquired property on the Campanian coast.[104] In short, evidence from the Bay of Naples confirms regionally the rise in freedmen's wealth and status, which is a familiar hallmark of the Claudian era.

Local sites and municipalities profited from Claudius' policies and attentions. He made repairs at the Lucrine Lake, stationed cohorts of *vigiles* both at Puteoli and Ostia to guard against fires

---

[101] Pliny *NH* 31.5: (*aquae*) *quae in Baiano Posidianae vocantur nomine a Claudii accepto Caesaris liberto obsonia quoque percocunt.* Cf. the phrase of Seneca (*Ep.* 86.7): *balnea libertorum.*

[102] Posides: *PIR* P 654; his building: Juv. 14.91; Positano: Della Corte, *Rivista Indo-Greco-Italica di Filologia, Lingua, Antichità* 20 (1936), 67; and *Rass. Stor. Salernitana* 1 (1937), 9. For the villa, see Maiuri in *RAAN* N.S. 29 (1954), 93–94, cited also in the following note.

[103] Mommsen registered the inscriptions under Salernum in *CIL* X (wrongly, since the entire peninsula belonged to Surrentum). See *CIL* X, 526–527, 549, 563, 607, 653, 654. Cf. Maiuri, "Le vicende dei monumenti antichi della Costa Amalfitana e Sorrentina . . ," *RAAN* N.S. 29 (1954), 87–98.

[104] *CIL* X, 2857: *Polybio Aug. lib. Amarantian. Perelia Gemella amico benemeren.* Mommsen had not seen the stone, which came to light only recently in Giugliano: V. Causa, "Segnalazioni epigrafiche nell'Agro Campano," *RAAN* N.S. 38 (1963), 19–22, with plate II.1. The editor writes (p. 20): "Sia per il *ductus* sia per i caratteri della decorazione, si può datare questo cippo alla metà del I secolo d. C." Noteworthy is Polybius' friendship with a free-born woman: see P. R. C. Weaver, *JRS* 54 (1964), 127, n. 79. Cf. *PIR* P 427, where the inscription is not mentioned.

at the imperial granaries; and he instructed the commander of the Misene fleet to replenish the supplies of fish along the Campanian coastline.[105] In August of 42, Claudius paid a special visit to Neapolis, where he presided over the *Sebasta*. He entered in the competitions a comedy in honor of, and quite possibly written by, his brother Germanicus, and in accordance with the decision of the local judges, awarded it the crown. During that Neapolitan sojourn, not surprisingly, Claudius and his associates took care to live and dress in a manner consonant with their Greek surroundings.[106]

Nero

Nero was in the habit of repairing to Baiae in March for the festival of the *Quinquatria*.[107] There the charms of at least two villas not originally his own proved irresistible, and by the end of his reign the property of his aunt Domitia and of C. Calpurnius Piso had helped to swell still further the territory of the imperial holdings at Baiae.[108] Like Caligula, Nero too is alleged by Suetonius to have enjoyed sailing about the *sinus Baianus*, with stops at frequent intervals for scandalous refreshments.[109] The captivating Acte will often have accompanied Nero on such pleasure cruises; she at some point acquired property of her own at Puteoli.[110] Acte gave way, in time, to Poppaea Sabina—the name of

[105] Pliny *NH* 36.125 (Claudian works of repair at the Lucrine Lake; on the significance of this passage see below, Chapter 5, p. 136). Suet. *Claud.* 25.2 (cohorts at Puteoli and Ostia). Pliny *NH* 9.62; Macrob. *Sat.* 3.16.10 (Optatus, freedman of Claudius and *praefectus classis Misenensis* distributed *scari* along the Campanian coast).

[106] Suet. *Claud.* 11.2; Cass. Dio 60.6.1–2. Neither authority explicitly asserts that Claudius presided over the games, but that must have been the case: the emperor's costume, as described by Dio, exactly corresponds with Domitian's dress when presiding over the Capitoline *Agon* (Suet. *Dom.* 4.4); Geer, "Greek Games," *TAPA* 66 (1935), 214, n. 29.

[107] Tac. *Ann.* 14.4.1. These festal days of Minerva commenced on the fifth day (reckoned inclusively) from the Ides, and lasted for five days: Varro *Ling.* 6.3.14; Aul. Gell. 2.21.7; Ov. *Fast.* 3.809–814.

[108] Domitia: Catalogue II, no. 17. C. Calpurnius Piso: Catalogue II, no. 9.

[109] Suet. *Nero* 27.3.

[110] *CIL* X, 1903: *Claudiae Aug. l. Actes*; the name appears upon a *fistula plumbea aquaria* found in the sea near Puteoli, and was therefore originally attached to a house or

one of her freedmen appears on pieces of lead pipe discovered in the territory of Baiae near the Lucrine Lake.[111]

Transportation of the emperor and members of the imperial family at the seaside was one of the duties discharged by the Misene fleet.[112] Under Nero the commander of its squadrons was suborned for more sinister service. When Agrippina boarded ship at Baiae after dining with the emperor in March of 59, Nero and his *praefectus classis*, Anicetus, had contrived that the journey was to be her last—the vessel was designed to collapse and sink suddenly in deep water.[113] Agrippina's destination was the imperial villa at Bauli,[114] which had been placed at her disposition earlier the same day when she had arrived from Antium. Suspicious and alert, she had elected to travel to dinner at Baiae in a sedan chair. There the pleasures of the table and the devoted attentions of her son helped to allay her fears; besides, Agrippina was accustomed

villa in the vicinity (so also Hirschfeld, *GRK*, 526, n. 4; Dubois, *PA*, 376, n. 7; and see also below, Catalogue II, no. 1). She possessed property also at Velitrae and in Sardinia: Stein, *PIR*² C 1067.

[111] *CIL* X, 1906: *C. Poppaei Aug. l. Hermetis.* Cf. Dubois, *PA*, 376, n. 7.

[112] Starr, *Roman Imperial Navy*², 177–179.

[113] Tacitus (*Ann.* 14.3.5–10.5) provides a full account of the matricide; cf. Suet. *Nero* 34.2–4; Cass. Dio 62.13.1–5.

[114] Tacitus *Ann.* 14.4.3–6: *venientem dehinc obvius in litore (nam Antio adventabat) excepit manu et complexu ducitque Baulos. id villae nomen est quae promunturium Misenum inter et Baianum lacum flexo mari adluitur . . . ac tum invitata ad epulas erat, ut occultando facinori nox adhiberetur. satis constitit . . . Agrippinam . . . gestamine sellae Baias (baulos:* MSS) *pervectam.* Cf. *Ann.* 14.5.7: *Agrippina silens eoque minus adgnita . . . nando, deinde occursu lenunculorum Lucrinum in lacum vecta villae suae infertur.* If the dinner party in honor of Agrippina was held at Bauli, the reading *Baulos* may be retained in 4.5, and Tacitus' account coheres more neatly with that of Dio, who places the entertainment at Bauli (62.13.1). But Suetonius (*Nero* 34.2) locates the feast at Baiae, and states that the boat collapsed during Agrippina's return to Bauli (*repetenti Baulos*): on this view the *villa sua* of *Ann.* 14.5.7 will refer to the villa at Bauli, described as *sua* because placed by the emperor at his mother's disposal. Despite the necessity for emendation, this latter seems the more likely alternative, because Agrippina's tomb was near Bauli (see following note) and not even a characteristic straining for brevity could permit Tacitus to write *villae suae*, thereby referring obliquely to a previously unspecified villa of Agrippina at the Lucrine Lake. But Bauli lay south of Baiae (see Catalogue I, no. 17, Q. Hortensius Hortalus); why therefore did the fishing boat convey Agrippina north, to the Lucrine Lake? Doubtless to enable her to escape detection; pursuers would not expect her to proceed north. The problem has been much discussed, most recently by P. J. Bicknell ("Agrippina's villa at Bauli," *CR* N.S. 13 [1963], 261–262), who also rejects the first alternative.

to travel in imperial triremes. She embarked, attended by Crepe-reius Gallus and Acerronia. The ship weighed anchor, initially heading east into the gulf of Puteoli. Then a leaded canopy crashed down upon the passengers, bringing instant death to Crepereius: Anicetus had had the foresight to equip the vessel with this auxiliary mechanism of destruction lest the calmness of the sea should prevent the ship's collapse from appearing accidental. Agrippina suffered a shoulder wound but escaped by swimming; rescued at last by sailing vessels, she was conveyed north to the Lucrine Lake, whence she made her way back to Bauli. There three naval officers burst into her bedroom; trierarch and naval centurion struck the fatal blows while their commander Anicetus stood menacingly by. For this and subsequent services, Anicetus collected handsome rewards, which illustrate Nero's concern to increase the power of the fleet at the expense of the Praetorians.[115] At Bauli a tomb was constructed in Agrippina's memory by loyal domestics.[116] The nearby Campanian towns offered sacrifices in the temples and dispatched legations to the emperor. Nero, feigning grief, departed for Neapolis.

Nero particularly enjoyed Neapolis' Hellenic amusements. He was there in 68 on the anniversary of his mother's murder enjoying an extended sojourn which not even news of the revolt of Vindex moved him to curtail.[117] Visits are also attested in 66 and 65.[118] Precisely because Neapolis was a *Graeca urbs*, Tacitus relates, she was singled out in 64 to witness Nero's first appearance

[115] In 62, Nero bribed Anicetus with the promise of *amoenos secessus* to feign confession of adultery with Octavia (Tac. *Ann.* 14.62.3; cf. Suet. *Nero* 35.2). Della Corte has argued that the luxurious retreats were properties in Campania (*Atti del IV Cong. Naz. di Studi Romani* II [1938], 299); but Anicetus was banished to Sardinia after his confession (Tac. *Ann.* 14.62.6). Cf. *PIR*² A 589. The fleet and the Praetorian Guard: D. Kienast, *Untersuchungen zu den Kriegsflotten der römischen Kaiserzeit* (Bonn, 1966), 48–81.

[116] Tac. *Ann.* 14.9.3: *mox domesticorum cura levem tumulum accepit, viam Miseni propter et villam Caesaris dictatoris* . . . The "tomb of Agrippina" is still pointed out to the curious in modern Bacoli; in fact the ruins appear to have served originally as the *cavea* of a small odeon attached to a Roman *villa maritima*: Maiuri, *Campi Flegrèi*, 88–89.

[117] Suet. *Nero* 40.4.

[118] In 66, Nero here welcomed and devised all manner of entertainments for prince Tiridates; most brilliant and costly was the gladiatorial exhibition at Puteoli, produced and directed by the freedman Patrobius (Cass. Dio 62.2.3–3.2). 65: Tac. *Ann.* 16.10.4–5.

as a musician on the public stage: he was preparing himself for competition next in the great games on the Greek mainland.[119] The Neapolitan engagement appears to have lasted for some days, despite the distractions of an earthquake which destroyed the theater.[120] Nero's debut brought crowds of spectators, and the audience was of an international flavor; Alexandrians from a fleet recently put into harbor enchanted the emperor by their rhythmic applause. Nero instructed his own clacque to emulate their style.[121]

For Nero's frequent trips to the Bay of Naples in these years, domestic considerations may have provided additional incentive. It is possible that the family of Poppaea Sabina, who became the emperor's second wife in 62, came originally from Pompeii: Poppaea had inherited property there; and she may have influenced the emperor to rescind the imperial decree of 59 which had prohibited, for the space of ten years, the holding of games in the local amphitheater. The esteem in which both Nero and Poppaea were held by the Pompeians is perhaps best explained by Poppaea's local ties.[122]

In his last years as *princeps* Nero might justly be called *incredibilium cupitor*, squandering immense sums on building projects of doubtful practicality.[123] In addition to the *domus aurea*, two water-

---

[119] Tac. *Ann.* 15.33.2.

[120] Suet. *Nero* 20.2; cf. Tac. *Ann.* 15.34.1-2.

[121] Suet. *Nero* 20.3.

[122] See Della Corte, *CeA*[3], 72-79, for the *gens Poppaea* at Pompeii. Poppaea Sabina *nomen avi materni sumpserat* (Tac. *Ann.* 13.45.1); that relative may have been C. Poppaeus Sabinus (*cos.* A.D. 9), a *novus homo*: Della Corte, *CeA*[3], 72 and cf. Maiuri, *La Casa del Menandro* (Rome 1933), 20-22. Her Pompeian property: Arangio-Ruiz and Pugliese Carratelli, " *Tabulae Herculanenses* IV," *PdP* 9 (1954), 56-57; and for epigraphical evidence relevant to the *gens Poppaea*, cf. R. Hanslik, "Poppaea Sabina," *RE* 22 (1953), 89-90, no. 4. Imperial decree of 59: Tac. *Ann.* 14.17.4, on which see A. W. Van Buren, "Pompeii-Nero-Poppaea," *Studies Presented to D. M. Robinson* II (St. Louis 1953), 970-974. Further evidence for the popularity of Nero and Poppaea in Pompeii: R. Étienne, *La Vie Quotidienne à Pompéi* (Paris 1966), 120-121. Note also that Pompeii attained colonial status during Nero's reign: see below, n. 126.

[123] Tac. *Ann.* 15.42.4 (*incredibilium cupitor*); cf. Suet. *Nero* 31.1-3; Tac. *Ann.* 15.42.1 (the *domus aurea*). See A. Boëthius, *The Golden House of Nero* (Ann Arbor 1960); J. B. Ward Perkins (*Antiquity* 30 [1956], 209) has conclusively demonstrated that Nero hereby intended to introduce the architectural typology of the *villa pseudourbana* into palace architecture in the city.

ways on the Campanian coast are attested among his works. The first reveals that the emperor had a better grasp of economic policy than has often been supposed. Nero's architects, Severus and Celer, undertook to dig a canal from Lake Avernus to the Tiber mouth, thereby enabling the journey to be made by ship yet not by sea. The length was to have been 160 Roman miles; the width sufficient to allow two quinquiremes to pass.[124] The project was scarcely feasible. Some of the enormous technical difficulties are noted by Tacitus, who however completely ignores the important economic advantages to have been gained by the canal's completion: the water way would have ensured the safe transport of corn and other commodities from Puteoli to Ostia, precluding shipwrecks and the other dangers of the open sea as well as the difficulties and delays of land conveyance.[125] Nero, whose full recognition of the commercial importance of Puteoli and of other Campanian cities is revealed by other evidence,[126] must here be credited with a policy of foresight, not irrational caprice.

The emperor's second scheme is suspiciously similar to the first in points of detail, and at first sight might appear to be the invention of Suetonius, who alone alleges that Nero began a covered pool extending from Misenum to Lake Avernus; into its enclosed colonnades he hoped to divert the waters from all the hot springs at Baiae.[127] Suetonius, however, stands confirmed: a topographical sketch of coastal terrain from Misenum to Baiae has been preserved on an ancient glass flask from Puteoli; individual monuments can

[124] Tac. *Ann.* 15.42.2–4; cf. Suet. *Nero* 31.3; Pliny *NH* 14.68; Stat. *Silv.* 4.3.7–8.

[125] Tacitus himself knew the hazards that awaited ships along the Campanian coast: *Ann.* 15.46.3. For a more just evaluation of Nero's scheme, see Frederiksen, *RE* 23 (1959), 2043–2044; R. Meiggs, *Roman Ostia* (Oxford 1960), 57–58.

[126] Puteoli's status was elevated to that of colony under Nero: Tac. *Ann.* 14.27.2; *CIL* X, 5369; IV, 2152; IV, 3525 (*Colonia Claudia Neronensis*); cf. Frederiksen, *RE* 23 (1959), 2041–2042. In the last named inscription, Pompeii and Tegianum are also listed as *coloniae* and described as owing their increased civic dignity to *iudic(i)is Aug(usti)*, surely Nero: see Mau's remarks on *CIL* IV, 3525; and cf. Rostovtzeff, *SEHRE*², 610, n. 25, with references *ad loc.*

[127] Suet. *Nero* 31.2: *Praeterea incohabat piscinam a Miseno ad Avernum lacum contectam porticibusque conclusam, quo quidquid totis Baiis calidarum aquarum esset converteretur.*

be identified by incised inscriptions, among them a *stagnum Neronis*.[128]

69 and the Flavians

While still a private citizen the future emperor M. Salvius Otho had a villa at Baiae, where he played host to Nero and Agrippina on that fatal evening in March of 59.[129] Aulus Vitellius too appears to have owned property on the Campanian coast before his elevation to the principate. His ties with the region were longstanding: his father came originally from Nuceria; Vitellius himself passed his boyhood and early youth on Capreae while Tiberius was master of the island; Vitellius' favorite freedman, Asiaticus, was his constant companion when both were young, and Vitellius encountered him later at Puteoli, where Asiaticus was living.[130] It is not surprising, in view of this familiarity with the Bay of Naples, that the partisans of Vespasian enticed a receptive Vitellius with the promise of a safe and luxurious retreat on Campania's bays, should he lay down his imperial powers in 69.[131]

Frugality and old-fashioned simplicity were the watchwords of the reign of Vespasian: the Campanian extravagances of the later

[128] For descriptions of the glass vase long housed in the Museo Borghiano in Rome, see Beloch, *Campanien*[2], 184; Dubois, *PA*, 208; for accessible reproductions see C. Picard, *Latomus* 18 (1959), 34–36 and plate 6; A. De Franciscis, *Archaeology* 20 (1967), 213. Maiuri, in an important study, scrutinized the coastal terrain from Misenum to Baiae in the light of the topographical designations on the vase (Maiuri, "La specola misenate," *RAAN* N.S. 25 [1949–1950], 259–285); while he rightly concluded that the designation *stagnu(m) Neronis* cannot refer to the inland waterway described by Tacitus, he failed to discuss the great Neronian *piscina* to which Suetonius alone alludes (Maiuri, *ibid.*, 273–275). The vestiges of that enterprise, however, are surely what are represented on the vase.

[129] Suet. *Otho* 3.1: *Omnium autem consiliorum secretorumque particeps die, quem necandae matri Nero destinarat, ad avertendas suspiciones cenam utrique exquisitissimae comitatis dedit.* There need be no incompatibility between this passage and Tac. *Ann.* 13.46.5, where Otho's removal from Rome to govern Lusitania is assigned to 58: Nero's orders may not have gone immediately into effect (so also Bicknell, *CR* N.S. 13 [1963], 262).

[130] Nucerian origin: Suet. *Vit.* 2.2. Capreae: *ibid.*, 3.2 (quoted above, n. 73). Asiaticus and Puteoli: Suet. *Vit.* 12.

[131] Tac. *Hist.* 3.63: *non omisere per eos dies Primus ac Varus crebris nuntiis salutem et pecuniam et secreta Campaniae offerre Vitellio, si positis armis seque ac liberos suos Vespasiano permisisset.* Cf. 3.66: *nunc pecuniam et familiam et beatos Campaniae sinus promitti . . .*

Julio-Claudian emperors find no parallel in the first decade of Flavian rule.[132] The fact is strikingly illustrated in the inscriptions: numerous imperial freedmen are attested in Campanian contexts from the Julio-Claudian period; but with the accession of Vespasian epigraphical testimony sharply diminishes.[133] Vespasian passed his summers at *Aquae Cutiliae* near Reate; this was his native region.[134] Nevertheless during the last year of his life he certainly spent some time in Campania.[135] Here as elsewhere the property accumulated by the earlier emperors passed by inheritance, despite the lack of a family connection, into the possession of the Flavians and became part of their patrimony: this was determined not by private law but by the emperor's public position. The gravity of economic crisis, rather than the desire to visit his villas, most likely drew Vespasian to Campania early in 79. In a famous passage the Elder Pliny declared that the *latifundia* had proved ruinous to Italy; small private farms were being swallowed up by increasingly vast estates where management was based upon different principles. In order to stem the tide the Flavians inaugurated important social and economic policies, empowering imperial officials to reclaim for the state those public lands which had been unjustly seized by private owners. These measures are reflected in the Campanian evidence: Vespasian's officials and their enactments are attested in inscriptions from Pompeii, Nola, and Capua.[136]

Some details of additional imperial policies and benefactions in Campania under Vespasian and Titus may be reconstructed from inscriptions from Puteoli, Salernum, Surrentum, and Neapolis.

[132] Tac. *Ann.* 3.55.5: *sed praecipuus adstricti moris auctor Vespasianus fuit, antiquo ipse cultu victuque.* For luxury under the Flavians see below, Chapter 5, p. 123–124.

[133] On Julio-Claudian freedmen see Della Corte, *Atti del IV Cong. di Stud. Rom.* II (1938), 297–302, and above, *passim*; for a Flavian freedman at Stabiae, see F. Di Capua, *RAAN* N.S. 19 (1938), 87–88.

[134] Suet. *Vesp.* 24.1; cf. 2.1.

[135] *Ibid.*, 24.1: *Consulatu suo nono temptatus in Campania motiunculis levibus protinusque urbe repetita* . . .

[136] For Flavian inheritance of Julio-Claudian estates, see P. A. Brunt, "The Fiscus and its Development," *JRS* 56 (1966), 79. *Latifundia*: Pliny *NH* 18.35. On the agricultural crisis and Flavian response, cf. Rostovtzeff, *SEHRE²*, 198–206. The Campanian evidence has been conveniently assembled and discussed by G. O. Onorato, *Iscrizioni Pompeiane* (Florence 1957), 111–112.

Puteoli, doubtless owing to her economic ties with the Orient, had declared for Vespasian in the civil wars; the rewards for her allegiance included territorial accessions and a change of title (to *Colonia Flavia Augusta*); increased prosperity ensued and is impressively commemorated by the city's construction, *pecunia sua*, of a vast new amphitheater, the third largest in Italy.[137] Titus was generous and prompt in his relief of the cities buried by the eruption of Vesuvius,[138] and restored at Surrentum an *horologium* which had been damaged by earthquakes.[139] Although a public timepiece might not appear to be an object worthy of imperial munificence, there was, as so often, the best of precedents for such a benefaction: Augustus had once presented Puteoli with a sundial and had erected a splendid meridian in Rome's *Campus Martius* in 10 B.C.[140]

Titus further displayed a continuing interest in Neapolis and the *Sebasta*. A Greek inscription set up there in the year 81 testifies to his repair of a public building (damaged, no doubt, by the earthquakes which accompanied the catastrophe of 79) and discloses that he presided thrice over the Neapolitan games.[141] He must therefore have been in Neapolis in 74 and 78, as well as upon some special occasion in an unknown year. That fact reveals the Flavians' concern to popularize the new dynasty in the city.[142] It also helps

---

[137] Puteoli in the civil war: Tac. *Hist.* 3.57. Territorial expansion: *CIL* X, 3750; 1807; 1873; 1894 (associated with the colony of Vespasian by Fredericksen, *RE* 23 1959], 2053–2054). Amphitheater: *Eph. Epigr.* VIII, 364; Maiuri, *Campi Flegrèi*, 39–51; Frederiksen *RE* 23 (1959), 2057–2058 (*q.v.* also for additional bibliography). Vespasian restored a building at Salernum: *AE* (1951), no. 200, with Degrassi's observations in *Atti d. Accad. Naz. dei Lincei, classe sci. mor. stor. filol.*, 8th ser., XI (1965), 274–276.

[138] Suet. *Titus* 8.3; cf. 8.4: *Curatores restituendae Campaniae e consularium numero sorte duxit; bona oppressorum in Vesuvio, quorum heredes non exstabant, restitutioni afflictarum civitatium attribuit*, Titus personally inspected the region in 80: Cass. Dio 66.24.1. A graffito proves that Apollinaris, Titus' physician (and perhaps also, therefore, the emperor himself), was in Herculaneum less than a month before the eruption of 79: see J. J. Deiss *Herculaneum—Italy's Buried Treasure* (New York 1966), 44.

[139] A. Sogliano, *Not. d. Sc.* (1901), 363–364.

[140] *CIL* X, 1617 (Puteoli); for the Roman meridian, its needle an obelisk from Heliopolis, see E. Nash, *Pictorial Dictionary of Ancient Rome*[2] II (New York 1968), 134.

[141] *IG* XIV, 729 (= *CIL* X, 1481).

[142] *CIL* X, 1481, with Mommsen's note *ad loc.* (p. 173); Geer, "Greek Games," *TAPA* 66 (1935), 215.

to confirm Suetonius' assertion that during Vespasian's reign Titus was both *particeps* and *tutor*, taking upon himself the greater part of the burden of official duties.[143]

With Domitian's accession resume the ancient notices of Baiae's luxuries and the inanities of the fishpond. Josephus pauses in his description of Gaius' visit to Baiae to observe that "the lordly palaces there abound with costly appointments, for each emperor is anxious to outdo his predecessor"; since the *Antiquitates* were published in 93 or 94, this passage manifestly applies also to Baiae in Domitian's day.[144] Martial presages dire consequences for poachers at the imperial fish preserves in the *Baianus lacus*; Domitian's fish, he adds, swim up at their master's bidding to nuzzle the imperial hand.[145] In the *Panegyricus* the younger Pliny contrasts Trajan's vigor with Domitian's distasteful habits during periods of leisure at Baiae,[146] where the emperor possibly increased the numbers of the imperial estates through enforced legacies and confiscations—his practice in this regard was particularly notorious.[147]

While at Baiae Domitian attended also to matters of economic policy, watching over the construction of the new roadway which was to bear his name. Extending along the coast from Sinuessa to Puteoli, the *Via Domitiana*, completed in 95, enabled commercial traffic between Rome and Puteoli to avoid the long detour through Capua on the *Via Appia*. Statius marvels that what was once a day's journey (from Sinuessa to Puteoli) now required but two hours; and even though the accuracy of the figures of the court

---

[143] Suet. *Titus* 6.1.

[144] Joseph. *AJ* 18.248–249: ἐν βαίαις . . . βασίλειοί τέ εἰσιν οἰκήσεις αὐτόθι πολυτελέσι κεχρημέναι κατασκευαῖς φιλοτιμηθέντος τῶν αὐτοκρατόρων ἑκάστου τοὺς προγεγονότας ὑπερβάλλεσθαι. Martial (5.1.1–6) lists six villas of Domitian, excluding that at Baiae. For a *procurator* of Domitian's wife at Baiae, see below, n. 182.

[145] Mart. 4.30.3–5. Cf. Stat. *Silv.* 1.5.60–61, very possibly an allusion to Domitian (Vollmer, *P. Papinii Statii Silvarum Libri* [Leipzig 1898], 301 *ad loc.*).

[146] Pliny *Pan.* 82.1: *quantum dissimilis illi, qui non Albani lacus otium Baianique torporem et silentium ferre, non pulsum saltem fragoremque remorum perpeti poterat, quin ad singulos ictus turpi formidine horresceret.*

[147] Suet. *Domit.* 12.2; Pliny *Pan.* 34.1; cf. Rogers, *TAPA* 78 (1947), 151–152.

poet is scarcely above suspicion, Domitian's new road was certainly a public utility of the first importance, diminishing greatly both distance and discomfort of travel between the capital and the towns on the Campanian coast.[148] Furthermore, there are signs that the *Via Domitiana* was but one part of that emperor's—and his predecessors'—ambitious scheme for improvements along the *Via Appia*; for these repairs, however, his successors were inclined to take the credit.[149]

The Second Century and After

Domitian's successors might justly wish to publicize their achievements. Concern for the communications of Italy, both internal and external, preoccupied both Nerva and Trajan, and the early years of the latter's principate were marked by an impressive series of improvements and repairs to the *Via Appia*, *Via Aemilia*, *Via Sublacensis*, and *Via Latina*. Along with these attempts to improve Italian economic arteries, Trajan in 102 completed the widening of the earlier road between Puteoli and Neapolis. The work had been begun by Nerva, who thereby revealed his appreciation of the importance of the roadway carried to Puteoli by his Flavian predecessor. Trajan also built bridges, it is alleged, in the region of Baiae, but these were probably designed to set his personal stamp upon the architecture of the imperial palaces.[150]

[148] The *Via Domitiana*: Stat. *Silv.* 4.3; Cass. Dio 67.14; Beloch, *Campanien*², 164; Maiuri, *Not. d. Sc.* (1928), 181; *Campi Flegrèi*, 103–106. The new roadway proves also the continuing economic importance of Puteoli in Domitian's day: *AE* (1941), no. 73.

[149] Cf. Syme, *JRS* 20 (1930), 56, n. 4, on the suppression of Domitian's name on milestones. Domitian is also conspicuously absent from the *collegium* of the *Augustales* (?), which was discovered by chance in February, 1968, near the southern extremity of the outer harbor at Misenum, and which contained statues of Vespasian and Titus in one chamber, an equestrian statue of Nerva in an adjacent room; for a preliminary report of these unpublished finds, see A. De Franciscis in *Il Mattino* (Naples), 5 July, 1968.

[150] On Nerva's and Trajan's road repairs (and other public works) see, e.g., R. P. Longden, *CAH* XI, 206–210; for the roadway from Puteoli to Neapolis, *CIL* X, 6926–6928, 6931; and especially W. Johannowsky, "Contributi alla topografia della Campania antica," *RAAN* N.S. 27 (1952), 83–146. There is also evidence that Trajan commemorated the completion of the work with an arch at Puteoli: see H. Kähler, *Studies Presented to D. M. Robinson* I(St. Louis 1951), 430–434. Bridges at Baiae: *S.H.A.*

For the second century and after, ancient references to the Campanian policies and properties of the emperors become still more scattered and diffuse, reflecting the decline in strength of the historiographical tradition. Hadrian departed for Campania in 119. The evidence suggests that the visit was a deliberate act of policy, and that he was as assiduous in his economic attentions to the towns of Italy as he was famous later for his subventions in the provinces: he aided towns in the district by numerous gifts and benefactions and made efforts to secure the friendship and support of persons prominent in the Campanian cities.[151] The emperor's philhellenic sentiments are well-known; in addition to the magistracies assumed by him in the Latin towns, he became archon at Athens and, not surprisingly, demarch in Neapolis.[152] Hadrian was staying in the imperial villa at Baiae when he died in July of 138;[153] and although there was a tradition that he found burial at Cicero's villa near the Lucrine Lake, other evidence asserting that Pius bore his predecessor's remains to the gardens of Domitian at Rome is to be preferred: the mention of Puteoli is doubtless due to subsequent commemorative gestures on the part of Pius— he arranged for the construction of a temple in Puteoli, sacred to

---

Alex. Sev. 25.11. The testimony of "Aelius Lampridius" should probably be accepted, although the bridges to which he here alludes may have stood elsewhere. Cf. Hirschfeld, *GRK*, 538.

151 *S.H.A. Hadr.* 9.6: *Summotis his a praefectura, quibus debebat imperium, Campaniam petiit eiusque omnia oppida beneficiis et largitionibus sublevavit, optimum quemque amicitiis suis iungens.* On this Campanian excursion, cf. Syme, *Tacitus*, 487, 524. Expenditures in provincial cities: Cass. Dio 69.5.2–3. In Campania, inscriptions testify to the variety and scope of his munificence. Hadrianic brickstamps have been discovered among the vaulted ruins of baths (*balneum Faustines*) near the amphitheater of Puteoli (Frederiksen, in *RE* 23 [1959], 2059; see Chapter 5, n. 112); the same emperor had a hand in restoration of Puteoli's harbor works: *CIL* X, 1640. *CIL* X, 1496 discloses Hadrian's name in Naples on ruins of the Serino aqueduct; *CIL* X, 3832 proves imperial subvention in construction of the amphitheater at Capua. For Hadrian's building projects in Italy and the provinces, see T. Frank, *ESAR* V, 71–74; for his connections with Pausilypon, cf. below, n. 180. A milestone indicates Hadrianic road repairs near Stabiae: L. D'Orsi, *Gli Scavi Archeologici di Stabiae*² (Milan 1965), 35–36.

152 *S.H.A. Hadr.* 19.1; on this magistracy, cf. Strab. 5.4.7 (C 246), discussed below, Chapter 5, p. 143.

153 *S.H.A. Hadr.* 25.5–7: *Post haec Hadrianus Baias petiit Antonino Romae ad imperandum relicto. ubi cum nihil proficeret, accessito Antonino in conspectu eius apud ipsas Baias periit die VI iduum Iuliarum. Invisusque omnibus sepultus est in villa Ciceroniana Puteolis.*

Hadrian's memory, and introduced Greek games—appropriately entitled the Εὐσέβεια—in the city.[154]

Antoninus Pius, his biographer asserts, sold off *species imperatorias superfluas et praedia*, preferring to live on his own private estates, among which he varied his residence in accordance with the seasons. But Pius' properties included estates in Campania,[155] and he accepted legacies from freedmen who had served him in those parts: an inscription from Neapolis records a financial bequest made by a certain Fortunatus to the emperor, *optimo et indulgentissimo patrono*. It was also in that city that the freedman Strenion, *cubicularius* to Faustina, paid tribute to his mistress at some date between 140 and 160.[156] These inscriptions seem to reflect the necessity for increasing imperial intervention at Neapolis in the economic and administrative spheres, a process which culminated in the transformation of the city's status from *municipium* to *colonia* in the Antonine Age.[157] They further suggest that none of the emperors' properties in Neapolis was jettisoned in Pius' sales of superfluous luxury estates. Nor were those at Baiae: in 143 Pius' adoptive successor Marcus Aurelius, then in his twenty-second

---

[154] Burial in Cicero's villa (cf. preceding note) is a most suspicious detail (accepted, however, by Dubois, *PA*, 372) of precisely the sort that might recommend itself to an inventive historiographer with a taste for early tradition; cf. Syme, *Antiquitas*, Reihe 4 (Beiträge zur *Historia Augusta* Forschung, 3 [1966]), 269. But there is no need to reject the statement that Hadrian died at Baiae; that fact would have been widely recorded and well-known. Taking fact as his starting point, "Aelius Spartianus" will have been easily and naturally led to burial—and to embellishment. For the more plausible account of Hadrian's burial, cf. *S.H.A. Pius* 5.1, *Marc.* 6.1; for the temple at Puteoli (itself above suspicion) *S.H.A. Hadr.* 27.3, with *CIL* X, 1784. Εὐσέβεια: *S.H.A. Hadr.* 27; Artemidorus, *Oneir.* 1.26; *IG* XIV, 737, line 7. Cf. Frederiksen in *RE* 23 (1959), 2052.

[155] *S.H.A. Pius* 7.10: *species imperatorias superfluas et praedia vendidit et in suis propriis fundis vixit varie ac pro temporibus. nec ullas expeditiones obiit, nisi quod ad agros suos profectus est et ad Campaniam, dicens gravem esse provincialibus comitatum principis, etiam nimis parci.* For an odd incident on Campania's coast cf. Aur. Vict. *Caes.* 16.2.

[156] A. Sogliano, *Not. d. Sc.* (1892), 479–481: *Imp. Caesari T. Aelio Hadriano Antonino Aug. Pio p. p. optimo et indulgentissimo patrono Fortunatus lib. ex* HS $\overline{CCC}$ *testamento fieri iussit.* A. De Franciscis, *Archeologia Classica* 6 (1954), 279: *Divae Faustinae Antonin. Strenion lib. a cubic.*

[157] *Colonia Aurelia Augusta Antoniniana Felix Neapolis: Eph. Epigr.* VIII, 871. On the date and significance of this and other Antonine developments, see E. Lepore in *Storia di Napoli* I, Società Editrice Storia di Napoli (Naples 1967), 296, with n. 11 (p. 363).

year, was journeying up and down the Campanian coast, dispatching from the imperial villas at Baiae and Neapolis affectionate communications to his tutor in Latin Rhetoric.[158] Marcus Aurelius retained as emperor his liking for *peregrinatio* in these coastal regions. He was known to have travelled all the way from Campania to introduce proposals in the Roman senate; perhaps some concerned the alimentary schemes which flourished under the Antonines, and for which there is some Campanian evidence.[159] A lead pipe bearing the name of Commodus was found near Baiae, where that emperor presumably carried out new building at the imperial villa.[160] And the imperial villa on the southern coast of the Sorrentine peninsula was still in operation through the Antonine period, the last for which epigraphical evidence is available.[161]

Herodian affirms that after the fall of Plautianus in 205, Septimius Severus passed most of the remainder of his life on the imperial estates near the city and along the Campanian coast because he feared for his sons' corruption by the luxuries of Rome.[162] Clodius Albinus, it is alleged, consulted the oracle at Cumae, where his imperial destiny was disclosed. He then enriched the votive deposits at Apollo's temple with an arresting offering—the purple horns of a snow-white bull.[163] Alexander Severus entertained Dio Cassius in Campania in 229 at the time when Alexander was almost certainly holding court at Baiae. Dio knew Baiae well,

[158] Fronto, *ad M. Caes.* 2.6.3 (Naber, p. 30 = Haines I, 142); 2.8 (Naber, p. 32 = Haines I, 146); 1.4.2 (Naber, p. 9 = Haines I, 92): *Nunc, quando apud Baias agimus in hoc diuturno Ulixi labyrintho.* The emperor's mother was staying in Neapolis on her birthday in 143: see Catalogue II, no. 16 (M. Cornelius Fronto).

[159] *S.H.A. Marc.* 10.7: *Semper autem, cum potuit, interfuit senatui etiam si nihil esset referendum, si Romae fuit; si vero aliquid referre voluit, etiam de Campania ipse venit.* Alimentary schemes: see R. Duncan-Jones, *PBSR* N.S. 20 (1965), 296, no. 637.

[160] F. Colonna, *Not. d. Sc.* (1891), 320–321.

[161] For that villa, possibly constructed by Claudius, see above, p. 93. Antonine freedmen: *CIL* X, 526; 563.

[162] Herodian *Hist.* 3.13.1: ὁ δὲ Σεβῆρος . . . τὰ πλεῖστα τοῦ βίου διέτριβεν ἐν τοῖς βασιλικοῖς προαστείοις καὶ τοῖς παραλίοις τῆς Καμπανίας χωρίοις, δικάζων τε καὶ πολιτικὰ διοικῶν . . .

[163] *S.H.A. Clod. Alb.* 5.4. But neither the incident nor the oracular response inspires confidence: see A. Momigliano, *Studies in Historiography* (New York 1966), 147–148.

and independent evidence attests that his host there made arrangements for the construction of a number of new monuments: a palace and a pond (filial homage to Alexander's mother Mamaea), notable public works in honor of his kinsmen, and huge pools into which ran the waters of the sea. These details should perhaps be viewed within the larger context of local Severan benefactions, which included repairs to the coast road between Puteoli and Neapolis, as well as harbor works at Puteoli.[164]

When the aged Tacitus was proclaimed emperor in 275, an escort was sent to fetch him from Baiae, whither he had repaired two months before. This notice is exceptional; there can have been but few sojourners at Baiae in this period. Indeed, the sharp decline in inscriptional evidence throughout Campania after the Severans should be seen as symptomatic of the years of crisis through which the entire Empire was passing, and for which, paradoxically, the almost universal scarcity of literary, documentary, and archaeological source materials is the historian's chief evidence. *Correctores Campaniae* appear in the inscriptions from the time of Carus and Carinus (282–283), and soon are succeeded by *consulares Campaniae*: the presence of these officials confirms locally Italy's loss of preferential tax status and her provincialization. In contrast, later documents record notable public works of Constantine, and thereby bear witness to economic revival on the Bay of Naples after the uncertainties of the third century; repairs were made at

---

[164] Cass. Dio 80.5.2: καὶ οὕτω μετὰ ταῦτα ἔς τε τὴν Ῥώμην καὶ ἐς τὴν Καμπανίαν πρὸς αὐτὸν (sc. Ἀλέξανδρον) ἦλθον, καὶ συνδιατρίψας τινὰς ἡμέρας αὐτῷ . . . His knowledge of Baiae: 48.50–51; he had seen the constructions himself. The works of Alexander Severus at Baiae: *S.H.A. Alex. Sev.* 26.9–10: *In matrem Mamaeam unice pius fuit, ita ut Romae in palatio faceret diaetas nominis Mamaeae, quas imperitum vulgus hodie 'ad Mammam' vocat, et in Baiano palatium cum stagno, quod Mamaeae nomine hodieque censetur. Fecit et alia in Baiano opera magnifica in honorem adfinium suorum et stagna stupenda admisso mari.* Confirmed by Amm. Marc. 28.4.19: *Dein cum a Silvani lavacro vel Mamaeae aquis ventitant* (sc. *nobiles) sospitalibus;* and see further A. De Franciscis in *Archaeology* 20 (1967), 212–215: lead pipes bearing the name of Alexander Severus have been found at Baiae. That Dio and Alexander Severus met at Baiae was conjectured also by F. Millar, *A Study of Cassius Dio* (Oxford 1964), 24; cf. *ibid.*, 11. Dio had a villa in Capua: see below, Chapter 5, n. 32. Severan benefactions: *CIL* X, 6929 (Neapolis); *CIL* X, 1650–1654 (Puteoli).

5

the harbor and elsewhere in late fourth century Puteoli.[165] The last evidence for an emperor in a villa is still later. At the outset of the last quarter of the fifth century, the infant emperor Augustulus was stripped of his powers by Odovacar and driven into exile in Campania. He and his family took up residence on an estate whose history could be traced back to the days of the great *piscinarii* of the late Republic—the Neapolitan villa of L. Licinius Lucullus.[166]

It is only too obvious from the foregoing chronological survey that the literary evidence is inadequate to permit the history of most imperial villas in Campania to be reconstructed in detail. This, after all, is to be expected: *otium* and privacy are intimately connected. Splendid new coastal buildings might occasionally excite public curiosity, and an imperial death at Misenum or at Baiae would be certain to find its way into the biographical record; but at the imperial villas in Campania an emperor's administrative concerns and his personal enjoyment were neither generally known nor widely circulated. There is no reference to a *princeps'* presence at the villas at Misenum or Surrentum subsequent to the deaths of Tiberius and Claudius, respectively; similarly, Capreae is mentioned only once thereafter—as the place of exile for Lucilla, sister of the emperor Commodus.[167] Perhaps by the late second century the villas on Pandateria and Ponza had been abandoned; at any

[165] Tacitus at Baiae: *S.H.A. Tac.* 7.5–6: *Hoc loco tacendum non est plerosque in litteras rettulisse Tacitum absentem et in Campania positum principem nuncupatum; verum est, nec dissimulare possum. Nam cum rumor emersisset illum imperatorem esse faciendum, discessit atque in Baiano duobus mensibus fuit. Sed inde deductus huic senatus consulto* ... The statements are uncontroversial; additional grounds for credence are provided by Zonaras 12.28. For a recent account of the third-century crisis see F. Millar *et al., The Roman Empire and its Neighbours* (London 1967), 239–248. *Correctores Campaniae, consulares Campaniae*: R. Thomsen, *The Italic Regions from Augustus to the Lombard Invasion, Classica et Mediaevalia*, Diss. 4 (Copenhagen 1947), 200–201; 210–212. Constantine and the Bay of Naples: *CIL* X, 6932, cf. 6930; and see Frederiksen, in *RE* 23 (1959), 2045 (Puteoli); E. Lepore, in *Storia di Napoli* I, Società Editrice Storia di Napoli (Naples 1967), 326 (Neapolis). Late repairs at Puteoli: *CIL* X, 1690–1694.

[166] Marcellinus Comes, *Chron.* a. 476 (= *Mon. Germ. Hist., AA* XI, p. 91). Cf. M. Napoli, *Napoli Greco-Romana* (Naples 1959), 22; Catalogue I, no. 22b.

[167] *S.H.A. Comm.* 5.7: *ipse autem Commodus Lucillam sororem, cum Capreas misisset, occidit*; so also Cass. Dio 73.4.6, where Commodus' wife Crispina is included in the relegation to Capreae.

rate, the villa on the southern coast of the Sorrentine peninsula yields no inscriptions after the Antonine period.

Only at Baiae can a definite pattern of continuing imperial possession be traced from Julio-Claudian days to the reign of Alexander Severus—a continuity to which, as has been seen, Josephus bears independent witness when he remarks late in Flavian times that at Baiae each emperor was anxious in his buildings to surpass the works of his predecessor.[168] Here the archaeological evidence, clearly reflecting various phases of construction, lends general support to Josephus' statement. The excavations of the past twenty years have unearthed the most elaborate and monumental architectural complex yet recovered in the Phlegraean Fields (Plates 4–7). A complicated network of terraces, *exedrae*, *nymphaea*, pools, and porticoes, which are interconnected by means of ramps and stairways, descend in gradual stages from the western heights of the "Sella di Baia" (where huge cisterns were fed by the Augustan aqueduct) to the curving shores of the *sinus Baianus*.[169] In Maiuri's plan this vast area is designated as the baths of Baiae.[170] But the current superintendent for Campanian antiquities, observing that the complex lacks many of the usual characteristics of Roman *thermae*, believes that this was actually the site of the imperial palace at Baiae and that the so-called temple of Mercury, much the earliest of three domed buildings in the precinct, functioned as the grand bath of the palace.[171] Topographical support for this view has been adduced from two ancient glass vases, one of which has already been mentioned.[172] These flasks were manufactured at Puteoli, where they were doubtless sold as souvenirs; their surfaces depict scenes

[168] See above, n. 144.

[169] For the modern excavations, see Maiuri, *Campi Flegrèi*, 72–86.

[170] Maiuri's plan (cf. *Campi Flegrèi*, 70–71) is reproduced below, Plate 8.

[171] A. De Franciscis, "Underwater Discoveries Around the Bay of Naples," *Archaeology* 20 (1967), 212–214. For the "temple of Mercury," cf. below, Chapter 5, n. 109.

[172] For the vase formerly located in the Museo Borghiano, see above, n. 128; on the so-called Piombino vase, see Dubois, *PA*, 199–201. The former reproduces the major monuments of the coastline from Misenum to Baiae, the latter the coastal strip from Baiae to Puteoli.

of the coastal monuments at Baiae, including oyster beds flanked by two domed buildings above which, on the Piombino flask, the word *palatium* is clearly legible.[173] De Franciscis believes also that the numerous works of sculpture and wall decorations recovered at the site—and these include several portraits of Roman emperors—are all of a quality worthy of display in an imperial palace rather than in baths; the architectural remains range in date from the late sixth century B.C. to the reign of Severus Alexander.[174] Further study of these remarkable and complicated excavations—and additional inscriptions—may enable De Franciscis to present and document his hypothesis in more detail; at present conclusions can be only tentative because much needs to be explained. The public baths at Baiae can have been scarcely less elaborate than the imperial holdings—four centuries of constant and enthusiastic public patronage stands in confirmation;[175] but if the portions of Baiae currently excavated should be regarded as imperial domain, where did the general public amuse itself? The baths at Baiae, as will be seen, were regarded by Romans as a paragon, and as such they can be expected to have differed, both in overall design and in individual architectural forms, from other thermal establishments elsewhere. Architectural originality, therefore, is an inadequate criterion for determining which sectors of the baths were public, which reserved for the private enjoyment of the emperor and his family. And until private and public sectors are differentiated, it is of course impossible to distinguish how far individual emperors

---

[173] The suggestion that *palatium* on the vase was intended to designate an imperial palace at Baiae was first advanced by De Rossi (*Bollettino Napol.* II [1854], 155); cf. Dubois, *PA*, 200. It should be observed that the word does not appear on the vase from the Museo Borghiano, which is in other respects a more detailed representation of the Baian sector; the two vases correspond, however, in depicting domed buildings on either side of a complex labelled *ostriaria*. *Palatium* is used of the imperial palace at Baiae only once in the literary sources: *S.H.A. Alex. Sev.* 26.9–10 (quoted above, n. 164).

[174] A. De Franciscis (see above, n. 171), 212–214. For discussion of a remarkable system of underground corridors and caverns at Baiae, and of masonry above ground belonging apparently to a temple which has been securely dated to the late sixth century B.C., see R. F. Paget, "The 'Great Antrum' at Baiae: a Preliminary Report," *PBSR* N.S. 22 1967), 102–112.

[175] See below, Chapter 5, pp. 119–120.

transformed their predecessor's estates to suit their personal pleasure or integrated new constructions with earlier buildings.

Baiae, however, is a special case. Epigraphical evidence, where it has chanced to survive, may occasionally assist and control inquiry into the fates of imperial estates elsewhere in Campania, also providing some insight into the ways in which these properties were administered. L. Annaeus Seneca was the Elder Pliny's source for the statement that a fish, which was introduced into the emperor's ponds at Posillipo by Vedius Pollio, expired sixty years later.[176] There is some confusion here, for as has been seen, Augustus only acquired the ponds and the property after Pollio's death in 15 B.C.;[177] but why should Pollio have performed this act during the last year of his life? Seneca must therefore have heard the tale at some point before A.D. 45; and at that date the villa Pausilypon must still have belonged to the emperors. Inscriptions confirm and further extend this verdict. Three inscriptions from Posillipo, dated securely to the year 65, mention a *Macrinus Diadumeni Aug. lib. proc(uratoris) Antoniani [servus] disp(ensator)*.[178] At the same site epigraphical evidence from the reign of Trajan is still more explicit: *M. Ulpius Aug. lib. Euphrates qui procuravit Pausilypo*.[179] Further, a piece of lead water pipe has been discovered at the same location, stamped with the name of the emperor Hadrian; repairs or additions to the buildings presumably occurred during his reign.[180] The conclusion is inescapable: the villa of Vedius Pollio remained continuously within the imperial domain at least until the death

---

[176] Pliny *NH* 9.167: *Pausilypum villa est Campaniae haut procul Neapoli; in ea in Caesaris piscinis a Pollione Vedio coniectum piscem sexagensimum post annum expirasse scribit Annaeus Seneca . . .*

[177] See above, p. 76.

[178] *Eph. Epigr.* VIII, 335–337. The text of 337 runs as follows: *Macrinus Diadumeni Aug(usti) l(iberti) proc(uratoris) Antoniani disp(ensator) hic ambulavit a villa Polli Felicis, quae est epilimones usque ad emissarium Paconianum Nerva et Vestino cos.* (that is, 65). On Pollius Felix and his villa, see Catalogue II, no. 34. As Hirschfeld suggests (*GRK*, 518, n. 10), Diadumenus Antonianus may well have been earlier attached to the villa at Bauli occupied by Antonia minor, and subsequently charged with the management of Pausilypon (see above, p. 85).

[179] *CIL* VI, 8584.

[180] Günther, *Pausilypon*, 214, n. 14; see also Scherling, "Pausilypon," *RE* 18 (1949), 2420; Hirschfeld, *GRK*, 518, n. 10.

of Hadrian, administered by an imperial freedman of procuratorial rank. And, since it is most unlikely that the history of Pausilypon was without parallel elsewhere, a second conclusion emerges: even though a particular villa of the emperors may be alluded to but rarely in the ancient literature, the possibility of a pattern of continuing imperial possession, in any case through the Antonine Age, ought not to be rejected.

A small number of inscriptions, included by Mommsen among those of Puteoli, reveal the names of other procuratorial *liberti* who were very probably charged with the management of imperial estates in the coastal area, and in addition, the existence of a certain *procurator patrimonii*, the extent of whose official competence is uncertain.[181] A procurator of the wife of Domitian is named in an inscription found at Baiae, suggesting that the empress may have presided over a part of the imperial holdings there.[182] *Dispensatores*, invariably of servile status, regularly served as financial agents at the larger imperial villas; in addition to Macrinus, treasurer at Posillipo, *dispensatores* are attested at Misenum, Neapolis, and at the imperial villa once owned by Agrippa Postumus at Boscotrecase near Pompeii.[183] Imperial *cubicularii* (chamberlains) tended to be freedmen.[184] Other officials of the emperors served in coastal Campania, though they were probably not attached to any particular imperial estate; those attested include two *ingenui* (an *architectus Augustorum* and a bookbinder to Tiberius Caesar) and a Flavian freedman (who was *supra velarios de domu Augusti*).[185] *Caesaris vilici* (imperial bailiffs of servile status), subordinate to whom were the *familiae* of local slaves, recur still

[181] CIL X, 1737, 1739, 1747; *Not. d. Sc.* (1922), 460 (on which see Catalogue II, no. 46, M. Vipsanius Agrippa; the man managed the estate, but does not appear to have been a *procurator*); *Eph. Epigr.* VIII, 367; CIL X, 1740 (= ILS 1488). Cf. Dubois, *PA*, 378–379. For the *procuratores* on private estates see above, Chapter 3, n. 61.

[182] CIL X, 1738; cf. Dubois, *PA*, 379.

[183] Misenum: CIL X, 1732 (this *dispensator* of Claudian date married an *ingenua*, *Titacia C. f. Procula*: cf. P. R. C. Weaver, *JRS* 54 [1964], 127). Neapolis: CIL X, 1730–1731. Boscotrecase: CIL IV, 6997; cf. Rostovtzeff, *SEHRE²*, 552, n. 31. See in general N. Vulic', '*dispensator*,' *Dizionario Epigrafico* (1913), 1920.

[184] CIL X, 695; A. De Franciscis, *Archeologia Classica* 6 (1954), 279 (cited above, n. 156).

[185] CIL X, 1757, 1735, 1745 (on which see Dubois, *PA*, 379).

more frequently in the epigraphical texts; an inscription from Baiae records a dedication to the wife of a certain Mystes, *Caesaris vilicus,* by the *familia quae sub eo est.*[186]

The *familia* (a villa's slaves) was charged with a wide variety of duties which devoted survivors often thought fit to designate on the sepulchral epitaph of the deceased—titles were a mark of status. The imperial cemetery at Surrentum has yielded a sizable harvest of slaves' titles and official functions: we know of a gardener, a watchman, a mason, a gatekeeper, and a painter; more unusual are a *verna a memoria* and *servi a possessionibus* and *a valetudine.*[187] Whether the slaves attached to the imperial estates were collectively organized into units larger than that of the *familia* remains an open question, despite Mommsen's ingenious interpretation of three inscriptions discovered long ago at Bauli. One stone discloses the name of a freedman of Tiberius and the initials *D.D.E.F.V.L.* Mommsen restored the phrase as *decreto decurionum e familia villae Lucullanae* and plausibly suggested that the imperial villa at Misenum retained the name of its famous late Republican proprietor.[188] A more difficult problem is posed, however, by his restoration *decreto decurionum* and by the mention in two other local inscriptions of a *collegium* and *ordo Baulanorum*: Bauli is not known ever to have comprised an independent *municipium,* but like Baiae was administratively dependent upon Cumae.[189] Mommsen therefore concluded that the *decuriones, collegium,* and *ordo* were congregations of imperial slaves and

[186] *CIL* X, 1750 (but cf. *ILS* 7368 with Dessau's note *ad loc.*). Other *vilici: CIL* X 1561, 1749, 1751; *Not. d. Sc.* (1928), 208, no. 5.

[187] *Topiarius: CIL* X, 696 (cf. 1744, another gardener from Puteoli); *circitor: CIL* X, 711; *structor: ibid.,* 708; *aedituus: Not. d. Sc.* (1928), 207, no. 1; *pictor: CIL* X, 702; *a memoria: Not. d. Sc.* (1928), 207, no. 2 (cf. *CIL* VI, 1727, from Puteoli); *a possessionibus: Not. d. Sc.* (1928), 207, no. 3; *a valetudine: CIL* X, 703.

[188] *CIL* X, 1748: *Lalus Aug. L. Fecit Ti. Iulio Sp. F. Heliconi Filio Suo Et Sibi Et Suis L.D.D.D.E.F.V.L.* For Mommsen's theory, see *CIL* X, p. 213; on Lucullus' villa, see Catalogue I, no. 22a.

[189] *CIL* X, 1747, 1746. Bauli's dependent status: Mommsen, *CIL* X, p. 213. Beloch (*Campanien*[2], 177) did not concur: "Ursprünglich zum Gebiet von Cumae gehörig, ist es nicht unmöglich, dass Bauli unter Augustus als selbstständige Gemeinde constituirt worden ist."

freedmen which had been organized into these units and charged with the administration of local estates and villas which were the personal property of the emperor. Mommsen's theory has found general acceptance, but it should be observed that the meager evidence of three inscriptions is the sole support for his hypothesis.[190] Certainly at Surrentum, where more than twenty sepulchral inscriptions pertain to slaves and freedmen employed on the imperial estates, there is no trace of such collective organization. We continue to await further epigraphical indication that the imperial slaves and freedmen at Bauli were in fact so numerous as to justify their borrowing, for purposes of administration, the political terminology characteristic of the *municipium*.

Employing language fulsome and unctuous, Symmachus in 369 addressed a *laudatio* to the first Valentinian, wherein he dilated upon the contrast between his emperor's ceaseless labors and the luxurious languor of earlier masters of the Roman world: he censured Augustus for straining the imperial exchequer by his constructions at Baiae and at the Lucrine Lake, Tiberius for swimming and sailing *in deversoriis insularum*.[191] Ancient accounts of the Campanian extravagances of those emperors, as has been seen, seem restrained when set beside the references to the wasteful follies of Gaius and Nero, under whom the territorial extent of imperial holdings on the Bay of Naples presumably reached its culmination; and to Pliny in the *Panegyricus* the reign of Domitian seemed par-

---

[190] Mommsen has been followed by Hirschfeld (*GRK*, 535), and Dubois (*PA*, 378); to Schneider (*'vilicus,' RE* 8 A [1958], 2138) there seemed to be no controversy. It may be that a fourth inscription should be included among the others: observe the *curator . . . embaenitariorum III piscinensium* mentioned in an inscription found in 1897 near Baiae (A. Sogliano, *Not. d. Sc.* [1897], 13; cf. H. B. Walters, *CR* 11 [1897], 367). It has been suggested that *embaenitarii* were imperial boatmen attached to the local imperial domains (so Dubois, *PA*, 377). But the word, although unquestionably connected with the phrase *embaeneticam facere* used by Caelius of Q. Pompeius Rufus (at Bauli in 51 B.C.: Cic. *Fam.* 8.1.5; cf. Catalogue I, no. 33), remains hopelessly obscure: any attempt at elucidation must deal with both the Ciceronian passage and the inscription. Cf. *TLL* V.2.449, *s.v. embaeneticam*.

[191] Symmachus (ed. Seeck), *Laud. in Valentinianum* 1.16: *Hi sunt illi triumfales viri, delicatis negotiis frequentibus occupati, amoena litorum terrarumque opima sectantes. Vis petam proximae aetatis exempla? Ecce Baias sibi Augustus a continuo mari vindicat et molibus Lucrinis sumptus laborat imperii; Tiberius in devorsoriis insularum natans et navigans adoratur . . .*

ticularly notorious—Symmachus may indeed have drawn inspiration for his own animadversions from Pliny's words. The Campanian domiciles and diversions of the emperors (and their families) were a commonplace, an easy target for rhetoricians and self-proclaimed guardians against luxury and vice. But the moralists, as has been seen, often tended to distort and to ignore important facts, and their opinions require correction. Emperors were drawn to Campania by matters of real consequence, not simply by desire for recreation. Inscriptions have permitted glimpses of imperial acts of policy and administration (including public works and benefactions) which fostered Campania's prosperity during the early empire, bound the Bay of Naples more closely to Rome, and rendered the pleasures of that coast equally familiar to large numbers of the emperors' prominent contemporaries. To an account of those pleasures and their other devotees we now turn.

FIVE · *The Bay of Naples in the Imperial Age*

Introduction

The vicissitudes of the forties, followed in the next decade by the gradual concentration of all political power into the hands of Caesar's heir, brought, along with absolutism, the return to peace and order of which Augustan poets sang. Widespread prosperity too attended the birth of the restored Republic. To be sure, the wealth of the emperors and the increase of the imperial estates were outstanding features of the economic life of the Roman Empire, and as Rostovtzeff has shown, those imperial holdings grew at the expense of the great private landowners and proprietors of luxury estates.[1] But this was in large part a third century phenomenon. During the first two centuries of imperial peace, Rome's economic boundaries steadily expanded. Through the harbors, arteries of overseas trade, the wealth and produce of the provinces poured into Italy, creating the substantial fortunes upon which numerous beneficiaries, themselves increasingly of extra-Italian origin, could base their luxurious living. Thus, notwithstanding the concentration of wealth—through provincial exploitation and conquests, imperial confiscations, and individual legacies—in the hands of Roman emperors, the foundations of private fortunes stood for a time secure and unshaken, as did the monumental witnesses to those fortunes: luxury villas glittered on the hills and seashores throughout the Antonine Age;[2] they rose

[1] Rostovtzeff, *SEHRE²*, 702–703 (n. 34); cf. Frank, *ESAR* V, 300: "... Septimius Severus dealt the fatal blow to the empire by his confiscations and by his centralization of vast estates under imperial ownership."

[2] Rostovtzeff, *SEHRE²*, 30. See in general, Hor. *Carm.* 2.15.1–5: *Iam pauca aratro iugera regiae / moles relinquent ..*; Tac. *Ann.* 3.53.5 (Tiberius alludes to *villarum infinita spatia*); 3.54.7; Suet. *Gaius* 45.3 (*amoenos secessus*).

again in the fourth century, when the Empire enjoyed a temporary revival and recovery from the social and economic insecurities of the preceding years. The following pages present an attempt to visualize the workings of these familiar imperial tendencies in one local context.

Partly in order to facilitate the reader's comparison of late Republican with imperial developments, partly because the nature of the evidence precludes the possibility of a strictly chronological treatment, in the following pages I have resumed the topical method of presenting subject matter, and the titled sections, which were adopted above in chapter three.

Imperial Prosperity and the Crater Delicatus

Tacitus is explicit: Rome's period of greatest luxury extended from the battle of Actium to the accession of Vespasian, who was able to check general extravagance rather by personal example than by decrees or statutes.[3] After the confiscations of Domitian, the younger Pliny noticed with approval what his correspondence confirms: during the reign of Trajan ample houses and lovely villas returned to the hands of private owners.[4] Many wealthy contemporaries shared—if on a more modest scale—their rulers' addiction to buying and building showy villas and adorning them with exotic statuary and imported marbles; the strictures of both Martial and Juvenal prove that the *aedificator* was a familiar target for the moralists.[5] The aesthetic extravagances of Silius Italicus at his villas near Neapolis elicited censure from the younger Pliny—whose own villas numbered six.[6]

---

[3] Tac. *Ann.* 3.55.1–6 (discussed below, p. 123–124).

[4] Pliny *Pan.* 50.2: *est, quod Caesar non suum videat, tandemque imperium principis quam patrimonium maius est.* Cf. the further contrast with Domitian (50.6): *tum exitialis erat apud principem huic laxior domus, illi amoenior villa; nunc princeps in haec eadem dominos quaerit, ipse inducit; ipsos illos magni aliquando imperatoris hortos, illud numquam nisi Caesaris suburbanum licemur, emimus, implemus.*

[5] E.g., Mart. 9.46; Juv. 14.86–95: *aedificator erat Caetronius . . .* Cf. *ibid.*, 274–275: *tu propter mille talenta / et centum villas temerarius . . .* Cf. Sen. *Ep.* 89.21.

[6] Silius Italicus: Catalogue II, no. 12; Pliny's villas: Pliny *Ep.* 2.17 (Laurentum), *Ep.* 5.6 (Tuscan villa); for the *plures villae* at Lake Como, cf. *Ep.* 9.7.1–2. The evidence for

In the Augustan age, Strabo could affirm that an unbroken succession of houses and villas garnished the Bay of Naples from Misenum to Surrentum, presenting the aspect of a single city.[7] Prominent Romans with a taste for rich living continued to gratify it in their villas along Cicero's *crater delicatus*, which during the first centuries of the Christian era retained and strengthened its earlier reputation as Rome's most fashionable resort. The younger Seneca, subjecting to philosophical analysis men's restless discontent with their current lot and their consequent hankering for travel, makes them say when the delights of rich living beckon *nunc petamus Campaniam*; the Stoic caps his discussion with an apposite quotation from Lucretius cited earlier in this study.[8] Approximately eighty years after Seneca, Aulus Gellius passed summer holidays at Puteoli *in voluptatibus pudicis honestisque*, thereby implying that in those coastal parts less salutary diversions could be assumed to be the rule.[9] Again in the late fourth century the luxury of the "Crater" became a familiar literary theme: Ammianus Marcellinus once digressed to review the various delinquencies of the *nobiles*, and provides a vivid vignette of languid grandees sailing from Lake Avernus to Puteoli in painted boats adorned with silken canopies and gilded fans.[10] But Sym-

---

estates at Tusculum, Praeneste, and Tibur (*Ep.* 5.6.45) is inconclusive: A.N. Sherwin-White, *The Letters of Pliny* (Oxford 1966) *ad loc.*, 329–330. For an excellent discussion of Pliny's villas and economic status, see R. Duncan-Jones, "The Finances of the Younger Pliny," *PBSR* N.S. 20 (1965), 177–188.

[7] Strab. 5.4.8 (C 247): μέχρι μὲν δεῦρο ἔχει τέλος ὁ κόλπος ὁ κρατὴρ προσαγορευόμενος, ἀφοριζόμενος δυσὶν ἀκρωτηρίοις βλέπουσι πρὸς μεσημβρίαν, τῷ τε Μισηνῷ καὶ τῷ Ἀθηναίῳ. ἅπας δ' ἐστὶ κατεσκευασμένος τοῦτο μὲν ταῖς πόλεσιν, ἃς ἔφαμεν, τοῦτο δὲ ταῖς οἰκοδομίαις καὶ φυτείαις, αἳ μεταξὺ συνεχεῖς οὖσαι μιᾶς πόλεως ὄψιν παρέχονται.

[8] Sen. *Tranq. an.* 2.13: *Inde peregrinationes suscipiuntur vagae et litora pererrantur et modo mari se, modo terra experitur semper praesentibus infesta levitas. Nunc Campaniam petamus . . .* 2.14: *Aliud ex alio iter suscipitur et spectacula spectaculis mutantur. Ut ait Lucretius: Hoc se quisque modo semper fugit.* (See above, Chapter 3, p. 40).

[9] Aul. Gell. 18.5.1.

[10] Amm. Marc. 28.4.18: *aut si a lacu Averni lembis invecti sunt (sc. nobiles) pictis Puteolos, velleris certamen, maxime cum id vaporato audeant tempore. Ubi si inter aurata flabella laciniis sericis insederint muscae, vel per foramen umbraculi pensilis radiolus irruperit solis, queruntur quod non sunt apud Cimmerios nati. Naumachiae* are attested at Cumae and Lake Avernus in the fourth century: Auson. *Mos.* 208–219.

machus' Campanian deportment, he hastened to assure a correspondent, was exemplary: *ubique vitam agimus consularem et in Lucrino serii sumus*—and more in the same vein.[11]

Baiae

"So numerous were the contiguous luxury palaces that another city had suddenly come into being, not inferior in size to Puteoli."[12] Strabo thus describes Augustan Baiae, easily the first among Roman resorts in Italy, a city whose very existence constitutes formidable proof of the prompt resurgence of luxury after years of civil war. Favored site of the emperors' Campanian recreation, boasting exceptional natural endowments in her curving shores, sparkling waters, myrtle groves and mineral springs, Baiae also offered exotic delights to uninhibited seekers after pleasure, and, as in the late Republic, a favorite topic to denouncers of luxury and corruption. The love poets knew and feared this Bay's attraction. Propertius cursed her waters, *crimen amoris*.[13] Now as in Varro's day, Baiae was replete with hazards for members of both sexes: a man might come for a thermal cure and leave with a broken heart; a woman might arrive a Penelope and leave a Helen.[14] Seneca once visited Baiae. He promptly departed, pronouncing it a *deversorium vitiorum*.[15] But he saw fit to record his disagreeable impressions—drunkards on beaches, riotous sailing parties, lakes resounding with choral songs.[16] The Christian apologists, not surprisingly, were no more friendly in their judgments: St. Jerome expatiates on the city's immorality in a passage which consciously echoes Cicero's

[11] Symmachus *Ep.* 8.23.3: *non vereor, ne me lascivire in tanta locorum amoenitate et rerum copia putes. Ubique vitam agimus consularem et in Lucrino serii sumus. Nullus in navibus canor, nulla in conviviis helluatio, nec frequentatio balnearum nec ulli iuvenum procaces natatus. Scias nullum esse in luxuria crimen locorum.*

[12] Strab. 5.4.7 (C 246): ἐκεῖ γὰρ (*sc.* ἐν βαίαις) ἄλλη πόλις γεγένηται, συνῳκοδομημένων βασιλείων ἄλλων ἐπ᾽ ἄλλοις, οὐκ ἐλάττων τῆς Δικαιαρχείας.

[13] Prop. 1.11.30.

[14] Ov. *Ars Am* 1.283; Mart. 1.62.1–6.

[15] Sen. *Ep.* 51.3.

[16] *Ibid.* 51.4: *Videre ebrios per litora errantes et comessationes navigantium et symphoniarum cantibus strepentes lacus et alia quae velut soluta legibus luxuria non tantum peccat sed publicat, quid necesse est?*

language in the *Pro Caelio*;[17] Baiae is mentioned once and made synonymous with illicit pleasure in the works of St. Augustine.[18]

Horace proclaimed *nullus in orbe sinus Baiis praelucet amoenis*; a thousand verses, says Martial, would not suffice for the praise of this golden shore of Venus.[19] The poets did not greatly exaggerate. Baiae was indeed a paragon; her villas, baths, and entertainments became the acknowledged models not merely for Italy but for the entire empire. The shores of Altium in Venetia attracted Martial, for they vied in beauty with Baiae's villas, to which Cassiodorus in the fifth century also likened the *praetoria* of Istria.[20] When the younger Pliny discussed the emplacements of his villas at Comum, *Baiano more* is the phrase employed to describe both elevated and seaside sites.[21] A traveler from Campania who visited the Moselle, predicted Ausonius, would want for none of the delights of his own region; indeed, he might believe that Baiae and Baiae's oysters had been transplanted.[22] Still later in the fourth century Eunapius ranks the warm baths of Gadara in Syria "second only to the Roman baths at Baiae, to which none can compare."[23] A mosaic recovered from a Roman estate near Utica discloses that the owner had named his property from the famous Campanian resort; other African inscriptions and passages from Sidonius Apollinaris reveal that the name of Baiae had become a generic term for baths or mineral springs.[24]

[17] Hieron. *Ep.* 45.4.1: *Baias peterent, unguentia eligerent, divitias et viduitatem haberent, materias luxuriae et libertatis* ... The passage directly echoes Cicero, *Pro Caelio* 27: see J. F. Gilliam, *HTR* 46 (1953), 103–107.

[18] August. *Contra Acad.* 2.2.6.

[19] Hor. *Epist.* 1.1.83; Mart. 11.80.3–4.

[20] Mart. 4.25.1; Cassiod. *Var.* 2.22.3–5: Istria the Campania of Ravenna.

[21] Pliny *Ep.* 9.7.3: *Altera imposita saxis more Baiano lacum prospicit, altera aeque more Baiano lacum tangit.* There is no implication here (despite Sherwin–White, *The Letters of Pliny*, 486, *ad loc.*) that Pliny's correspondent had a villa at Baiae—Baiae simply set the standards.

[22] Auson. *Mos.* 345–348: *quod si Cumanis huc adforet hospes ab oris, / crederet Euboicas simulacra exilia Baias / his donasse locis: tantus cultusque nitorque / adlicit et nullum parit oblectatio luxum.*

[23] Eunap. *Vitae Soph.* 26.

[24] *CIL* VIII, 25425: *splendent tecta Bassiani fundi cognomine Baiae*; cf. *CIL* VIII, 25362 (= *ILS* 8960); Sid. Apoll. *Ep.* 5.14.1; *Carm.* 23.13. For Baiae's baths, see below, pp. 139–140; and Plates 4–7.

Proprietors

Nunc petamus Campaniam. To villas in the Bay of Naples came: senatorial proprietors, usually *novi homines* who owed wealth and status to a particular imperial benefactor under whom they had served with distinction; occasional sojourners, like Seneca, Martial, and the younger Pliny, who relied upon the hospitality of wealthy friends; affluent natives of the region; and resident intellectuals, often of foreign extraction.[25] Literary and epigraphical evidence stands in confirmation: the *testimonia* for the coastal properties of forty-seven imperial proprietors have been collected and presented alphabetically in a second catalogue.[26] Although the entries date from the Augustan age to the days of Symmachus, the distribution of evidence is uneven, concentrated, as we might expect, within the first and second centuries; our information is most meager for the period which extends from the second quarter of the third century through the middle decades of the fourth. Here arguments *e silentio* are particularly hazardous. That we happen to know little of Campania in these years is in itself no proof that little was happening. Yet the independent evidence of economic decline throughout the empire in the third century invests the silence of our sources with a certain significance, inviting the conclusion that the wealth of Campanian proprietors and the numbers of Campanian estates then dwindled and decreased; in the fourth century, however, there is evidence from Campania and elsewhere of temporary economic revival.[27] As

[25] On the *studiosi*, see below, pp. 142–152.

[26] See below, pp. 202–232.

[27] Economic decline in the third century: see in general F. Oertel in *CAH* XII, 259–270; T. Frank, *ESAR* V, 296–304; and see above, Chapter 4, n. 165. That Plotinus' Campanian "city of philosophers" lay in ruins in the mid-third century (see below, n. 146), is not, perhaps, without general economic interest. Fourth century revival: for evidence from Ostia, cf. the comments of Meiggs, *Roman Ostia*, 3: "One of the most striking contributions of the recent excavations has been the revelation of the handsome houses of the late Empire; Ammianus Marcellinus in his diatribes against the extravagant living of the nobility in Rome illuminates the Ostian picture." No such archaeological revelations have confirmed Ammianus' descriptions of the diversions of the *nobiles* on the Bay of Naples (quoted above, n. 10), but the numerous local estates possessed by Symmachus and his prominent contemporaries are good evidence for economic revival

with the *testimonia* for the catalogue, so also with sources pertinent to the discussions in this chapter: our information remains abundant only for the one hundred and fifty years subsequent to the reign of Augustus; consequently in the following pages (although every effort has been made to incorporate later evidence, both literary and archaeological) the arguments and conclusions unavoidably depend largely upon the works of first and second century authors.

An inspection of the catalogue will reveal a few instances of continuity between late Republic and early empire: the Cumaean villa of P. Servilius Vatia, who died during the reign of Tiberius, was perhaps built by his grandfather, the Sullan consular of 79 B.C.[28] Other imperial villa owners (C. Calpurnius Piso, Domitia, Appius Claudius[29]) could claim illustrious consular forebears for whom, however, no Campanian properties are attested. But the instances of aristocratic connections are extremely rare. The imperial villas belong as a rule to members of families newly risen to political prominence and influence, such as Agrippa under Augustus, or L. Publilius Celsus under Trajan.[30] Herein lies a major, if by no means unexpected, point of similarity between this catalogue and its Republican counterpart: in both lists the current social and political fluctuations of the city are reflected in the names and in the status of owners of properties on the coast.

in the late fourth century (Catalogue II, no. 42), when Baiae's popularity is also amply attested (above, nn. 22–24). Indeed, renewed prosperity seems indicated in Campania at a still earlier date: the best evidence is the Constantinian inscription recording repairs of the great Serino aqueduct and listing the coastal cities which its waters then supplied (I. Sgobbo, *Not. d. Sc.* [1938], 75–97; cf. above, Chapter 4, p. 79); Constantine was also honored by Surrentum (*CIL* X, 677, 678); and important evidence from fourth century Puteoli still awaits publication (but for a preliminary survey, see M. Napoli in *Bollettino d'Arte* 44 (1959), p. 113, n. 1). This general pattern of affluence, decline, and revival is further supported by evidence from Roman Britain, where the chronological distribution of villas is similar. Of the total number of villas (some seven hundred) thus far identified, roughly one hundred belong to the second century, fifty to the third, and then, impressively, two hundred to the fourth: see now J. Liversidge, *Britain in the Roman Empire* (London 1968), pp. 236, 288–290.

[28] P. Servilius Vatia: Catalogue II, no. 39; see above, Chapter 2, p.34, and Catalogue I, no. 39.

[29] Catalogue II, nos. 9, 17, 13.

[30] Catalogue II, no. 46 (Agrippa), no. 37 (L. Publilius Celsus).

The catalogue reflects as well the growing influx of provincial participation in Roman political life. Trajan prescribed that one third of the property of all senators be invested in Italian land, on the grounds that it seemed shameful that those who held Roman magistracies should regard the capital and Italy *non pro patria sed pro hospitio aut stabulo quasi peregrinantes*. Marcus Aurelius later reduced the requirement to one quarter.[31] In the early Empire, however, there is no very clear indication that the growing numbers of non-Italian senators, at whom Trajan's regulation was chiefly directed, opted for a return to their towns of ultimate origin when their active careers were at an end. On the contrary, many of the new senators joined the rush to buy and build in Campania, thereby adopting forms of recreation which made them indistinguishable from Italians: Valerius Asiaticus, Silius Italicus, and M. Cornelius Fronto all owned villas on the Bay of Naples. Dio Cassius, it is true, went home to Bithynia at the close of his career; but as a senator it was to a villa in Campania that he retired to think and write.[32]

Silius Italicus' Neapolitan holdings are of particular interest because they reveal that not every new provincial senator from the Flavian period conformed to Tacitus' famous description of their type: men who retained their frugal habits however great their wealth, stern and steady foes of luxurious living. The question thus naturally suggests itself: does an analysis of the list of owners of Campanian villas support Tacitus' further contention that luxury declined under the Flavians? Of the catalogue's forty-seven names, forty-five can be dated securely to a particular period: and

[31] Trajan's measures: Pliny *Ep.* 6.19.4, on which see Sherwin–White, *Letters of Pliny, ad loc.*, 377–378: "The measure was made necessary by the steady increase in the numbers of senators from the provinces, both of the Romanized western empire, and from Trajan onwards of the hellenized East." Sherwin–White then offers a useful bibliographical conspectus, to which now add, on the hellenizing of the senate, G. W. Bowersock, *Augustus and the Greek World* (Oxford 1965), 141–145. Marcus Aurelius: *S.H.A. Marc.* 11.8. For subsequent developments and statistics for senatorial Greeks with properties in Italy, cf. F. Millar, *A Study of Cassius Dio* (Oxford 1964), 10.

[32] Catalogue II, nos. 43, 12, 16. For provincial senators and their tastes, cf. Syme, *Tacitus*, 446–447; V. A. Sirago, *L'Italia agraria sotto Traiano* (Louvain 1958), 5–8. Dio's holdings: Cass. Dio 77.2.1.

of the names in this latter category, seventeen are of Julio-Claudian, as compared with twelve of Flavian date.[33] But our sources are somewhat fuller for the Julio-Claudian period, which in any case was more than three times the length of the Flavian epoch. So small a discrepancy in numbers can hardly be considered statistically significant; much more noteworthy (even allowing for the reduction in bulk of available evidence) is the contrast between numbers of owners from the Flavian period and those from Trajan's reign—the latter has yielded the name of only one proprietor. Therefore Tacitus' claim that luxury declined under the Flavians is not supported by the surviving Campanian evidence. Neither, it might be argued, does the historian's claim derive much more support from the contemporary literature bearing upon Roman society as a whole.[34]

Comparison of the two catalogues reveals instructive differences. The family of the emperor Vitellius was of Campanian origin; it seems that at least one other proprietor native to the coast was an imperial consular; T. Eprius Marcellus (*cos. suff.* II, 74) hailed from Capua.[35] In contrast with the late Republic, when Roman senators of coastal Campanian provenance are a rarity

[33] Tacitus' description, and his assertion that luxury declined (*Ann.* 3.55.4): *simul novi homines e municipiis et coloniis atque etiam provinciis in senatum crebro adsumpti domesticam parsimoniam intulerunt, et quamquam fortuna vel industria plerique pecuniosam ad senectam pervenirent, mansit tamen prior animus.* Julio–Claudian personages: Catalogue II, nos. 6, 9, 15, 17, 20, 23, 24, 25, 26, 29, 32, 39, 41, 43, 44, 45, 46. Flavians: nos. 1, 8, 11, 12, 19, 21, 22, 31, 34, 35, 37, 38.

[34] Trajanic proprietor: Catalogue II, no. 7. Five names are datable to the Antonine period (nos. 14, 16, 18, 30, 40); two belong to the third century (nos. 13, 33); seven contemporaries of Symmachus (no. 42) are attested: nos. 2, 3, 4, 5, 27, 28, 47. Two names (nos. 10 and 36) cannot be dated, but belong in all probability to the second century. For Flavian luxury, see above, p. 117; cf. the villas at Surrentum and Stabiae discussed below, pp. 127–129; add also, for luxury elsewhere, Mart. 10.30 (Formiae), 12.57 (Rome). The latest building in Pompeii reveals that luxury had not declined: the house of the Vettii is but one example. Observe also the increasing popularity of the coast of Latium as a setting for elaborate villas: Van Buren in *RE* 8 A (1958), 2156–2157. In Roman Britain the magnificent Fishbourne palace was begun in Flavian times; see J. Liversidge, *Britain in the Roman Empire* (London 1968), 288–289.

[35] Vitellius: above, Chapter 4, p. 99. T. Eprius Marcellus from Capua: Tac. *Dial.* 8.1; cf. *CIL* X, 3853 (= *ILS* 992). Coastal Campanian senator: Catalogue II, no. 1 (L. Acilius Strabo); and cf. no. 21, Iulius Menecrates, for whose children Statius presaged *dignitas senatoria* (Stat. *Silv.* 4.8.59–62).

and not one can be shown to have retained property on the coast,[36] it is somewhat more common to discover the Campanian senators of the Empire maintaining their regional ties in the form of houses or villas. The reason is easily divined: with the extinction of the old Republican families, the emperors turned to the towns of Italy to recruit fresh political and administrative talent, and new senators or *equites* felt no need to mask the relative obscurity of their origins by severing connections with their native *municipia*. Besides, the towns of the Bay of Naples, Puteoli in particular, attained new heights of importance and prosperity under the early principate: Augustus had seen to that.[37]

Of the three great *piscinarii* of the Ciceronian age, one traced his lineage back to the regal period, and the other two, although scions of families more lately risen to prominence, could point to consular forebears.[38] In contrast, P. Vedius Pollio, harsh master of the ponds at Pausilypon, was a Roman knight of libertine parentage—but a valued agent in Augustus' government.[39] Cicero's friends Marius and Paetus, humane and pleasure-loving, lived in comfort at Pompeii and Neapolis in the late Republic.[40] Cluvius and Vestorius were local men, wealthy but without cultural pretensions.[41] In the early empire local fortunes and luxurious refinements had perceptibly increased. The author of the *Satyricon* localized the prodigious wealth and pseudo-sophistication of Trimalchio in an opulent villa on the Campanian coast; he had made his fortune in commerce, agriculture, and banking.[42] The sources of wealth of Pollius Felix (*Puteolanus*, Epicurean, and benefactor of

---

[36] Republican senators from Campania: Manilius Cumanus (*tr. pleb.* 52 B.C.: Ascon *Mil.* [ed. Clark] 32) has been tentatively placed in the *tribus Falerna* by L. R. Taylor, *Voting Districts*, 229; likewise Granius Petro, quaestor designate probably for 46 B.C.: *Voting Districts*, 218.

[37] See above, Chapter 4, pp. 79–83.

[38] On L. Marcius Philippus (*cos.* 56 B.C.), cf. Catalogue I, no. 28. Q. Hortensius Hortalus: Catalogue I, no. 17. L. Licinius Lucullus: Catalogue I, no. 22.

[39] Catalogue II, no. 44.

[40] Catalogue I, nos. 29, 30.

[41] See above, Chapter 3, pp. 52–53.

[42] See Rostovtzeff, *SEHRE*[2], 57–58. The scene of the *Cena* is almost certainly Puteoli: see Catalogue II, no. 32 (*Petronius*).

Statius) were not perhaps so very different, although the poet has glorified Pollius' origins and stressed the refinement of his tastes.[43] Pollius owed his villa at Surrentum, as doubtless other prosperous members of the local gentry owed coastal villas like it, to the vigorous economic state of coastal Campania in the first century A.D.

The Villas; Amoenitas

It was shown above that by the Ciceronian age, coastal villas, whether elevated or constructed at the sea's edge, were designed to take full visual advantage of the natural surroundings.[44] Imperial proprietors followed and further refined the practice, while exhibiting a preference for the symmetrical disposition of the villa's quarters. General confirmation comes from Vitruvius' architectural prescriptions for private houses and from the younger Pliny's detailed descriptions of his Laurentine and Tuscan villas; explicit literary testimony from Campania is found in Seneca's and Statius' discussions of *villae maritimae* at Cumae and Surrentum, respectively.[45] Moreover, the archaeological evidence is abundant and constantly increasing. More than two centuries of excavations in the environs of Pompeii and studies by such scholars as Comparetti, Rostovtzeff, Swoboda, Della Corte, Carrington, Maiuri, Van Buren, Lehmann, Mustilli, D'Orsi, and Boëthius have revealed that the Roman luxury villas—Vitruvius' term is *villa pseudourbana*[46]—were of two basic architectural

[43] Catalogue II, no. 34; see further E. Lepore, *PdP* fasc. 25–27 (1952), 328–329.

[44] See above, Chapter 3, pp. 45–46.

[45] Vitr. *De arch.* 6. *praef.* 7: *Igitur, quoniam in quinto de opportunitate communium operum perscribsi, in hoc volumine privatorum aedificiorum ratiocinationes et commensus symmetriarum explicabo.* The chapters which follow fulfill the author's promise; observe especially 6.2.1: *nulla architecto maior cura esse debet, nisi uti proportionibus ratae partis habeant aedificia rationum exactiones.* Pliny *Ep.* 2.17, 5.6; cf. in general H. H. Tanzer, *The Villas of Pliny the Younger* (New York 1924); Sherwin-White, *The Letters of Pliny, ad loc.* (esp. pp. 186–189, where the originality of Pliny's exact descriptions is stressed and bibliography critically surveyed). Sen. *Ep.* 55 (on which see Catalogue II, no. 39, P. Servilius Vatia); Stat. *Silv.* 2.2 (on which see Catalogue II, no. 34, Pollius Felix).

[46] Vitr. *De arch.* 6.5.3. On the distinction between *villa rustica* and *villa urbana* or *pseudourbana*, see above all the discussion by Maiuri, *La Villa dei Misteri* (Rome 1931), 101–104.

types: peristyle and portico.[47] It has been demonstrated that the former, of which the villa of Publius Fannius Synistor near Boscoreale and the "villa dei misteri" at Pompeii are excellent examples, were derived originally from royal Hellenistic palaces; a main entrance gives access to a large central court, the peristyle, which may have an *exedra* directly behind it. Off these central spaces were arranged, on at least three sides, living rooms and other private apartments (*diaetae, cubicula*).[48] Equally luxurious and contemporaneous with estates of the peristyle type were the portico villas, which, as Swoboda has observed, evolved from a long narrow row of rooms which opened onto a road or court.[49] This primitive arrangement was Hellenized by the construction of a colonnaded gallery, the *porticus*, parallel to the row of rooms; the doors of the various chambers opened onto the portico in such a way that an architectural shape with pronounced longitudinal axis resulted.

The *porticus* villa became especially popular along the coast, where the long colonnades were designed to front directly on the sea.[50] Statius describes at length the portico of Pollius Felix: the covered colonnade climbed at an oblique angle from the buildings at the seaside to the heights of the Sorrentine cliff.[51] In the third century Philostratus mentions a villa near Neapolis where there

[47] See especially Rostovtzeff, "Pompeianische Landschaften und römische Villen," *Jahrb. d. Kais. Deutsch. Archäol. Inst.* 19 (1904), 103–126; —— "Die Hellenistisch-römische Architekturlandschaft," *Rom. Mitt.* 26 (1911), 1–185; K. M. Swoboda, *römische und römanische Paläste*[2] (Vienna 1924); D. Mustilli, "La villa pseudourbana ercolanese," *RAAN* N.S. 30–31 (1956), 77–97; M. E. Blake, *Roman Construction ... through the Flavians* (Washington 1959), 150–151; K. Schefold, "Origins of Roman Landscape Painting," *Art Bulletin* 42 (1960), 93; A. Boëthius, *The Golden House of Nero* (Ann Arbor 1960), 94–102. Among recent studies, that of H. Drerup, "Die römische Villa," *Marburger Winckelmann-Programm* (1959), 1–17 is of particular importance.

[48] P. W. Lehmann, *Roman Wall Paintings from Boscoreale* (Cambridge, Mass. 1953), pp. 4 (fig. 1), 16 (n. 43). Cf. Vitr. *De arch.* 6.5.1–3; Boëthius (see above, n. 47), 99.

[49] Swoboda (see above, n. 47), 29–34; Boëthius (see above, n. 47), 100. *Porticus*, as employed in the ancient texts, is ambiguous: the word can mean both "(covered) colonnade" or "arcade." See W. L. MacDonald, *The Architecture of the Roman Empire* I (New Haven 1965), 29; Maiuri, *PdP* 1 (1946), 306–307.

[50] The portico finds its place among the signs of Roman luxury deplored by Horace: *Carm.* 2.15.14–16.

[51] Stat. *Silv.* 2.2.30–33.

was a portico built on four or five terraces, open to the west wind and looking out upon the sea.[52] The imperial estate at Torre Damecuta on Capreae (Plate 9), and houses situated on the south slope of Pompeii, are well known examples of villas of this type.[53] More recently, Libero D'Orsi's dramatic rediscovery of ancient Stabiae has brought two further specimens to light. The Elder Pliny states that in his day Stabiae consisted entirely of handsome villas; with at least one of these Pliny was personally acquainted.[54] In the eighteenth century, although no systematic excavations were attempted, many priceless paintings, marbles, and mosaics were unearthed and appropriated by Charles III, first of the Bourbons; some found their way into the private collections of other contemporary European potentates.[55] In early 1950, D'Orsi began his own excavations. He could claim no professional competence; he lacked financial support and official endorsement. Today the results have surpassed even D'Orsi's optimistic expectations: two large villas have been unearthed and partially restored; a small museum in Castellammare can no longer contain the wall paintings, mosaics, stuccos, coins, together with more than 3500 artefacts of clay and bronze, which have been temporarily consigned there for preservation and display.[56]

At the first villa (scavo A, provisionally entitled villa di Arianna) which stood southeast of modern Castellammare and commanded

---

[52] Philostr. *Imag.* 1. *praef.* 4.

[53] Damecuta villa: Beloch, *Campanien*[2], 292; Maiuri, *Capri*, 60–69. Pompeii: see in general F. Noack and K. Lehmann-Hartleben, *Baugeschichtliche Untersuchungen am Stadtrand von Pompeji* (Berlin and Leipzig 1936). The portico in the suburban villa at Porta Marina extended for more than eighty meters: Maiuri, *Pompeii*, 106. For an immense *porticus tri[umphi]* belonging probably to a private villa near Baiae, see *Eph. Epigr.* VIII, 374, and the comments of Beloch, *Campanien*[2], 468.

[54] Pliny *NH* 3.70: *In Campano autem agro Stabiae oppidum fuere usque ad Cn. Pompeium L. Catonem coss. pr. kal. Mai., quo die L. Sulla legatus bello sociali id delevit quod nunc in villas abiit.* For the history and archaeology of ancient Stabiae see above all F. Di Capua, "Contributi all'Epigrafia e alla Storia della Antica Stabia," *RAAN* N.S. 19 (1938), 83–124. For the villa known to Pliny, cf. Catalogue II, no. 35 (Pomponianus).

[55] L. D'Orsi, *Gli Scavi Archeologici di Stabia*[2] (Milan 1965), 18–19.

[56] Cf. D'Orsi's own account in *Come Ritrovai l'Antica Stabia*[2] (Milan 1962); for the antiquities and museum, D'Orsi, *Gli Scavi Arch. di Stabia*[2], 23–24, 25–33; K. Schefold, *Antike Kunst* 3 (1960), 46–47.

an extraordinary view of the Bay and of Mt. Vesuvius, the principal portico overlooked an *ambulatio* (terrace) nearly seventy meters in length. The rooms opening off the portico were fitted with large windows; Boëthius well compares Cicero's description of the *cubiculum* and window of M. Marius mentioned in an earlier chapter.[57] Approximately five hundred meters from these excavations a second and still more elaborate villa has come to light (scavo B, villa "San Marco"). The monumental complex (Plates 10–11) had two principal sectors, of which the first was itself divided into two levels, one 5.30 meters above the other. On the upper level seventeen painted columns with spiral flutings were found *in situ*—they comprised a part of a *porticus* which extended for seventy meters. On the lower level stood a second colonnade parallel to the first. Living rooms opened off these galleries too. If this was, as D'Orsi believes, a private villa it was of unparalleled magnificence. In the second sector a huge pool (*natatio*) was discovered, 30 meters by 5.90, located in the center of an open garden which was flanked by finely decorated colonnades and a cryptoporticus; the arcades formed a *porticus triplex*, with a central *oecus* opening towards the sea.[58]

The Campanian *villa maritima* still awaits, and surely requires, a specialized study from architects and from architectural historians. Although it undoubtedly incorporated features common to both peristyle and portico villas, this species was typologically distinct: its unique position on terrain contiguous to the seashore required individualistic, often idiosyncratic, architectural designs and intricate artificial terracing for substructural supports. Picturesque sites predominated. The very intractability of the terrain, as one scholar has recently observed, served to challenge and to stimulate the builders of *villae maritimae*: verses of Statius represent the finished architectural product as a symbol of man's domination of nature. Remains of such villas (Plate 12) still abound along the

<hr />

57 Villa di Arianna: D'Orsi, *Scavi*, 19–20; Boëthius (see above, n. 47), 100. Marius' window: see above, Chapter 3, p. 46; Boëthius (see above, n. 47), 101.
58 D'Orsi, *Scavi*, 20–21, with plates 3–6.

Italian coastline, although the prospects of their remaining indefinitely accessible to surveyors are not encouraging.[59] Fortunately, ancient murals from houses in Herculaneum, Pompeii, and Stabiae (Plates 13-15) provide excellent indications of the typology of the *villa maritima* and confirm incidentally its great popularity, for these representational paintings of elegant *villae maritimae* were certainly inspired by villas standing on the nearby coast shortly before the disaster of 79.[60] Boats and the sea are visible in two foregrounds; the quay in one painting is built out over the water on piers, *Baiano more*, and follows the curves of the shoreline, while in another it is set back at no great distance from the sea. In the murals long and spacious porticoes dominate the scene; other buildings are visible in one background, staggered at different levels on a low sloping hill. All doubtless formed part of the complex of the same estate. A villa built during the first century and excavated some years ago at Torre del Greco near Naples exhibits a similar cluster of buildings, each set on a slightly higher slope; the entire villa thus descended to the sea by gradual stages.[61] The murals studied by Rostovtzeff further reveal that the portico villas permitted a number of variations on the standard longitudinal shape;[62] and from the second century with increased

[59] Remains of some *villae maritimae* in the Bay of Naples: for a ground plan of the villa del Capo di Sorrento, see Mingazzini and Pfister, *Surrentum* (*Forma Italiae, Regio* I, vol. 2 [Florence 1946]), carta IV, together with the authors' discussion, 121-132; and see below, Plate 12, for the protected landing place. A detailed publication of this villa is currently being prepared by Dr. F. Rakob. Additional remains on three stories are visible near Naples at Marechiaro, Posillipo. A plan of the well-known *villa maritima* at Astura was published recently by G. Schmiedt, "Contribution of photo interpretation to the reconstruction of the geographic topographic situation of the ancient ports in Italy," 10th *Congress of the International Society of Photogrammetry* (Lisbon 1964), 28-32. Statius' verses: *Silv.* 2.2.45-59; on which see the excellent remarks of H. Drerup, *Gymnasium* 73 (1966), 190-191.

[60] Rostovtzeff, *SEHRE²*, plates 8 and 9. Rostovtzeff first studied these paintings at length in *Jahrb. d. Kais. Deutsch. Archaeol. Inst.* 19 (1904), 103-126.

[61] L. Breglia, "Avanzi di una villa romana a Torre del Greco," *Camp. Rom.* I, 91-98, and especially p. 96. For another villa with arcaded portico at Minori, see Maiuri, in *RAAN* N.S. 29 (1954), 89-92.

[62] Rostovtzeff, *Jahrb. d. Kais. Deutsch. Archäol. Inst.* 19 (1904), 103-126; and the subsequent study in *Röm. Mitt.* 26 (1911), 72-78 ("Die Villenlandschaft"), where the various types of villas and their settings are distinguished and surveyed. Since Rostovtzeff wrote, excavations on the Bay of Naples and elsewhere have produced a number of fresh

refinement in techniques of concrete, curvilinear porticoes might follow a sinuous strip of shoreline: Symmachus speaks of a *geminam porticum*, continuous and curved, at his Neapolitan estate.[63] Even in its early and less developed form, the portico villa may well have been the architectural type preferred by Cicero and his prominent contemporaries—the orator's own *Cumanum* and the villa at Bauli of Q. Hortensius boasted famous colonnades.[64]

The construction and decoration of villas brought profits to local craftsmen. *Marmorarii* and mosaicists are attested in the inscriptions from Puteoli, where also the shop of a marble worker, containing 40 pseudo-Corinthian capitals and 33 bases of Attic columns, has been discovered.[65]

Porticoes, windows, gardens, and terraces all point to an architectural obsession with space, light, and panorama;[66]

---

examples of wall decorations which depict *villae maritimae*. In Pompeii, the *atrium* of the House of the Menander contains two unusually large specimens: see Maiuri, *La Casa del Menandro* (Rome 1933), 32 with figure 12. Another was removed from its wall during D'Orsi's excavations and may currently be seen in the antiquarium in Castellammare di Stabia, while another Stabian example is still *in situ* in a *cubiculum* northeast of the *porticus triplex* of Villa S. Marco (see Plate 10A): the living quarters in this painting are arranged on four sides of an open court, and the entire complex rests on a platform supported by arcades which are partially submerged. One chamber of the *domus aurea* in Rome contained paintings of villas (some now damaged almost beyond recognition) on all four walls; the room is situated at the extremity of the east wing, along the corridor which runs north–south and connects with the passage leading to the octagonal domed hall: see the plan in E. Nash, *Pictorial Dictionary of Ancient Rome* I², 339, no. 407.

[63] Symmachus, *Ep.* 2.60.2: *geminam porticum solido et incorrupto opere curvatam multis in longitudinem passibus explicari* . . . Cf. Catalogue II, no. 42 (Symmachus).

[64] Cicero's portico: Pliny *NH* 31.7 (on which see Catalogue I, no. 43b). Hortensius: Catalogue I, no. 17.

[65] *Marmorarii*: Dubois, *PA*, 130. Mosaicists: *ibid.*, 123.

[66] Cf. M. W. Frederiksen, "Towns and Houses," *The Romans*, ed. J. P. V. D. Balsdon (New York 1965), 157–167. In addition to the individual villas discussed in the foregoing pages and the imperial estates treated above in Chapter 4, many others on the Bay of Naples have been thoroughly or partially excavated. On remains near Misenum see Maiuri, *Campi Flegrèi*, 98–99; for the *ambulatio* of a Roman villa on the "sella di Baia," see P. Mingazzini in *Not. d. Sc.* (1932), 293–303. Remains of another coastal estate, dated to the second half of the first century A.D., have come to light near the "Castello di Baia": see P. Mingazzini, *Not. d. Sc.* (1931), 353–355. On the evidence from Puteoli, see Dubois, *PA*, 355–366. Submerged remains of villas between Neapolis and Pausilypon were detected and described early in this century by Günther, *Pausilypon*, 145–162; but cf. L. Jacono, "Note di archeologia marittima," *Neapolis* I (1913), 365–367. In the

builders of villas strove for the harmonious integration of architectural elements within a particular scenic context on the Naples Bay. It is thus fully comprehensible, though noteworthy, that coastal Campania, whose topography even today so perfectly answers to the natural definition of *amoenitas* and where Roman *villeggiatura* enjoyed its greatest vogue, should have acquired the epithet *amoena* by Cicero's time and retained it still in the days of Symmachus. It has been seen that Horace pronounced Baiae *amoenae*; so elsewhere he described Surrentum.[67] Velleius remarks on the *amoenitas* of both Cumae and Neapolis; Pomponius Mela noticed the *amoena Campaniae litora*.[68] The Elder Pliny, marvelling at the beauties of Italy, felt inadequate to describe *Campaniae ora per se felixque illa ac beata amoenitas*; Statius claimed that the construction of Pollius Felix' *porticus* brought *amoenitas* to the Sorrentine cliffs; and he too calls Baiae *portus amoenus*.[69] Juvenal writes of Cumae, *ianua Baiarum est et gratum litus amoeni/secessus*.[70] In Tacitus, summer on Capreae is described as *peramoena* (the compound is both original and unique in Latin), and Nero as *captus amoenitate* of Piso's villa at Baiae.[71] Servius comments that Augustus by his works at Lake Avernus *amoena reddidit loca*.[72] Symmachus, at leisure in his villa at Puteoli, speaks of himself as

---

contrada S. Rocco di Capodimonte at Naples the nucleus of a villa has been discovered and published by G. Chianese (see *Camp. Rom.* I, 81–87). Recently, Piso's villa at Herculaneum has been extensively restudied by Mustilli: see below, Catalogue I, n. 5. Rostovtzeff (*SEHRE*², 551–553, n. 26) lists thirty six estates (most of them *villae rusticae*) recovered from the environs of Pompeii; see also the plan in Della Corte, *CeA*³, appendix 2, p. 463, for a topographical guide to the villas in the suburbs. Mingazzini and Pfister register eighteen villas on the Sorrentine peninsula: see *Surrentum* (*Forma Italiae, Regio* I, vol. 2 [Florence 1946]), 100–160 (nos. 20–37), with map I (carta archeologica della Penisola Sorrentina). On villas situated along the southern coast at Positano and Minori, see Maiuri in *RAAN* N.S. 29 (1954), 87–92.

[67] Baiae: see above, n. 19; Surrentum: Hor. *Epist.* 1.17.52. For *amoenitas* in the late Republic, see above, Chapter 3, pp. 47–48.

[68] Vell. Pat. 1.4.2: *Utriusque urbis eximia semper in Romanos fides facit eas nobilitate atque amoenitate sua dignissimas.* Cf. Pomponius Mela 2.70.

[69] Pliny *NH* 3.40 (cf. Pliny *Ep.* 6.16.9). Stat. *Silv.* 2.2.33; 4.7.18–19.

[70] Juv. 3.4–5.

[71] Tac. *Ann.* 4.67.3 (on which cf. Syme, *Tacitus*, pp. 349, 722); *Ann.* 15.52.1.

[72] Serv. *ad Aen.* 3.442.

circumsessum Campaniae amoenitatibus.[73] So much loveliness might even have its disadvantages. When Cicero argued in the *De Re Publica* that maritime cities are peculiarly prone to moral degeneracy and corruption, he urged the *amoenitas* of their sites as a contributing factor.[74] The cities which he there named do not include Baiae. Seneca was more explicit: in his famous denunciation of that notorious town he asserts: *effeminat animos amoenitas nimia.*[75]

Variae Oblectamina Vitae

In ninety-three Statius bade his wife retire from Rome and take up permanent residence with him in his native Neapolis. Recurrent ill-health was the poet's own principal inducement. Lest his consort not find that argument sufficiently compelling, Statius marshaled an eloquent case in hexameters, therein extolling the abiding charms of his native district.[76] His wife need not, he says, restrict herself merely to the neighborhood of Neapolis: *nec desunt variae circa oblectamina vitae*; and there follows a list of the places most likely to delight a sightseer—Baiae, Cumae, Misenum, Gaurus, Capreae, Surrentum, Aenaria, and Stabiae.[77] To move among the various attractions of the various coastal towns, to divert the eye with changing scenery, was one of the chief pleasures of *peregrinatio*—so at least the younger Pliny held.[78] The younger Seneca, as has been seen, took a more jaundiced view: frequent scurrying about was the outward sign of an unstable spirit. Although this is a recurrent sentiment in the *Epistulae Morales*,[79]

[73] Symm. *Ep.* 8.25; cf. 1.5.1.
[74] Cic. *Rep.* 2.8. The *topos* is of course Platonic: Plato, *Leg.* 704 d-e.
[75] Sen. *Ep.* 51.10.
[76] Stat. *Silv.* 3.5. For the date, see Vollmer, *P. Papinii Statii Silvarum Libri* (Leipzig 1898), 18; and R. Helm, "P. Papinius Statius," *RE* 18 (1949), 985, no. 8.
[77] *Silv.* 3.5.95–104. Aenaria's place in the list is curious: see A. W. Van Buren, *AJP* 51 (1930), 378–379.
[78] Pliny *Ep.* 3.19.4: *habet etiam multum iucunditatis soli caelique mutatio ipsaque illa peregrinatio inter sua.* Cf. Tac. *Ann.* 3.47.5 (*peregrinatio suburbana*). On *peregrinatio* in the late Republic, see above, Chapter 3, n. 29.
[79] Sen. *Ep.* 2.1; 69.1: *Mutare te loca et aliunde alio transilire nolo; primum, quia tam frequens migratio instabilis animi est.* And see above, n. 8.

Seneca's practice gives the lie to his thesis: he was frequently in Campania between 63 and 65; he visited on separate occasions Liternum, Cumae, Baiae, Puteoli, Neapolis, and Pompeii, and at each location he found inspiration for the lofty and improving themes which dominate the letters addressed to Lucilius Junior.[80]

To reach the coastal cities from Rome before completion of the *Via Domitiana* in 95, a traveller had first to proceed along the *Via Appia* as far as Capua, whence diverse roads led to Puteoli and Neapolis.[81] The journey required an overnight stop enroute, for Statius' proud claim that with the completion of Domitian's new road Baiae could be reached in a day from Rome is misleading: only a courier could have traversed 141 Roman miles in fourteen hours.[82] Evening ship service was regularly provided between Ostia and Puteoli. The journey took three days, whereas four days were needed for the voyage between Rome and Stabiae.[83] As during the late Republic, sightseeing expeditions within the Bay of Naples could be made by land or sea, by litter or by pleasure boat. Seneca, when bilious, welcomed the jerks and jostlings of the litter.[84] Small pleasure craft were the choices of nocturnal revelers at Baiae.[85] They could be hazardous in a rough sea. A seasick Seneca once ignored the warnings of his boatman during a stormy trip from Puteoli to Neapolis and insisted upon being put ashore

---

[80] Liternum: Sen. *Ep.* 86; Cumae: *ibid.*, 5; Baiae: *Ep.* 51, 57; Puteoli: *Ep.* 53, 77; Neapolis: *Ep.* 49, 53, 57, 76; Pompeii: *Ep.* 49, 70. For the date of Seneca's prolonged Campanian excursion, see Stein, *PIR*[2] A 617. In view of his obvious familiarity with the coastal Campanian towns, it is remarkable that Seneca has left no clue to his places of residence there; if he owned no property himself he must have ordinarily put up with friends, and possibly even rented lodgings from time to time (a legitimate inference from *Ep.* 56.1). Note, however, that the graffito *Lucius Annaeus Senecas* (sic) appears on a wall in Pompeii: *CIL* IV, 4418; on which see A. W. Van Buren, "Pompeii," *RE* 21 (1952), 2037.

[81] Capua to Puteoli: *Via Consularis Campana* (Pliny *NH* 18.111; Frederiksen in *RE* 23 [1959], 2054). Capua to Neapolis (a later road): Lepore, in *PdP* fasc. 25–27 (1952), 302. See also above, Chapter 4, p. 103, for the road between Puteoli and Neapolis.

[82] Stat. *Silv.* 4.3.112–113.

[83] Ostia-Puteoli: Philostr. *Vit. Apoll.* 7.16. Rome-Stabiae: Galen 10.363; on all this, see further L. Friedländer, *Sittengeschichte Röms*[9] I, 335–336.

[84] Sen. *Ep.* 55.1–2.

[85] Sen. *Ep.* 51.4 (quoted above, n. 16). For fourth-century evidence, cf. above, n. 10.

before he had reached his destination.[86] Mindful of that bitter experience, he later opted to return to Neapolis by land through the *crypta Neapolitana* where, however, his constant struggles with mud and dust seemed scarcely an improvement upon the dangers of the sea.[87] Martial knew of a lady who had drowned during a trip from Bauli to Baiae; her fate reminded him of the shipwreck of Agrippina.[88]

In the vicinity of Baiae the imperial fishponds were probably situated along the shore outside the confines of a villa's private quarters to facilitate the steady flow of both salt and fresh water which circulated in the ponds.[89] It is certain that these ponds and the arresting antics of the emperors' favorite fish were accessible to public view: it has already been observed that when Antonia affixed gold rings to a favorite *murena*, crowds of sightseers flocked to the ponds at Bauli, and that Martial warned poachers away from Domitian's ponds at the *lacus Baianus*.[90] At Lake Lucrinus in the Augustan age Rome and all Italy turned out to see a fish that was under the sway of Aphrodite.[91] A dolphin used regularly to convey a schoolboy on its back across the *Sinus Baianus* to his lessons at Puteoli. When the boy died, the devoted fish also languished and expired; and it found burial in the same tomb. Both the Elder Pliny and Aulus Gellius knew versions of this tale, and they cite as guarantors for its authenticity no fewer than

---

[86] *Ibid.*, 53.1–5.
[87] Sen. *Ep.* 57.1–2. For the road between Neapolis and Puteoli, the so-called *Via Antiniana*, see above, Chapter 4, n. 150; Frederiksen in *RE* 23 (1959), 2054, ll.43–44.
[88] Mart. 4.63.
[89] Columella (*De Re Rust.* 8.17) distinguishes two types of fishponds, those built along a coastal strip (*piscinae in litore constructae*) and those cut out of rock (*in petra excisae*). The first systematic attempts to relate Columella's distinction to archaeological evidence from Campanian coastal villas were made by L. Jacono, "Note di archeologia marittima," *Neapolis* I (1913), 353–367; and "*Piscinae in litore constructae*," *Not. d. Sc.* (1924), 333–340; for his study of the ponds belonging to the imperial villa at Pontiae, see above, Chapter 4, n. 26. Mingazzini and Pfister have now catalogued the archaeological evidence in accordance with Columella's categories: see *Surrentum* (*Forma Italiae, Regio* I, vol. 2 [1946]), 43–44; cf. Rostovtzeff, *SEHRE*², 689–690, n. 100.
[90] See above, Chapter 4, nn. 60 and 145.
[91] Aul. Gell. 6.8.5.

four different authors, all contemporaries of Augustus and all eyewitnesses.[92]

Generally it was shellfish rather than dolphins that continued to attract crowds to Lake Lucrinus and kept their praises on the lips of diners in the capital. The epicures adjudged the oysters delectable; the truly discriminating knew at first bite whether an oyster had matured in the beds of Lucrinus, Circeii, or Rutupiae.[93] In the days of the Elder Pliny it had become fashionable to transport young oysters from Brundisium and allow them to fatten in the Lucrine Lake; the resulting blend of two piquant flavors more than compensated for the effort.[94] A truly sumptuous dinner was scarcely complete without oysters from Lucrinus, but the host ran the risk of being thought a slave to luxury—or even anxious for a legacy.[95] The fishing interests at the Lucrine Lake watched zealously over their source of immense profits: Julius Caesar is alleged to have made repairs along the *Via Herculanea*, the narrow strip of land which divided Lucrinus from the *Sinus Baianus*; the emperor Claudius is known to have done the same.[96] It is small wonder therefore that soon after the wars with Sextus Pompey Agrippa's naval works at the *Portus Iulius* were abandoned in favor of the harbor at Misenum: ships at Lucrinus meant the ruin of the oyster beds. It is true that the ancient sources are virtually silent about both the date and pretext of this important and seemingly swift decision; and that Strabo, who speaks of the lake's abundant supplies of oysters, also terms it useless as a place to moor boats.[97] From this most scholars have inferred that silting

---

[92] Pliny NH 9.25; cf. Pliny's aside, ad loc.: *pigeret referre ni res Maecenatis et Fabiani et Flavi Alfii multorumque esset litteris mandata*; Aul. Gell. 6.8.4–7, where the *Egyptian History* of Apion (FHG III, 510) is quoted.

[93] Juv. 4.140–143.

[94] Pliny NH 9.169.

[95] Mart. 3.60.1–4, 12.48.1–4; cf. Sen. *Ep.* 78.23, Mart. 6.11.5, 13.82.1–2, Macrob. *Sat.* 3.15.

[96] Caesar: Servius on Virg. G. 2.161; for the *Via Herculanea*, see above, Chapter 3, n. 73. Claudius: Pliny NH 36.125 (cited above, Chapter 4, n. 105): *Nam portus Ostiensis opus praetereo, item vias per montis excisas, mare Tyrrhenum a Lucrino molibus seclusum . . .*

[97] Strab. 5.4.6 (C 245): εἴσπλουν δ' ἔχει πλοίοις ἐλαφροῖς, ἐνορμίσασθαι μὲν ἄχρηστος, τῶν ὀστρέων δὲ θήραν ἔχων ἀφθονωτάτην. Careful topographical study

at Lucrinus occasioned the construction of a new harbor at Misenum, which in its situation and land-locked inner harbor certainly did possess strong natural advantages as a base for maritime operations.[98] Nevertheless it is significant that Lake Lucrinus was renowned for her oysters long before the construction of the *Portus Iulius* and that the beds were replanted and in flourishing condition immediately thereafter; it would be strange indeed if the combined pressures exerted by the fishing interests and the rich gourmands had not been a factor in the decision to keep Lake Lucrinus free for the cultivation of the oyster. That Agrippa proved unsusceptible to these pressures in the early thirties B.C. is characteristic of the man and itself not perhaps without significance: in a public speech he once proclaimed that paintings and other works of art should be made the public property of the state, rather than be hidden away in the villas of the rich.[99] A man like that—*vir rusticitati propior quam deliciis*[100]—would not concern him-

of the terrain by R. F. Paget has now revealed unmistakable traces of large and elaborate harbor installations at Cumae to the southwest of the ancient acropolis; Paget plausibly identifies these works as part of the *Portus Iulius*, constructed by Agrippa to complement the harbor at Lakes Lucrinus and Avernus: R. F. Paget, "The Ancient Ports of Cumae," *JRS* 58 (1968), 159–169. The author offers no explanation, however, for the Romans abandoning these imposing water works in favor of the new harbor at Misenum (see next note).

[98] Although Tacitus (*Ann.* 4.5.1) and Suetonius (*Aug.* 49.1) reveal that Misenum had become the main naval base in the west in Augustan times, date and circumstances of these installations have remained elusive, obscured by that biographical conception of Augustus' reign which has been recently deplored by Syme, *JRS* 51 (1961), 28. It may be that the prominent place assigned to Misenum in the *Aeneid* (6.156–182; 212–235, especially the final lines) may be invoked to confirm, but it alone cannot establish, a *terminus ante* of 19 B.C. (cf. A. G. McKay, *Greece and Rome*, N.S. 14 [1967], 8). Starr (*Roman Imperial Navy*[2], 14) states that "the Misene fleet was another result of the same energetic systematization (as had occurred at Ravenna) from 27 to 15 B.C." But epigraphical evidence provides strong grounds for believing that the Misene installations were prior to 27 B.C.: C. Iulius Caesaris l. Automatus, the trierarch mentioned in *CIL* X, 3357, must have received his freedom from Octavian as triumvir, for the abbreviation "Aug." does not occur. For the topography of the site, see in general Beloch, *Campanien*[2], 194–202; Maiuri, *Campi Flegrèi*, 95–98; A. G. McKay, *Greece and Rome*, N.S. 14 (1967), 8. For the lighthouse see Maiuri, "La specula misenate," *RAAN* 24/25 (1949–1950), 259–285.

[99] Pliny *NH* 35.26: *exstat certe eius oratio magnifica et maxumo civium digna de tabulis omnibus signisque publicandis, quod fieri satius fuisset quam in villarum exilia pelli.*

[100] *Ibid.*, 35.26.

self overmuch if wealthy epicures in Campania and elsewhere were denied their supplies of succulent oysters from Lucrinus.

Puteoli occupies a special place in the list of Campanian sites commended by Statius to his wife's attention; here were cosmopolitan shores: *litora mundi hospita*.[101] Seneca successfully captures some of the excitement generated by a mid-summer spectacle which was greatly significant in the life of that commercial emporium and well worth the notice of Romans vacationing in those parts: the appearance on the horizon of Alexandrian despatch boats, sent ahead to announce the coming of the grain fleet.[102] *Gratus illarum Campaniae aspectus est*; all of Puteoli gathered at the docks, having recognized the Alexandrian ships by their distinctive rigging. Seneca, although he was soon to receive letters from his friends, was less anxious to learn the condition of his investments abroad; therefore he could regard the bustle of the crowds with cool detachment. On neither of these counts was the local citizenry indifferent: the economic and social ties between Alexandria (and the East generally) and the Bay of Naples remained particularly close until Trajan's new harbor at Ostia attracted eastern shipping away from Puteoli in the second century.[103] Thereafter the prosperity of Puteoli declined, and the epigraphical evidence for her Eastern ties diminishes.[104] But when Seneca

[101] Stat. *Silv*. 3.5.75–76.

[102] Sen. *Ep*. 77.1: *Subito nobis hodie Alexandrinae naves apparuerunt, quae praemitti solent et nuntiare secuturae classis adventum: tabellarias vocant. Gratus illarum Campaniae aspectus est: omnis in pillis Puteolorum turba consistit et ex ipso genere velorum Alexandrinas quamvis in magna turba navium intellegit; solis enim licet siparum intendere, quod in alto omnes habent naves*. The corn fleet departed from Alexandria in June, returing from Puteoli in August: Starr, *Roman Imperial Navy*², 176, n. 36. Northwesterly winds prevailed, and as many as seventy days were required for the voyage from Alexandria to Puteoli; but the outward journey could be made in less than three weeks: see L. Casson, "The Isis and her Voyage," *TAPA* 81 (1950), 43–45; —— *The Ancient Mariners* (New York 1959), 234–235.

[103] See R. Meiggs, *Roman Ostia* (Oxford 1960), 60, for economic consequences at Puteoli of Trajan's harbor at Ostia; see also Frederiksen, *RE* 23 (1959), 2044. Earlier prosperity and ties with the east: Philo *Leg. ad Gaium* 143; Frederiksen, *RE* 23 (1959), 2043–2044, 2048–2049; Dubois, *PA*, 83–110 ("Les Orientaux à Pouzzoles"); Meiggs, *Roman Ostia*, 56–57.

[104] Frederiksen, *RE* 23 (1959), 2044–2045; Meiggs, *Roman Ostia*, 60.

1. *Capreae, Palazzo a Mare, "Bagni di Tiberio."*

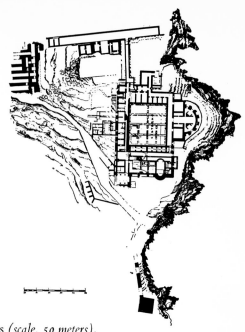

2. *Capreae, plan of* Villa Iovis *(scale, 50 meters).*

3. *A. Capreae, aerial view of* Villa Iovis.

3. *B. Capreae*, Villa Iovis, *cisterns 1 and 2.*

4. *Baiae, the baths. View NW, from* piscina.

5. *Baiae, the baths. View N, from SW corner of* piscina.

6. *Baiae, the baths. View N towards the "terma di mercurio"; exedra in foreground.*

7. *Baiae, the baths. View SW along* ambulatio *on the* "*Sella di Baia.*"

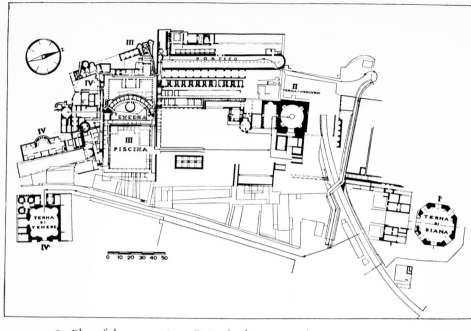

8. *Plan of the excavations, Baiae (scale, 50 meters).*

9. *Capreae (Anacapri), portico of the "villa di Damecuta."*

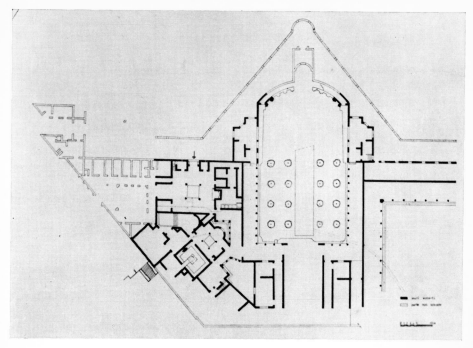

10. *A. Stabiae, ground plan of Villa S. Marco (scale, 10 meters).*

10. *B. Stabiae, Villa S. Marco.* Porticus triplex *with* natatio.

11. *A. Stabiae, Villa S. Marco.* Porticus triplex *with* natatio; *view NW to-wards* oecus *overlooking the sea.*

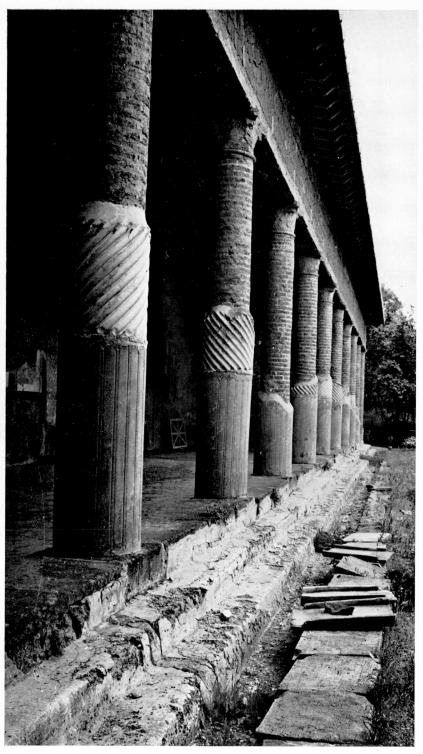

11. B. Stabiae, *Villa S. Marco. South side of small peristyle. Steps lead to stuccoed columns with spiraled flutings.*

12. *Villa del Capo di Sorrento. Roman masonry at the landing place, with view N across the Bay.*

13. Villa maritima *in the Bay of Naples. Part of wall decoration of a house in Stabiae. Museo Nazionale, Naples.*

14. *Group of buildings of a* villa maritima, *with terracing and steps to the sea (left). Wall painting from* tablinum *of the House of M. Lucretius Fronto, Pompeii.*

15. *A.* Villa maritima *in the Bay of Naples with curved portico in two stories. Part of wall decoration from a house in Stabiae.*

15. B. Villa maritima *in the Bay of Naples; construction of three stories with artificial terracing. Wall decoration from the same Stabian house.*

wrote in the last five years of Nero's reign, Puteoli was a flourishing cosmopolitan center. Merchants from Egypt, Asia, and Syria, whose prominence during the Augustan age has been noticed in the preceding chapter, rented permanent trading stations (*stationes*) in Puteoli and worshipped their national gods at local shrines which were maintained at their own expense.[105] Doubtless on the day in question oriental and local traders were on hand in large numbers to greet the Alexandrian mail ships—and so were members of the imperial fleet, for Egypt placed more recruits in the *classis Misenensis* than any other country, and the sailors were eager for news of family and friends: there survives on papyrus an affectionate letter to his father from a young Egyptian recruit, written shortly after his assignment to Misenum.[106]

Finally, coastal Campania's volcanic soil, and man's ingenuity, provided imperial visitors with a unique attraction: the baths, patronized both by invalids who hoped for thermal cures and by healthy sojourners who were satisfied to tone their bodies and to improve their digestions. Most widely acclaimed were the sulphurous sweat baths in the myrtle groves on the hills between Cumae and Baiae. In all probability these were the *Aquae Cumanae* mentioned as the destination of Cornelius Scipio Hispallus in 176 B.C.[107] Later, with the rise in Baiae's fortunes, their geographical designation changed; in the first century of the Empire the

[105] Cf. the famous letter dispatched by Tyrians at Puteoli to their own senate in 174 (*IG* XIV, 830 = Dittenberger, *Orientis Graeci Inscriptiones Selectae* [1905], 287, no. 595; Dubois, *PA*, 83–85): "As nearly all of you know, there are trading stations in Puteoli besides our own; but ours, in respect to both adornment and size, is superior to the others. In earlier days the Tyrians who lived in Puteoli were responsible for the station's upkeep: they were numerous and wealthy. But now we are but a small number, and, because of the expenses which we must meet for sacrifices and worship of our national gods, who have their own temples here, we have not the necessary resources to pay to rent the station, a sum of 100,000 denarii a year . . ." For the amount of the rent, the largest surviving cost from Puteoli, see R. Duncan Jones, *PBSR* N.S. 20 (1965), pp. 193, 302 (no. 1185a). On the Heliopolitani, see *CIL* X, 1579; Dubois, *PA* 97–98. *Berytenses qui Puteolis consistunt*: *CIL* X, 1634. *Germellenses*: *CIL* X, 1578. See further Frederiksen, *RE* 23 (1959), 2049; and for oriental religions and cult, R. M. Peterson, *The Cults of Campania*, *Papers and Monographs of the Amer. Acad. in Rome* I (1919), 131–159.

[106] Hunt and Edgar, *Select Papyri* I (1932), no. 112. Egyptian recruitment: Starr, *Roman Imperial Navy*[2], 75; Fitzhardinge, *JRS* 41 (1951), 19.

[107] See above, Chapter I, pp. 3–5.

7

groves are said to stand *super Baias*.[108] There buildings were constructed to confine the hot sulphurous vapor which emanated from
the earth: circulation of the steam was abetted by pipes placed
inside the walls and floor. It was also aided by domed roofs, for,
as is now coming to be more generally recognized, the baths at
Baiae constitute early evidence for originality and experimentation
in Roman vaulting.[109] In twenty-three B.C., with Antonius Musa's
spectacular cure of Augustus by cold medications, Baiae's myrtle
groves suffered an eclipse in popularity; accordingly in a famous
epistle, Horace urged his horse past Baiae, not perhaps without a
wistful backward look.[110] The decline, however, was temporary.
It has been seen that in the days of Claudius a favorite freedman
gave his name to sulphurous *thermae* at Baiae; Seneca did not care
for *sudatoria*; Martial knew the myrtle groves.[111]

In addition to sweat baths there were other public *thermae*—and
a wealth of mineral sources—both at Baiae and in all other coastal
cities: there are extensive remains in the forum of Roman Cumae,
west of the amphitheater in Puteoli; the forum and suburban baths
at Herculaneum—and the three large establishments at Pompeii—
are too well known to require comment.[112] Seneca took lodgings

[108] Celsus *Med.* 2.17.1; 3.21.6; Cass. Dio 48.51.1–5.

[109] Celsus *Med.* 2.17.1: *Sudor etiam duobus modis elicitur, aut sicco calore aut balneo.
Siccus calor est et harenae calidae et Laconici et clibani et quarundam naturalium sudationum,
ubi terra profusus calidus vapor aedificio includitur, sicut super Baias in murtetis habemus.* Cf.
Sen. *Quaest. Nat.* 3.34.3. The domed building at Baiae known commonly as the "Tempio
di Mercurio" is very probably of Augustan date: see R. Salinas, "Le cupole nell'
architettura della Campania," *Atti del VIII Conv. Naz. di Stor. dell'Architettura* (Rome
1956), 289–291; for a detailed description, and an appreciation of the monument's
architectural originality, see W. L. MacDonald, *The Architecture of the Roman Empire* I
(New Haven 1965), 11–12. For the exterior of the dome see Plate 6, below.

[110] M. Antonius Musa: Suet. *Aug.* 81.1; Cass. Dio 53.30.3; see below, n. 153. Hor.
Epist. 1.15.2–5: *nam mihi Baias | Musa supervacuas Antonius, et tamen illis | me facit invisum,
gelida cum perluor unda | per medium frigus. Sane myrteta relinqui . . .* Cf. R. G. M. Nisbet,
JRS 52 (1962), 285.

[111] *Aquae Posidianae:* Chapter 4, n. 101. Seneca's views: *Ep.* 51.6: *quid mihi cum istis
calentibus stagnis? Quid cum sudatoriis, in quae siccus vapor corpora exhausurus includitur?
Omnis sudor per laborem exeat.* Cf. Mart. 3.58.1–2.

[112] On the waters in the *sinus Baianus* see above all Pliny *NH* 31.4–5: *nusquam tamen
largius (sc. emicant aquae) quam in Baiano sinu nec pluribus auxiliandi generibus, aliae sulpuris
vi, aliae aluminis, aliae salis, aliae nitri, aliae bituminis, nonnullae etiam acida salsave mixtura.
vapore ipso aliquae prosunt tantaque est vis, ut balneas calefaciant ac frigidam etiam in solis*

above public baths in one coastal Campanian city; the continual din distressed him.[113] Neapolis had hot mineral springs and bathing establishments less numerous than those of Baiae, but inferior in no other respects; the emperor Nero found them to his taste.[114] Invalids seem to have had a preference for Neapolis.[115] But in general, if a person suffered from rheumatism or gout, one Campanian spa would serve as well as another; thus Agrippina in 54, finding it convenient to remove Narcissus from his master's side, showed sudden concern for the freedman's gout and sent him to the waters ἐς Καμπανίαν.[116] Some baths bore famous names: according to Ammianus Marcellinus, both the waters of Mamaea (built, as has been seen, by her son Alexander Severus) and an obscure *Silvani lavacrum* enjoyed brisk patronage by members of the nobility in fourth century Baiae.[117] The smaller thermal establishments owned by private citizens might draw upon both salt and fresh water and were located at the sea's edge. Near Pompeii a notice advertised: *thermae M. Crassi Frugi aqua marina et balneum aqua dulci*; the same man was apparently the owner of a

---

fervere cogant. See further Dubois, *PA*, 385–393; I. Sgobbo, "Terme flegree e origine delle terme romane," *Atti I Cong. Naz. di Studi Romani* (1928), 1–24; for a more recent catalogue of the archaeological remains of Campanian baths in which heating systems exploited local mineral deposits, see B. Crova, "Le terme romane nella Campania," *Atti del VIII Conv. Naz. di Stor. dell'Architettura* (Rome 1956), 277–285. Cf. Maiuri, *Campi Flegrèi*, 72–86. Baths at Cumae: Maiuri, *ibid.*, 144; at Puteoli: Frederiksen, *RE* 23 (1959), 2059; Herculaneum: Maiuri, *Herculaneum*[6] (tr. V. Priestley), *Istituto Poligrafico dello Stato* (1961), 36–40, 68–70. Pompeii: R. Étienne, *La Vie Quotidienne à Pompéi* (Paris 1966), 411–425.

[113] Sen. *Ep.* 56.1–2.

[114] Strab. 5.4.7 (C 246): ἔχει δὲ καὶ ἡ Νεάπολις θερμῶν ὑδάτων ἐκβολὰς καὶ κατασκευὰς λουτρῶν οὐ χείρους τῶν ἐν βαίαις, πολὺ δὲ τῷ πλήθει λειπομένας. τὸ πλῆθος must, in the context, mean "number of bathing establishments," despite H. L. Jones, The Geography of Strabo (Loeb Classical Library) II, *ad loc.* (451). Their location: I. Sgobbo (see n. 112), 6. Nero's tastes: Suet. *Nero* 20.2 (although these may have been baths attached to the imperial residence in Neapolis).

[115] See below, pp. 142–143.

[116] Cass. Dio 61.34.4. Compare Pliny, solicitous for Calpurnia's health in 107 (*Ep.* 6.4.1–2): *Numquam sum magis de occupationibus meis questus, quae me non sunt passae aut proficiscentem te valetudinis causa in Campaniam prosequi aut profectam e vestigio subsequi. Nunc enim praecipue simul esse cupiebam, ut oculis meis crederem, quid viribus, quid corpusculo adparares, ecquid denique secessus voluptates regionisque abundantiam inoffensa transmitteres.*

[117] Amm. Marc. 28.4.19 (quoted above, Chapter 4, n. 164).

comparable complex near Baiae. And at the Sorrentine villa of Pollius Felix, baths at the seaside poured forth steam from twin domes.[118]

Learning and Culture: the Studiosi

An attempt was made in an earlier chapter to set forth the various reasons why cultivated Romans and learned Greeks were drawn to visit and to settle in Republican Neapolis and the nearby cities.[119] The geographer Strabo, an Apamesian Greek fully sensitive to the ways of the Romans, vividly reviews the chief characteristics of Augustan Neapolis. He first notices the city's tenacious devotion to Greek institutions, mentions that the local *Sebasta* rivaled the most famous musical and gymnastic competitions on the Greek mainland, and concludes with revealing observations on some of the components of Neapolitan society: "The Greek mode of life at Neapolis finds special favor with the men who make their living by educating the young and who withdraw there from Rome for the sake of peace and quiet (ἡσυχίας χάριν), or else with still others who, on account of their old age or infirmity, long to live without effort (ἐν ἀνέσει ζῆν). And some of the Romans too, delighting in this way of life and observing the great numbers of men—cultured like themselves—residing there, happily frequent the city and take up permanent residence."[120]

Evidence pertaining largely to first and second century Neapolis confirms conclusively, and in turn, each one of Strabo's major points. First, the surviving inscriptions from Neapolis are predominantly Greek and testify to the existence of *gymnasia*,

[118] Catalogue II, no. 23 (M. Licinius Crassus Frugi); no. 34 (Pollius Felix).

[119] Chapter 3, pp. 59–60.

[120] Strab. 5.4.7 (C 246): ἐπιτείνουσι δὲ τὴν ἐν Νεαπόλει διαγωγὴν τὴν Ἑλληνικὴν οἱ ἐκ τῆς Ῥώμης ἀναχωροῦντες δεῦρο ἡσυχίας χάριν τῶν ἀπὸ παιδείας ἐργασαμένων ἢ καὶ ἄλλων διὰ γῆρας ἢ ἀσθένειαν ποθούντων ἐν ἀνέσει ζῆν· καὶ τῶν Ῥωμαίων δ᾽ ἔνιοι χαίροντες τῷ βίῳ τούτῳ, θεωροῦντες τὸ πλῆθος τῶν ἀπὸ τῆς αὐτῆς ἀγωγῆς ἐπιδημούντων ἀνδρῶν, ἄσμενοι φιλοχωροῦσι καὶ ζῶσιν αὐτόθι. For Strabo in the west, see G. W. Bowersock, *Augustus and the Greek World*, 123–130, 132–134.

ephebia, phratries, and to the *demarchia*, the chief Neapolitan magistracy; as Tacitus observed, Neapolis was indeed a *Graeca urbs*.[121] It has already been seen that the *Sebasta*, instituted by Neapolis in honor of Augustus, were patronized by subsequent emperors; inscriptions elucidate certain aspects of both their organization and their content.[122] Further, Strabo's emphasis upon the life of peace and quiet finds its echo in the epithet *otiosa* bestowed upon Neapolis by Augustan poets, by Statius in his expressive commemoration of his native district, and by Silius Italicus.[123] The learned pursuits continued to flourish in imperial Neapolis, practised precisely by the men described by Strabo as "making their living by educating the young": along with *otiosa* a second poetic epithet gained currency in the first century, for Columella refers to *docta Parthenope*, Martial to *docta Neapolis*.[124] That Statius and Silius Italicus chose to retire permanently to Neapolis in their declining years is sufficient indication that the city functioned as a haven for the aged and infirm.[125] Finally, cultivated Romans did indeed continue to seek out the one city in Italy where Greek institutions, leisure, and learning could be found in combination:

[121] *IG* XIV, 714–828; cf. *CIL* X, 1478–1543 (five of which are all or partly in Greek). For the tenacity of the Greek language into the third century in official documents and epitaphs, see *IG* XIV, 803, 809, 794 (= *CIL* X, 1504); for hellenized Latin, cf. *Not. d. Sc.* (1892), 99: *Dis Manibus Iuliaes Rodopes*. On phratries, see M. Napoli, *Napoli Greco-Romana* (1959), 166–182. Magistracies and constitutional problems: F. De Martino, *PdP*, fasc. 25–27 (1952), 333–343; Sartori, *Problemi*, 43–55; and cf. above, Chapter 3, p. 59. Tacitus' remark: above, Chapter 4, n. 119.

[122] See the examples in Geer, "Greek Games," *TAPA* 66 (1935), 209–213; the single most important inscription represents an attempt on the part of the senate of Neapolis to define the regulations of the games at Olympia and so to publicize the *Sebasta* among the spectators at the prestigious contests on the Greek mainland: Dittenberger and Purgold, *Die Inschriften von Olympia* (Berlin 1896), no. 56. Observe the important additions of L. Robert, *Études Anatoliennes* (1937), 143–144, and see further L. Moretti, *Iscrizioni Agonistiche Greche* (Rome 1953), index, s.v. "Σεβαστά."

[123] Virg. *G.* 4.563–564: *illo Vergilium me tempore dulcis alebat / Parthenope studiis florentem ignobilis oti;* Hor. *Epod.* 1.5.43: *otiosa Neapolis;* Ov. *Met.* 15.711–712: *in otia natam Parthenopen.* Stat. *Silv.* 3.5.85; Sil. Ital. 12.31–32.

[124] Columella *De Re Rust.* 10.134; Mart. 5.78.14. On all this, see A. Rostagni, "La cultura letteraria di Napoli antica nelle sue fasi culminanti," *PdP* fasc. 25–27 (1952), 344–357; and, more recently, F. Sbordone, *Storia di Napoli* I, Società Editrice Storia di Napoli (Naples 1967), 543–570; but neither author has fully exploited the available evidence.

[125] Catalogue II, no. 31 (P. Papinius Statius); no. 12 (Ti. Catius Silius Italicus).

Aulus Gellius once speaks of passing summer holidays in Neapolis; there he encountered in residence a rich young Roman, studying with tutors in both languages preparatory to taking up a career in the courts of Rome.[126]

All that Strabo found to be significant of Augustan Neapolis appears to converge in the career of a man who, but for the attainments of his son, would remain utterly obscure. The father of the poet Statius—the son's *Epicedion* is our single source[127]—was born at Velia to parents of good stock and of moderate fortune; from an early age, however, his *patria* was Neapolis, where he apparently passed the remainder of his life and died at the age of sixty-five, not long after the eruption of Mt. Vesuvius.[128] The elder Statius made his living as a tutor. To him flocked southern youths (from Lucania and Apulia), local pupils (from Surrentum, Misenum, Cumae, Puteoli, and Baiae), and the sons of the Roman great, in order to learn *mores et facta priorum*.[129] To this learned gentleman, Statius proudly sings, Roman *pontifices*, provincial governors, pleaders in the courts, and military commanders all owed their subsequent renown. For purposes of instruction he produced a literal translation of the Homeric poems in Latin prose; and the works of all the major Greek poets were included in the curriculum.[130] No doubt the majority of his pupils were drawn by their master's own poetic achievements: from early youth he had won prizes for his original compositions at the *Sebasta* in Neapolis and added victories at the major competitions on the Greek mainland. He lamented in verse the horrors of the Civil War of 69, and shortly before his death was planning a poem on the hapless cities buried by the eruption of Vesuvius.[131] Quite clearly, then,

---

126 Aul. Gell. 9.15.2: *Atque ibi erat adulescens tunc quispiam ex ditioribus cum utriusque linguae magistris meditans et exercens ad causas Romae orandas eloquentiae Latinae facultatem* . . .

127 Stat. *Silv.* 5.3.

128 *Ibid.*, 104–130, 205–208, 252–254; cf. F. Vollmer, *P. Papinii Statii Silvarum Libri* (Leipzig 1898), 15–16.

129 *Silv.* 5.3.145–177.

130 Specifically, the *Iliad* and *Odyssey*, Hesiod, Theognis, Pindar, Ibycus, Alcman, Stesichorus, Sappho; the elder Statius also unraveled for his pupils the complexities of Callimachus, Lycophron, Sophron, and Corinna: *Silv.* 5.3.146–161.

131 *Silv.* 5.3.205–208.

it was not merely the hopes of victory in the *Sebasta* which induced Statius' father to remain in Neapolis, but neither was he content to devote his life entirely to his students. Similarly, the existence of the *Sebasta* and the presence of poets were not the sole criteria of the city's Hellenism, any more than Neapolis existed solely to provide learned tutors for the sons of Roman grandees. The point was rather, as Strabo asserted, the Romans realized, and as the career of the Elder Statius proves, that in this *Graeca urbs* all such persons and pursuits could flourish in combination.

The atmosphere remained ripe for learning. *Docta Neapolis* and other coastal cities could claim as settlers or sojourners a remarkably large number of the cultured and the erudite in imperial times; they include rhetors and poets, philosophers and scholars, physicians, actors, and musicians, some known little more than by name. Antonius Julianus was a Spaniard by origin, a rhetor by profession, and seems to have plied his trade principally in Rome.[132] But he sought out the Bay of Naples in hot weather; Aulus Gellius accompanied him to Puteoli one summer in the early 140's, and to Neapolis in a later year. There they occupied their days entirely in literary pursuits, once attending the theater to hear a reading of Ennius' *Annales*, once listening, when importuned, to private *declamationes*, not of the highest quality.[133] Julianus' fellow countryman, M. Cornelius Fronto, some years before he held a suffect consulship in 143, was appointed tutor in Latin Rhetoric to the future emperors, M. Aurelius and L. Verus; he owned property in the environs of Surrentum.[134] M. Aurelius reported to his *magister* that he did not think highly of the rhetorician Polemo when the latter declaimed in Neapolis in 143, but he formed a higher—and more just—estimate of Polemo's abilities in later life.[135] The speech *De Fortuna*, transmitted among the

[132] Aul. Gell. 19.9.2; see further *PIR*² A 844.
[133] Puteoli: Aul. Gell. 18.5.1–3; Neapolis: Aul. Gell. 9.15.2 (quoted above, n. 126).
[134] Catalogue II, no. 16 (M. Cornelius Fronto).
[135] Fronto, *ad M. Caes.* 2.5 (= Naber p. 29; Haines I, 116). The later estimate: Philostr. *Vit. Soph.* ed. Kayser, 231.

writings of Dio Chrysostom but now plausibly attributed to the rhetor Favorinus, has recently been shown from internal evidence to have been delivered in Neapolis during the reign of Hadrian.[136]

The poet Virgil's connections with Neapolis are attested first in his early manhood. He maintained them throughout his life and found burial in the city.[137] More than a century later two lesser poets worshipped at his shrine: Statius, the first Campanian native since Lucilius to enrich the national literature; and Silius Italicus, whose *Punica* was composed in the several Neapolitan villas which he successively fancied.[138] The lyric poet Caesius Bassus, it is alleged, owned a villa near Mt. Vesuvius; the house and its master were buried in the catastrophe of 79.[139] Of the poets Blaesus (of Capreae) and Castricus (who entertained Martial at Baiae), few particulars beyond the names survive.[140]

At least occasionally the lectures of resident philosophers were attended by persons of comparable erudition. During a sojourn in Neapolis the younger Seneca faithfully frequented the school of the Greek Metronax, whose daily disputations began in his own house punctually at two.[141] Apollonius of Tyana, the itinerant Neo-Pythagorean sage, put into port at Puteoli during the reign of Domitian.[142] There, according to his biographer Philostratus, he met Demetrius, who had a reputation for being the boldest of philosophers, merely because he made his residence so close to Rome. Apollonius at once accused Demetrius of living in luxury in the most beautiful part of Italy. The two men, it is then reported, walked to the villa which Cicero had possessed of old and there initiated an animated discussion.[143] Their conversation would have

---

[136] A. Barigazzi, "Un'orazione pronunziata a Napoli ai tempi di Adriano," *Athenaeum* N.S. 29 (1951), 3–11.

[137] Catalogue II, no. 45 (P. Vergilius Maro).

[138] Catalogue II, no. 12 (Italicus), no. 31 (Statius). Their local devotions to Virgil: Mart. 11.48, 49; Stat. *Silv.* 4.4.51–55.

[139] Catalogue II, no. 8 (Caesius Bassus).

[140] Blaesus: Steph. Byz. *s.v.* Καπρέαι; Castricus: Catalogue II, no. 11.

[141] Sen. *Ep.* 76.4. The philosopher's death is mentioned in *Ep.* 93.1.

[142] Philostr. *Vita Apollon.* 7.10 (= p. 259, 27 Kayser). For the date, see F. Grosso, "La 'Vita di Apollonio di Tiana' come fonte storica," *Acme* 7 (1954), 468–469.

[143] Philostr. *Vita Apollon.* 7.11: "Ἄγει δὲ αὐτοὺς εἰπὼν ταῦτα ἐς τὸ Κικέρωνος

dealt only partially with abstractions. Demetrius had graver matters to discuss: these were anxious times for philosophers.[144] In the third century the Neoplatonist Plotinus repaired to Campania at the end of his life, having inherited a villa from a friend.[145] But his interest in the region had been keen also in earlier years. From the emperor Gallienus and his wife Salonina, Plotinus had sought financial support for a singular project. In Campania a city of philosophers was said to have existed once; at that time however, perhaps around the year 260, it lay languishing in ruins. Plotinus enthusiastically urged the revival of the city, proposing to rename it Platonopolis and to repeople it with the wise: all would live there in accordance with Plato's laws. Spiteful and small-minded ministers of the emperor, Porphyry relates, were prompt to thwart the scheme.[146]

τοῦ παλαιοῦ χωρίον, ἔστι δὲ τοῦτο πρὸς τῷ ἄστει. If the conversation in Cicero's villa is not the invention of Philostratus, the *Cumanum* must be meant (so also Frederiksen, *RE* 23 [1959], 2059).

[144] Grosso (see above, n. 142), 469; Domitian's purge explains the presence of Demetrius in Puteoli, and Philostratus' remark that residence near Rome was a sign of boldness. See further *PIR*² D 39.

[145] Porph. *Plot.* 2; cf. Catalogue II, no. 33.

[146] Porph. *Plot.* 12: ἐτίμησαν δὲ τὸν Πλωτῖνον μάλιστα καὶ ἐσέφθησαν Γαλιῆνός τε ὁ αὐτοκράτωρ καὶ ἡ τούτου γυνὴ Σαλωνίνα. Ὁ δὲ τῇ φιλίᾳ τῇ τούτων καταχρώμενος φιλοσόφων τινὰ πόλιν κατὰ τὴν Καμπανίαν γεγενῆσθαι λεγομένην, ἄλλως δὲ κατηριπωμένην, ἠξίου ἀνεγείρειν καὶ τὴν πέριξ χώραν χαρίσασθαι οἰκισθείσῃ τῇ πόλει, νόμοις δὲ χρῆσθαι τοὺς κατοικεῖν μέλλοντας τοῖς Πλάτωνος καὶ τὴν προσηγορίαν αὐτῇ Πλατωνόπολιν θέσθαι, ἐκεῖ τε αὐτὸς μετὰ τῶν ἑταίρων ἀναχωρήσειν ὑπισχνεῖτο. Καὶ ἐγένετ' ἂν τὸ βούλημα ἐκ τοῦ ῥάστου τῷ φιλοσόφῳ, εἰ μή τινες τῶν συνόντων τῷ βασιλεῖ φθονοῦντες ἢ νεμεσῶντες ἢ δι᾽ ἄλλην μοχθηρὰν αἰτίαν ἐνεπόδισαν. Various attempts have been made to identify both the city and its prospective inhabitants: for a summary see G. Della Valle, *RAAN* N.S. 19 (1938), 237–263. But J. M. Rist (*Plotinus: The Road to Reality* [Cambridge 1967], 12–14) rightly stresses the scantiness of our knowledge while noting that the scheme might well have appealed to "senatorial adherents of philosophy" (p. 14). Other coastal residents cultivated their philosophical interests: much earlier, Lucilius Junior may have migrated from Pompeii to the more congenial cultural climate of Neapolis (Catalogue II, no. 24). Certainly Pompeii offered little in these years to men with intellectual appetites: note the observation of M. Gigante, "La cultura letteraria a Pompei," *Pompeiana* (*Raccolta di Studi per il Secondo Centenario degli Scavi di Pompei* [Naples 1950]), 110: "Una 'villa dei papiri' non è stata scoperta, e nessun indigio ci ha potuto mettere sulla traccia di circoli letterari o filosofici." Very different was Puteoli; note the *Epicureius chorus* attested in a local inscription (*CIL* X, 2971; cf. Dubois, *PA*, 61).

The *desidis otia vitae* in the coastal cities did not distract scholars from their diverse works of erudition. On the contrary, they found in that unruffled municipal calm a positive incentive to private creativity. Apion recorded an arresting sight at Augustan Puteoli in the fifth book of his Egyptian History, which he was very possibly writing at the time; Maecenas, Fabianus, and Alfius Flavus all witnessed and transcribed the same events.[147] Such was the accuracy of Strabo's knowledge of Augustan Neapolis, and such his sensitivity to its atmosphere, that some scholars plausibly contend that Strabo had stayed at length in the city, where he may have been revising his geography as late as 19.[148] The distinguished grammarian Herodian lived in Rome during the reign of Marcus Aurelius, but it was to Puteoli that he retired to compose his *Convivium*.[149] Philostratus, author of the earlier collection of *Imagines*, asserted that the occasion of his discussions was a visit to Greek Neapolis where the people exhibited a characteristically Greek enthusiasm for discussion. There follows a rhetorical description of the paintings displayed on the open terrace of a Neapolitan villa in which Philostratus was currently a guest. As he moved from painting to painting the master was surrounded by a crowd of young listeners, his host's ten-year-old son among the most attentive.[150] In the fourth century the scholar Victorius died in Cumae, whither he had crossed by ship from Sicily.[151] One wonders where such numbers of scholars consulted books. Perhaps their hosts' villas were equipped with private libraries comparable—on a more modest scale—to that of Piso at Herculaneum, where the collection of Epicurean writings remained intact until 79.[152]

---

[147] Above, nn. 91, 92.

[148] E. Honigmann, *RE* 4 A (1931) 84, no. 3; Bowersock, *Augustus and the Greek World*, 132. On the date of composition of the *Geography*, see J. G. C. Anderson, *Anatolian Studies presented to Ramsay* (London 1923), 1–2.

[149] Steph. Byz. 230 20 M (cited by Friedländer, *Sittengeschichte Roms*9 I, 401).

[150] Philostr. *Imag.* 1.4 (= 295, Kayser).

[151] Auson. 5.22.19–20.

[152] Catalogue I, no. 5. Silius Italicus had quantities of books in Naples: see Catalogue II, no. 12.

A few physicians, too, had local connections, although the ancient evidence for their activities is meager. The recurrence in Campanian graffiti and inscriptions of the name M. Antonius Musa proves that the famed physician of Augustus was well known also in these parts.[153] Q. Stertinius of Cos and his more famous brother Xenophon amassed huge fortunes from their Roman medical practice in the reign of Claudius and drew heavily upon them to beautify the public buildings at Neapolis, where presumably, therefore, they had purchased estates.[154] Eustochius, a physician from Alexandria with a taste for philosophical abstractions, attended Plotinus during his later years and was residing in Puteoli while Plotinus struggled with his final illness elsewhere in Campania.[155]

The younger Seneca remarked that in order to reach the house of the philosopher Metronax he had to pass the theater of the

[153] CIL IV, 5730 (= ILS 8594): *Faecula Aminea Musae ab Varia Potita*. The words were painted upon a terracotta jug discovered in the 'isola dei Vetti' at Pompeii. Later five graffiti bearing the *cognomen* Musa—four from the "villa dei misteri"—were published and discussed by Della Corte (*Not. d. Sc.* [1921], 435, [1922], 482–485); these are the sole instances of the *cognomen* recorded at Pompeii. Della Corte had already proposed to identify this Musa with the Augustan physician (*Atti del'Accad. di Arch. Lett. e Belle Arti di Napoli*, N.S. 13 [1933], 82–84), when there came to light, among the graffiti from the cryptoporticus of the Augustan theatre at Suessa Aurunca, a name read by Della Corte as M. A[ntonius] Musa (Della Corte, *Camp. Rom.* I, 195). Since the physician's *cognomen* renders Campanian origin doubtful in the extreme, the Campanian graffiti should be interpreted as a reflection of local interest in, and gratitude to, the physician who brought Augustus back from the point of death in 23 B.C. (Cass. Dio 53.30.3; Suet. *Aug.* 81.1; *PIR*[2] A 853; and see above, p. 140). The freedman Musa was rewarded with gold rings, money, and an honorary statue (Cass. Dio 53.30.3, Suet. *Aug.* 59), but Augustus' previous physician, C. Aemilius, was discredited; the incident may even have occurred in Campania (Ps. Acro on Hor. *Ep.* 1.15.3; Pliny *NH* 19.128). For all his skill, Antonius Musa failed M. Claudius Marcellus, nephew of Augustus, who died at Baiae later in the same year (Prop. 3.18.1–16, cited above, Chapter 4, n. 21; cf. Cass. Dio 53.30.3).

[154] Pliny *NH* 29.7–8: Q. *Stertinius inputavit principibus quod sestertiis quingenis annuis contentus esset, sescena enim sibi quaestu urbis fuisse enumeratis domibus ostendebat. Par et fratri eius merces a Claudio Caesare infusa est, censusque, quamquam exhausti operibus Neapoli exornata, heredi HS $\overline{ccc}$ relinquere, quantum aetate eadem Arruntius solus*. For Q. and C. Stertinius of Cos, see Kind, *RE* 3 A (1929), 2450–2451 (nos. 2, 3).

[155] Porph. *Plot.* 1.7, 2.7. On the place occupied by doctors, rhetors, philosophers, and intellectuals in Neapolitan society, see E. Lepore, "Per la storia economico-sociale di Neapolis," *PdP* fasc. 25–27 (1952), 329; and see now Lepore's discussion in *Storia di Napoli* I, Società Editrice Storia di Napoli (Naples 1967), 312–313. Other physicians: *CIL* X, 1497, 1546; *IG* XIV, 809.

Neapolitans, where the quality of the musical entertainment stirred sharp controversy among the spectators.[156] Seneca must here refer to the smaller covered auditorium which stood next to an unroofed theater—Neapolis, like Pompeii, possessed two adjacent theatrical halls, and the smaller, which had its parallels in the covered Odeon at nearby Pausilypon and later in second century Athens, was the scene of musical competitions.[157] In these two structures were housed the dramatic and musical contests of the quinquennial *Sebasta*, as well as the entertainments and competitions which occurred regularly at other times. Crowds in the *theatrum Neapolitanum* were habituated to unusual performances. They had once heard an emperor's voice raised in song;[158] and Nero's cultivated consular contemporary, Calpurnius Piso, may also have appeared there: Piso had something of a reputation as a singer of tragic parts, and the author of the *Laus Pisonis*, noting that Greek culture flowed forth from Piso's lips, states explicitly that eloquent Neapolis could bear witness.[159]

Certainly by the middle years of the second century, and probably much earlier, pantomimic dances were a regular feature of the musical and dramatic portion of the *Sebasta*. This is quite clear from a reference in Lucian's *De Saltatione* to the inclusion of pantomime in the games "of a city in Italy, the fairest that belongs to the Chalcidian race"—the allusion to Neapolis and to the *Sebasta* is unmistakable—and from one of the Neapolitan victory lists which mentions a L. Aurelius Apolaustos, certainly a pantomimist.[160] Lucian's dialogue, as L. Robert has rightly re-emphasized, is to be dated to the years 162–165;[161] exactly when

[156] Sen. *Ep.* 76.4.

[157] The two theaters of Neapolis: Stat. *Silv.* 3.5.91; the site of the larger has long been known; see M. Napoli, *Napoli Greco-Romana* (Naples 1959), 184–189. Parallels at Pompeii and in Athens: Mau-Kelsey, *Pompeii* (New York 1899), 135–149; Pausilypon: Günther, *Pausilypon*, 40–47.

[158] Chapter 4, pp. 96–97.

[159] Catalogue II, no. 9 (Calpurnius Piso).

[160] Lucian *Salt.* 32: ἐῶ λέγειν ὅτι πόλις ἐν Ἰταλίᾳ τοῦ Χαλκιδικοῦ γένους ἡ ἀρίστη καὶ τοῦτο ὥσπερ τι κόσμημα τῷ παρ᾽ ἑαυτοῖς ἀγῶνι προστέθεικεν. L. Aurelius Apolaustus: *Not. d. Sc.* (1890), 41.

[161] L. Robert, "Pantomimen im Griechischen Orient," *Hermes* 65 (1930), 120.

pantomimists were admitted to the *Sebasta* cannot be determined, but that Neapolis should have been the first Greek competition to open its lists to these dramatic dancers is excellent evidence for their local popularity. Inscriptions further strengthen the hypothesis: the earliest evidence for pantomimic acting outside Rome is precisely Campanian. The Pylades who performed in Pompeii in 3 B.C. may well be identical with the Cilician Pylades of Augustan times, who founded pantomimic dancing of the tragic type.[162] The name of L. Domitius Paris, tragedian and favorite of the emperor Nero, recurs among the *dipinti* of Pompeii: it seems that he paid a visit to the city in 59. One pantomimist even rose to the highest magistracies in Neapolis in the Antonine Age—striking testimony to the local importance attached to such performances.[163]

The followers of Pylades tended to assume his name. One such successor in second century Campania was L. Aurelius *Aug. lib.* Pylades, characterized as the first among pantomimists of his day; his praises are sung, and his local benefactions gratefully attested, by a century of the *Augustales* of Puteoli.[164] Another inscription from Puteoli records a *C. Ummidius Actius Anicetus pantomimus.*[165] He must surely be connected with Ummidia Quadratilla, who kept a troupe of pantomimists in her town house for private delectation and thereby earned the disapproval of the younger Pliny.[166] Her native district was Casinum in southern Latium; there her theatrical enthusiasms led her to construct an amphitheater for the

---

[162] CIL X, 1074 (= ILS 5053); and see also G. O. Onorato, *Iscrizioni Pompeiane* (Florence 1957), no. 91, with the commentary, pp. 152–153. The founder: Sen. *Quaest. Nat.* 7.32.3; Hanslik, *RE* 23 (1959), 2082–2083.

[163] On Paris, see L. Richardson, Jr., *Pompeii: The Casa dei Dioscuri and its Painters* (*MAAR* 23 [1955]), 93–95; but he should perhaps be identified instead with the Domitianic archmime: Onorato (see above, n. 162), no. 108, with the commentary, pp. 166–167. In Neapolis, the pantomimist P. Aelius Antigenides served as both *demarch* and *lauchelarch*: *IG* XIV, 737, on which see E. Lepore, in *Storia di Napoli* I, Società Editrice Storia di Napoli (Naples 1967), 300.

[164] *Eph. Epigr.* VIII, 369 (= ILS 5186); cf. Mommsen in *Röm. Mitt.* (1888), 79; Hanslik in *RE* 23 (1959), 2083.

[165] CIL X, 1946 (= ILS 5183).

[166] Pliny *Ep.* 7.24.4: *Habebat illa pantomimos fovebatque effusius, quam principi feminae convenit.* For Pliny's disapproval, cf. *Pan.* 46.4.

citizens' entertainment.[167] C. Ummidius Actius Anicetus was very likely a resident of Puteoli, where the substantial foreign population certainly included professional actors and musicians. M. Turranius Hermonicus *Puteolanus*, whose name proves him native to the East, was crowned in 79 for his achievements with the lyre at the Pythian games.[168] Local entertainers, as in the days of Sulla and Julius Caesar, included mimes.[169] Some might even have influence in high places. When Josephus arrived in Puteoli in 64, he struck up friendship with a certain Aliturus, a μιμολόγος of Jewish origin; he smoothed Josephus' approach to Poppaea.[170] Given such elements in her population, Puteoli's own introduction of Greek games in 138 should appear quite understandable, but all the more impressive: by now, it will be remembered, her economic ties with the East were weakening, and her prosperity was on the wane.[171]

In an excellent recent study of Roman Greece in the Age of Augustus, place was rightly found for a consideration of Neapolis. The author there observes that the professional foreign athletes who competed in the *Sebasta* carried a breath of the Greek East into the Hellenized sectors of Italy.[172] As has been seen in the foregoing paragraphs, that observation can be extended to include men of culture and of learning. They also traveled to the Bay of Naples from the civilized centers of the East; and, as they would readily have conceded, Campania's own cultural climate provided a chief incentive for the journey.

---

[167] *CIL* X, 5183 (= *ILS* 5628). For her family and connections, see Sherwin–White, *The Letters of Pliny*, 430; to which should now be added the observations of R. Syme, "People in Pliny," *JRS* 58 (1968), 150–151, with the references *ad loc.*

[168] *SIG* 817.

[169] See above, Chapter 2, p. 33; Chapter 3, p. 60. The bronze bust of C. *Norbanus Sorex, secundarum* (*sc. partium actor*: *CIL* X, 814 = *ILS* 5198), found in the temple of Isis at Pompeii, belongs not to Sullan times but to the epoch of Augustus: see A. De Franciscis, *Il Ritratto Romano a Pompei* (Naples 1951), 27–31; cf. Onorato (above, n. 162), 120–121 (no. 21).

[170] Joseph. *Vit.* 16.

[171] *Eusebeia*: Chapter 4, n. 154. Economic decline: see above, p. 138.

[172] Bowersock, *Augustus and the Greek World*, 83.

Hazards; Leisure and Politics

Certain recurrent hazards, both those of nature and those of man's devising, assailed the owners of properties in coastal Campania during the empire. Earthquakes were frequent. A severe earthquake affected the region of Neapolis and Pompeii in 62; the younger Seneca reported that at Neapolis, although losses sustained by the city were negligible, damage to private villas was serious and widespread.[173] Herculaneum and Pompeii were less fortunate; many of the major municipal monuments required radical structural renovation, and in some instances complete rebuilding.[174] In seventy-nine, alterations were still in progress when the cities were struck by disaster compared to which earthquakes were as nothing: in two days Mt. Vesuvius emptied her contents, heaping seven meters of porous *lapilli* and ashes upon Pompeii; Herculaneum was left buried beneath strata of lava which in places attained to a depth of twenty meters. It has been estimated that Pompeii lost three quarters of her population of 20,000 citizens; in Herculaneum, despite her situation at the very foot of the mountain, there seem to have been many fewer victims.[175] The Elder Pliny, *praefectus classis Misenensis*, hastened to the scene during the crisis, first making for the Herculanean villa of Rectina, wife of Cascus. But the boat could not safely approach; Pliny prudently altered his course to Stabiae, where he passed the night and ultimately expired from suffocation at the villa of his friend

[173] Regularity of earthquakes: Pliny *Ep.* 6.20.3. That of 62: Sen. *Quaest. Nat.* 6.1.2: *Neapolis quoque privatim multa, publice nihil amisit leniter ingenti malo perstricta, villae vero prorutae, passim sine iniuria tremuere.* For the date, see G. O. Onorato, "La data del terremoto di Pompei, 5 febbraio 62 d.Cr.," *Rendiconti Accad. dei Lincei, classe sci. mor.,* ser. 8, 4 (1949), 644–661. For a *turbo ventorum* which damaged Campanian villas in 65, cf. Tac. *Ann.* 16.13.1.

[174] Cf. Onorato (above, n. 173), 644–661 (correcting the date in Mau-Kelsey, *Pompeii* [New York 1899], 19); see further the excellent discussion by R. Étienne, *La Vie Quotidienne à Pompéi* (Paris 1966), 11–22. The temple of *Mater Deum* in Herculaneum was restored by Vespasian: *CIL* X, 1406.

[175] Pompeii: A. Rittman, *Pompeiana, Raccolta di Studi per il Secondo Centenario degli Scavi di Pompei* (Naples 1950), 456–474; R. Étienne (above, n. 174), 23–37. Herculaneum: Maiuri, *Herculaneum*[6] (tr. V. Priestly), *Istituto Poligrafico dello Stato* (Rome 1962), 7–8.

Pomponianus.[176] Stabiae recovered temporarily; Statius refers to the site as *Stabiae renatae*.[177]

Conspiracies were occasionally uncovered, and political suspects apprehended in villas on the Campanian coast. In forty-seven the commander of the Praetorian Guard, acting upon Claudius' orders, seized Valerius Asiaticus at Baiae and returned with him in chains to Rome.[178] As has been seen, the *sinus Baianus* witnessed Nero's matricidal contrivings of 59. The Baian estate of C. Calpurnius Piso figured prominently in the conspirators' machinations against Nero in 65: that lovely villa was actually singled out as the site for the emperor's assassination.[179] In the next year Petronius was at Cumae, where he was apprehended and, with wit and elegance, embraced a Stoic death.[180] The Campanian territory played some part in the maneuvers during the Civil War in 69.[181] And when four consulars were accused of conspiracy against Hadrian and executed by order of the senate in 118, L. Publilius Celsus, then at Baiae, was among the victims.[182]

On superficial inspection, the presence in coastal Campania of persons adjudged politically dangerous or suspicious might seem unexceptionable, a natural consequence of the popularity of the Bay of Naples among persons socially and politically prominent in Rome. In fact, Campania's towns offered a safe haven to persons in exile; for those attractive beaches stood beyond the one hundredth milestone from the city. Tacitus realized the implications of that location. In 56, senatorial spokesmen against the abuses of ex-slaves are made to observe with sarcasm that the former owners' only current legal reprisal was to dispatch a freedman

[176] Catalogue II, no. 35 (Pomponianus).

[177] Stat. *Silv.* 3.5.104. A few traces of construction subsequent to 79 have come to light in Pompeii; but she never regained her role of commercial emporium. Stabiae's recovery consisted largely of her assumption of control of trade routes previously commaded by Pompeii: see Di Capua, *RAAN* N.S. 19 (1938), 113–114; cf. Van Buren, *AJP* 51 (1930), 379–380.

[178] Catalogue II, no. 43 (Valerius Asiaticus).

[179] Catalogue II, no. 9 (C. Calpurnius Piso).

[180] Catalogue II, no. 32 (Petronius).

[181] Tac. *Hist.* 3.57–60.

[182] Catalogue II, no. 37 (L. Publilius Celsus).

beyond the hundredth milestone—to the Campanian beaches.[183] In the midst of such luxurious surroundings a man might almost be beguiled into forgetting his disgrace, the more so if he owed banishment to the whims of a despotic emperor. Thus, the father of Claudius Etruscus, a freedman from Smyrna who lived to see ten emperors and whose splendid career culminated in the award of equestrian status by Vespasian, was banished early in the reign of Domitian. Statius notes that he made for the *molles Campani litoris oras . . . atque hospes, non exsul erat.*[184]

There was excellent Republican precedent for Roman magistrates' looking toward the Greek world for refuge in times of crisis.[185] Neapolis, being Greek, occupied a special place in the eyes of the politically troubled; she was one of a few *civitates foederatae* to possess a mutual right of *exsilium*, which guaranteed asylum for political refugees.[186] Although there can be no question of the constitutional survival of such immunity after Neapolis became a *municipium*, the tradition was remembered and did not die: it will be recalled that at least two prominent politicians of the late Republic availed themselves of Neapolitan residence as their response to troubles in the capital.[187] Parallels can be adduced from later years. The father of the emperor Tiberius after the seige

[183] Tac. *Ann.* 13.26.3: *Quid enim aliud laeso patrono concessum quam ut centesimum ultra lapidem in oram Campaniae libertum releget?* The practice was doubtless widespread; Petronius satirizes it in *Satyricon* 53, where one of Trimalchio's slaves is described as *atriensis Baias relegatus.*

[184] Stat. *Silv.* 3.3.160–164: *. . . cumque horrida supra / aequora curarum socius procul Itala rura / linqueret, hic molles Campani litoris oras / et Diomedeas concedere iussus in arces / atque hospes, non exsul, erat.* Cf. *PIR*² C 763.

[185] Thus, Rutilius Rufus and Marcus Marcellus had retreated to Mitylene; T. Pomponius Atticus retired discreetly to Athens during the days of Cinna: see Bowersock, *Augustus and the Greek World*, 77. Cato went off to Rhodes in 49 B.C.: Catalogue I, no. 13 (L. Domitius Ahenobarbus). Milo enjoyed the mullets of Marseilles (Cass. Dio 40.54.3)—but Marseilles too was a fashionable Greek city: Strab. 4.1.5 (C 181); cited also by Bowersock, *Augustus and the Greek World*, 80.

[186] Polyb. 6.14.8 (on the Roman citizen's right to forestall capital sentence by voluntary exile): ἔστι δ' ἀσφάλεια τοῖς φεύγουσιν ἔν τε τῇ Νεαπολιτῶν καὶ Πραινεστίνων, ἔτι δὲ Τιβουρίνων πόλει, καὶ ταῖς ἄλλαις, πρὸς ἃς ἔχουσιν ὅρκια. See in general Walbank, *Historical Commentary on Polybius* I (Oxford 1957), ad loc. (p. 683); and for Neapolis, Sartori, *Problemi*, 45; F. de Martino, *PdP* fasc. 25–27 (1952), 324.

[187] Namely, P. Sulla and the family of L. Domitius Ahenobarbus: Catalogue I, nos. 12, 13.

of Perusia in 41 B.C. escaped first to Praeneste, later to Neapolis.[188] When it was discovered that Fannius Caepio had conspired against Augustus, the author of that plot found it expedient to flee the city. An anecdote of Macrobius reveals that Caepio made first for his father's villa in the Laurentian territory; subsequently a loyal slave hid him from the authorities in Neapolis, where neither threats nor bribes could induce the servant to betray his master.[189] Under Nero, Antistia Pollitta had witnessed the assassination of her husband Rubellius Plautus; in 65 her father L. Antistius Vetus was in grave danger. At the bidding of the father, his daughter journeyed to Neapolis, where Nero was currently in residence; perhaps Antistius hoped that supplications in that city would be more likely to secure his pardon. If so, he was disappointed. From Neapolis word came back to the parent at Formiae: he should abandon hope and accept the inevitable.[190]

But if some persons were obliged to select Campania's coast during political upheavals, others made a deliberate choice to live permanently among her blandishments. That way of existence could seem altogether preferable even to the tangible distinctions of a political career. To be sure, there was widespread gratitude to Augustus who, in Tacitus' words, *cunctos dulcedine otii pellexit*.[191] But the principate, far from bringing an end to political uncertainties, merely shifted them to a different sphere: scions of the consular families of the late Republic might resent the fact that

---

[188] Suet. *Tib.* 4.2.

[189] Macrob. *Sat.* 1.11.21: *Caepionem quoque qui in Augusti necem fuerat animatus, postquam detecto scelere damnatus est, servus ad Tiberim in cista detulit pervectumque Ostiam inde in agrum Laurentum ad patris villam nocturno itinere perduxit. Cumis deinde navigationis naufragio una expulsum dominum Neapoli dissimulanter occuluit, exceptusque a centurione nec pretio nec minis ut dominum proderet potuit adduci.* According to Cass. Dio (54.3.3–8) the conspiracy occurred in 22 B.C.; Dio's testimony has recently been vindicated, and the case for 23 B.C. effectively demolished, by M. Swan, "The Consular *Fasti* of 23 B.C. and the Conspiracy of Varro Murena," *HSCP* 71 (1966), 235–247. Della Corte (*CeA*[3], 432) suggests that Caepio was one of the owners of a famous villa near Boscoreale, but this is most unlikely: see the discussion by H. Bloch in P. Lehmann, *Roman Wall Paintings from Boscoreale* (Cambridge 1953), 214–217.

[190] Tac. *Ann.* 16.10–11.1.

[191] Tac. *Ann.* 1.2.1.

an emperor, or the creatures who had his ear, controlled and sometimes capriciously blocked the avenues of political advancement. Not all men were willing or able to display the patience of an Agricola or a Manius Lepidus, who learned to steer that prudent and delicate course *inter abruptam contumaciam et deforme obsequium*.[192] The alternative was *quies*, or else to renounce politics altogether. P. Servilius Vatia, *nulla alia re quam otio notus*, chose the latter course. He attained the praetorship in 25 B.C., then retired permanently to his Campanian villa until his death late in the reign of Tiberius.[193] This was proof to the younger Seneca that Vatia knew only how to hide, not how to live. But when others were ruined by ill-chosen political friendships or animosities people cried out *o Vatia, solus scis vivere*.[194]

Viewed from Seneca's Stoic perspective, Vatia's choice had been for a life not *otiosa* but *ignava*. Augustus contemptuously named one of Capreae's adjacent isles ἀπραγόπολις, such was the *desidia* of his Roman companions who sojourned there; that energetic *princeps*, even on holiday in the midst of Greek surroundings, could distinguish leisure from lassitude.[195] But, as was seen above in a discussion of Cicero's reactions to the leisure of his final years,[196] the line cannot be drawn so confidently in every case. Bitterness in the face of the frustrations of political life, as well as a strong personal desire to live as he liked, influenced Tiberius' decision to withdraw to Capreae; which was the controlling factor cannot be easily determined. Bruttius Praesens, indolently roving Campania and Lucania in 103/104, seemed to the younger Pliny to be too much caught up in the delights of leisure, too little concerned with his political career; Pliny implies that Praesens

[192] Tac. *Ann.* 4.20.5; cf. *Agr.* 42.4–5; T. Eprius Marcellus: *Hist.* 4.8. Cf. Memmius Regulus under Nero: *Ann.* 14.47.1–2.

[193] Sen. *Ep.* 55.3; cf. Catalogue II, no. 39 (P. Servilius Vatia). Not so very different is *quies*, the pursuit of equestrian advancement free from the dangers of a senatorial career: see Syme, *AJP* 58 (1937), 8–9: Sherwin–White, *The Letters of Pliny*, 118 (*Ep.* 1.14.5).

[194] Sen. *Ep.* 55.4.

[195] Suet. *Aug.* 98.4 (quoted above, Chapter 4, n. 10).

[196] Chapter 3, pp. 70–72.

was an Epicurean, and cautioned that pleasures might pall if constantly indulged.[197] But Praesens was capable of more energy than Pliny implied. Here is the rare instance of political accomplishment superseding Campanian retirement, for an inscription discloses that Praesens belatedly achieved a brilliant career under Hadrian, attaining a first consulship in 124 and a second under Pius in 139.[198] We unfortunately know nothing of the reasons behind a certain Stertinius' retirement to Baiae; but since Aurelius, who records the fact, mentions Tiberius and Capreae in the same context, political frustrations may reasonably be presumed.[199] These certainly lay behind senatorial *secessus* in Campania under Aurelian. The author of the biography of Tacitus quotes from a joyous letter written by Claudius Sapilianus to Cereius Maecianus upon the accession of the aged Tacitus.[200] Certain excerpts are revealing: "The senate is restored to its ancient position. We now create the emperors . . . away with retirement to Baiae and Puteoli. Present yourself in the city, present yourself in the senate house."[201] *Mutatis mutandis*, these sentiments would certainly have commended themselves to Cicero, anxious in his final years to renounce his learned studies and to resume the political role of earlier, happier times. *Negotium* will normally be found to take precedence to *otium* in a Roman senator's mind.

---

[197] Pliny *Ep.* 7.3.3.
[198] Catalogue II, no. 7 (C. Bruttius Praesens).
[199] Catalogue II, no. 40 (Stertinius).
[200] *S.H.A. Tac.* 19.3.
[201] *Ibid.*, 19.5: *Abice Baianos Puteolanosque secessus, da te urbi, da te Curiae. Floret Roma, floret tota res publica. Imperatores damus, principes facimus; possumus et prohibere qui coepimus facere. Dictum sapienti sat est.* "Cereius Maecianus" cannot be admitted to the catalogue of Campanian property owners. His name, as well as that of his correspondent, is almost certainly a fabrication: "Maecianus" is a recurrent and favorite *cognomen* in the *S.H.A.*, and "Sapilianus" seems possibly a perversion of "Sapidianus," *Vicarius* of Africa in the year 399; see R. Syme, "The Bogus Names in the *Historia Augusta*," *Antiquitas*, 4te Reihe (Beiträge zur *Historia-Augusta* Forschung [Bonn 1966]), 260, 265. But the reference to senatorial retirement to Baiae and Puteoli ought not therefore to be impugned; on the contrary, the very casualness of its introduction is itself some guarantee of authenticity, and the notion is entirely consonant with the general reverence towards the senate revealed so consistently in the *S.H.A.* See Syme, "Bogus Names," 270–272.

Luxury Expenditure and Local Conditions

Thus *peregrinatio*, essentially a social and cultural phenomenon, has been examined in its Campanian setting. It may now be profitable, by drawing together some of the evidence discussed above in different contexts, to confront the larger implications raised by the presence of this privileged society and its villas on the Bay of Naples. What did this villa elite mean in social and economic terms? In particular, how far did this luxury expenditure affect local conditions? It must be admitted at the outset that answers to such questions are bound to seem speculative: the quantity of Campanian evidence after the Flavian period is too small, and its quality too uneven, to permit other than tentative conclusions. But the outlines of answers may nonetheless be traced, and thereby an attempt may be made to visualize local conditions within the wider context of known historical developments.

It might seem, *prima facie*, that owners of luxury villas played a major role in the economic life of the region and influenced also the pattern of social relationships, particularly in the coastal towns. After all, permanent residents, such as Silius Italicus, satisfied their demands for consumer and luxury goods in local markets, increasing, in the construction and decoration of their villas, the profits of the builders and *marmorarii* attested in local inscriptions. Rich Roman proprietors and occasional sojourners enjoyed vastly improved communications between Rome and the Campanian coast after Flavian and Trajanic efforts on the great roadways, first to Puteoli and subsequently on to Neapolis. Pollius Felix, although a local proprietor, was prodigal with his great riches: he contributed to the beautification of both Neapolis and his native Puteoli.[202] Social historians have detected an increase in population in the coastal cities of Neapolis and Puteoli through the Flavian period and beyond; can one not fairly presume some causal

---

[202] Silius Italicus: Catalogue II, no. 12. *Marmorarii*: see above, n. 65. For the *Via Domitiana* and the *Via Antiniana* (a modern name), see Chapter 4, pp. 102–103. Pollius Felix: Catalogue II, no. 34; his largesse: Statius *Silv.* 3.1.91–93.

connection between population growth and the large numbers of luxury villas on the coasts and hills?

Caution is required; we shall do well to reserve judgment. In the first place, it should here be re-emphasized that these villas were essentially non-productive estates, designed not for *fructus* but (to draw again from the terminology of late jurists) for *voluptas*. Moreover, their owners, with but few exceptions, were city-dwellers who expended their energies in Rome and owed their wealth almost exclusively to landed investments outside the coastal territory: the wife of Bruttius Praesens, it is a fair presumption, had estates elsewhere in Campania; other owners possessed lands beyond her borders, often in the provinces. It is not in the coastal *villae pseudourbanae* that one should look for large scale agricultural productions, tenant farmers, or the great households of rural slaves; on the contrary, it is doubtful in the extreme whether these estates contributed anything of substance to Campania's economic health.[203]

It should next be asked: how much time did these owners spend during any given year in their luxurious palaces on the Bay of Naples? The aged and disaffected who lived permanently in their villas were relatively few in number; the majority of owners were busily engaged in their affairs elsewhere. Here an epigram of Martial's provides evidence of the first importance. Having listed the charms of a seaside villa at Formiae, the poet then observes that the villa's owner is seldom in residence, so closely is he chained to the pursuits of the city; Martial finally exclaims, "Happy gate keepers and bailiffs; the delights provided for your masters are enjoyed by you."[204] There can be no doubt that the villas in Campania too stood vacant for large parts of the year, with no more than the *vilicus* and a few slaves to tend them. Furthermore,

---

[203] For juristic definitions of luxury estates, cf. *Digesta* 50.16.198 (quoted above, Chapter 1, n. 41). The estates of the wife of Bruttius Praesens are inferred from Pliny *Ep.* 7.3.1. Cf. Catalogue II, no. 7.

[204] Mart. 10.30.25–29: *Frui sed istis quando, Roma, permittis? / Quot Formianos imputat dies annus / negotiosis rebus urbis haerenti? / O ianitores vilicique felices! / Dominis parantur ista, serviunt vobis.*

on those occasions when the master came for visits, he brought with him a company of city slaves and regularly imported from the Roman markets his own exotic foods, instead of relying upon produce available in the local towns: Martial's poems bear frequent witness to both practices.[205] Unusual indeed was the coastal estate which yielded produce sufficient even for it master's needs: Faustinus' villa at Baiae interested the poet precisely because its character differed so sharply from that of most *praedia suburbana*; and even on that model farm the master had taken pains to secure all the comforts of the city. A company of sleek town-bred slaves had accompanied him from Rome.[206]

Even though the luxury estates only rarely housed their affluent owners, it may well be that in indirect ways those owners contributed to regional economic decline. Already in late Julio-Claudian times there are signs at Capua of economic stagnation, consisting principally in the disappearance of the local middle class landowners of the type familiar from Pompeii. These conditions accelerated, as has been seen, under the Flavians. Pompeii and Herculaneum found it difficult to recover from the earthquake of 62, and after the catastrophe of 79 neither city was rebuilt, despite the prompt intervention of the government—striking testimony, as Rostovtzeff has emphasized, to the decline of economic forces in Campania as a whole. Nor was the process arrested, so far as can be determined from fragmentary evidence, under the Antonines, when alimentary schemes and imperial benefactions at Capua suggest stagnant conditions in the local economy.[207] Now, it is a reasonable inference that this stagnation was indirectly abetted by economic parasites like Antistius Vetus, Pollius Felix, Julius

[205] E.g., Mart. 3.47; 7.31; 12.72. See further W. E. Heitland, *Agricola* (Cambridge 1921), 307–312, where it is rightly stressed (307) that Martial is a reliable witness for agricultural conditions.

[206] Faustinus' farm: Catalogue II, no. 19; and see also the observations of Heitland, *Agricola*, 309–310.

[207] Capua's decline: Frederiksen, *Rep. Cap.*., 124. Flavian conditions: above, Chapter 4, p. 100; Rostovtzeff, *SEHRE*[2], 194–195. Benefactions of the Antonines in Capua: *CIL* X, 3832, discussed above, Chapter 4, n. 151. Alimentary schemes: see above, Chapter 4, p. 106, and R. Duncan-Jones, *PBSR* N.S. 20 (1965), pp. 246 (no. 637), 296.

Menecrates, and Bruttius Praesens. These men, no different from the luxury-loving speculators whom Cicero knew in Campania in 63 B.C., helped to drive off the holders of smaller properties by accumulating great farms in Campania's cultivable regions, and subsequently used their riches to support their luxury establishments on the coast.[208]

Population increased in certain of Campania's coastal cities; to what extent was this process dependent upon the local presence of luxury villas, their owners, and their guests? Certainly in Neapolis, and doubtless too at Baiae (where, however, the evidence is insufficient to permit a close analysis), the two factors were to some degree connected, resulting in social and economic consequences of significance. Imperial Neapolis constitutes the paradigmatic case of an economy and society based upon luxury and large consumption; her economic life was rooted in her attractions as a residential and tourist center—for Roman grandees, participants and spectators at her various contests, and cultivated foreigners. When farmers on the small productive estates outside the city felt increasingly the pressures of agricultural crisis, or suffered losses from earthquake and eruption, they migrated as a matter of course to the city of Neapolis, where (like Statius' father) they helped to supply those goods and services upon which tourist centers thrive. To this extent the increased density of the city's population and the luxury economy were indubitably linked. But the steady influx of new citizens sufficed neither to reinvigorate the local economy nor to reestablish a healthy equilibrium in social life. On the contrary, the uniquely Greek civic institutions, whose flourishing condition Strabo had noted in Augustan Neapolis, show signs of gradual debasement and decay. Numerous acts of imperial munificence, recorded from Flavian times, led increasingly to public inertia; under the Antonines came a major change in the city's status; by the third century the Latin language had gained ascendancy over Greek in official documents. The pantomimist P. Aelius Anti-

[208] Catalogue I, no. 2; II, nos. 34, 21, 7. Cicero on coastal Campanian luxury: *Leg. Agr.* 2.78 (quoted above, Chapter I, n. 48).

genides, it will be recalled, became *demarch* and *lauchelarch* in the Antonine Age—an excellent indication of the contemporary alterations in the social fabric in the city.[209]

At neighboring Cumae and Puteoli, however, the local effects of villa owners, tourists, and their wealth are much less clearly visible. After ninety-five, Cumae was located upon the major highway between Rome and Puteoli; yet lines of Juvenal's reveal that early in the second century her population had dwindled and that the city was in decline.[210] Puteoli grew steadily more affluent and populous until the middle years of the second century; gradually thereafter her prosperity waned, until in late antiquity her citizens found their way to Neapolis, whose walls were more strongly fortified. Nevertheless Puteoli's rise was neither accelerated, nor her fall arrested, by the presence of Roman luxury. Her economic strength was grounded not upon tourism but upon commerce, and upon the industries connected with overseas trade. So long as goods from the provinces poured into her harbor, her economic position was secure; completion of the *Via Domitiana* doubtless brought her an influx of new citizens from Capua, whose own industries and signs of wealth were dealt a further blow when she was by-passed by the traffic between Rome and the Campanian coast. After Trajan built his new harbor, and Ostia in turn monopolized the eastern trade and received the grain fleet, Puteoli's days of greatest affluence were at an end.[211] A graphic illustration of her reduced circumstances is contained in an inscription from 174 which has already been cited in a different context.[212] Luxury expenditures and consumption by villa owners certainly

[209] On economic and social conditions in imperial Neapolis, see above all E. Lepore, *Storia di Napoli* I, *Società Editrice Storia di Napoli* (Naples 1967), 289–329. Population figures and decay of civic institutions: *ibid.*, pp. 297 (with n. 12), 300. *Colonia Aurelia Augusta Antoniniana Felix Neapolis*: above, Chapter 4, p. 105, and n. 157. Decline of Greek: see the texts collected by Nenci, *PdP* fasc. 25–27 (1952), 403–404; Lepore, *Storia di Napoli*, 289–290; and see also above, n. 121. P. Aelius Antigenides: see above, n. 163.

[210] Juv. 3.1–3.

[211] Puteoli's prosperity and decline: above, p. 138. Her new citizens from Capua: Frederiksen, *Rep. Cap.*, 124.

[212] The letter of the Tyrians in 174 is translated above ,n. 105. See also Frederiksen *RE* 23 (1959), 2045.

continued; surprisingly, they are attested even during the crisis of the third century, and again in the days of Symmachus and Ammianus Marcellinus. The entertainers and philosophers from the East continued also to find the city congenial. But the economic effects of such expenditures were trivial compared to the commercial wealth which Eastern trade brought into the harbor; and foreign traders, rather than foreign *studiosi*, gave Puteoli her cosmopolitan social character.[213]

Those conclusions will not seem surprising: the luxurious habits of the rich can hardly have affected, to any appreciable degree, the directions in which the economic and social forces of the Campanian region were tending. Indeed, these local forces derived their momentum from the more general pressures affecting Italy as a whole. Throughout the Italian peninsula during the first two centuries of the Christian era, production and industry declined as a direct consequence of the economic exploitation of the provinces. Agricultural crises were chronic; they in turn prompted a shift of population away from the country towns and towards the cities, which showed a corresponding density of population. Italy's harbors, through which the provincial imports poured, attained new heights of prosperity. At the same time, wealth was being transferred steadily from the private sector into the control of the emperors; imperial subventions, public works, and benefactions in the cities reflected the transition. This imperial munificence helped to promote, in turn, the decay of civic institutions in local towns and led to the gradual blurring even of regional differences and distinctions: thus the Romanization of Italy proceeded. The Bay of Naples illustrates clearly the working of most of these processes; indeed, it provides excellent local evidence for the irresistibility of their force. The privileged classes who sought out Campanian shores were quite powerless to influence the course of change.

---

[213] Later luxury at Puteoli: *S.H.A. Tacitus* 19.5 (quoted above, n. 201); Amm. Marc. 28.4.18 (quoted above, n. 10). On the foreign population of Puteoli and its distribution, see above, pp. 138–139; cf. Frederiksen, *RE* 23 (1959), 2050–2051 for social patterns. A *marmorarius* belonged to the *collegium* of *Augustales*: *CIL* X, 1873. Entertainers and philosophers: above, n. 155, and pp. 146–152.

EPILOGUE

O. E. Schmidt believed that three basic considerations—economic, hygienic, and "spiritual-aesthetic"—led to the development of *peregrinatio* among the Roman aristocracy.[1] A confluence of these factors (the tendency to identify wealth with landed property, the desire to escape the hot, crowded, and unsanitary conditions of the city, and a heightened sense of individualism in private life) may be detected in Campania and elsewhere from the days of the earliest pleasure villas to the days of Symmachus.[2] However, Schmidt's views fail in one important respect to do full justice to the Romans who built their villas on the Bay of Naples: place must be found for a consideration of Hellenic influences because Greeks are inextricably linked with each of the major themes developed in the foregoing pages.

In the first place, when luxury invaded the Roman world, it came not from the Gallic north, Africa, or Spain, but precisely from the civilized centers of the Greek East, *fons et origo* of all manner of delicate and pleasurable refinements. The Romans were entranced and responsive. Secondly, although both then and subsequently it was the fashion to deride the Greek nation as the collective embodiment of *mollitia* and *otium*, the pleasures of Hellenic ease, once sampled by the Roman senatorial class, were found far too attractive to renounce. Already in the days of Scipio and Laelius *negotium* and *officium* were yielding, at carefully specified intervals and under certain conditions, to periods of leisure and

[1] Schmidt, 330: "Das Bedürfnis nach einer ausgebildeten Villeggiatur wurzelte aber, wie ich meine, in drei Gruppen von Ursachen, in wirtschaftlichen, sanitären und geistig-ästhetischen."

[2] See Aul. Gell. 1.2.1–2, the Athenian estate of Herodes Atticus; cited also by Van Buren, "*Villa,*" *RE* 8 A (1958), 2149, to illustrate the manifold attractions of villa life.

relaxation. "Intervals" and "conditions" are the operative words.
A total embrace of leisure was always deemed incompatible with
senatorial *dignitas*, but when a man mixed *negotium* and *otium*, no
opprobrium need be attached: two Calpurnii Pisones thus kept
their political and private lives in successful balance; it was considered one of the distinguishing characteristics of Neapolis that
Romanus honos and *Graia licentia* could commingle to mutual
advantage.[3] Third, Greek tutors and house philosophers, as well as
resident Hellenic *studiosi*, were an important part of villa life in
Campania from the time of Cornelia, mother of the Gracchi, until
well into the imperial era. For alongside Greek luxury and leisure,
Greek learning flourished in the towns and Roman villas on the
Bay of Naples. Indeed, the three factors are intimately connected:
erudition demanded leisurely and luxurious conditions as its own
peculiar requisites for nutriment and growth.[4] With the phrase
hospita Musis otia Silius Italicus explicitly links learning to leisure in
imperial Neapolis.[5]

Once the younger Pliny, upon discovering a surprising degree
of cultivation in an acquaintance who had eschewed a public career
and embraced the life of leisure, was prompted to remark:
Athenis vivere hominem, non in villa putes.[6] But in fact, among cultivated Romans with a taste for leisured luxury, relatively few made
the decision to live permanently abroad: all foreign refinements
could be savored privately in the villa. There, if so disposed, a
proprietor might—with his works of art and his library, on his
walks along porticoes and in his gardens, in his cuisine and conversation—nearly recapture the atmosphere of Athens. After all,
ancient Rome possessed neither Stoa nor Academy; revealingly,

---

[3] Vell. Pat. 2.98.3 (on the son of the consul of 58 B.C.): *vix quemquam reperiri posse,
qui aut otium validius diligat aut facilius sufficiat negotio; Laus Pisonis* 81–177 (on the Neronian
consular). Neapolis: Stat. *Silv.* 3.5.93–94: *quid laudem litus libertatemque Menandri | quam
Romanus honos et Graia licentia miscent?*

[4] Cf. Bowersock, *Augustus and the Greek World*, 75: "erudition was nourished in an
atmosphere of luxury and leisure, time to savor experience and then to reflect upon it."

[5] Sil. Ital. 12.27–39.

[6] Plin. *Ep.* 7.25.4.

Cicero referred to his Cumaean villa as his *Academia*.[7] Indeed, the villa, a distinctly Roman invention,[8] holds a place of no meager significance in Roman social and cultural history. In these fixed seats many of the best traditions of Old Greece were transplanted. They enjoyed renewed vigor on Roman soil. And for this fusion of Greek and Roman culture, conditions were particularly propitious in and near the cities on the Bay of Naples, where Hellenic institutions had long pervaded the municipal structures and Romans were thus encouraged to imbibe Greek culture and even to adopt Greek ways: here Greek *otium* and Roman villas enjoyed their greatest vogue. In these pages the aim has been to identify the owners of those villas and to describe the quality of that leisure, and thereby to illustrate one aspect of the social and cultural history of ancient Rome.

[7] On private education and Roman villas in the second century B.C., see above, Chapter I, p. 15 with n. 65. Cicero: Catalogue I, no. 43b. In the time of Hadrian C. Claudius Pollio Frugianus, who belonged to that most distinguished intellectual institution, the Alexandrian *mouseion*, donated a notable work of art from his private villa to the sanctuary of Apollo at Cumae: see A. De Franciscis, "Chi era C. Claudio Pollione Frugiano?", *Mélanges André Piganiol* I (Paris 1966), 229–232; and cf. the important remarks of L. Robert, *Revue des Études Grecques* 80 (1967), 567, together with De Franciscis' second thoughts, *RAAN* N.S. 42 (1967), 155–158.

[8] Stressed also by Van Buren, *RE* 8 A (1958), 2142.

Appendix · *Select Bibliography* · *Index*

APPENDIX

CATALOGUE I · *The Roman Owners of Pleasure Villas or Private Houses on the Bay of Naples, CA. 75–31 B.C.*

The following Catalogue purports to be a complete list, for the Ciceronian age, of Romans prominent in the political and social life of the capital, who owned villas or houses on the Bay of Naples. Freedmen (e.g. M. Tullius Tiro) and persons apparently native to the Campanian *municipia*, however great their local influence (e.g. Cluvius and Vestorius of Puteoli) have not been included (for Tiro, see below, 43 c; Cluvius *et al.* are discussed above, Chapter 3 pp. 52–54, and n. 82).

Names of owners are presented in alphabetical order according to *gentilicia*. For although the Catalogue embraces a period of fifty years and two generations of Roman social life, a chronological listing is impracticable. The earliest references to a villa rarely include information pertinent to the date of acquisition, nor do career statistics (e.g., consular dates) of near contemporaries provide useful clues to so variable and private a matter as the year in which an estate was purchased.

Owners' names are followed on the same line first by the Roman name of the geographical district in which the estate was located. The ancient designation is somewhat misleading in the case of Cumae. The *Cumanum* of Cicero lay near the Lucrine Lake on the *Sinus Puteolanus*. It was therefore nearer to Puteoli and Baiae than to the *municipium* of Cumae, situated northwest of Misenum—thus beyond the natural northern boundary of the Bay of Naples. Next follows the year in which the villa is first mentioned; these and all other dates, unless otherwise noted, are B.C. The ancient *testimonia* are then presented, the most important quoted in full. Discussion of this evidence is contained in the ensuing paragraph(s). Different villas belonging to the same owner are designated a), b), and so on.

1. C. Anicius   Cumae or Puteoli   55

   Q.Fr. 2.8.3 (T &P 123): *Apud Anicium videbimus ut paratum sit* (from Cumae, 55).

   When Cicero's friend M. Marius visited him in the only partially completed *Cumanum* in 55, Cicero wrote to Quintus saying that he intended to put Marius up, for his comfort's sake, with Anicius. Of Anicius little is known (cf. Klebs, *RE* 1 [1894], 2196), but he must have had property nearby. He was a senator (Broughton, *MRR* II, 487), and it should probably therefore be presumed that he was a sojourner from Rome rather than a local man (but *Anicia* occurs twice in an inscription from Puteoli: *CIL* X, 2321). He was on good terms with Cicero, *Fam.* 7.26 (T&P 94), 12.21 (T&P 698); and a friend of P. Cornelius Lentulus Spinther (see below, no. 10), and of M. Fabius Gallus (*Fam.* 7.26; see below, no. 14).

2. C. Antistius Vetus (*cos. suff.* 30)   Cumae   imperial times

Pliny *NH* 31.6: *dignum memoratu, villa est ab Averno lacu Puteolos tendentibus imposita litori, celebrata porticu ac nemore, quam vocabat M. Cicero Academiam ab exemplo Athenarum; ibi compositis voluminibus eiusdem nominis . . . huius in parte prima exiguo post obitum ipsius Antistio Vetere possidente eruperunt fontes calidi perquam salubres oculis, celebrati carmine Laureae Tulli, qui fuit e libertis eius, ut protinus noscatur etiam ministeriorum haustus ex illa maiestate ingenii. Ponam enim ipsum carmen, ubique et non ibi tantum legi dignum: ' . . . atque Academiae celebratam nomine villam | nunc reparat cultu sub potiore Vetus.'* See below, no. 43 b.

For the career of Vetus and a suggestion as to how he came to acquire Cicero's *Cumanum*, see above, Chapter 3, p. 70; cf. *PIR*² A 770. Antistii are frequently attested in the inscriptions of Campania; see *CIL* X, index, p. 1025; *AJA* 2 (1898), 375 (Antistii at Puteoli); and the name Antistius Vetus has appeared among the graffiti of Pompeii: *Not. d. Sc.* (1933), 290, no. 136, included by Groag among the *addenda* in *PIR*² II, p. xiii. For a contemporary L. Antistius Campanus, see Frederiksen, *Rep. Cap.*, 119, n. 207. This branch of the *gens* may well have been local; but for a senatorial L. Antistius C.f. Vetus from Gabii, cf. *ILS* 948, with Dessau's note *ad loc.* Syme (*RR*, 499) notes that the family of Vetus, elevated to nobility by Augustus, lasted down to the consul of A.D. 96 in direct succession. But ownership of the *Cumanum* cannot be traced after Cicero's successor. For Ciceronian *iugera* later bought by Silius Italicus somewhere in the vicinity, see Catalogue II, no. 12.

3. M. Antonius (*cos.* II, 34)   Misenum   49

Att. 10.8.10 (T&P 392; SB 199): *Cum Antonio item est agendum . . . is ad Misenum VI Non. venturus dicebatur . . .* (May 2, 49); *Att.* 10.13.1 (T&P 399; SB 205): *ad villam eius* (May 7, 49, from Cumae); *Att.* 15.1a.2 (T&P 730; SB 377): *venit enim Misenum cum ego essem in Pompeiano . . .* (Puteoli, May

17, 44); cf. *Att.* 10.16.5 (T &P 402; SB 208); *Phil.* 2.73: *Qui risus hominum, tantam esse tabulam, tam varias, tam multas possessiones, ex quibus praeter partem Miseni nihil erat, quod, qui auctionaretur, posset suum dicere; Phil.* 2.48: *Domum dico? Quid erat in terris ubi in tuo pedem poneres praeter unum Misenum . . .*

The villa of Antony belonged earlier to his grandfather, the orator, and to his father, M. Antonius Creticus; see above, Chapter 2, pp. 21–22; it is one of the few examples of an estate which appears to have been handed down in direct succession for three generations (for another, see Catalogue II, no. 39). After Antonius' death in the east in 30 (Groebe, *RE* 1 [1894], 2611, no. 30), the villa, last mentioned in Cicero's 2nd Philippic, presumably became part of the imperial domain. Nothing is known of its location (see Beloch, *Campanien,*[2] 199); of its appointments only the bath is mentioned: *Att.* 10.13.1 (T &P 399; SB 205).

4. (?) Q. Caecilius Metellus Celer (*cos.* 60)   Baiae

Varro *Rust.* 1.13.7: *Nunc contra villam urbanam quam maximam ac politissimam habeant dant operam ac cum Metelli ac Luculli villis pessimo publico aedificatis certant*; Cic. *Cael.* 38, for which see below on Clodia (no. 7), wife of Metellus Celer.

5. L. Calpurnius Piso Caesoninus (*cos.* 58)   Herculaneum   *ca.* 55

The writings of the Epicurean Philodemus of Gadara, comprising two thirds of the Epicurean works deciphered from carbonized rolls of papyrus discovered at Herculaneum in 1752, were found in the library of a splendid Roman *villa pseudourbana*, which had been built unquestionably around the middle of the first century B.C. (see Mustilli, *RAAN* N.S. 31 [1956], 77–97; the villa is still underground). From Cicero's *in Pisonem* it is quite clear that L. Calpurnius Piso Caesoninus (*cos.* 58), the father of Caesar's wife Calpurnia, was the chief patron of Philodemus (Cic. *Pis.* 68). Thus it could be conjectured long ago that the villa at Herculaneum (the so-called "villa dei papiri") belonged to Piso; this view, revived by Comparetti, inpugned by Mommsen and, on his authority, long resisted in Germany and elsewhere, was convincingly re-argued in 1940 by H. Bloch, who examined afresh all the relevant literary and archaeological evidence (*AJA* 44 [1940], 490–493; *q.v.* also for the history of the controversy and earlier bibliography). Among the spectacular collection of bronzes recovered from the villa are three stylistically similar busts of Epicureans: Epicurus, Hermarchos, and the more obscure Zeno of Sidon, whose inclusion in the series is best explained by his having been the teacher of Philodemus (D. Comparetti, *La Villa Ercolanese dei Pisoni* [Turin 1883], 4; plate XII, nos. 4, 7-9; Bloch, *AJA* 44 [1940], 491). The papyri themselves (though only a small proportion of the more than 1000 rolls discovered have in fact been opened, read, and published) corroborate the conjecture: one fragment seems to link Philodemos with Herculaneum, and Croenert has shown that marginal notes from one papyrus were written into the text of another (*Pap. Herc.* 312, on which see above, Chapter 3, n. 95, and refs. *ad loc.*)

Some scholars remain unconvinced. While admitting that "the disproportion of Philodemos' writings is remarkable," Nisbet holds that the works might have belonged to "any Epicurean centre" (R. G. M. Nisbet, ed., *Cicero, in L. Calpurnium Pisonem oratio* [Oxford 1961], 188). This extreme caution is unwarranted. In the first place, the collection of Philodemus' writings, deliberately compiled, was still intact in 79 A.D., over a century after Philodemus' death; and as Bloch (*Gnomon* 37 [1965], 561) has subsequently observed, "This attitude of respect is best explained if the villa was still in the hands of the same family in 79." In the second place, Nisbet was unaware of evidence which links Piso with Herculaneum. L. R. Taylor was the first to point out that Piso's tribe was the Menenia, into which Herculaneum was placed after the Social War: and Miss Taylor has suggested that "the assignment of Herculaneum and its region to (Piso's) tribe resulted from special associations with the district" (L. R. Taylor, *Voting Districts*, pp. 200, 311). It thus seems highly probable that the villa at Herculaneum was constructed by Piso and the library deliberately placed by him at Philodemus' disposition: the varied testimony of art, archaeology, papyri, and classical texts here combines in almost unique fashion to support a conjecture first advanced nearly two hundred years ago and increasingly strengthened by the work of successive generations of scholars. Further excavations at Herculaneum may yet unearth inscriptions with clinching evidence; we should like especially to know to whom the villa passed after the death of Caesoninus. Until then however, we may presume with Bloch (*AJA* 44 [1940], 493) that *Pisones* retained possession.

6. C. Claudius Marcellus (*cos.* 50)   Liternum   49

Att. 10.13.2 (T &P 399; SB 205): *Servius prid. Non. Mai. Minturnis mansisse dicitur, hodie in Liternino mansurus apud C. Marcellum*; May 7, 49.

Marcellus, a cousin of the two Marcelli who were the consuls of 51 and 49, was Octavia's first husband and father of Augustus' heir apparent, whose death Virgil celebrated in *Aeneid* 6; for details, see Münzer, *RE* 3 (1899), 2734–2736, no. 216. Though a partisan of Pompey, he appears to have remained neutral during the civil wars (*Att.* 10.15.2 [T&P 401; SB 207], 10.12.3 [T&P 397; SB 203]), and probably kept to his villa in isolated Liternum—we hear of no other villas here during the Ciceronian age. He maintained good terms with Caesar, as later with Octavian; see *Att.* 15.12.2 (T&P 745; SB 390). He died in 40; it is not known what became of the *Literninum.*

7. Clodia (wife of Metellus Celer, *cos.* 60)   Baiae   56

Cic. *Cael.* 38: . . . *cuius in hortos, domum, Baias iure suo libidines omnium commearent* . . .

When Caelius became Clodia's lover (by 58: R. G. Austin, *Pro Caelio*[3] [Oxford 1960] introduction, p. vi), the affair flourished in Clodia's town house (*Cael.* 55, 57), in her pleasure gardens on the Tiber (36, 38), and at Baiae (27: . . . *qui Baias viderit* . . ., 35: . . . *Accusatores quidem* . . . *Baias* . . . *iactant,* 49: . . . *si in Baiarum illa celebritate* . . .). In these three passages Baiae = "the town of Baiae," but the form *Baiae,—arum,* in Cicero, is also used to mean "a villa at Baiae." While villas are ordinarily designated by means of a neuter adjective formed from the name of the nearest town (thus regularly *Cumanum, Puteolanum, Neapolitanum, Pompeianum*), villas at Baiae and Misenum are *Baias, Misenum*; for the meaning of *Baias* in 38 Austin rightly compares *Att.* 11.6.6 (T&P 418; SB 217): *Lentulus Hortensi domum sibi et Caesaris hortos et Baias desponderat,* where *domum, hortos, Baias* are parallel to *hortos, domum, Baias* in the *Pro Caelio*: the possessive genitives preclude all doubt; cf. *Att.* 12.40.3 (T&P 584; SB 281): *Baias habebat.* Clodia was not just a casual visitor at Baiae, but had a villa there; Austin (p. 101, *ad loc.*). translates "a woman to whose grounds, house, estate at Baiae, there was an automatic right of way for every lecherous person." The villa is not mentioned by Münzer, *RE* 4 (1900), 105–107, no. 66. As one of six children of Ap. Claudius Pulcher (*cos.* 79), Clodia is unlikely to have inherited the villa, (for the family, cf. Münzer, *Röm. Adelsparteien* [Stuttgart 1920], 302; Syme, *RR*, 20 n. 5); possibly it belonged originally to her husband Metellus Celer who, after his consulship in 60, was appointed governor of Transalpine Gaul but died in 59: see Münzer, *RE* 3 (1899), 1208–1210, no. 86. Yet Clodia and her husband had been on bad terms only a year before his death: *Att.* 2.1.5 (T&P 27; SB 21); there were doubtless more likely heirs. Neither Clodia nor her villa at Baiae is mentioned later than the *Pro Caelio* (delivered in April of 56; see Austin, appendix iv, 151).

8. L. Cornelius Balbus (*cos.* 40) Puteoli? 44

Att. 14.9.2–3 (T &P 712; SB 363): *Hic turba magna est eritque, ut audio, maior . . . et Balbus hic est multumque mecum* (Puteoli, April 17, 44); *Att.* 14.20.4 (T &P 727; SB 374): [*Hirtius*] *vivit habitatque cum Balbo* (Puteoli, May 11, 44); cf. *Fam.* 9.19.2 (T &P 478), *Att.* 14.10.3 (T &P 713; SB 364).

We know Balbus to have prospered and built under Caesar's dictatorship (*Att.* 12.2.2 [T &P 459; SB 238]); coastal Campania was a choice location for a villa. Cicero's letters in 46 and again in 44 show that Balbus was at Puteoli for some days; though there is no explicit mention of his estate, the circumstantial evidence that he was a proprietor is strong. He was with Paetus at Neapolis in 46; that occasion appears to have been a dinner visit (*Fam.* 9.19.1–2 [T &P 478]; cf. 9.17.1 [T &P 480]). But Cicero states that at Puteoli in 44 Hirtius lived and stayed with Balbus. *Vivere cum* need not always mean "stay with," "put up with"; see SB VI, 240, on *Att.* 14.20.4; cf. *Att.* 10.7.3 (T &P 388; SB 198). But when reinforced by *habitatque*, a reference to Balbus as host and Hirtius as guest seems unequivocal, despite the fact that we have independent evidence that Hirtius too owned a villa in the area (see below, no. 16). The town in which the villa of Balbus was located, however, is not known. Balbus' extraordinary energies carried him far, and made him rich, in the service of Caesar; for details, cf. Münzer, *RE*4 (1900), 1260–1261, no. 69. Other evidence attests his presence, and his patronage of Caesar's colony, at Capua (Suet. *Iul.* 81; *CIL* X, 3854; cited also by Frederiksen, *Rep. Cap.*, p. 122, n. 227).

9. P. Cornelius Dolabella (*cos. suff.* 44) Baiae 45

Att. 13.52.2 (T &P 679; SB 353): *Dolabellae villam cum* [*Caesar*] *praeteriret, omnis armatorum copia dextra sinistra ad equum nec usquam alibi* (from Puteoli, Dec. 19, 45); *Fam.* 9.12.1 (T &P 680): *Gratulor Baiis nostris, si quidem, ut scribis, salubres repente factae sunt* (Cicero to Dolabella, Dec. 17, 45); *Att.* 15.13 a.1 (T &P 795; SB 417): . . . *venisse eum ad Baias audiebam* . . . (Oct. 28, 44).

Dolabella's villa is first mentioned late in 45, when Caesar ordered his armed escort to present arms as they passed the house; as How (II, 441, *ad loc.*) observes, "This may have been a special mark of honour to Dolabella, whom Caesar intended to be consul next year, though he was under the requisite age and had not held the praetorship." The passage further shows that the villa lay on a main road or street, though it probably fronted on the sea; the context reveals only that the site was in the area of Cumae and Puteoli.

Baiae is specified explicitly by the other two references; for Dolabella's other material rewards, including villas of Pompey, from Caesar, see above, Chapter 3, p. 68; cf. Münzer, *RE* 4 (1900), 1300–1308, no. 141.

10. P. Cornelius Lentulus Spinther (*cos.* 57)   Puteoli   49

Att. 9.11.1 (T&P 367; SB 178): *Lentulum nostrum scis Puteolis esse?* ... *Inventus est vix in hortis suis (se) occultans*... (spring of 49); cf. *Att.* 9.13.7 (T&P 369; SB 180), 15.4 (T&P 373; SB 183).

The villa at Puteoli is mentioned only in the months after Corfinium, when Spinther was released by Caesar (Caes. *BCiv.* 1.23); later he left to join Pompey in Epirus (*BCiv.* 3.83). But part of his property appears to have been in danger in the previous year: *Att.* 6.1.23 (T&P 252; SB 115), with SB III, 252 *ad loc.* After Pharsalus Spinther fled with Pompey to Rhodes (*BCiv.* 3.102), and soon after was probably executed (Cic. *Phil.* 13.29; *Brutus* 268; see further Münzer, *RE* 4 [1900], 1397–1399, no. 238). He may have bought the *Puteolanum* after his three years as governor of Cilicia (56–53); it was ripe for appropriation by Caesar's supporters after his death.

11. Faustus Cornelius Sulla (*quaestor* 54)   Cumae?   55

Att. 4.10.1 (T&P 121; SB 84): *Ego hic pascor bibliotheca Fausti* (May, 55).

This is our only reference to a villa, whose location must have been not far from Cicero's *Cumanum*, belonging to Faustus Sulla, son of the dictator by Caecilia Metella and born before 86 (Plut. *Sull.* 22.2). It may well be the same estate occupied by Sulla during his Campanian retirement: Appian says Sulla's villa was located at Cumae (cf. Chapter 2, p. 31), and we know that Faustus inherited from his father since he apparently squandered much of his patrimony and put up some of his possessions for sale (Plut. *Cic.* 27.3; Cic. *Sull.* 54). Faustus was Pompey's follower; deep in debt, he welcomed civil war: *Att.* 9.1.4 (T&P 353; SB 167), 9.11.4 (T&P 367; SB 178). He was slain by Caesar's soldiers in Mauretania after Thapsus in 46 (Caes. *BAfr.* 94–96; *Fam.* 9.18.2 (T&P 473)); presumably the villa was then seized or came upon the market at a low price. See further, Münzer, *RE* 4 (1900), 1515–1517, no. 377.

12. P. Cornelius Sulla   Neapolis   63

Cic. *Sull.* 17: *hic contra ita quievit, ut eo tempore omni Neapoli fuerit* ...; *ibid.*, 53; *Fam.* 9.15.5 (T&P 481): *Domum Sullanam desperabam iam, ut tibi proxime scripsi, sed tamen non abieci* (to L. Papirius Paetus at Neapolis, late in 46).

P. Cornelius Sulla, perhaps a nephew of the dictator (Cic. *Off.* 2.29: *P. Sulla cum vibrasset dictatore propinquo suo*; cf. Cass. Dio 36.44.3) was defended in 62 by Cicero and said by him to have remained quietly in Neapolis during the previous years. During this time he helped to recruit a band of gladiators, apparently based in Campania, for Faustus Sulla (Cic. *Sull.* 54–55; cf. Münzer, *RE* 4 [1900], 1520, no. 386); his collaborators in this project included L. Julius Caesar and Q. Pompeius Rufus, whose presence (and properties) on the Bay of Naples are attested by independent evidence (Cic. *Sull.* 55; see below, nos. 20, 33). But Sulla's connections with Campania antedate the Catilinarian period: it will be remembered that he was cofounder with the dictator of the veteran colony at Pompeii (see above, Chapter 2, p. 34; Cic. *Sull.* 62); and while residing at Neapolis he seems to have maintained his influence there, for he was a *patronus coloniae* (Cic. *Sull.* 61) and was charged with having incited the citizens of Pompeii to join the Catilinarian conspiracy (Cic. *Sull.* 60–61). In July of 46 Cicero contemplated moving to Neapolis and showed interest in buying a *domum Sullanam*; Paetus was seeing to such details as the soundness of the roof and walls: *Fam.* 9.15.5 (T&P 481). That the *domus* mentioned in 46 was Sulla's residence in 63 (see above, Chapter 2, p. 35) is the natural inference. Both during the Sullan proscriptions and the confiscations of Caesar, Sulla, who fought on Caesar's side during the Civil War (Caes. *BCiv.* 3.51, 89), acquired an unsavory reputation as one of the *sectores* (*Pro Rosc. Amer.* 80), or bidders in confiscated property: *Off.* 2.29; *Fam.* 9.10.3 (T&P 537). He died late in 46 (*ibid.*); and the house at Neapolis had apparently come on the market (*Fam.* 9.15.5 [T&P 481]; for the date, cf. How II, *ad loc.* pp. 416, 418).

13. L. Domitius Ahenobarbus (*cos.* 54) Neapolis? 49

Att. 9.3.1 (T&P 358; SB 170): *Domiti filius transiit Formias VIII Id. currens ad matrem Neapolim mihique nuntiari iussit patrem ad urbem esse . . .* (March 9, 49).

After capitulation at Corfinium, Ahenobarbus was released by Caesar and reached Rome safely; his son passed by Formiae on March 8 on his way to his mother Porcia at Neapolis (cf. Münzer, *RE* 5 [1903], 1340–1341, no. 27). Ahenobarbus may have had a villa there: he was the owner of huge estates throughout Italy (Caes. *BCiv.* 1.17, 56). Alternatively, Porcia may have been seeking temporary refuge with family. She was the sister of M. Cato Uticensis (Plut. *Cat. Min.* 41), who, upon the death of L. Licinius Lucullus in 56 or 55, became the official guardian of Lucullus' son and trustee of his property; Cato sold the fish from Lucullus' Neapolitan ponds at a great profit (Varro *Rust.* 3.2.17). At the beginning of the Civil War, Cato left Italy with Lucullus' son and widow; he sought safety at Rhodes (Miltner, *RE* 22 [1953], 197, no. 16) but it may be that Cato's sister Porcia retired to the Neapolitan villa of Lucullus, presently under the trusteeship of Cato, to wait out the war.

14. M. Fabius Gallus   Herculaneum   50

Fam. 9.25.3 (T &P 246): . . . *repente percussus est atrocissimis litteris, in quibus scriptum erat fundum Herculanensem a Q. Fabio fratre proscriptum esse, qui fundus cum eo communis esset* (to L. Papirius Paetus, February, 50).

Shackleton Bailey has demonstrated conclusively that the occurrences of this man's *nomen* in *MSS* of the letters require his re-identification as Fabius, and that the usual reading Fadius be abandoned: see *CR* N.S. 12 (1962), 195–196. His property at Herculaneum is described as a farm (*fundus*), rather than as a villa, and was perhaps therefore situated inland, rather than on the coast. Why Gallus' brother was moved suddenly to sell the property does not emerge from the letter; but it is noteworthy, and appropriate, that Cicero entreated Paetus, a Neapolitan resident, to look out for Gallus' interests in the affair. Gallus was a friend of C. Cassius Longinus (*Fam.* 15.14.1 [T &P 241]) and of C. Anicius (above, no. 1), and held Epicurean views: cf. *Fam.* 7.26.1 (T &P 94): *Epicurum tuum*; *Fam.* 9.25.2: . . . *in iis controversiis, quas habeo cum tuis combibonibus Epicuriis, optima opera eius uti soleo*; see further Münzer, *RE* 11 (1909), 1958, no. 6, where the *fundus* is not mentioned; above, Chapter 3, p. 58.

15. M. Fonteius   Neapolis   67

Att. 1.6.1 (T &P 2; SB 2): *Domum Rabirianam Neapoli, quam tu iam dimensam et exaedificatam animo habebas, M. Fonteius emit HS* ccclↃↃↃ$\overline{\text{xxx}}$ (Jan. 67).

As propraetor of Gallia Narbonensis (74–72), M. Fonteius was charged with maladministration and defended by Cicero in 69; the event to which *Fontei causa* (*Att.* 4.15.6 [T &P 143; SB 90]) refers is not known. Atticus appears to have had a keen interest in the property of Rabirius (see below, no. 35), but Fonteius anticipated him (cf. Münzer, *RE* 6 (1909), 2845, no. 12). The cost of the house, 130,000 sesterces, leaves little scope for inference, for we have no other Neapolitan real estate figures with which to compare it; Lepore (*PdP* fasc. 25–27 [1952], 320–321) thinks the price modest, though not so very small. Lucullus' villa at Misenum, it will be remembered, cost

10,000,000 sesterces (Plut. *Mar.* 34); Cicero paid 3,500,000 for his town house on the Palatine (*Fam.* 5.6.2 [T &P 16]; cf. Frank, *ESAR* I, 393), and his little lodges, the *deversoria*, seem to have cost between thirty and forty thousand sesterces each (*Att.* 10.5.3 [T &P 384; SB 196]). We have no figures for any of his villas. But in 57 the senate voted a compensation of 500,000 for the plundered *Tusculanum*, and 250,000 sesterces for the *Formianum*: *valde illiberaliter*, complained Cicero (*Att.* 4.2.5 [T &P 91; SB 74]). The indemnity voted Cicero for his Palatine house was 2,000,000 sesterces; if the discrepancy between cost and compensation for the town house holds for the villas as well (cf. J. Carcopino, *Cicero—The Secrets of his Correspondence* I [London 1951], 53–54), the *Tusculanum* might have been worth 875,000 sesterces and the *Formianum* 437,500 sesterces (the calculations of Carcopino are inaccurate). The villa at Formiae was not apparently luxurious; its price is probably most comparable to Fonteius' new property at Neapolis, and 130,000 sesterces would thus not seem to be a high price to pay for a *domus*.

16. A. Hirtius (*cos.* 43) Puteoli? 44

Att. 14.21.4 (T &P 728; SB 375): *Postridie apud Hirtium cogitabam et quidem Πεντέλοιπον* (from Puteoli, May 11, 44); *Fat.* 2: *nam cum essem in Puteolano, Hirtiusque noster consul designatus eisdem in locis . . . cum ille ad me venisset . . .*

Hirtius was on the Campanian coast for some weeks during the spring of 44, staying now with Balbus (*Att.* 14.20.4 [T &P 727; SB 374]), now with Cicero (*Att.* 15.1a.2 [T &P 730; SB 377]); the phrase *apud Hirtium* shows conclusively that he owned this villa: cf. *apud Anicium, QFr.* 2.8.3 (T &P 123); *apud Paetum, Att.* 4.9.2 (T &P 122; SB 85); *apud me, Att.* 15.1a.2 (T &P 730; SB 377). The location of the estate is difficult to determine from the vague phrase *eisdem in locis* in the *De Fato*. On the fifteenth of April, Cicero promised to write Atticus of *Baiana negotia chorumque illum* (*Att.* 14.8.1 [T &P 710; SB 362]), which T &P (*ad loc.*) take to refer "to Hirtius, Pansa and Balbus who were living at this time in Baiae." But there is no other evidence to render Baiae more likely as a villa site than Cumae or Puteoli; Hirtius, Pansa (no. 44), and Balbus (no. 8) all had estates in this region, but their precise whereabouts are unknown. Hirtius was an Epicurean: Cicero characterizes Hirtius and Dolabella as *dicendi discipulos . . . cenandi magistros* (*Fam.* 9.16.7 [T &P 472]); and elaborate sauce and peacock were two dishes in which Cicero's cook did not attempt to imitate Hirtius' luxury (*Fam.* 9.20.2 [T &P 475]; cf. 9.18.3 [T &P 473]). It is not known what became of Hirtius' villa after his death (at Mutina: cf. Von der Mühll, *RE* 8 (1913), 1961–1962, no. 2).

17. Q. Hortensius Hortalus (*cos.* 69)   Bauli   63–60

Cic. *Acad. Pr.* 2.9: ... *in Hortensii villa quae est ad Baulos*; cf. *ibid.*, 125, 145. *Att.* 5.2.1 (T &P 185; SB 95): *In Cumano cum essem, venit ad me, quod mihi pergratum fuit, noster Hortensius.* Varro *Rust.* 3.17.5: Q. *Hortensius, familiaris noster, cum piscinas haberet magna pecunia aedificatas ad Baulos* . . . Pliny *NH* 9.172: *Apud Baulos in parte Baiana piscinam habuit Hortensius orator, in qua murenam adeo dilexit, ut exanimatam flesse credatur.* Cf. Symmachus *Ep.* 1.1.5–6.

The question of the location of ancient Bauli has been much discussed. Beloch (*Campanien*[2], 176–177) followed by Huelsen ("Bauli," *RE* 3 [1897], 154–155) rejected previous identifications of the site with modern Bacoli, the village two kilometers north of Misenum, and instead supposed that the villas of Hortensius and others were on the promontory called "punta dell' epitaffio," which forms the natural boundary of the Bay of Baiae some four kilometers northeast of Misenum. However, a more recent discussion by Maiuri (*Atti della Reale Accademia d'Italia, Rendiconti*, 7th Series, vol. II [1941], 249–260), successfully vindicates the earlier view, which is more in accord with the ancient topographical testimony (Cass. Dio 59.17.1; Symmachus, *Ep.* 1.1.11–12; Maiuri, *Atti ... Accad. d'Italia*, 257–258). To Maiuri's arguments in favor of Bacoli may be added the statement of Cicero (*Acad.* 2.80) that from Hortensius' villa at Bauli one could see Puteoli and nothing intervened to block the sight of Pompeii; but from the "punta dell' epitaffio" the hills of Puteoli and the ridge of Posillipo entirely obstruct the view of any land beyond, whereas Pompeii is easily visible, on a clear day, from Bacoli. Maiuri (*Atti ... Accad. d'Italia*, 255; *Campi Flegrèi*, 89–91) further argues, with some plausibility, that remains of Hortensius' villa form a part of the elaborate network of cisterns now known as "cento camerelle," on the heights of modern Bacoli. Like the *Cumanum* of Catulus and the *Neapolitanum* of Lucullus, Hortensius' villa is first mentioned in the *Academica*, but his wealth and costly holdings elsewhere in Italy were extensive (cf. Pliny *NH* 14.96, 35.130: villa at Tusculum; Varro *Rust.* 3.13.2: villa at Laurentum with a deer park; see further Von der Mühll, *RE* 8 [1913], 2475, no. 13), and nothing precludes his having acquired the estate at Bauli several years before Cicero mentions it, perhaps during the Sullan confiscations (see J. D'Arms, *AJP* 88 [1967], 199). The last time that Cicero saw his famous adversary was at Cumae in 51 (*Att.* 5.2.2 [T &P 185; SB 95]). At Hortensius' death in 50 his son inherited the villa (see below, on no. 18, *q.v.* also for his contacts, property, and interests at Puteoli).

18. Q. Hortensius (son of the above)   Bauli   49

Att. 10.16.5 (T &P 402; SB 208): *Sed cum redeo, Hortensius venerat et ad Terentiam salutatum deverterat . . . Iam eum, ut puto, videbo; misit enim puerum se ad me venire* (Cumae, May 14, 49). Cf. *Att.* 10.17.1 (T &P 403; SB 209).

After the elder Hortensius' death in 50, Cicero wrote Atticus that he was informed of the legacies which the young Hortensius would have to pay from the estate, and that he was eager to know what properties Hortensius would put up for auction (*Att.* 7.3.9 [T &P 294; SB 126], December 50). This passage shows that Hortensius was his father's principal heir, and the two sections from *Att.* 10.16 and 17 cited above show that Hortensius first had property of his own (in the area of Cicero's *Cumanum*) shortly after the death of his father: the property, beyond reasonable doubt, is the villa at Bauli. Cf. Münzer, *RE* 8 (1913), 2468–2469, no. 8; and, for the subsequent history of the villa, see above, Chapter 3, pp. 68–69.

In addition to the luxury villa at Bauli, the Hortensii had business connections and property in Puteoli. Hopeful that the young Hortensius' financial entanglements were extensive and the legacies large, Cicero added: *nescio enim cur, cum portam Flumentanam Caelius occuparit, ego Puteolos non meos faciam* (*Att.* 7.3.9 [T &P 294; SB 126]): Cicero was interested in property at Puteoli which belonged to Hortensius. Those holdings are archaeologically attested. An *Hortensiana Ripa* is designated on an ancient glass flask which depicts the major monuments of imperial Puteoli: see J. D'Arms, *AJP* 88 (1967), 195–198. And other evidence links the Hortensii with the business men of Puteoli: in the *Academica* (2.80), Cicero refers to a Gaius Avianius of Puteoli, in a context which suggests that Avianius is as well known to the orator Hortensius as to himself. The Avianii, known from both literature and inscriptions, were among the most important commercial families of Puteoli (for details, see Dubois, *PA*, 46); the connection of their name with that of the Hortensii, when taken together with Cicero's reference to the holdings of the family in Puteoli, shows that the luxury villa at Bauli did not comprise the whole of this great family's interests in Campania. Shrewd local investments, in fact, might help to contribute to the cost of maintaining the palace at Bauli nearby.

19. C. Julius Caesar (the Dictator)   Baiae   48

Cic. *Att.* 11.6.6 (T &P 418; SB 217): *L. vero Lentulus Hortensi domum sibi et Caesaris hortos et Baias desponderat* (Nov. 48); Sen. *Ep.* 51.11: *Illi quoque . . . C. Marius et Cn. Pompeius et Caesar extruxerunt quidem villas in regione Baiana, sed illas imposuerunt summis iugis montium*; Tac. *Ann.* 14.9.3: *mox domesticorum cura levem tumulum accepit, viam Miseni propter et villam Caesaris dictatoris quae subiectos sinus editissima prospectat.*

It is curious that Caesar's villa at Baiae, to which there are two unequivocal references in imperial times, is explicitly mentioned but once in the entire Ciceronian corpus; but that passage (on which see SB V, *ad loc.*, 274) reveals that the property had been acquired before the Civil Wars. When the dictator dined with Cicero at Cumae in 45, it was the villa of L. Marcius Philippus (see below, no. 28) which housed Caesar and his vast retinue. Beloch (*Campanien*², 185) believed that Cicero's *is qui optimas Baias habebat* (*Att.* 12.40.3 [T &P 584; SB 281]) referred to Caesar, but that passage is a hopeless conundrum. Cicero, at Astura at the time (45), had said to Atticus: "I am in the same place where he who had a splendid villa at Baiae used to spend this time of year"; but there is no evidence that Caesar had property at Astura, and the use of the imperfect tense suggests that whoever fitted the description was no longer alive. Hortensius and Lucullus have both been suggested (cf. T &P, *ad loc*; Schmidt, 476, n. 2), but the evidence is equally deficient. A somewhat more likely clue to Caesar's having built a villa at Baiae (cf. Sen. *Ep.* 51.11: *extruxerunt*) may lie in a passage of a letter to Quintus written in 54; Cicero praised his brother's villa at Arcanum "as worthy of Caesar or of someone still more tasteful" (*QFr.* 3.9.7 [T &P 160]). T &P (*ad loc.*) find "the mention of Caesar as one who would give advice on the adornment of a country house somewhat strange." But if Caesar were then in the process of building, or had recently built at Baiae, the comment would be apposite. Again, after visiting Cicero in 45, *Caesar Puteolis se aiebat unum diem fore, alterum ad Baias* (*Att.* 13.52.2 [T &P 679; SB 353]); this could mean either "at Baiae" or "at his villa at Baiae" (see above, on no. 7). See further Drumann-Groebe III², 658–659; and for the possible location of the villa, Beloch, *Campanien*², 185, with plan V.

20. L. Julius Caesar (*cos.* 64)　　　　Neapolis　　　　　　　　44

Att. 14.17a.3 (T &P 722; SB 371 A): *L. quidem Caesar, cum ad eum aegrotum Neapolim venissem, quamquam erat oppressus totius corporis doloribus* . . . (Pompeii, May 3, 44); *Att.* 14.17.2 (T &P 724; SB 371): *L. Caesari videbatur, quem pridie Neapoli adfectum graviter videram* . . .

The uncle of M. Antonius (his sister Julia had married M. Antonius Creticus, to whom she bore the triumvir) attempted to mediate between the senate and Antony after the assassination of Caesar; although proscribed by the triumvirs, he was saved by his sister's intercession (Cic. *Phil.* 8.1, 12.18; Appian, *BCiv.* 4.12, 4.37; cf. Münzer, *RE* 10 [1917], 468–469, no. 143). In 44 he seems to have been in Neapolis for the sake of his health; since Neapolis was a favorite retreat for the aged and infirm (see above, Chapter 5, p. 143, with n. 125), he very probably owned property there (cf. *ad eum* above).

21. M. Junius Brutus (*praetor* 44)　　　Cumae　　　　　　　46

　　Cic. *Brut.* 300: *Vero, inquam, Brute; sed in Cumano aut in Tusculano aliquando, si modo licebit, quoniam utroque in loco vicini sumus.*

This is the only reference to a villa of Brutus near Cicero's *Cumanum*; from the letters we know that Brutus was on the Campanian coast in the summer of 44, but staying at Lucullus' villa at Nesis (*Att.* 16.1.1 [T &P 769; SB 409]; and see below, no. 23). In 45 Brutus refused Cicero's offer to use his *Cumanum* (*Att.* 12.36.2 [T &P 578; SB 275]); and see above, Chapter 3, p. 50); this is, of course, no proof that Brutus was not himself a property owner in the area. The estate was presumably appropriated after Philippi.

22. L. Licinius Lucullus (*cos.* 74)　　　Misenum, Neapolis　　　63–60

　　a) *Misenum*: Plut. *Mar.* 34.2: καὶ γὰρ ἦν ἐκεῖ περὶ Μισηνοὺς τῷ Μαρίῳ πολυτελὴς οἰκία τρυφὰς ἔχουσα καὶ διαίτας . . . ταύτην λέγεται . . . Κορνηλία πρίασθαι. χρόνου δ᾽ οὐ πάνυ πολλοῦ γενομένου Λεύκιος Λεύκολλος ὠνεῖται μυριάδων πεντήκοντα καὶ διακοσίων . . . Phaedr. 2.5.18: *Caesar Tiberius quum petens Neapolim | in Misenensem villam venisset suam | quae monte summo imposita Luculli manu | prospectat Siculum et prospicit Tuscum mare.* Tac. *Ann.* 6.50.2: *mutatisque saepius locis tandem apud promunturium Miseni consedit in villa cui L. Lucullus quondam dominus.* Varro *Rust.* 3.17.9: *In Baiano autem aedificans tanta ardebat cura, ut architecto permiserit vel ut suam pecuniam consumeret . . .*

Plutarch, the only source to give some indication of date, says that Lucullus bought the villa at Misenum "not long after" Cornelia had acquired it (probably, as has been seen above, Chapter 2, p. 29, during the Sullan proscriptions). The eastern campaigns of Lucullus kept him out of Italy certainly from 73, possibly from late 74, until 67 or 66: Ooteghem, *L. Licinius Lucullus, Mémoires de l'Académie Royale de Belgique,* (Namur 1959), 57–58; Gelzer, *RE* 13 (1926), 376–377, no. 104. He may have bought the villa at Misenum before or during his consulship but could not have occupied it during these years. After his return, political enemies postponed the triumph of Lucullus for three years, until 64 or 63: Cic. *Acad. Pr.* 2.3. Plutarch (*Pomp.* 46.6, *Luc.*

38.2) states that Lucullus in his last years retired from political life and gave himself over to the enjoyment of his vast wealth. It is thus to the years after 67, which established Lucullus' reputation for leisured luxury, that the buying and building of his villas should probably be ascribed. The price of 10,000,000 sesterces paid by Lucullus to Cornelia is staggering; only the Tusculan villa of Scaurus is known to have cost more (30,000,000 sesterces: Frank, *ESAR* I, 393).

Phaedrus' statement that the villa at Misenum *prospectat Siculum et despicit Tuscum mare* fixes the location more securely than that of any other Lucullan estate. Beloch and subsequently Maiuri have argued that the northwest ridge of "Monte Miseno," above the so-called "Grotta della Dragonara," was the probable site; but the area has been so heavily quarried for pozzuolana and tufa that recovery of the villa's position is impossible: Beloch, *Campanien*[2], 198–199; Maiuri, *Campi Flegrèi*, 99; ———, *Passeggiate Campane*, 45; and cf. Maiuri's letter quoted (in translation) by Ooteghem, *Lucullus*, 191, n. 3. Tiberius died in the villa, which must by then have comprised a part of the imperial domain (cf. Phaedr. 2.5: . . . *villam venisset suam*; and see above, Chapter 4, p. 86. To the villa at Misenum should also be referred Varro's remark (*Rust.* 3.17.9, quoted above). There is no other evidence that Lucullus had a villa at Baiae; the phrase *regio Baiana*, as has been seen, is elsewhere employed to designate a general area of which Misenum is a specific part (see Chapter 2, p. 23); *aedificare* need not contradict Plutarch's statement that Lucullus bought an already existing villa from Cornelia, but may imply only that Lucullus made further additions to an earlier structure (cf. Gelzer, *RE* 13 [1926], 411).

b) *Neapolis*: Cic. *Acad. Pr.* 2.9: *Quo quidem etiam maturius venimus quod erat constitutum, si ventus esset, Lucullo in Neapolitanum . . . navigare*; Varro *Rust.* 3.17.9: *contra ad Neapolim L. Lucullum, posteaquam perfodisset montem ac maritumum flumen immisisset in piscinas, quæ reciproce fluerent ipsae, Neptuno non cedere de piscatu*; Vell. Pat. 2.33.4: *Lucullus . . . quem ob iniectas moles mari et receptum suffossis montibus in terras mare haud infacete Magnus Pompeius Xerxen togatum vocare adsueverat*; Pliny *NH* 9.170: *Lucullus exciso etiam monte iuxta Neapolim maiore impendio quam villam exaedificaverat euripum et maria admisit*; Plut. *Luc.* 39.3: τὰ δ' ἐν τοῖς παραλίοις καὶ περὶ Νέαν πόλιν ἔργα, λόφους ἀνακρεμαννύντος αὐτοῦ μεγάλοις ὀρύγμασι καὶ τροχοὺς θαλάσσης καὶ διαδρομὰς ἰχθυοτρόφους τοῖς οἰκητηρίοις ἐναλίους κτίζοντος. . . ; ibid., 44.5.

From the reference to the *Neapolitanum* in the *Academica*, it may be deduced that Lucullus owned it by the late sixties; Cicero and Pliny imply that it was his single piece of property in the Neapolitan area; Varro, Pliny, Velleius, and Plutarch show that construction required mammoth feats of engineering, which included the tunneling of a mountain in order to admit sea water for fish ponds. It follows that the elaborate complex of buildings cannot have been situated on a flat stretch of coast. But the actual location of the *Neapolitanum*, by all accounts the most sumptuous of the Republican villas in Campania, is most uncertain. Beloch (*Campanien* ², 81–82), following the antiquarians Giordano and Chiariti, held that the villa of Lucullus comprised the island of Megaris, where in the middle ages rose the "Castel dell'Ovo,' associated by local tradition with Virgil and necromancy. A *castrum Lucullanum* is first mentioned as the site of the emperor Romulus Augustulus' imprisonment in 476 A.D. (see above, Chapter 4, n. 166), and frequently thereafter; Cocchia (*La Tomba di Virgilio* [Naples 1889], 56) used medieval documents to establish the identification of the *castrum* with Megaris; his conclusions are today generally accepted (for finds on the Via S. Lucia, possibly connected originally with the villa, see W. Johannowsky, *RAAN* N.S. 26 [1952], 121, n. 7; cf. Napoli, *Napoli Greco-Romana* [Naples 1959], 22). Despite the lateness of the testimony, and the incongruity (owing to the many alterations of the ancient shoreline since antiquity) between the mountain and tunnel attested in the ancient sources and the present aspect of the terrain, this view may well be correct. Yet the passage which Beloch cites to show that Lucullus' Neapolitan villa was at Megaris (Cic. *Phil.* 10.8 [Beloch, *Campanien* ², 81]) unquestionably refers instead to the island of Nesis, in the gulf of Puteoli; Marcus Licinius Lucullus seems to have inherited this island from his father (see below, no. 23). Since the accuracy of Cicero's testimony is in this instance beyond question, medieval documents become the only real evidence that Lucullus' villa was on Megaris. But it is doubtful that Cicero would have referred (in the *Academica*) to the estate at Nesis as a *Neapolitanum*. The matter stands thus: Lucullus certainly owned the island of Nesis, and a sumptuous villa as well at Neapolis; the site of the latter villa, however, is by no means so certain as Beloch implied.

23. M. Licinius Lucullus (son of the consul of 74)   Nesis   44

    Att. 14.20.1 (T &P 727; SB 374): *E Pompeiano navi advectus sum in Luculli nostri hospitium ... A Lucullo postridie ... veni in Puteolanum.* (May 11, 44); *Phil.* 10.8: *... in insula clarissimi adulescentis, Luculli, propinqui sui; Att.* 16.1.1 (T &P 769; SB 409): *iens ad Brutum in Nesidem haec scripsi* (July 8, 44, on Cicero's way from Puteoli); cf. *Att.* 16.2.3 (T &P 772; SB 412); 16.3.6 (T &P 773; SB 413); 16.4.1 (T &P 771; SB 411).

In the first few letters of *Att.* 16 (July, 44) Cicero repeatedly mentions conversations with Brutus held on the island of Nesis (Nisida) west of the headland of Posillipo in the gulf of Puteoli. In the 10th Philippic, he says that his conversations with Brutus at this time took place on the island of Lucullus. A comparison of these passages demonstrates that Nesis and the "island of Lucullus" are identical and that the one-day visit with Lucullus which interrupted Cicero's boat trip from Pompeii to Puteoli in May of 44 (*Att.* 14.20.1 [T &P 727; SB 374]) also took place at Nesis. Beloch's identification (*Campanien*², 81) of *insula Luculli* with Megaris at Neapolis must be rejected. Though we have no explicit testimony that the island was part of Lucullus' inheritance from his father (see above no. 13, for details of that inheritance), that seems a safe conjecture, since the young Lucullus was barely twenty in 44, too young to have begun to accumulate property on his own. He was probably a nephew of Brutus (Münzer, *RE* 13 [1926], 418, no. 110) and died on the side of Brutus and Cassius at or after Philippi in 42 (Vell. Pat. 2.71.2–3). In 44, Brutus and Cassius may have found Lucullus' Nesis a strategic base owing to its natural defenses; certainly it was not easily accessible. Poseidonius recorded that he had observed numerous *cuniculi* on an island between Puteoli and Neapolis: surely Nesis is meant (Athenaeus 9.401; cf. Beloch, *Campanien*², 87–88).

24. L. Lucceius   Puteoli   45

Fam. 5.15.2 (T &P 587): *sed certe adhuc non fuimus, cum essemus vicini in Tusculano, in Puteolano . . .*

After his accusation of Catiline *inter sicarios* and unsuccessful coalition with Caesar for the consulship of 59 (*Att.* 1.17.11 [T &P 23; SB 17]; Suet. *Iul.* 19.1), Lucceius embraced literary pursuits, and was asked by Cicero in 56 to write down and glorify the orator's deeds as consul (*Fam.* 5.12 [T &P 109]). The implication of *Fam.* 5.15.2 is that in 45, he and Cicero were no longer neighbors at Tusculum and at Puteoli (cf. Münzer, *RE* 13 [1927], 1554, no. 6), but Cicero had kept his villas in both districts (his villa in the latter territory is elsewhere regularly called *Cumanum*; the exception here proves that the estate of Lucceius lay within the district of Puteoli): Lucceius must therefore no longer have owned his. As early as 50, part of his property seems to have been in danger (*Att.* 7.3.6 [T &P 294; SB 126]); since Lucceius was a committed Pompeian (Caes. *BCiv.* 3.18.3; *Att.* 9.1.3 [T &P 353; SB 167]; 9.11.3 [T &P 367; SB 178]), it is probable that the villa at Puteoli had been confiscated by 45. Lucceius is a gentile name of some prominence in coastal

Campania: forty-three instances are listed in the index of *CIL* X. One Cn. Lucceius, apparently an agent of Brutus, was encountered by Cicero at Puteoli in 44 (*Att.* 16.5.3); Münzer (*RE* 13 [1927], 1553, no. 3) connects this man with the *praetores Gnaeii Lucceii*, who, in an inscription from Cumae dated 7 A.D., are recorded as vowing to restore the cult of Demeter (*CIL* X, 3685 [*ILS* 4040]; cf. 3687, 3697); and Cicero attended the funeral of the mother of Cn. Lucceius (Chapter 3, p. 51). Thus, it may be that L. Lucceius, who narrowly missed the consulate in 59, came himself from Puteoli (as argued by Annecchino, *Storia di Pozzuoli* [Pozzuoli 1960] 92–93); the frequent recurrence of the gentile name in those parts shows that at least one branch of the family was of local provenance. Alternatively, it is possible that L. Lucceius and the Cn. Lucceii could point to common ancestry in another place.

25. C. Lucilius Hirrus (*tr. pl.* 53)   Location unknown

Varro *Rust.* 3.17.3: *Hirrus circum piscinas suas ex aedificiis duodena milia sestertia capiebat . . . uno tempore enim memini hunc Caesari duo milia murenarum mutua dedisse in pondus et propter piscium multitudinem quadragies sestertio villam venisse*; cf. Pliny *NH* 9.171.

Hirrus, a kinsman of Pompey (Cichorius, *Röm. Stud.* 67–70; A. B. West, *AJP* 49 [1928], 240–252; cf. Syme, *RR*, 31, n. 1) was the owner of great estates in Bruttium (Varro *Rust.* 2.1.2) as well as of the fishponds and villa recorded above. Syme (*RR* 195) suggests that the ponds would have been ripe for confiscation by the triumvirs in 42; but Varro states explicitly that the high price brought by Hirrus' villa was owing to the value of his fish. Since we rarely find references to fishponds outside of Campania, it may well be that those of Hirrus were also on the Bay of Naples (so also Beloch, *Campanien*², 186); the passage from Varro speaks in favor of a location not far distant from Rome (cf. Münzer, *RE* 13 [1927], 1642–1645, no. 25).

26. Q. Lutatius Catulus (*cos.* 78)   Cumae   62–61

Cic. *Acad. Pr.* 2.80: *Ego Catuli Cumanum ex hoc loco cerno et e regione video, Pompeianum non cerno . . .*; cf. 2.9: *. . . et quondam in Hortensii villa quae est ad Baulos, cum eo Catulus et Lucullus nosque ipsi postridie venissemus quam apud Catulum fuissemus.* The imaginary date of the *Academica* must fall between 63 (the year of Cicero's consulship alluded to in 2.62) and 60 (the year of Catulus' death; cf. J. S. Reid, *Academica* [London 1885], 418; Philippson, *RE* 7 A [1939], 1129–1130).

Although the *Cumanum* is not mentioned before the *Academica*, it is highly probable that Catulus (who returned to Italy with Sulla, was praetor in 81, gained the consulship for 78 with Sulla's support, and struggled against his colleague Lepidus' attempts to invalidate the Sullan constitution [Münzer, *RE* 13 (1927), 2083–2094, no. 8]) in fact acquired the villa at least by the early 70's; he is listed by Frank (*ESAR* I, 398) among Romans who probably then increased their wealth by bidding on confiscated properties. Nor should the possibility be excluded that he inherited the villa from his father (*cos.* 102), who knew the Bay of Naples (see Chapter 2, n. 75). Reid (*ad loc.*, 273) and Münzer (*RE* 13 [1927], 2094) believed that the *Pompeianum* of *Academica* 2.80 referred to another piece of Campanian property owned by Catulus; but it is more probable that Cicero was here referring to his own villa at Pompeii, mentioned explicitly earlier in the same book of the *Academica* (2.9); omission of the possessive adjective, though somewhat harsh, is not uncommon (so also Schmidt, 491, n. 1). On Catulus' villa at Tusculum, later acquired by Cicero, cf. Münzer, *RE* 13 (1927), 2094.

27. L. Manlius Torquatus (*praetor* 49)   Cumae?   48

   Cic. *Fin.* 2.107: *omitto dignitatem honestatem, speciem ipsam virtutum, de quibus ante dictum est; haec leviora ponam ... signum, tabula, locus amoenus, ludi, venatio, villa Luculli (nam si tuam dicerem, latebram haberes ...)* Cf. *Fin.* 1.14: *nam cum ad me in Cumanum salutandi causa uterque venisset ...*

   The villa of Torquatus, an Epicurean (*Fin.* 1.13; cf. *Att.* 7.2.4 [T &P 293; SB 125]: *Lucius noster et Patron*; see further Münzer, *RE* 14 [1928], 1203–1207, no. 80), is mentioned only casually in the *De Finibus*; Cicero does not elucidate its site. But the setting of the dialogue was Cicero's own *Cumanum*, and the preface makes clear that Torquatus was not staying with Cicero at Cumae but merely stopped in *salutandi causa*. Presumably therefore his own villa was nearby, at no great distance from the Campanian bases of the Epicurean philosophers Philodemus and Siro (see above, Chapter 3, pp. 56–57) with whom Torquatus was intimately acquainted (*Fin.* 2.119). Early in 49 Torquatus was with Cicero at Formiae (*Att.* 7.23.1 [T &P 321; SB 147]; cf. *Att.* 8.11b. 1 [T &P 327; SB 161B]), but later joined Pompey (*Att.* 9.8.1 [T &P 363; SB 175]), and was killed by Sittius in 46 at Hippo Regius in Africa (*BAfr.* 96.2). For his possible financial interest in granaries at Puteoli, see Chapter 3, p. 55.

28. L. Marcius Philippus (*cos.* 56)   Puteoli   60?

   Att. 1.18.6 (T &P 24; SB 18), 1.19.6 (T &P 25; SB 19), 1.20.3 (T &P 26;

SB 20), 2.9.1 (T &P 36; SB 29): Cicero's contempt for the *piscinarii*, in the year 60; whence Macrob. 3.15.60: *nobilissimi principes Lucullus, Philippus, et Hortensius, quos Cicero piscinarios appellabat. Att.* 14.11.2 (T &P 714; SB 365): *Modo venit Octavius et quidem in proximam villam Philippi* (Cumae, April 21, 44), *Att.* 13.52.1 (T &P 679; SB 353): *Sed cum . . . ad Philippum vesperi venisset, villa ita completa a militibus est ut vix triclinium ubi cenaturus ipse Caesar esset vacaret; quippe hominum* CIƆ CIƆ (Cumae, Dec. 19, 45). Cf. Varro *Rust.* 3.3.9–10; Pliny *NH* 9.170.

If Cicero's sarcastic allusions to *piscinarii* refer, as Macrobius thought, to Philippus as well as to Lucullus and Hortensius—and they may well have, for we have other evidence that Cicero took little pleasure in the company of Philippus (*Att.* 12.16 [T &P 548; SB 253]; 12.18.1 [T &P 549; SB 254]: he disturbed Cicero's peace and quiet at Astura)—Philippus must have owned his Cumaean villa and fishponds by 60. Their location is securely fixed as next to Cicero's own *Cumanum*: *Att.* 14.11.2 (T &P 714; SB 365); cf. Schmidt, 482 n. 7; How II, 438–439 on *Att.* 13.52. It was at the villa of Philippus that Caesar and his retinue of 2000 were entertained in 45: if Cicero has not exaggerated the numbers, the estate must have been as vast as Philippus' general reputation for luxury would lead us to believe. Son of the more famous and equally wealthy consul of 91, Philippus married Atia and became the stepfather of Octavius. At the outbreak of the Civil War in 49, he was given permission by Caesar to live where he liked (Cic. *Fragmenta Ep.* [T &P VI², 354, no. 15—to Octavian]: *Quod mihi et Philippo vacationem das, bis gaudeo*; but cf. *Att.* 10.4.10 [T &P 382; SB 195], April 14, 49, which shows that Philippus had already obtained the *vacatio* for which Cicero had not yet dared to ask) and was at Neapolis at least for a time in the spring (*Att.* 9.15.4 (T &P 373; SB 171). Philippus may have owned property in the Greek town (cf. Münzer, *RE* 14 [1930], 1570, no. 76). The family's Campanian interests and contacts ranged widely; an inscription from Herculaneum honors a "Marcius Phi[lippus]" as one of the first two *duoviri* of Herculaneum. The stone cannot be dated exactly but the new constitution will have been instituted either under Caesar or Augustus; although the initial of the *praenomen* is missing, it is highly probable that either the consul of 56 or his homonymous son, *consul suffectus* in 38, received this special honor from the *decuriones* of Herculaneum because of their special associations with the Bay of Naples (A. Degrassi, *Scritti Vari di Antichità* 1 [Rome 1962], 189–190; H. Bloch, *Gnomon* 37 [1965], 561–562). As with Hortensius, the Campanian interests of L. Marcius Philippus do not appear to have been confined to

luxury villas and fishponds. Philippus' villa at Puteoli may have passed sub-
sequently to Octavian, but Annecchino's arguments for the survival of
Octavian's name in the modern place name Teano are unconvincing: R.
Annecchino, *Atti del V Congr. Naz. di Studi Romani* II (1940), 176–179.

29. M. Marius   Pompeii   56

QFr. 2.8.3 (T &P 123): *Nam illorum praediorum scito mihi vicinum Marium
lumen esse* (the year is 56 or 55; see T &P II², 100); *Fam.* 7.1.1 (T &P 127):
tu in illo cubiculo tuo, ex quo tibi Stabianum perforasti et patefecisti sinum (to
Marius, in 55); *Fam.* 7.3.1 (T &P 464): *cum in Pompeianum vesperi venissem,
tu mihi sollicito animo praesto fuisse* (in 46, describing spring of 49).

Like L. Papirius Paetus (no. 30), Marius had eschewed politics and led a
life of cultivated leisure (*humaniter vivere, Fam.* 7.1.5 [T &P 127]), principally
at Pompeii. Presumably wealthy, he was of weak health and gentle disposition (*QFr.* 2.8.3 [T &P 123]: *Marius et valetudine est et natura imbecillior*), and
nearly died of fright when Cicero, conveying him from Neapolis to Baiae
by litter, suddenly revealed that their escort consisted of 100 armed men
(*QFr.* 2.8.2). Yet he visited Cicero at Cumae (*Fam.* 7.1.5 [T &P 127]); at
Pompeii his house was close by that of Cicero (cf. *vicinum* above, *QFr.*
2.8.3; *Fam.* 7.3.1). It may even have been owing to the influence of Marius,
an older man than Cicero, that the orator came to buy his villa in those parts.
His charm lay in sophisticated and cultured conversation (*QFr.* 2.8.2 [T &P
123]: *subtilitatem veteris urbanitatis et humanissimi sermonis*); his leisurely way
of life, like that of Paetus, the more ambitious Cicero not only approved
(*Fam.* 7.1.5 [T &P 127]: *istam rationem oti tui et laudo vehementer et probo*) but
also occasionally envied (*ibid.*). Marius is last mentioned late in 46, when
Cicero notified him of an imminent trip to Pompeii (*Fam.* 7.4 [T &P 503]).
The Marian *gens* participated actively in the municipal life of Pompeii (see
Della Corte, *CeA*³, no. 193, p. 125, n. 1); Münzer suggests that the M.
Marius recorded in *CIL* I², 1656 a-g, as a candidate for the local aedileship,
may even have been Cicero's good friend and correspondent (*RE* 14 [1930],
1820, no. 25).

30. L. Papirius Paetus   Neapolis   55

Att. 4.9.2 (T &P 122; SB 85): *eo die Neapoli apud Paetum.* (May 26, 55);
Fam. 9.15–26, *passim.*

Paetus was learned, apolitical, wealthy, and cultivated; he resided permanently in Neapolis (cf. Hanslik, *RE* 18 [1942], 1071, no. 69). He is men-

tioned first in 60 (*Att.* 1.20.7 [T&P 26; SB 20]; cf. *Att.* 2.1.12 [T&P 27; SB 21]), when he presented Cicero with some books which had been left him by his cousin (not brother: *Fam.* 9.16.4 [T&P 472]), Servius Clodius, whom Cicero calls *literatissimum* (*Fam.* 9.16.4 [T&P 472]), and whose proficiency as a grammarian and curious death are mentioned by Suetonius (*Gram.* 3). In sixty Paetus was an acquaintance rather than a friend of Cicero (*Att.* 1.20.7 [T&P 26; SB 20]: *vir bonus amatorque noster*, not a strong expression of affection), but Cicero stayed with him in 55. By 46, partly because Paetus was at a safe remove from Roman politics, sympathetic to the political difficulties of Cicero, and no admirer of Caesar (since he feared for his landed property near Neapolis, *Fam.* 9.16.7 [T&P 472]; 9.17.1 [T&P 480]; 9.20.1 [T&P 475]), the two had become fast friends. Paetus' humor was in the Campanian grain—it reminded Cicero of the Granii and Lucilii, but also of more aristocratic wits (*Fam.* 9.15.2 [T&P 481]; see further J. D'Arms, *AJP* 88 [1967], 200–202). He had historical, philological, and philosophical interests. The latter included a sympathy with Epicureanism (*Fam.* 9.20.1 [T&P 475]), but he was probably an eclectic (see Chapter 3, p. 58). Cicero visited Paetus frequently, and when in 46 Paetus was unable to find a house in Neapolis to suit him, Cicero resolved to take up quasi-permanent residence with his friend; for the reasons, see above, Chapter 3, p. 65. Architectural details of Paetus' house are never mentioned—we hear only of the bath (*Fam.* 9.16.9 [T&P 472]). Paetus was still alive early in 43, though apparently not in good health (*Fam.* 9.24.2 [T&P 820]). For the presence of the *cognomen* on a Neapolitan tile, cf. *CIL* X, 8042. 84.

31. Cn. Pompeius Magnus (*cos.* 70)   Cumae   55

   Att. 4.10.2 (T&P 121; SB 84): *Pompeius in Cumanum Parilibus venit* . . . (April 22, 55); *Att.* 4.9.1 (T&P 122; SB 85): *Nos hic cum Pompeio fuimus* (April 27, 55). Sen., *Ep.* 51.11: *Illi quoque* . . . *C. Marius et Cn. Pompeius et Caesar extruxerunt quidem villas in regione Baiana, sed illas imposuerunt summis iugis montium.*

Pompey was proverbial for his wealth and ostentation (Plut. *Pomp.* 40; Joseph. *BJ* 1.155; Sen., *Tranq. an.* 8.6: *quem non puduit locupletiorem esse Pompeio*) and was offended, according to Plutarch, at being the only Sullan supporter not mentioned in Sulla's will (Plut. *Sull.* 38.1). He probably acquired the *Cumanum* some years before Cicero mentions it. Seneca (*Ep.* 51.11) says that Pompey, like Marius and Caesar, built the villa on a height *in regione Baiana*; but though Seneca knew the site (cf. *Ep.* 51.11: *aspice, quam positionem elegerint quibus aedificia excitaverint locis et qualia*) it will be remembered that "the Baian district" is topographically imprecise (see above, Chapter 2, p. 23); the villa of Marius was in fact at Misenum, and Baiae comprised Bauli and part of the administrative district of Cumae. Thus, the villa called *Cumanum* by Cicero and built, according to Seneca, *in regione Baiana*, was almost certainly the same villa (but cf. Miltner, *RE* 21 [1952], 2210). We have no information about the fate of Pompey's *Cumanum* after Pharsalus. It may have been confiscated; we are told that much of Pompey's property went to M. Antonius (*Phil.* 2.64) and that his villas at Alba and Formiae were bought by Dolabella during Caesar's dictatorship (*Phil.* 13.11, where it is also said that Antonius acquired Pompey's *Tusculanum*). Perhaps it was plundered and left unoccupied until, by the treaty of Misenum in 39, Sextus Pompey redeemed it—we do not know.

32. Sex. Pompeius Magnus   Pompeii   ?

CIL X, 8157: *Sex. Pompeius Sex. l. Ruma Neptuno v. s. l.*

Late nineteenth-century excavations in the south suburb of Pompeii revealed "un' edicoletta votiva ricavata dal muro"; within were found a travertine bust and the dedicatory inscription, on marble, quoted above (Della Corte, *CeA*³, 444–445, citing A. Sogliano, "Pompei e la *gens Pompeia*," *Atti della R. Accad. Arch. Lett. di Napoli*, N.S. 8 [1924], 17–31). Sogliano (29) and Della Corte (*CeA*³, 445) have identified the Ruma of the inscription with a freedman of Sextus Pompeius Magnus, younger son of Pompey the Great, and argued that the *aedicula* comprised a part of the complex of a sumptuous *villa maritima* owned originally by the same Sextus; neither the inscription nor the villa is mentioned by F. Miltner, *RE* 21 (1952), 2213–2250, no. 33. While there are literary references to Sextus' presence and piratical raids in the gulf of Naples in the early thirties (Cass. Dio 48.36.1–38.1; App. *BCiv.* 5.72–73; cf. Miltner, *RE* 21 [1952], 2225–2226, on the treaty of Misenum in 39), no ancient author directly links Sextus Pompeius with Pompeii. Yet there may be a hint of such a connection in a letter of Cicero which shows that L. Scribonius Libo, father-in-law to Sex. Pompeius, was on intimate terms with M. Marius (*Fam.* 7.4 [T &P 503]: *in Cumanum veni cum Libone tuo vel nostro potius*; to M. Marius, 46 B.C.). Marius lived permanently in Pompeii, and may well have met Libo there, either at the villa of Sex. Pompeius, or possibly at a house belonging to Libo himself. Cf. *Att.* 16.4.1 (T &P 771; SB 411), which shows that Libo was at Puteoli in July of 44. For other freedmen of Sex. Pompeius at Pompeii, cf. Della Corte, *CeA*³, 445.

33. Q. Pompeius Rufus (*tr. pl. 52*) Bauli 51

Fam. 8.1.4 (T &P 192): . . . *maximus rumor fuit te a Q. Pompeio in itinere occisum. Ego qui scirem Q. Pompeium Baulis embaeneticam facere, et usque eo ut ego misererer eius esurire non sum commotus* . . . (June 51, Caelius to Cicero).

Rufus, grandson of Sulla and of his consular colleague of 88, Q. Pompeius Rufus, was tribune in 52; he incited the people against Milo as Clodius' murderer, and thereby incurred the hostility of Cicero (Ascon. *Mil.* 33, 37, 42, 49; see also Miltner, *RE* 21 [1952], 2252–2253, no. 41). Prosecuted for *vis* by Caelius after his tribunate (Val. Max. 4.2.7), he was convicted and appears to have retired to Bauli, where Caelius says that he *embaeneticam facere* to the point of near starvation. (For a cognate form of this curious word in an inscription from Baiae, see Chapter 4, n. 190.) It is possible that Rufus owned property at Bauli: his mother Cornelia had once presided at a famous villa at Misenum (see above, Chapter 2, p. 27); she later refused to restore to the rightful possession of her son estates temporarily entrusted to her (Val. Max. 4.2.7). Those estates, conceivably, were near Bauli; certainly the fashionable Campanian coast seems a curious retreat for so impoverished and politically discredited a personality as Rufus appears by now to have been (cf. How II, 242, *ad loc.*).

34. Pontius Neapolis 44

Att. 14.21.3 (T &P 728; SB 375) (May, 44): *Ponti Neapolitanum a matre tyrannoctoni possideri!*

For a discussion of how Servilia, the mother of M. Junius Brutus, came to acquire the villa of Pontius, see above, Chapter 3, p. 67. Pontius has regularly been identified with the friend of Cicero who also owned an estate at Trebula: Münzer, *RE* 22 [1953], 34–36, no. 17; Cichorius, *Röm. Stud.*, 171; but cf. SB VI, 241, *ad loc.*

35. C. Rabirius Neapolis 67

Att. 1.6.1 (T &P 2; SB 2): *Domum Rabirianam Neapoli quam tu iam dimensam et exaedificatam animo habebas, M. Fonteius emit HS cccl* $\overline{\text{ɔɔɔ}}\overline{\text{xxx}}$ (Jan. 67).

The aged senator C. Rabirius was prosecuted in 63 for the murder of Saturninus in 100 (cf. Von der Mühll, *RE* 1A [1914], 24–25, no. 5), and was defended by Cicero. *Domum Rabirianam*, as T &P have observed, seems to imply that the house was the principal family seat rather than a simple dwelling (in which case Cicero might have written *domum Rabiri*; cf. *domum*

Sullanam, "Sulla's house at Neapolis," *Fam.* 9.15.5 [T &P 481]). How (II, *ad loc.*, 418) compares *domus Anniana*, *Att.* 4.3.3 (T &P 92; SB 75), for a house at Rome; cf. *domus Seliciana*, *Fam.* 9.16.10 (T &P 472). But the latter is a mistake for *villa Seliciana* and so not a true parallel. SB (I, 280–281, *ad. loc.*) rightly observes that Rabirius "may have been the name either of the vendor (of the house) or of a previous owner." In either case, Cicero will have been referring to his former client, who in 63 was supported *cum tanto studio . . . totius Apuliae, singulari voluntate Campaniae* (Cic. *Rab. perd.* 8). His Campanian connections were thus clearly long-standing; but his tribe, the Galeria (Taylor, *Voting Districts*, 250), renders it doubtful that he was a local man. (Cf. Lepore, *PdP* fasc. 25–27 [1952], 320.) He adopted his nephew C. Rabirius Postumus (Cic. *Rab. Post.* 45), who was active in trade at Puteoli (*ibid.* 40).

36. C. Scribonius Curio (*tr. pl.* 50)   Cumae   49

Att. 10.4.7 (T &P 382; SB 195): *Cum haec scripsissem, a Curione mihi nuntiatum est eum ad me venire. Venerat enim is in Cumanum vesperi pridie, id est Idibus* (from Cumae, April 14, 49).

The younger Curio was at first the great hope of the *optimates* (*Att.* 2.18.1 [T &P 45; SB 38]) but a profligate, whose debts Caesar paid in return for his support, which was then wholehearted (*Att.* 1.14.5 [T &P 20; SB 14]; App. *BCiv.* 2.26; Suet. *Iul.* 29; and see in general Münzer, *RE* 2A [1921], 867–876, no. 11). He fell in battle in Africa in 49. The *Cumanum* is very probably the same villa of Marius which the elder Curio had acquired during the Sullan proscriptions (see above, Chapter 2, p. 29), and which young Curio inherited upon his father's death in 53 (*Fam.* 2.2 [T &P 168]). Cicero implies that the estate of the father was near Baiae (*Or. in Clod. et Cur.* ed. Klotz-Schoell, fr. 21); the Bobiensian scholiast refers to it simply as *fundus in Campania* (T. Stangl, *Cic. Orat. Schol.* II [Leipzig 1912], 89). But since Baiae was officially a part of Cumae, and since neither the fragments of Cicero's speech nor the Bobiensian scholiast provide exact topographical description, the *Cumanum* mentioned in *Att.* 10.4.8 may well be the same villa.

37. Q. Selicius   Neapolis   46

Fam. 9.16.10 (T &P 472): *De villa Seliciana et curasti diligenter et scripsisti facetissime. Itaque puto me praetermissurum; salis enim satis est, †sannionum† parum* (July 46, to Paetus at Neapolis).

Along with the *domus Sullana* (see above, no. 11) Cicero considered purchasing the villa of Selicius when he thought he might move to Neapolis in 46; again L. Papirius Paetus was his local consultant. From Paetus' description, Cicero apparently felt that the villa, though attractive enough, lacked the more essential advantages. Selicius watched closely over the interests of Lentulus Spinther (*Fam.* 1.5a.4 [T &P 99]) during Spinther's proconsulship in Cilicia, and was known to Cicero as a moneylender as early as 61 (*Att.* 1.12.1 [T &P 17; SB 12]); how long the villa had been in his possession is not known. Selicius, who was probably a senator (SB I, 298, on *Att.* 1.12.1), is not mentioned later than the letter to Paetus; his death in 46 would explain the availability of his Neapolitan villa (so also Münzer, *RE* 2A [1921], 1259, no. 1). The *MSS* of the letters mention a "Selicia," apparently of Puteoli, in October, 44 (*Att.* 15.13.4 [T &P 794; SB 416]; cf. Münzer, *RE* 2A [1921], 1259, no. 2). But the *gens* may have been Praenestine: *CIL* I², 294–299; on which see R. Syme, *Historia* 13 (1964), 122–123.

38. Servilia, mother of M. Junius Brutus   Neapolis   44

Att. 14.21.3 (T &P 728; SB 375): *Ponti Neapolitanum a matre tyrannoctoni possideri!* (May, 44; cf. above, no. 34).

For a discussion of how Servilia, the mother of M. Junius Brutus, came to acquire the villa of Pontius from Caesar, see above, Chapter 3, p. 67. If the reading *Servilia* be adopted in place of the *Selicia* of the *MSS* at *Att.* 15.13.4 (T &P 794; SB 416)—see above on no. 37, and cf. SB VI, 296, *ad loc.*—Brutus's mother was probably at the villa in Naples in October of this same year: Cicero at Puteoli looked to her, and to her visitors, for some news of Brutus (but cf. Münzer, "Selicia," *RE* 2A [1921], 1259, no. 2). For the extent of her political interests and influence, cf. Münzer, "Servilia," *RE* 2A (1923), 1817–1821, no. 101.

39. P. Servilius Isauricus (*cos.* II, 41)   Cumae   ?

See Catalogue II below, no. 39 (P. Servilius Vatia).

40. Servius Sulpicius Rufus (*cos.* 51)   Cumae   49

Fam. 4.2.1 (T &P 389): ... *Postumia tua me convenit et Servius noster. His placuit ut tu in Cumanum venires, quod etiam mecum ut ad te scriberem egerunt* (April 49, Cumae: to S. Sulpicius Rufus). Cf. *Att.* 10.9.3 (T &P 393; SB 200); 10.13.2 (T &P 399; SB 205); 10.14.1 (T &P 400; SB 206).

Postumia his wife and his son Servius were awaiting Servius Sulpicius Rufus, the eminent jurist, in the family villa at Cumae in 49; he finally joined them on the 8th of May. A moderate and a man of peace, he expressed a desire to die in his bed (*Att.* 10.14.3 [T &P 400; SB 206]); but his wife was energetic and his son supported Caesar. After Pharsalus he was governor of Greece after living and lecturing in Samos (Münzer, *RE* 4 A [1931], 855–856, no. 95); he survived until 43, when he was sent along with L. Calpurnius Piso Caesoninus (no. 5) and L. Marcius Philippus (no. 28) as ambassador to Antony before Mutina, and died before his return. It is perhaps more than coincidence that each of these four consulars owned villas on the Bay of Naples: the three ambassadors may have been selected in part as a result of the closeness of their personal relations with Antonius—relations which flourished during periods of leisure in coastal Campania. The villa, mentioned only in the spring of 49, probably remained in the hands of Sulpicius' family after his death. He numbered a Capuan, Ofillius, among his legal pupils; Frederiksen, *Rep. Cap.*, p. 119.

41. M. Terentius Varro   Cumae   46

Fam. 9.1.2 (T &P 456): *Quam ob rem sive in Tusculano sive in Cumano ad te placebit* . . . (early in 46); *Fam.* 9.15.3 (T &P 481); *Acad. Post.* 1. 1: *in Cumano nuper* . . . *nuntiatum est a M. Varrone venisse eum Roma* . . . *itaque confestim ad eum ire perreximus, paulumque cum ab eius villa abessemus ipsum ad nos venientem vidimus.*

Varro's *Cumanum*, like that of Cicero, was near the Lucrine Lake; it is the imaginary setting of the second edition of the *Academica*, and a fragment of the third book shows that it could not have been set on an elevated piece of ground (Nonius, fr. 65: *Et ut nos nunc sedemus ad Lucrinum pisciculosque exultantes videmus* . . . (Reid, *Academica*, 164, fr. 13). Varro was over forty in 75 (by which time the Campanian coast was fashionable) and wealthy: he had family estates at Reate, a luxurious farm at Casinum, and a villa at Tusculum in addition to the *Cumanum*. It is probable, therefore, that he acquired the *Cumanum* long before its first mention in 46. Having served as an officer in the east under Pompey, and as Pompey's legate in Spain, he was nonetheless pardoned by Caesar, and his property seems to have remained intact. Although the villa at Casinum was plundered by Antony in the spring of 44 (*Phil.* 2.103–105; cf. Dahlmann, *RE* Suppl. 6 [1935], 1178), Cicero's outraged comment in section 104 suggests that such harsh treatment was not repeated. Varro seems to have visited the *Cumanum* in October of 44 (*Att.* 15.13a.6 [T &P 795; SB 417]), and in May of 43 he was still rich: D. Brutus refers to the *Varronis thensauros* (*Fam.* 11.10.5 [T &P 854]). The *migratio et emptio* of Varro in 45 (*Fam.* 9.8.2 [T &P 641]) remain mysterious, nor may it be said with certainty that he continued to own the *Cumanum* until his death in 27.

42. M. Terentius Varro Lucullus (*cos.* 73)　　　　?　　　　　　　　?

Varro, *Rust.* 3.3.10: *Quis enim propter nobilitates ignorat piscinas Philippi, Hortensi, Lucullorum? Ibid.* 3.17.8: *Etenim hac incuria laborare aiebat M. Lucullum ac piscinas eius despiciebat, quod aestuaria idonea non haberet . . .*

The ponds of M. Lucullus, denigrated by Hortensius, were probably somewhere on the Campanian coast, where the famous owners of *piscinae* (Varro *Rust.* 3.3.10: the plural *Lucullorum* shows that M. Lucullus is included) all had their preserves and luxury villas; the exact location is unknown. M. Lucullus outlived his more celebrated brother (Plut. *Luc.* 43) and is last mentioned early in 56 (*Fam.* 1.1.3 [T &P 951]); cf. How II, *ad loc.*, 185.

43. Marcus Tullius Cicero (*cos.* 63)　　　Pompeii (after 63), Cumae (56), Puteoli (45)

a) *Pompeianum* (Schmidt, 489–491): Cicero owned this villa, his first on the Bay of Naples, before 60 (*Att.* 1.20.1 [T &P 26; SB 20]); it is mentioned first in the *Academica* and last at the end of 44 (*Att.* 16.11.6 [T &P 799; SB 420]); he thus seems to have had it still at the time of his death. His friend M. Marius (no. 29) was one of the major attractions of Pompeii and could have been the first one to interest Cicero in the site. But Cicero's familiarity with the town very possibly began during the Social War: see G. O. Onorato, "La partecipazione di Cicerone alla guerra sociale in Campania," *RAAN* N.S. 25 (1950), 415–426. Although the villa has not been found, it was probably situated in the northwest suburb of the city which became the *Pagus Augustus Felix Suburbanus* (Della Corte, *CeA*[3], 438–439); it was on elevated terrain with a view of the sea (*Acad. Pr.* 2.80, where the setting is the villa of Hortensius at Bauli). Cicero traveled from Cumae or Puteoli to Pompeii by boat (e.g., *Acad. Pr.* 2.9; *Att.* 16.7.8 [T &P 783; SB 415]); it was quieter than the more fashionable resorts in the northwest corner of the Bay of Naples (*Att.* 5.2.2 [T &P 185; SB 95]; 15.13.6 [T &P 794; SB 417]), and it was probably for this reason that Cicero, no recluse, preferred his other villas: he rarely seems to have spent more than a few days at a time in the *Pompeianum.*

b) *Cumanum* (Beloch, *Campanien*[2], 175–176; Schmidt, 478–486; Dubois,

PA, 366–370; Frederiksen, *RE* 23 [1959], 2059): Cicero did not buy the *Cumanum* before his return from exile; it is first mentioned in 56, when it may not have been ready to occupy (*QFr.* 2.5.4 [T &P 106]). Vestorius of Puteoli (Schmidt, 479, n. 3) helped with details of the purchase; the architect Cyrus with necessary renovations. The next April Cicero was in residence and entertained Pompey (*Att.* 4.9.1 [T &P 122; SB 85]). The Roman *municipium* of Cumae lay well to the west, but the town's official territory comprised both *Lacus Lucrinus* and *Lacus Avernus* (Beloch, *Campanien*[2], 163–176, with pl. I); Cicero's *Cumanum*, which had a view of the sea, lay on the eastern slope of Lucrinus (*Att.* 14.16.1 [T &P 721; SB 370]: *villam ad Lucrinum*) in the area now occupied by Monte Nuovo. The western border of ancient Puteoli was nearby, Pliny *NH* 31.6: *digna memoratu villa est ab Averno lacu Puteolos tendentibus imposita litore* [*sc. Lucrini Lacus*] *celebrata porticu ac nemore, quam vocabat Cicero Academiam.* The villa's nearness to Puteoli allowed Cicero to refer to it in one instance as *Puteolanum* (*Fam.* 5.15.2 [T &P 587]; for the reason, see above, no. 24). In addition to the portico and grove mentioned by Pliny, there was a garden at the villa (*QFr.* 2.8.4 [T &P 123]) and apparently a permanent resident staff of slaves and freedmen for maintenance (*Att.* 14.16.1 [T &P 721; SB 370]: *vilici et procuratores*; on the significance of Cicero's use of the plurals, see above, Chapter 3, n. 61). One of the procurators was undoubtedly Tullius Laurea, who sang the praises of the villa and its eloquent master during the proprietorship of C. Antistius Vetus (Pliny *NH* 31.7; see above, no. 2), and who composed verses describing a grim accident which befell a fisherman—a subject very possibly inspired by a scene witnessed in nearby Puteoli (*Anth. Lyr. Graec.* 7.294). To own a luxury villa at Cumae was a mark of status which Cicero would not have been inclined to forego. In fifty-six there were still *nobiles* who resented his purchase of the *Tusculanum* of Catulus (*Att.* 4.5.2 [T &P 108; SB 80]); although Cicero nowhere hints that he was slighted by his aristocratic neighbors, there are signs that he derived some satisfaction from owning a villa in their midst (*Att.* 5.2.2 [T &P 185; SB 95]: to be called upon by Hortensius was particularly gratifying; on the entire question of Cicero's relationship with the *nobiles*, see especially W. Kroll, *Die Kultur der Ciceronischen Zeit*, 37–44). He spent at least some time in the *Cumanum* in 55, 53, 52, 51, 50, 49, 46, 45, and 44 (Schmidt, 482); Caesar was his most difficult guest (*Att.* 13.52.1–2 [T &P 679; SB 353]). There was a rumor in the spring of 44 that he might sell the *Cumanum*—but he had no such intentions then (*Att.* 14.13.5 [T &P 718; SB 367]) and refused an offer made through the agent Pindarus in mid-summer (*Att.* 16.1.5 [T &P 769; SB 409]). After Cicero's death Vetus was the proprietor of the villa (see above, no. 2). Later Silius Italicus appears to have purchased part of the connected lands (see Catalogue II, no. 12); and Hadrian is alleged to have found burial there (but see above, Chapter 4, n. 154). It was seen by Flavio Biondo in the 15th century (Annecchino, *Camp. Rom.* I, 25; Frederiksen, *RE* 23 [1959], 2059), and it probably was preserved in some form until the eruption of Monte Nuovo in 1538 buried it beyond recovery.

c) *Puteolanum:* (Schmidt, 486; Annecchino, *Camp. Rom.* I, 17–43): this villa must be identified with the *horti Cluviani* (*Att.* 13.46.3 [T&P 663; SB 338]; 14.16.1 [T&P 721; SB 370]), part of Cicero's inheritance from the businessman Cluvius of Puteoli who died in 45 (for details see above, Chapter 3, pp. 52–53). By the spring of 44 the property was ready for his occupancy and is subsequently called *Cluviana* (*sc. praedia*): *Att.* 14.9.1 (T&P 712; SB 363), or simply *Puteolanum* (*Att.* 14.7.1 [T&P 709; SB 361]; 15.1b.1 [T&P 731; SB 378]; *Fat.* 2). Cicero at Puteoli was close to the local businessmen who were his friends, drew substantial profits from the rentable property which was part of the inheritance from Cluvius (see above, Chapter 3, p. 53), and at a port town could get news of important happenings elsewhere more quickly than at either Cumae or Pompeii (*Att.* 16.14.1 [T&P 805; SB 425]). It appears that the *Puteolanum* was located almost at the sea's edge (*Att.* 14.13.1 [T&P 718; SB 367], discussed above, Chapter 3, p. 46; *Att.* 14.16.1 [T&P 721; SB 370]: *conscendens ab hortis Cluvianis in phaselum epicopum*) in the western sector of the city (Annecchino, *Camp. Rom.* I, 22, 25; Schmidt, 488). Cicero may have bequeathed the *Puteolanum* to his favorite freedman, M. Tullius Tiro: Suet., ed. Roth (Teubner 1904), p. 289, lines 14–16: *M. Tullius Tiro Ciceronis libertus . . . in Puteolano praedio suo usque ad centesimum annum consenescit.*

44. C. Vibius Pansa Caetronianus (*cos.* 43)   Baiae? Pompeii?   44

Att. 14.20.4 (T&P 727; SB 374): *Cum Pansa vixi in Pompeiano* (May 11, 44); *Att.* 15.1a.3 (T&P 730; SB 377): *cum a me xvii Kal. de Puteolano Neapolim Pansae conveniendi causa proficisceretur Hirtius . . .* (May 17, 44).

Cicero was in his villas on the Campanian coast from mid-April through mid-May in 44; like Hirtius and Balbus, Pansa is mentioned frequently in his letters and appears to have been on the coast himself throughout this period. On April 21 and 22 he was staying with Cicero at Puteoli and, together with Hirtius, was insisting that he be given exercises in rhetoric; Cicero jokingly complained that he thus got no rest even at the seaside (*Att.* 14.11.2 [T&P 714; SB 365]; 14.12.2 [T&P 715; SB 366]; Ensslin, *RE* 8 A

[1958], 1959, no. 16). Inasmuch as on the 11th of May Cicero reported having seen much of Pansa at Pompeii, and six days later Pansa and Hirtius were to meet in Neapolis, it seems highly likely that Pansa had his own house somewhere on the coast; Baiae is a possibility, but so is Pompeii, where the Vibii later became an important family (see Della Corte, *CeA*³, 153–154, nos. 271–273; cf., on the provenance of Pansa, Ensslin, *RE* 8 A [1958], 1954–1955). Pansa rose to prominence under Caesar; Cicero's private opinion of that comfortable Epicurean was not high (*Att.* 16.1.4 [T &P 769; SB 409]; cf. *Fam.* 16.27.2 [T &P 815]; Ensslin, *RE* 8 A [1958], 1964–1965).

CATALOGUE II · *The Owners of Pleasure Villas or Private Houses on the Bay of Naples during Imperial Times (30 B.C. – A.D. 400)*

The format of the present Catalogue follows in most essentials that of its late Republican counterpart (explained above, pp. 44, 171). In this list, however, certain persons native to the Campanian *municipia* have been included; this is entirely compatible with the social changes which were ushered in during the early Empire: see above, Chapter 5, pp. 124–125. It should be noted further that although each contemporary of Symmachus has a separate entry (see nos. 2, 3, 4, 5, 27, 28, 47) discussion of those men will be found under Symmachus' own name (no. 42). All dates, unless otherwise specified, are A.D.

1. L. Acilius Strabo (*cos. suff.* 71)   Cumae or Puteoli   after 71(?)

Not. d. Sc. (1893), 211 (Cumae); *ibid.* (1902), 630 (Puteoli); *AJA* 2 (1898), 391 (= *AE* [1899], 34), Puteoli: *L. Acili Strabonis.*

In 1893 F. Colonna reported the recurrence of the name *L. Acili Strabonis*, stamped upon eight pieces of lead pipe found among others "in territorio cumano" (*Not. d. Sc.* [1893], 211). Fifteen such pieces were at Pozzuoli in 1898 in the possession of Canon De Criscio (the owner of a large collection of local inscriptions, many of which were made available to Mommsen during the preparation of the tenth volume of the *Corpus*; cf. *CIL* X, p. 189, xxxvii); W. Dennison examined eight of these and concluded that they were all made with the same stamp (W. Dennison, *AJA* 2 [1898], 391; it is highly probable that some of the inscriptions inspected by Colonna and Dennison were identical; cf. also *Not. d. Sc.* [1902], 629). The presence of a name stamped in the genitive is of course a characteristic feature of *fistulae plumbeae aquariae* (see R. Cagnat, *Cours d'Epigraphie Latine* 2 [Paris 1889], 303; de Ruggiero, *Dizionario Epigrafico* I [1895], 585); the name denotes either the manufacturer of the pipe or, more regularly, the owner of the property through which the pipe ran. Colonna was therefore almost certainly correct to conclude that L. Acilius Strabo owned a villa in the vicinity of Cumae or Puteoli. Of this proprietor something more is known. A Greek inscription from Neapolis (*ILS* 6460) provides evidence for the date of his consulship, and Groag plausibly suggests that he is identical with the praetorian Acilius Strabo, sent by Claudius to adjudicate upon estates in Cyrene and subsequently (in 59) accused by the Cyrenaeans (Tac. *Ann.* 14.18.2–4; cf. Groag, *PIR*² A 82). It cannot be determined whether Acilius Strabo came originally from Campania, although the tribe of his (apparently) adopted son may provide a clue: see below, no. 41.

2. Acyndinus (*cos.* 340)   Bauli   375
   Symmachus *Ep.* 1.1.2; cf. *CIL* X, 1995; 8061.
   Discussed below, no. 42 (Symmachus).

3. Vettius Agorius Praetexatus   Baiae   before 385
   (elected to consulship of 385)
   Symmachus *Ep.* 1.47, 1.48.
   Discussed below, no. 42 (Symmachus).

4. Caecina Decius Albinus (*praef. urb.* 402)   Neapolis   ?
   Symmachus *Ep.* 7.36.
   Discussed below, no. 42 (Symmachus).

5. Priscus Attalus (*praef. urb.* 409)   Baiae   397
   Symmachus *Ep.* 7.16.2; 7.24.
   Discussed below, no. 42 (Symmachus).

6. M. Bennius Rufus   Cumae   Augustan Age
   1) *CIL* X, 3713, Cumae: *M. Benni Rufi.* 2) *CIL* X, 1684 (*ILS* 1375), Neapolis: [*M.*] *Bennio M. f. Ru[fo] procuratori* [*i*]*mp. Caesaris Augu[sti*], *Oenses ex provinc. Afr[ica].*

A lead water pipe (1) bearing the name of M. Bennius Rufus was reported by Mommsen (*ad loc.*) to have been found at Cumae in 1851; it is thus highly probable that this man possessed a house or villa in the vicinity. A second inscription (2) strengthens the hypothesis: discovered at Neapolis, it was there seen and transcribed by Mommsen, who was able to supply the initial of the *praenomen* and the final two letters of the *cognomen* by comparison with the name on the pipe. That Africans from Oea (modern Tripoli) should have expressed gratitude to this equestrian procurator in an inscription displayed at Neapolis strongly suggests that M. Bennius Rufus was

9+

native to that district (so also Stein, *PIR*² B 107, *q.v.* also for Carthaginian inscriptions of the slaves of Rufus). He is the earliest attested *procurator Provinciae Africae* (H. G. Pflaum, *C. Proc. Équestres*, 1092). *Bennius Proculus* is attested in an inscription which came to light recently in Naples (see A. De Franciscis, "Le recenti scoperte in Santa Chiara e la topografia di Napoli romana," *Archeologia Classica* 6 [1954], 281–282; and for Bennii from Puteoli, see Dennison in *AJA* 2 [1898], 377).

7. C. Bruttius Praesens L. Fulvius Rusticus (*cos.* II, 139)   ?   *ca.* 103

Pliny *Ep.* 7.3.1: *Tantane perseverantia tu modo in Lucania, modo in Campania?* '*ipse enim,*' *inquis,* '*Lucanus, uxor Campana.*'

It is not known in which of the Campanian towns the wife of Praesens had her property; the estate may not have been located on the coast. Whatever its precise situation, the attractions proved abiding; Pliny goes on to rebuke his friend for having become so enveloped in leisure as to neglect the senate, and urges him to return to Rome and thereby to intermit, if not to renounce altogether, the pleasure of *peregrinatio* (*ibid.*, 2–5; see above, Chapter 5, pp. 157–158). A recently discovered inscription from Africa strikingly confirms the testimony of Pliny by revealing that Praesens long held no political office but later enjoyed a distinguished career under Hadrian (*AE* [1950], 66; on which see Sherwin–White, *The Letters of Pliny, ad loc.*, 404; add also, for his career, the acephalous inscription from Lepcis: J. M. Reynolds and J. B. Ward Perkins, *The Inscriptions of Roman Tripolitania*, no. 545). Other epigraphical evidence shows that the tribe of the family was the *Pomptina* (*ILS* 1117); this fact coheres neatly with Pliny's notice of the Lucanian origin of Praesens (cf. Sherwin–White, *The Letters of Pliny*, 404; *q.v.* also for the letter's date). And Praesens' wife's name is now known, Laberia Crispina, grandmother of the empress Crispina and daughter of the M'. Laberius Maximus who encountered disgrace at the end of Trajan's reign (see M. Torelli, *Epigraphica* 24 [1962], 55–58; J. M. Reynolds, *JRS* 56 [1966], 119). Her father has been supposed to have come from Lanuvium (Syme, *Tacitus*, p. 599, n. 7); instead Campania will have claimed him (if, that is, Laberia is identical with Pliny's *uxor Campana*, as Torelli assumed; but cf. the doubts of R. Syme, *JRS* 58 [1968], 150). Mommsen assigned three inscriptions of the *gens Laberia* to Puteoli: *CIL* X, 1725, 2634, 3135; and it will be remembered that the well-known *eques*, Decimus Laberius, was probably native to that city: see above, Chapter 3, p. 60.

8. Caesius Bassus   near Mt. Vesuvius   79

Schol. on Persius 6.1: *hanc satiram scribit Persius ad Caesium Bassum poetam lyricum, quem fama est in praediis suis positum ardente Vesuvio . . . et late ignibus abundante cum villa sua ustum esse.*

Only the scholiast informs us that Caesius Bassus, lyric poet and friend of Persius, perished on his estate during the eruption of Mt. Vesuvius; the villa was very likely situated somewhere on the coast between Neapolis and Stabiae. Relying upon the authority of the scholium, O. Jahn ingeniously emended "Caesi" for "Casci," husband of the Rectina whose villa lay beneath Vesuvius and who sent a plea for help to the Elder Pliny at Misenum in 79 (Pliny *Ep.* 6.16.8; see below, no. 38, Rectina). But "Casci" seems the *lectio certa* (cf. the discussion below, no. 38), and the wife of Caesius Bassus perhaps bore the name Sulpicia: the phrase *Sulpicia T. f. Pia Caesi Bassi* appears upon a small marble vessel from Neapolis (*CIL* X, 2991). Mommsen may well have erred in assigning that inscription to Puteoli. His normally valid grounds were that most of the local *tituli* which give no indication of their exact provenance must have originated in that city (Mommsen, *CIL* X, 183). Among lyric poets, Caesius Bassus is classed just beneath Horace by Quintilian, who speaks of him as recently dead (Quint. *Inst.* 10.1.96 *quem nuper vidimus*); he was also very probably the author of the didactic poem *de metris* (cf. *PIR*[2] C 192). From the opening verses of Persius' 6th satire, it appears that Caesius Bassus, in addition to his Campanian villa, owned a farm in the Sabine country, whither he repaired to compose during the winter months. For a T. Caesius Anthianus at Puteoli, and for the presence of the *gens Caesia* in other local inscriptions, see Ch. Huelsen, *Röm. Mitt.* 23 (1908), 71–73; esp. 72, n. 1.

9. C. Calpurnius Piso (*suff. ann. inc.*)   Baiae   65

Tac. *Ann.* 15.52.1: *coniuratis . . . placitum maturare caedem apud Baias in villa Pisonis, cuius amoenitate captus Caesar crebro ventitabat balneasque et epulas inibat . . .*

The villa at Baiae (cf. Beloch, *Campanien*[2], 186) may have been a part of Piso's vast inheritance from his mother (Schol. on Juv. 5.109), but since his parentage is unknown (see *PIR*[2] C 284), the earlier history of the property cannot be traced. Before the owner's suicide in 65, he doubtless bequeathed his villa either to his second wife Atria Galla (an *Atria* occurs in an inscription from Nola: *CIL* X, 1288), or, more probably, to Nero himself, who took such manifest pleasure in the villa's chambers and baths: Piso's will contained gross flattery of the emperor (Tac. *Ann.* 15.59.8). Figurehead of the conspiracy against Nero in 65, Piso nonetheless (in Tacitus' view) lacked the gravity and self-discipline for imperial leadership (*Ann.* 14.48.4). His were other accomplishments. Noble and comely, eloquent and accessible, he was generous with his wealth and cultivated in his tastes (*Ann.* 14.48.2–3). The author of the *Laus Pisonis* supplies further evidence for Piso's Campanian diversions; noting that Greek culture flowed forth from Piso's Roman lips, he adds that eloquent Neapolis could bear witness (*Laus Pisonis* 89–92). When at leisure Piso composed verses and played the lyre: *Mira subest gravitas inter fora, mirus omissa | paulisper gravitate lepos (ibid.,* 162–168). He even took part in theatrical productions. Tacitus records the rumor that to Subrius Flavus it mattered little in point of disgrace whether Nero or Piso reigned— the one a player of the lyre, the other a singer of tragic parts (*Ann.* 15.65.2, confirmed by Schol. on Juv. 5.109). For the possible scene of his performances, see above, Chapter 5, p. 150.

10. C. Cassius Camillus   Baiae   ?

CIL X, 1902: *C. Cassi Camilli*

The name appears upon a *fistula plumbea aquaria* discovered at Baiae; Mommsen did not himself examine the inscription, which was described to him by Friedländer (Mommsen, *CIL* X, *ad loc.*, 232). The person named on the pipe was presumably the owner of a house or villa at Baiae (so also Dubois, *PA*, 363); he has no entry in *PIR*². Pliny once refers to a *villa Camilliana* in Campania, owned by L. Calpurnius Fabatus (Pliny *Ep.* 6.31.2); a Camillius was probably the previous proprietor (see above, Catalogue I, no. 37). But that estate was in the country, not on the coast (Pliny *Ep.* 6.31.4).

11. Castricus   Baiae   90–91

Mart. 6.43.1–6: *Dum tibi felices indulgent, Castrice, Baiae | canaque sulphureis nympha natatur aquis, | me Nomentani confirmant otia ruris | et casa iugeribus non onerosa suis. | hoc mihi Baiani soles mollisque Lucrinus, | hoc sunt mihi vestrae, Castrice, divitiae.*

Castricus—a curious *cognomen*; this may be the *gentilicium*—is unknown save from the epigrams of Martial, who counted himself inferior to his friend in both wealth and poetic skill (Mart. 7.42.1–2; cf. *PIR*² C 545). From Martial's contrast of his friend's expensive pleasures with those of his own rural retreat at Nomentanum, it is clear that Castricus was familiar with

Roman society and owned an estate at Baiae. There he consorted with his favorite Eutychus, until that youth met death by drowning in Baiae's waves; Martial proffered verses of consolation, instructing the Naiads of the Lucrine Lake to mourn (6.68.1–12). Although mentioned first in the 6th book of the epigrams (composed by 90–91: see 6.3.5–6; and cf. *PIR* V 77), Castricus may have been among Martial's hosts during the latter's stay on Campania's coast in the summer of 88 (cf. 4.30, 4.44, 4.57, 4.63; cf. *PIR* V 77).

12. Ti. Catius Asconius Silius Italicus (*cos.* 68)   Neapolis   *ca.* 95

Pliny *Ep.* 3.7.1: *Modo nuntiatus est Silius Italicus in Neapolitano suo inedia finesse vitam.* Pliny *Ep.* 3.7.6: *Novissime ita suadentibus annis ab urbe secessit, seque in Campania tenuit ac ne adventu quidem novi principis inde commotus est* Pliny *Ep.* 3.7.8: *Plures isdem in locis villas possidebat, adamatisque novis priores neglegebat. Multum ubique librorum, multum statuarum, multum imaginum, quas non habebat modo, verum etiam venerabatur, Vergili ante omnes, cuius natalem religiosius quam suum celebrabat, Neapoli maxime, ubi monimentum eius adire ut templum solebat.*

An inscription from Aphrodisias reveals the full name of the author of the *Punica* (W. M. Calder, *CR* 49 [1935], 217; cf. *ILS* 5025); it has been suggested that he came originally from Cisalpine Gaul (see G. E. F. Chilver, *Cisalpine Gaul* [Oxford 1941], 109–111; cf. Sherwin–White, *The Letters of Pliny*, 227). If so, it is noteworthy (albeit characteristic of some imperial senators from the provinces; cf. Valerius Asiaticus, no. 43 below) that in retirement the *novus homo* Silius Italicus sought out, in place of his native district, the most fashionable portion of the Italian coast. The last of his public offices appears to have been the proconsulship of Asia, which he held in 77 (Pliny *Ep.* 3.7.3; cf. *PIR* C 474); but he will probably have owned property (perhaps inherited: Chilver, *Cis. Gaul*, 110) in Neapolis before retiring permanently to that region at some point during the early nineties; once in residence, not even the accession of Trajan could induce him to return to Rome (*Ep.* 3.7.6). Although one reason for his retirement may have been his precarious health, the intellectual climate of Neapolis was certainly to his taste, and his activities while in Campania prove that he was neither a total invalid nor a total recluse. He lavished much energy upon the decoration and appointments of his various villas, incurring reproach for the extravagance of his aesthetic enthusiasms (*ibid.*, 7: *erat* φιλόκαλος *usque ad emacitatis reprehensionem*). By ninety-five, Silius had purchased from an impoverished former owner the tomb of Virgil, located by Donatus before the second milestone from

Neapolis along the *Via Puteolana* (Mart. 11. 49.1–4; Donatus *Vita Vergili* 36). The monument became the focus of the poet's devotion to Virgil, and Statius also worshipped at its threshold (*Silv.* 4.4.51–52). Martial's statement that Silius owned *iugera Ciceronis* as well as the *monumenta Maronis* (Mart. 11.48.1–2), when taken together with Pliny's ascription to Silius of many villas in the same region, permits the inference that Silius also purchased Cicero's *Cumanum* (above, Catalogue I, no. 43b) doubtless from a descendant of C. Antistius Vetus (see Catalogue I, no. 2). Somewhere on that property Demetrius and Apollonius of Tyana may have conversed during the reign of Domitian: see above, Chapter 5, p. 146. See further Klotz, *RE* 5 A (1934), 80.

13. (Appius?) Claudius (*cos.* ?)   Neapolis   3rd century (?)
    CIL X, 1688 (*ILS* 1184):
        [*Qui dedit*] *Aeneadum fastis ex ordine consul*
        [*nomi*]*na, progenies Claudius Appiadum,*
        [*al*]*ta Sabinillae dat dulci moenia natae*
        [. . .]*anus genitor de rude coepta solo,*
        [*sospes ubi an*]*noso mea Claudia lucis in aevo*
        [*prospicia*]*t lepidam pulchra anus in subolem.*

The above inscription in elegiacs was examined in Neapolis by Mommsen; the initial letters in each line are Beucheler's restorations (whence *Carmina Latina Epigraphica* [Leipzig 1897], no. 888). A consular Claudius (probably of the third century; cf. the comment of Mommsen, *CIL* X, *ad loc.* p. 207: *litteris magnis aetatis sequioris*) herein presents his daughter Claudia Sabinilla with a new house or villa within whose walls, the donor hopes, she may in time witness her grandchildren around her; Mommsen was almost certainly correct to conjecture that the inscription originally adorned not a sepulchral monument, but the house itself, built for the daughter perhaps on the occasion of her marriage. The identity of the consul remains in doubt, owing to the lacuna in line 4. Against Borghesi's restoration [*Iuli*]*anus*, Beucheler advanced sound metrical objections, and instead proposed [*germ*]*anus* (*Carmina Latina Epigraphica, ad loc.*); but this entails the omission of *cognomen*, which Mommsen regarded as most improbable. The *praenomen*, however, will probably have been Appius; as Groag observed (*PIR*² C 762), no consular Claudius who lacked it would have dared claim descent from one of the most famous patrician *gentes* of the Republic. (It should nonetheless be admitted that fanciful genealogies were going about in the third century: see *S.H.A. Alex Sev.* 44.3). The consular donor's family origins, then, mark him as very probably a sojourner on, rather than a native of, the Bay of Naples; further, the fact that the new house or villa was being constructed upon ground where no building had previously stood (cf. *CIL* X, 1688, vv. 3–4 quoted above: *moenia . . . de rude coepta solo*) suggests that the new edifice was built upon land already owned by Claudius; he may have had a villa of his own in the same territory. An Ap[pius] Claudius, apparently a priest, is mentioned in an early third-century inscription from Puteoli: see *Not. d. Sc.* (1954), 285. And a much earlier, and more famous, Appius Claudius (Pulcher) also had Campanian connections: the consul of 38 B.C. was honored after his death with a statue and inscriptions at Herculaneum (*CIL* X, 1423, 1424).

14. Cocceia Galla   Baiae   ?

   Not. d. Sc. (1932), 293–303: *Cocceiae Gallae C. F.*

   The name of this *clarissima femina* appears upon a *fistula plumbea* discovered among the remains of a Roman villa situated on the "Sella di Baia," the hill which divides the Bacoli peninsula from the territory of Lake Fusaro and Cumae to the west. Due to the frequency of the *gentilicium* in coastal Campania (see below, no. 15, L. Cocceius Nerva, for examples), neither the identity of the owner nor the date of the lead pipe can be securely fixed. The editor, Mingazzini, tentatively assigned the inscription to the first century, noting that the reticulate and brick work of the villa lend circumstantial support to such a date (P. Mingazzini, *Not. d. Sc.* [1932], 303). But in the year after Mingazzini's report appeared, Paribeni published a badly damaged inscription from the forum of Augustus in Rome; the stone elucidates the career of C. Aufidius Victorinus (on whom see below, no. 16, M. Cornelius Fronto) and includes a name which Groag has restored as Cocceius Gallus (*Not. d. Sc.* [1933], 468–470; *PIR*[2] C 1233, with Groag's *addendum*, in the same volume, to A 1393). If this man was the husband of Cocceia Galla, the date of the *fistula* must be brought well into the second century, controlled by the career of C. Aufidius Victorinus, who attained a first consulship probably in 155, a second certainly in 183 (*PIR*[2] A 1393). The abbreviation *C. F.* does not become common in inscriptions until the middle of the second century (see below on no. 30), and so lends further support to the later date.

15. L. Cocceius Nerva   ?   ?

   CIL X, 1614 (*ILS* 7731): *L. Cocceius L. C. Postumi l. Auctus architect[us]*.

   The *gens Cocceia* claimed Narnia as its place of origin (Syme, *Tacitus,*

576). There are no explicit indications that L. Cocceius Nerva owned property on the Bay of Naples, but circumstantial evidence, while far from conclusive, lends some support to such a view. L. Cocceius Auctus, the architect of the Augustan temple at Puteoli (*CIL* X, 1614, with Mommsen *ad loc.*, p. 200), was almost certainly his freedman (for the other patron, cf. *ILS* 7731, *PIR*² C 1213); it seems also that he played a major part in the design and execution of Agrippa's works of engineering at the *Portus Iulius* in 38/7 B.C., and constructed a tunnel from Puteoli to Neapolis (Strab. 5.4.5 [C 245]; cf. H. W. Benario, *Class. Bull.* 35 [1959], 40–41). The freedman's various operations thus seem to have been confined to the Bay of Naples, and suggest that his former master may have had a villa in the vicinity; further, Cocceii are prominently represented in local inscriptions: *CIL* X, 3707 (a L. Cocceius at Cumae); *ibid.*, 1764, 2308–2311, 2451 (Puteoli); 3568 (Misenum); 3803 (L. Cocceius C. L. M. l. Papa, from Capua, perhaps a freedman of the three brothers Gaius, Lucius, and Marcus Cocceius: cf. *PIR*² C 1223); 4088–4089, *Eph. Epigr.* VIII, 489 (Capua); *Not. d. Sc.* (1932), 303 (a Cocceia Galla : see above, no. 14); *PdP* fasc. 25–27 (1952), 408 (L. Cocceius Priscus of Neapolis, 154 A.D.); and *RAAN* N.S. 19 (1938), 97 (a L. Cocceius at Stabiae). L. Cocceius Nerva (cf. *PIR*² C 1223) was also the owner of the *plenissima villa* at Caudium in Samnium, mentioned by Horace as a stopping place during the journey to Brundisium (Hor. *Sat.* 1.5.50–51; cf. Porphyrio, *ad loc.*). It is doubtful that the family's interests in Campania had anything to do with Tiberius' selection of M. Cocceius Nerva, grandson of Lucius, as one of his companions for the Campanian excursion of 26 (Tac. *Ann.* 4.58.1; cf. *PIR*² C 1225). L. Cocceius Nerva was never consul; the *Fasti* record another member of the *gens* as *cos. suff.* in 39 B.C.: see Syme, *RR*, 200, n. 4.

16. M. Cornelius Fronto (*cos. suff.* 143)   Surrentum   144–145

Fronto *ad M. Caes.* 4.4 (Naber, p. 67 = Haines I, 176): *Nunc tu postquam inde profectus es, utrumne in Aureliam an in Campaniam abiisti? Fac scribas mihi ... an ad villam multitudinem librorum tuleris ... Epigraphica* 2 (1940), 214: *Corneliae Cratiae M. Corneli Frontonis.*

M. Cornelius Fronto of Cirta, tutor in Latin rhetoric to the sons of Antoninus Pius, reveals in his correspondence a close familiarity with the seaside places of Campania (cf. *ad M. Caes.* 3.8 [Naber, p. 45 = Haines I, 34]; *ibid.*, 1. 3 [= Haines I, 86]); during his absence in Rome as suffect consul in 143, Fronto promised to send his wife Gratia to Neapolis to celebrate with M.

Aurelius the birthday of the future emperor's mother (*ibid.*, 2.8 [Naber, p. 32 = Haines I, 144, 146]). In 4.4 (quoted above), Aurelius inquired of his *magister* whether he had made for Campania where, it is fair to assume, Fronto had estates. Assumption now gives way to certainty; a fragment of an inscription found at Sorrento in 1937 discloses the names of Fronto and of his daughter (Gratia minor: *ad M. Caes.* 2.13 [= Haines I, 152]), and Mustilli, surely rightly, interpreted the epigraphical evidence to mean that Fronto owned a villa in the vicinity of Surrentum (D. Mustilli, "Iscrizione di M. Cornelio Frontone rinvenuta a Sorrento," *Epigraphica* 2 [1940] 214–216: cf. *Epigraphica* 1 [1939], 49): Stein's entry in *PIR*² (C 1364) now requires a minor addition. Gratia minor (cf. *PIR*² G 219) married C. Aufidius Victorinus whose career is elucidated by a mutilated inscription found in the forum of Augustus (Paribeni, *Not. d. Sc.* [1933], 468–470); it is perhaps significant that Groag (*PIR*² A 1393) has restored the tribe as "Macc(ia)," in which Neapolis was enrolled (Taylor, *Voting Districts*, 273). The North African Fronto had a splendid career: he enjoyed imperial patronage, held the consulship, and owned *hortos Maecenatianos* (*ad M. Caes.* 1. 8 [Naber p. 23 = Haines I, 122]) as well as a villa in fashionable—and salubrious—Campania. There he might nurse the ill health of which he so constantly complained (cf. *PIR*² C 1364).

17. Domitia   Baiae   55

    Cass. Dio 61.17.2: καὶ ἔσπευσε γε τοῦτο ποιῆσαι διὰ τὰ κτήματα αὐτῆς τὰ ἐν ταῖς βαίαις καὶ ἐν τῇ 'Ραβεννίδι ὄντα . . . Tac. *Ann.* 13.21.6: *Nam Domitiae inimicitiis gratias agerem, si benevolentia mecum in Neronem meum certaret . . . Baiarum suarum piscinas extollebat . . .* Cf. Suet., *Nero* 34.5.

So eager, according to Dio, was Nero to acquire his aunt Domitia's estates at Baiae and Ravenna, that he poisoned her a few days before she would have died naturally of old age. From Tacitus' account of the speech of Agrippina in 55, it appears that Domitia devoted particular attention at Baiae to the equipment of her fishponds (*Baiarum suarum* means "her villa at Baiae"; see Catalogue I above, no. 7). The actual location of Domitia's villa cannot be determined, but the name of one of her ex-slaves may be included among the numerous local inscriptions in which her *nomen* is attested (cf. *CIL* X, 1738, 2366–2373). Domitia was the daughter of L. Domitius Ahenobarbus (*cos.* 16 B.C.) and the first wife of the elegant and politically adroit C. Passienus Crispus (*cos.* II, 44), who ultimately abandoned her for Agrippina (*PIR* P 109). Perhaps she was also the owner of the *horti Domitiae* across the

9*

Tiber (cf. *PIR*² D 171); all of her property, including the estate at Baiae, will have passed to Nero after her death in 59. Her great-grandfather, the consul of 54 B.C., may have possessed property in Neapolis (Catalogue I, no. 13); perhaps Domitia Lepida's fishponds came down to her from the *Ahenobarbi* of the late Republic.

18. C. Egnatius Certus (*suff. ann. inc.*)   Puteoli   after 168(?)

Eph. Epigr. VIII, 376: *Egnati Certi et fil. cl. vir.*

De Criscio (on whom see above, no. 1, Acilius Strabo), supplied Mommsen with the above inscription after the publication of the tenth volume of the *Corpus*; a *fistula plumbea*, it was discovered near the Flavian amphitheater of Pozzuoli (*Eph. Epigr.* VIII, *ad loc.*, p. 101). The evidence of the *fistula* alone is nearly sufficient to establish that the two senatorial *Egnatii Certi* possessed a house or villa in this elevated district of Puteoli (so also Groag, *PIR*² E 20; Dubois, *PA*, 363). The matter has now been placed beyond dispute owing to the more recent discovery, in precisely the same district of Pozzuoli, of a sepulchral inscription, dedicated by A. Egnatius Alypus to his wife, Egnatia Euthenia (*Not. d. Sc.* [1924], 84); Aurigemma, the editor, observed that the Greek *cognomina* point to the "condizione libertina" of the persons named but failed to consider the relevance of the *fistula* to the nomenclature of the inscription (*ibid.*, 84). Euthenia and Alypus will have been the *liberti* of the Egnatii Certi: the coincidence of the *nomina*, when taken together with the identical locations of pipe and inscription, precludes all reasonable doubt (for a preliminary report of still more recent excavations near the amphitheater of Pozzuoli, cf. *Not. d. Sc.* [1954] 283). C. Egnatius C. f. Certus was *consul suffectus* in an unknown year (*CIL* IX, 1578). That this consular Egnatius Certus should be identified with the first person named on the *fistula* is highly probable because a C. Egnatius C. f. Certus C(*larissimus*) V(*ir*) is mentioned in an inscription from Abellinum, where this person was *patronus coloniae* (*Eph. Epigr.* VIII, 862; accepted by Groag in *PIR*² E 20). The abbreviation *cl. v.* probably points to a date after 168: cf. below, on no. 30, P. Octavius Lutatius Quintilianus.

19. Faustinus   Baiae   87–88

Mart. 3.58.1–5: *Baiana nostri villa, Basse, Faustini / non otiosis ordinata myrtetis / viduaque platano tonsilique buxeto / ingrata lati spatia detinet campi, / sed rure vero barbaroque laetatur.*

The first verses of Martial's epigram establish the theme of the whole:

at the villa of Faustinus at Baiae are to be found none of the idle luxuries of the *villa pseudourbana*, but the wholesome regimen and simplicity of the farm. The poem is thus something of a *tour de force*. Nowhere else in the ancient sources is a villa at Baiae celebrated for its rustic glories: her palaces offered more civilized pleasures; her shores enticements to corruption. Here the springtime was ordinarily the fashionable season; Martial, in his account of his friend's Baian villa, makes early mention of the winter (vv. 7–8). Bulls roar fiercely in the valley, and the barnyard fowl crow and cackle. The domestic staff—*vilicus, vilica, vernae*—are models of industry and native vigor (vv. 20–32). A cheerful local neighbor is invited to dine: genial host, guests, and attendants partake of the same fare (vv. 41–42). Despite the poet's emphasis upon simplicity, there are indications, both internal and external, that Faustinus at Baiae did not want for more luxurious comforts. Peacocks and flamingos are listed among the occupants of the barnyard (vv. 13–14); the villa's staff included, in addition to the native personnel, *servi urbani capillati* and a *delicatus eunuchus* (vv, 39–42). Further, that Faustinus was extremely wealthy is manifest from other of Martial's epigrams: he had villas at Tibur (4.57.3, 7.80.12) and near Trebula (5.71.1–5). The date of publication of the third book of the epigrams (cf. *PIR* V 77) proves that Faustinus (to whom Martial dedicated books 3 and 4: cf. 3.1, 4.10; and further *PIR*² F 127) owned his villa at Baiae by 87/88; and it was doubtless with Faustinus that Martial passed much of his Campanian sojourn in the summer of 88 (cf. 4.30, 4.44, 10.57, 10.63; for another possible host on that occasion see above, no. 11, Castricus). In an inscription from Sperlonga a Faustinus, just possibly Martial's friend, alludes to the now celebrated sculptures which were discovered in fragments in the grotto of the imperial villa: see G. Iacopi, *L'Antro di Tiberio a Sperlonga* (Rome 1963), 42–45. One might presume that Martial's friend was a senator; conveniently, a Minicius Faustinus, *suffectus* in 91, is now attested by the *Fasti Potentini*.

20. Agrippa Iulius Caesar (earlier M. Vipsanius Agrippa Postumus)

Near Pompeii

The evidence for Agrippa Postumus' acquisition by inheritance of his father's villa at Boscotrecase is presented below, no. 46, M. Vipsanius Agrippa.

Born after the death of his father in B.C. 12, banished permanently to the island of Planasia by 8 A.D., and executed at the outset of the reign of Tiberius, Agrippa Postumus (on whom see *PIR*² I 214) can have spent little time actually in residence at his Pompeian villa. But before his confinement on Planasia, he had been sent away to Surrentum, probably in 6 (Suet. *Aug.* 65.1: *Agrippam brevi ob ingenium sordidum ac ferox abdicavit seposuitque Surrentum*; for the date, cf. *PIR*² I 214). Although inscriptions indicate the presence of an imperial villa there (see Chapter 4, pp. 75–76), it is most unlikely that Augustus' grandson was restricted to its confines; on the contrary, he was clearly permitted a certain freedom of movement while on the Bay of Naples, for his conduct continued to give offense and subsequently caused his permanent relegation to Planasia (Suet. *Aug.* 65.4: *Nihilo tractabilior in insulam transportatur et saepitur custodia militum*; cf. Tac. *Ann.* 1.3.4). Dio in fact reports that Germanicus rather than Agrippa was sent to the Dalmatian front in 7 because of Agrippa's abrasive disposition and his single-minded dedication to catching fish; the youth even called himself Poseidon and upbraided Augustus for refusing to allow him to come into full possession of his patrimony (Cass. Dio 55.32.1–2). The anecdote well coheres with Agrippa's period of residence in coastal Campania; while under mild surveillance for some three years on the coast, he will certainly have seen much of the Pompeian villa before his permanent banishment to Planasia. Dio (*ibid.*) further reports that Agrippa's property was finally given to the military treasury; for the subsequent history of the villa cf. above, Chapter 4, p. 76.

21. Iulius Menecrates   Neapolis   94
    Stat. *Silv.* 4, preface.

Discussed below, no. 34, Pollius Felix, who was his father-in-law.

22. C. Iulius Proculus   Puteoli   ?
    CIL X, 1904: *C. Iulii Proculi.*

This *fistula plumbea* was found at Puteoli where it was seen and transcribed by Mommsen; the property of the man named on the pipe was therefore presumably close by (so also Dubois, *PA*, 362). Several *Julii Proculi* are known; the most noteworthy, who also bore the *praenomen* Gaius, had a distinguished career under Trajan and was *consul suffectus* in 109 (cf. *PIR*² I 497, where however the *fistula* is not mentioned).

23. M. Licinius Crassus Frugi (*cos.* 64)   Pompeii   *ca.* 50 (?)
    CIL X, 1063: *THERMAE*
        M. Crassi Frugi
    aqua marina et baln[eum]
  aqna dulci, Ianuarius l[ibertus].

This inscription has been much discussed. It was discovered in March, 1749, during the earliest excavations at Pompeii, a few yards outside of the Porta Ercolano in the so-called "Villa di Cicerone," where it had been fitted horizontally into a niche of a shrine and was serving as a shelf (Mommsen, *CIL* X, *ad loc.* p. 122; Maiuri, "Note di topografia pompeiana," *RAAN* N.S. 34 [1959], 73–79, *q.v.* also for earlier bibliography). The text of the inscription is the clue to its original location. Since the baths of Crassus Frugi were supplied with sea water as well as fresh, they must of course have been situated along the shore of the coast near Pompeii (Maiuri, "Note di topografia pompeiana," 75; Della Corte, *CeA*³, 29–30). Mommsen was the first to observe a connection between the text of the inscription and a passage from Pliny (*NH* 31.5): *vaporant et in mari ipso quae Licinii Crassi fuere, mediosque inter fluctus existit aliquid valetudini salutare* (discussed above, Chapter 2, p. 22). Struck by the resemblance between owners' names and by the similarity of the baths described, Mommsen concluded (*CIL* X *ad loc.*) that the two texts refer to a single bathing establishment on the Campanian coast. This is unlikely; Pliny's discussion (as the context makes clear) is restricted to the waters *in Baiano sinu* (*NH* 31.4), whereas the baths of Crassus Frugi must have been situated on the Pompeian littoral near which the inscription was discovered; nor is there reason to suppose that *thermae* combining the use of salt and fresh waters were particularly remarkable in this region: those of Pollius Felix at Surrentum (see below, no. 34) were precisely of this variety (Stat. *Silv.* 2.2.18–19). More plausible is Mommsen's contention that the Pompeian (and Baian) waters were the property of the same man, M. Licinius Crassus Frugi (*cos.* 64), rather than of his homonymous father, the consul of 27 (so also Dessau, *PIR* L 131). The tenses in Pliny's sentence imply that Licinius Crassus was a contemporary recently deceased, and the consul of 64 died in the last years of Nero's reign (Pliny *Ep.* 1.5.3; Tac. *Hist.* 1.48; 4.42): it must however be admitted that the father cannot be excluded on these grounds (cf. Sen. *Apocol.* 11: he was put to death by the Emperor Claudius). That the younger Crassus was proprietor of these elaborate bathing establishments is conclusive evidence also for his ownership of coastal property on the Bay of Naples. He had further connections with this region. The tribe of his father (*PIR* L 130) and of his brother Cn. Pompeius Magnus (*PIR* P 477) was the Menenia, in which citizens of Pompeii, Herculaneum, and Stabiae were enrolled after the Social War, and those of Surrentum still earlier; cf. Taylor, *Voting Districts*, 225. (Miss Taylor also argues [p. 225] that the consul of 27 was very likely the grandson of L. Calpurnius Piso [*cos.* 58 B.C.], whose tribe was also the Menenia; for his sumptuous villa at Herculaneum see above, Catalogue I, no. 5. But the consul of 58 B.C. cannot have been a Frugi; see Syme, *JRS* 50 [1960], pp. 13–14.)

24. Lucilius Junior   Neapolis, Pompeii   63

Sen. *Ep.* 49.1: *Ecce Campania et maxime Neapolis ac Pompeiorum tuorum conspectus incredibile est quam recens desiderium tui fecerint . . . Ep.* 53.1: . . . *sed putavi tam pauca milia a Parthenope tua usque Puteolos subripi posse . . . Ep.* 70.1: *Post longum intervallum Pompeios tuos vidi. In conspectum adulescentiae meae reductus sum . . .*

From the above evidence—passages composed during the younger Seneca's Campanian sojourn which began in 63 (*PIR* [2] A 617)—scholars have regularly and reasonably concluded that Seneca's friend Lucilius was native to Campania, born either at Pompeii or Neapolis (see, e.g., Dessau in *PIR* L 286); from *Ep.* 70.1 it appears that Seneca may first have met Lucilius in Pompeii as a youth. But the *nomen* is not listed in Della Corte's index of the residents of Pompeii (cf. *CeA* [3], 476), and Seneca himself is our authority for the statement that Lucilius, despite his poverty and lowly origins, turned early to the composition of verses and the study of philosophy (Sen. *Nat. Quaest.* 4 *praef.* 14–15). For these pursuits Lucilius would have found the atmosphere of Neapolis particularly congenial, that of Pompeii less so (see above, Chapter 5, n. 146) and he may well have migrated there from Pompeii; certainly Lucilius was sufficiently well acquainted with the Neapolitan philospher Metronax to mourn his passing (*Ep.* 93.1). There is a good possibility that he retained property in the district, although this cannot be conclusively established. During Seneca's days of *peregrinatio* in Campania (see *Ep.* 49–51, 53–57, 70, 76, 77, 80, 84, 86), Lucilius was absent in Sicily as procurator; he had become an *eques Romanus* by dint of energy and hard work (*Ep.* 44.2).

25. Metilia Marcia   Puteoli   *ca.* 41 (?)

CIL X, 1905: a) *Metiliarum Marcia . . .*
              b) *Metiliarum Marciae . . .*
              c) *Metiliarum Marciae et Rufinae.*

Mommsen's *addendum* to *CIL* X, 1905 makes clear that these three *fistulae plumbeae* (only the text of "c" is complete) were found in the sea, some fifteen yards off the coast of Pozzuoli (cf. *CIL* X, p. 972); the pipes most probably belonged to a coastal villa in the vicinity, owned jointly by the two Metiliae (so also Dubois, *PA*, 362–363). Marcia and Rufina were apparently sisters, and the daughters of Cremutia Marcia, herself the daughter of the annalist A. Cremutius Cordus, and the recipient of Seneca's *Cons. Ad Marciam* (so Dessau in *PIR* M 395; followed by Dubois, *PA*, 362–363: for the date [*ca.* 41] of the dialogue cf. *PIR* M 382). For that Marcia, Seneca relates, had two sons and two daughters (Seneca, *Cons. Marc.* 16.5); since the son whom Marcia had lost was named Metilius (*ibid.*, 16.6), Dessau concluded that the *nomen* of her husband (not attested elsewhere) was also Metilius (*PIR* M 185). Alternatively, the sisters who owned the villa at Puteoli may have been Marcia's granddaughters: for two daughters of Metilius, as well as a grieving mother, are said by Seneca to have survived their father's death (*ibid.*, 16.6–8). Whether the sisters inherited the villa cannot, of course, be determined; the text of the inscription, however, does indicate that they owned the property in their own right.

26. Metilia Rufina   Puteoli   *ca.* 41

     CIL X, 1905: *Metiliarum Marciae et Rufinae*
     See above, no. 25 (Metilia Marcia).

27. Nicomachus Flavianus (son-in-law of Symmachus)   Near   Before
                                              Puteoli   395

     Symmachus *Ep.* 8.23.3.
     Discussed below, no. 42 (Symmachus).

28. Virius Nicomachus Flavianus (*cos.* 394)   Neapolis   Before 394

     Symmachus *Ep.* 2.60.1–2.
     Discussed below, no. 42 (Symmachus).

29. (Q.) Numonius Vala   Salernum   23–20 B.C.

     Hor. *Ep.* 1.15.1–2: *Quae sit hiems Veliae, quod caelum, Vala, Salerni | quorum hominum regio et qualis via . . . Ibid.*, 45–46: *vos sapere et solos aio bene vivere, quorum | conspicitur nitidis fundata pecunia villis.*

     In the fifteenth epistle of the first book (composed between 23 and 20 B.C.; see E. Fraenkel, *Horace* [Oxford 1957] 308–310), Horace addresses inquiries to Vala concerning the character of the coastal cities Velia and Salernum as winter resorts. That Numonius Vala (the *nomen* appears at the heading of several of the *MSS*) should be expected to have reliable information demonstrates that he owned property in the region; the final verses of the poem show that he was wealthy, and there is an explicit reference to *villae*; there is thus a strong probability that Vala had a villa at Salernum. The Horatian Vala may well be a local man: observe the Q. Numonius C. f. Vala, honored as *patronus coloniae* in an inscription from Paestum (*CIL* X, 481; cf. *PIR* N 194; inferred also by T. P. Wiseman, *CQ* N.S. 14 [1964], 124); Paestum is nearly equidistant between Velia and Salernum. Whether he was also the Vala Numonius who served under Varus as legate in Germany in 9 (Vell. Pat. 2.119.4) is more doubtful; cf. *PIR* N 193.

30. P. Octa(vius) Lutatius Quintilianus   Baiae   after 168 ?

Not. d. Sc. (1884), 430 (*Eph. Epigr.* VIII, 377): *P. Octa. Lutati Quintilian. c.v.*

Of this senator nothing is known beyond the fact that the name appears upon a *fistula plumbea* discovered in 1884 near the "Stufe de Nerone" on the heights of Bacoli; this permits the inference that he owned a villa somewhere on this hillside (so also Dubois, *PA*, 363). A rough *terminus a quo* is provided by the abbreviation *c.v.*: *clarissimus vir* became a formal designation of senatorial rank only after a regulation by Marcus and Verus (by 168; for the date cf. Mommsen, *Römisches Staatsrecht* III [Leipzig 1887], 471; cf. de Ruggiero, *Dizionario Epigrafico* II, pt. 1 [Rome 1900], 268). But the formula was in use much earlier. The first examples in documents belong to the years 56 and 69 (*ILS* 6043.24, 5947.13–14); and Pliny uses the title for Servilius Calvus in the correspondence with Trajan (*Ep.* 10.56.2, on which see Sherwin White, *The Letters of Pliny, ad loc.*, 637).

31. P. Papinius Statius   Neapolis   93–4

Stat. *Silv.* 1.2.260–261: *mea Parthenope; 3.5, passim.*

Although Neapolis was the adopted city of the poet's father, Statius repeatedly refers to it as his *patria* (cf. *Silv.* 2.2.6; 3. *praef.*); he was born there between 40 and 45 (since in 95 he states *vergimur in senium*, 4.4.70; cf. F. Vollmer, *P. Papinii Statii Silvarum Libri* [Leipzig 1898], 16). Vollmer (*ibid.*, 17) has plausibly suggested that it was owing to the great influence of his father—Statius mentions no other teacher—that the poet never seems to have considered a political career; poetic excellence was his first and abiding ambition, and great was the father's pride in Statius' early successes in *declamationes* at Neapolis (*Silv.* 5.3.215–219), where also he lived to witness his son's victory in the *Sebasta* (5.3.225–227). Shortly after his father's death (around 80: see above, Chapter 5, p. 144), Statius appears to have left Neapolis for Rome, where he remained until 93/94. There the *Thebaid*, begun at

Neapolis under his father's watchful eye (5.3.232–237), was completed; there too Statius met his wife Claudia who shared both her husband's triumph at the Alban competition of Domitian and his subsequent failure (a bitter disappointment) in the Capitoline games (3.5.28–33; cf. 5.3.227–230). During these years Statius' closeness to the imperial court may perhaps be illustrated by his purchase of an estate at Alba, to which Domitian appears to have contributed a running brook (3.1.61–64); but he returned to Neapolis for such occasions as the *Sebasta*, which he attended in 90 before going on to the Surrentine villa of his wealthy local patron, Pollius Felix (see below, no. 34). But in 93–94, broken in health, he resolved to return permanently to Neapolis, *patria senium componere terra* (3.5.13; see above, Chapter 5, p. 133): his wife was loathe to accompany him, deeming Rome to be a more auspicious location in the quest for a son-in-law (3.5.60–62). At Neapolis, the poet wrote, *pax secura locis et desidis otia vitae | et numquam turbata quies somnique peracti* (3.5.85–86). These artful verses were apparently persuasive: the fourth book of the *Silvae* was composed at Neapolis during 94 and 95 (*Silv.* 4. *praef.*; cf. *Silv.*, 4.4.1–11), and the poet does not seem to have returned to Rome before his death. Statius retained, however, his estate at Alba, where he summered in 95 (4.5.1–2). The location of Statius' property in Neapolis is not known, but it is unlikely that he settled in a house or villa inherited from his father: in *Silvae* 3.5, where one might have expected an explicit reference, no such ancestral property is mentioned, and those verses instead support the view that Statius may have purchased an estate expressly for his retirement. He seems to have enjoyed easier financial circumstances than his contemporary Martial (cf. R. Helm in *RE* 18 [1949], 985, no. 8. Aside from his wealthy benefactor Pollius Felix, Statius' local friends and contacts included Violentilla (*Silv.* 1.2.260–262) and Julius Menecrates (no. 21 above).

32. Petronius   Cumae   66

Tac. *Ann.* 16.19.1: *Forte illis diebus Campaniam petiverat Caesar, et Cumas usque progressus Petronius illic attinebatur.*

Nero's *elegantiae arbiter* was kept under surveillance at Cumae, where he subsequently committed suicide (Tac. *Ann.* 16.18.1–19.5); no imperial villa is attested at Cumae; the natural inference is therefore that Petronius possessed an estate there. The Tacitean Petronius should perhaps be identified with T. Petronius Niger (*cos. suff.* 62): see Syme, *Tacitus*, 387, n. 6; 538, n. 6. It is here assumed that Nero's friend and the author of the *Satyricon* are identical (cf. Syme, *Tacitus*, 336, n. 5, for a possible allusion to the work in

Tacitus' appreciation of the man). It will be recalled that the setting of the *Cena*, as well as the site of its author's villa, was in a coastal Campanian city, almost certainly Puteoli: see K. F. C. Rose, "Time and Place in the *Satyricon*," *TAPA* 93 (1962), 403–405, with bibliographical references *ad loc.*

33. Plotinus   ?   269

Porphyry *Plot.* 2: . . . εἰς δὲ τὴν Καμπανίαν ἐλθὼν εἰς Ζήθου χωρίον ἑταίρου παλαιου αὐτῷ γεγονότος καὶ τεθνηκότος κατάγεται.

Afflicted by a grotesque disease of the throat, Plotinus left Rome towards the end of his life and repaired to Campania, where the Neoplatonic philosopher had inherited a villa from Zethus, a friend of whom little is known; Plotinus' wants were provided partly from the estate of Zethus, partly from that of Castricius, another friend, who had property at Minturnae (Porph. *Plot.* 2). Eustochius of Alexandria, a doctor and Plotinus' philosophical disciple, was living in Puteoli at the time, and provided Porphyry with a detailed account of Plotinus' last days. When he died in 269/270 (for the date, see *PIR* P 379), only Eustochius was with him, and he reached Plotinus' bedside late, having made the journey from Puteoli (*Plot.* 2); this suggests that the villa of Plotinus was some distance away and that it need not have been situated on the coast. The philosopher's interest in Campania antedated the days of his final illness: see above, Chapter 5, p. 147.

34. Pollius Felix   Surrentum, Posillipo   90, 65
  a) Surrentum: Stat. *Silv.* 2.2, *passim.*

a) After attending the *Sebasta* at Neapolis in 90 (*Silv.* 2.2.6; for the date cf. F. Vollmer, *P. Papinii Statii Silvarum Libri*, 6–7), Statius sailed across the bay to Surrentum where, on the Punta della Calcarella between the Capo di Sorrento and the Capo di Massa, sprawled the vast and sumptuous villa of his patron Pollius Felix; for the possible location, see now Mingazzini and Pfister, *Forma Italiae Regio* I, vol. 2 (*Surrentum*), 54–70; but cf. Maiuri, *PdP* 1 (1946), 393. The poet has artfully contrived to unfold the successive stages of the villa's appointments in the order in which they would have appeared to a beholder who, like himself on that occasion, approached by sea. Beyond a spacious beach (no quay is mentioned) appeared smoke from the vaulted rooves of a double bath (2.2.17; 3.1.100–101), and fresh spring water mingling with that of the sea (2.2.18–19; cf. above, on M. Crassus Frugi, no. 23). Nearby was a small shrine dedicated to Hercules (2.2.23–25; the god's new edifice, the subject of *Silv.* 3.1, had not yet been constructed). From here a

mammoth *porticus,* presumably covered, ran at an oblique angle up the hillside and served to link the seaside with the chief living quarters on the
height above; Statius devotes six verses to this most characteristic feature of
the coastal Campanian villas set along the slopes (*Silv.* 2.2.30–35; cf. above,
Chapter 5, p. 127). To do full justice to the glories of the villa sorely taxed
the poet's powers: some rooms had eastern, some western exposure; in
some the sound of the sea was audible, others enjoyed the silence of the land;
nature and art vied and intermingled, but the owner had tamed the place,
and the cliff had learnt to bear the yoke (2.2.45–59). Rooms were fitted out
with the masterworks of bronze and marble sculpture; diverse windows
provided views of Aenaria, Procida, Misenum, Nesis, the shrine of Euploia
(on the heights of Pizzofalcone above Neapolis: Beloch, *Campanien*², 83),
Megaris, Limon (on which see b, below); one chamber, higher than all the
other *diaetae,* and fitted out with imported polychrome marbles, gave a view
of Neapolis (63–94). Here abided Pollius Felix in elegant Hellenic retirement, composing verses and contemplating in lavish comfort the doctrines
of Epicurus (2.2. 112–117). It had not been always thus. He was a *Puteolanus*
by birth (2.2.96,133–137; Beloch's hypothesis [*Campanien*², 269] that his
family went back to the foundation of the Roman colony at Puteoli in 194
B.C. is a plausible conjecture), and in his youthful days appears to have been
avid of poetic prizes; then he was the object of veneration of both *Puteolani*
and *Neapolitani,* with each city anxious to claim him as citizen (2.2.133–137).
But at some undetermined date he chose to retreat from the public gaze;
Statius represents his retirement to Surrentum as a victory for Greek culture
(2.2.95–97). He lavished his great wealth upon both persons and municipalities: Statius owed him much, dedicating the third book of the *Silvae* to
his patron (*Silv.* 3. *praef.*); and buildings adorning both Neapolis and Puteoli
were products of his largesse (3.1.91–93). Pollius Felix and his wife Polla had
been blessed with a *turba nepotum* by 94, when Statius celebrated the birth of a
third child to Julius Menecrates, son-in-law of Pollius Felix and, like Statius,
of Neapolitan origin: *Silvae* 4. *praef;* cf. 4.8.59–62 where also *dignitas senatoria*
is augured for the children of Menecrates (cf. also *PIR*² I 430). See also
Chapter 5, p. 126.

b) Posillipo: *Eph. Epigr.* VIII, 337 (*ILS* 5798): *Macrinus . . . hic ambulavit
a villa Polli Felicis, quae est Epilimones, usque ad emissarium Paconianum, Nerva
et Vestino cos.*

b) In addition to the Surrentine villa, and visible from it, Pollius Felix
possessed an estate at Posillipo which bore the name of Limon (Stat. *Silv.*

3.1.49; 2.2.82 with Vollmer, *P. Papinii Statii Silvarum Libri, ad loc.*; on the location, cf. Beloch, *Campanien²*, 466). That property is epigraphically attested. A graffito from Posillipo, bearing the names of the consuls of the year 65, mentions a *villa Polli Felicis quae est epilimones* (to be understood as an adjective, ἐπιλειμωνής: so Mommsen, *Hermes* 18 [1883], 158; cf. *Eph. Epigr.* VIII, 337 [*ILS* 5798]). *Limon* may have then belonged to the homonymous father of Pollius Felix, but it could equally well have been the property of Statius' patron himself; since he had been many times a grandfather by 94. See further *PIR* P 419, and Maiuri, *Vita d' Archeologo* (Naples 1959), 141–143.

35. Pomponianus	Stabiae	79

Pliny *Ep.* 6.16.8: *Egrediebatur domo: accipit codicillos Rectinae Casci imminenti periculo exterritae (nam villa eius subiacebat, nec ulla nisi navibus fuga): ut se tanti discrimini eriperet orabat. Ibid.*, 12: '*fortes*' *inquit*, '*fortuna iuvat, Pomponianum pete!*' *Stabiis erat diremptus sinu medio (nam sensim circumactis curvatisque litoribus mare infunditur)* . . .

Keen curiosity prompted Pliny's uncle, commander of the fleet at Misenum, to embark for a closer inspection of the eruption of Mt. Vesuvius. A sense of urgency was added to the mission upon his receipt of a terrified plea for help from Rectina, the wife of Cascus; her coastal villa lay beneath the mountain: Pliny *Ep.* 6.16.8, where the name is not Tascius, but Cascus, very possibly (as A. Sogliano suggested long ago) Cn. Pedius Cascus, *cos. suff.* 71; see C. P. Jones, *Phoenix* 22 (1968), 127, correcting Sherwin–White, *The Letters of Pliny, ad loc.*, 373; and cf. also Syme, *JRS* 58 (1968), 140. The Elder Pliny's small squadron proceeded at once to the point of danger; but hot pumice fell into the ships, and the rising of the sea-bed might have forced them to run aground (*Ep.* 6.16.11). To the pilot's counsel that his commander retreat, Pliny replied with a stirring maxim and commanded the helmsman to make for Pomponianus at Stabiae (*ibid.*, 12). Sherwin–White proposes to identify "Tascius" with Pomponianus, suggesting that he was "a son of the Elder's friend and protector Pomponius Secundus . . . who had changed his name by an act of adoption and become Tascius Pomponianus" (*The Letters of Pliny*, 373). Nomenclature aside, this explanation raises two major difficulties which Sherwin–White does not appear to have considered: 1) why does the younger Pliny refer no more to Rectina? The remainder of the letter chronicles the events from the time of the Elder Pliny's arrival at the villa of the agitated Pomponianus (afternoon of 24, August) through his attempted escape and suffocation (morning of 25, August); but there is no mention of the Rectina at whose behest Pliny undertook his voyage and to whom (had she been present) we might reasonably have expected a reference by name, particularly among those who waited out the night with Pomponianus *Ep.* 6.16.14: . . . *Pomponiano ceterisque qui pervigilaverant*). 2) There is, further, a topographical difficulty. On Sherwin-White's hypothesis, the villa of Rectina, which is described as having lain at the foot of the mountain and as having allowed escape only by sea (*ibid.*, 8) must be identical with the villa of Pomponianus, which was distant from Vesuvius by the width of the bay of Stabiae, and from which the inhabitants ultimately chose to flee through the fields (*ibid.*, 15–16). More important, if the estate of Pomponianus had been the Elder Pliny's destination from the start, why did he first make for the shore near Herculaneum (apparently his location in *Ep.* 6.6.11; so also Sherwin-White, *The Letters of Pliny*, 373), thereby adding approximately eight kilometers to the journey? In view of these considerations it must be concluded that Cascus, husband of Rectina, and Pomponianus were different persons, and that the former's villa (near Herculaneum) was inaccessible by the time the Elder Pliny had arrived. Rectina had undoubtedly perished in the dense hail of *lapilli* and *cineres* which threatened to overwhelm Pliny on shipboard off the coast. Giving her up for lost, Pliny made instead for the estate of Pomponianus at Stabiae. (The attempts to derive the name of modern Resina from Pliny's Rectina must be rejected: see Di Capua in *RAAN* N.S. 19 [1938], 112, n. 58). For the villas of Stabiae in the light of recent excavations, see above, Chapter 5, pp. 128–129.

36. Q. Pomponius Maternus (*cos. ann. inc.*)   Bauli   ?

Eph. Epigr. VIII, 378: Q. *Pomponi Matern.*

Near the "Stufe di Nerone" at Bacoli, on the western heights above the gulf of Pozzuoli, this *fistula plumbea aquaria* came to light in 1884; together with that of P. Octavius Lutatius Quintilianus (no. 30, above), which was found on the same property, it was published by Fiorelli in *Not. d. Sc.* (1884), 430. We may therefore presume that a Pomponius Maternus had a coastal villa in this attractive setting (so also Dubois, *PA*, 363). The name is extremely rare; the person should perhaps be identified, therefore, with the Q. Pomponius Maternus who was consular colleague in an unknown year with M. Junius Mettius Rufus (*ILS* 1622; *CIL* XV, 69, 939, 1409 [*tegulae*]; cf. *PIR* P 553).

37. L. Publilius Celsus (*cos.* II, 113)   Baiae   118

S.H.A. Hadr. 7.2: *quare Palma Tarracinis, Celsus Baiis, Nigrinus Faventiae,*

Lusius in itinere senatu iubente, invito Hadriano, ut ipse in vita sua dicit, occisi sunt.

During Hadrian's absence on the Danube during the winter and spring of 118, four consulars were accused of conspiracy against the emperor and put to death on the orders of the senate; L. Publilius Celsus was among them. Since Baiae was the scene of his demise, it is a reasonable presumption that he there owned a coastal estate. Cassius Dio (69.1.5) reports that Celsus and Nigrinus had plotted against Hadrian during a hunt, but supplies no topographical details of these deaths, which erased four persons prominent in the reign of Trajan. Nothing further is known of the conspiracy, nor of the origin of Publilius Celsus (cf. *PIR* P 782; and further, A. von Premerstein, *Klio*, Beiheft 8 [1908], 47–57).

38. Rectina, wife of Cascus   Herculaneum   79

Pliny *Ep.* 6.16.8: *Egrediebatur domo: accipit codicillos Rectinae Casci imminenti periculo exterritae (nam villa eius subiacebat, nec ulla nisi navibus fuga)* . . .

Discussed above, no. 35, Pomponianus.

39. P. Servilius Vatia (*praetor* 25 B.C.)   Cumae   63

Sen. *Ep.* 55.2: *ideo diutius vehi perseveravi invitante ipso litore, quod inter Cumas et Servili Vatiae villam curvatur et hinc mari, illinc lacu velut angustum iter cluditur. 3: In hac (villa) ille praetorius dives, nulla alia re quam otio notus, consenuit et ob hoc unum felix habebatur. 6: de ipsa villa nihil tibi possum certi scribere. Frontem enim eius tantum novi et exposita, quae ostendit etiam transeuntibus. 7: hoc tamen est commodissimum in villa, quod Baias trans parietem habet; incommodis illarum caret, voluptatibus fruitur . . . non stulte videtur elegisse hunc locum Vatia in quam otium suum pigrum iam et senile conferret.*

P. Servilius Vatia was the grandson of P. Servilius Vatia Isauricus (*cos.* 79 B.C.) and son of P. Servilius (*cos.* I, 48 B.C.); he rose only to the rank of praetor (25 B.C.) and died during the reign of Tiberius at an advanced age (for his name, career, and connections see above all, Münzer, *Röm. Adelsparteien*, 374–376; cf. Syme, *RR*, 492; and see above, Chapter 5 p. 157). Both Münzer (*Röm. Adels.*) and Maiuri (*Passeggiate Campane*, 50) believed that the villa was constructed by one of Vatia's forebears, probably his grandfather, the consul of 79 (see above, Chapter 2, p. 34). Although Seneca mentions no earlier owner, his description of Vatia's torpor fits particularly well with the view that he had inherited his wealth and comforts; and both Van Deman and Maiuri have claimed to have detected traces of Republican masonry at the villa's site (Blake, *Ancient Roman Construction in Italy . . . to Augustus*, 245; Maiuri, *Passeggiate Campane*, 50–51). It may be suggested therefore that the villa was acquired first by P. Servilius Vatia Isauricus (*cos.* 79 B.C.), that it passed subsequently to his son P. Servilius Isauricus (*cos.* II, 41 B.C.). The prudence of his politics (for which see Münzer, *RE* 2 A [1923], 1798–1802, no. 67; cf. Catalogue I, no. 39) doubtless helped to safeguard the villa during the confiscations of the 40's, and enabled Isauricus to bequeath it subsequently to his son, the idle praetorian.

40. Stertinius   Baiae   before 180

M. Aurelius, *Meditations* 12.27: συμπροσπιπτέτω δὲ καὶ τὸ τοιοῦτο πᾶν, οἷον Φάβιος Κατουλλῖνος ἐπ' ἀγροῦ καὶ Λούσιος Λοῦπος ἐν τοῖς κήποις καὶ Στερτίνιος ἐν βαίαις καὶ Τιβέριος ἐν Καπρέαις καὶ Οὐήλιος 'Ροῦφος . . .

In one passage of his *Meditations* Marcus Aurelius was moved to remember all those persons who had chafed greatly with indignation, all those greatly conspicuous for fame, calamities, enmities or fortunes of any description. There came to mind certain persons who had withdrawn from the public gaze to their private villas. Included in this curious list of malcontents are Stertinius (at Baiae) and the emperor Tiberius (at Capreae). Of Stertinius nothing further is known (cf. *PIR* S 656), but from the context it appears that he may have been a person of prominence in Roman political life, had suffered disappointment, and had withdrawn, embittered, to seek solace on the Bay of Naples. "Consider," the philosopher wrote, "where is it all now? Smoke and ashes and a tale that is told, or not so much as a tale."

41. L. Stertinius Quintilianus Acilius Strabo C. Curiatus Maternus Clodius Nummus   Neapolis (?)   See below

CIL X, 1486 (Neapolis): *L. Stertinio C. f. Maec. Quin[tiliano] Acilio Straboni C. Curiat[io] [Ma]terno Clodio Nummo Iulius Atticus Praef. Coh.*

Discovered at Neapolis, the above inscription must also be assigned to that city: the *Maecia* was the tribe of Neapolis (Mommsen, *CIL* X, p. 171; Taylor, *Voting Districts*, 273), and this Acilius Strabo must thus have been of Neapolitan origin. He dedicated a (sepulchral?) inscription at Ephesus to his natural father, C. Clodius Nummus, quaestor of Asia, whose tribe was also the *Maecia* (*CIL* III, 429); Groag has argued convincingly that he was adopted by L. Acilius Strabo (no. 1 above; see Groag on *PIR*[2] A 83); it is to the adoptive father that the name on the *fistula aquaria* should be referred (*Not. d. Sc.*

[1902], 637, whence wrongly Dubois, *PA*, 363). That he should have been honored in a Neapolitan inscription proves that Acilius Strabo maintained his contacts (and, like his adoptive father, doubtless also possessed property) in the vicinity of Neapolis. He governed Numidia as *legatus Augusti pro praetore* in 116 A.D. (*CIL* VIII 28063 b [*ILS* 5958 b], on which cf. Groag, *PIR*² A 83).

42. Q. Aurelius Symmachus Eusebius (*cos.* 391)

   a) Cumae: Symm. *Ep.* 2.4.2.

   b) Bauli: *Ep.* 1.1.2–5; 1.8; 8.23.3.

   c) Baiae: *Ep.* 6.9; 1.3.3–5; 2.26.1; 5.93; 7.24.

   d) Lucrinus: *Ep.* 1.1.2; 1.8.

   e) Puteoli: *Ep.* 6.66.3; 1.8; 2.26.1; 5.93.

   f) Neapolis: *Ep.* 2.60; 7.24.

a) Symmachus speaks (in 383; for the dates of the letters see O. Seeck, ed., *Symmachi Opera, MGH, Auctores Antiquissimi* VI [Berlin 1883], 60–66) of setting sail from his *Cumanum*; the villa must have been located at the sea's edge, but we have no further topographical details. A local boatman, apparently in the employ of either Symmachus or his father, is epigraphically attested: Ἐλπίδιος ναύκληρος Συμμάχων τῶν λαμπροτάτων ἐνθάδε κεῖται: *IG* XIV, 879 (Puteoli).

b) The villa at Bauli is mentioned in the first letter of Symmachus' correspondence in 375; he and Rusticiana, recently married, were in residence at the beginning of autumn (*Ep.* 1.1.1). The happy occasion moved Symmachus to the composition of elegiac verses, celebrating famous sojourners at Bauli; it is a highly exclusive list: Hercules, Hortensius (the orator), Acindynus (*cos.* 340, the builder of the villa: *Ep.* 1.1.2), Orfitus (the subsequent purchaser, and the poet's father-in-law), and himself (*Ep.* 1.1.5). As Seeck has suggested, *Symmachi Opera*, 50, the villa was undoubtedly part of Rusticiana's dowry; Symmachus was certainly the sole proprietor in 396 (see *Ep.* 8.23.3). At Bauli the young couple could be assured of an appropriate tranquility (cf. *Ep.* 1.8.1: *Bauli magnum silentes*).

c) When Symmachus speaks of his *praetorium* at Baiae, as Dubois has observed (*PA*, 373), it is as of property long familiar to him; his father had doubtless owned the estate before him. The *praetorium* is mentioned first in 375, when Symmachus was there enjoying aristocratic repose until the rumor reached him that the populace threatened to intrude with their earthly pleasures; he promptly made for Neapolis and Beneventum (*Ep.*

1.3.3). At Baiae again in November 385, he found stifling the very tran-
quillity which ten years earlier he had claimed to prize so highly (*Ep.* 2.26.1:
Baiarum solitudine vehementer offensus . . .). In 398 Symmachus became
involved in a boundary dispute at Baiae. *Inspectatores* had determined that a
wall which extended from a hill top and terminated apparently near the
shore divided his *praetorium* from that of his neighbor Censorinus, who seems
to have disputed the earlier adjudication on the grounds that the boundary
allowed him insufficient frontage on the sea. Symmachus compromised.
Permitting the neighbor a ten foot extension to his existing property, he
pressed for the completion of the dividing wall, lest additional encroachments recur in the future (*Ep.* 6.9; 6.11.3). Two further references to the
estate at Baiae confirm that the resort retained her notorious reputation in
the late fourth century (*Ep.* 5.93; 7.24).

   d) During the autumn of 375 Symmachus wrote to his father that he had
exchanged the delights of the villa at Bauli for those of a sojourn at Lucrinus
(*Ep.* 1.1.2); later, and possibly during the same Campanian visit, he urges
his parent to come to the lands where there is no limit to holiday enjoyment:
*iamdumdum vestri cupiunt Lucrina tacita et liquida Baiana et Puteoli adhuc celebres
et Bauli magnum silentes* (*Ep.* 1.8); the property at Lucrinus thus seems to have
been in the family's possession for some time (so also Dubois, *PA*, 373).

   e) The *praetorium* at Puteoli is mentioned before 376 (*Ep.* 1.8); it was doubtless family property. Symmachus was there also in 385, preferring its
salubris habitatio to the isolation of Baiae (*Ep.* 2.26.1), and proposed another
visit, from Formiae, in 399, when he was hesitant to confess that Baiae was
his actual destination (*Ep.* 5.93). The baths at the villa were reached from the
dwelling quarters by a steep incline; in 398 Symmachus enjoined his son-in-
law Nicomachus to see to the construction of a more gentle slope (*Ep.* 6.66.3).

   f) Symmachus and Virius Nicomachus Flavianus owned adjacent properties
at Neapolis where, at some point before 395, Symmachus had determined
to engage in additional building—*opera Lucullana*—on vacant ground of his
own estate. Flavianus offered to link the new constructions of Symmachus'
with his own, by means of a double colonnade (*geminam porticum*), continuous
and curved. Symmachus was delighted and grateful, if somewhat appre-
hensive of the costs (*Ep.* 2.60.1–2).

   In addition to the references in Symmachus' correspondence to the six
villas on the Bay of Naples, a *signaculum* from Neapolis reflects the presence
of the family in the district (*CIL* X, 8059, no. 389). Symmachus' word for
these properties is *praetorium*, and all references suggest that they were designed to provide *delectatio*, not *fructus* (cf. *Digesta* 50.16.198, quoted above,

Chapter 1, n. 41). While the holdings in Campania are alone sufficient to establish the great wealth of Symmachus and the members of his family, they are but a small fraction of their landed property; the full register of Symmachus' estates is staggering. He had three houses in Rome and, including the six villas on the Bay of Naples, fully fifteen properties in Italy. Three *villae suburbanae* lay in the environs of Rome (*Ep.* 2.59.1; 6.58.1; 6.66.1); there were villas besides at Ostia (*Ep.* 1.6), at Laurentum (4.44), Tibur (6.81), Praeneste (1.5.1), Cora (1.8), and Formiae (1.8). Other estates, in Samnium, Apulia, Sicily, and Mauretania Caesariensis, were valued primarily for their revenues (see further Seeck, *RE* 4 A [1931], 1151).

The Campanian letters contain frequent allusions to the family, friends, and distinguished contemporaries of Symmachus who owned villas near his on the Bay of Naples. At Bauli, Acyndinus (above, no. 2), *praefectus Orientalis* from 338 to 340 and consul in 340, had built the villa which eventually passed to Symmachus (*Ep.* 1.1.2); the name is attested also in a local inscription and on a precious stone from a signet ring (*CIL* X, 1995; 8061). The subsequent owner was Memmius Vitrasius Orfitus Honorius (below, no. 47; *praef. urb.* II, 357–359), Symmachus' father-in-law, who died in 369 or 370; the property had passed to Symmachus by 375, when he speaks of it as a possession recently acquired (*Ep.* 1.1.5; see further Seeck in *RE* 4 A [1931], 1144–1146, no. 16). Vettius Agorius Praetextatus (above, no. 3), who died before he could assume the consulship of 385, had a villa at Baiae; Symmachus once blames *Baianum otium* for Praetextatus' negligence as a correspondent (*Ep.* 1.47; 1.48; cf. Seeck, *Symmachi Opera*, 86–88). It has already been observed that Virius Nicomachus Flavianus (above, no. 28) had estates at Neapolis (*Ep.* 2.60). He was *praefectus praetorio per Italiam* from 389, and anticipated under Theodosius the consulship which was actually bestowed upon him by the usurper Eugenius (in 394; for his career cf. Seeck, *Symmachi Opera*, 113–114). A villa belonging to Nicomachus Flavianus (above, no. 27), the son-in-law of Symmachus, was located near Puteoli on *Mons Gaurus* (for the location, cf. Beloch, *Campanien*[2], 25), where Symmachus had been invited to visit in 396 (*Ep.* 8.23.3); Nicomachus and Symmachus' daughter left Rome for Campania in the autumn of 395 and there passed the entire winter. They were there again in the summer of 396, in 397, and in subsequent years (Seeck, *Symmachi Opera*, 162–163, 166; so also Dubois, *PA*, 375). Upon his son-in-law and daughter Symmachus more than once relied for the execution of instructions concerning the upkeep and redecoration of his own Campanian properties (cf. *Ep.* 6.66.3; 6.9; 6.11.3). Priscus Attalus (above, no. 5) had a place at Baiae (*Ep.* 7.16.2; 7.24); his family came originally from the east, but he was educated in Rome and was *praefectus urbi* in 409 (cf. Seeck, *Symmachi Opera*, 170–171). Caecina Decius Albinus (above, no. 4), *praefectus urbi* in 402, was one of Symmachus' neighbors at Neapolis (*Ep.* 7.26); for his career and a stemma, cf. Seeck, *Symmachi Opera*, 174–177. Finally, at Baiae, two other acquaintances of Symmachus are mentioned: a Censorinus, possibly Caelius Censorinus, *consularis Numidiae* between 375 and 378 (*Ep.* 6.9; 7.11; cf. Dubois, *PA*, 374), and a Pompeianus, possibly Gabinius Barbarus Pompeianus, *consularis Campaniae* and proconsul of Africa (*Ep.* 6.9; 6.11; cf. Seeck, *Symmachi Opera*, 203; *CIL* X, 1199 [Abella]).

43. (? D.) Valerius Asiaticus (*cos.* II 46) Baiae 47

Tac. *Ann.* 11.1.3: *At Claudius nihil ultra scrutatus citis cum militibus tamquam opprimendo bello Crispinum praetorii praefectum misit, a quo [Valerius Asiaticus] repertus est apud Baias vinclisque inditis in urbem raptus.*

In 47 Messalina was anxious for personal reasons to hasten the downfall of Valerius Asiaticus: Tacitus states that she believed him to have been the lover of Poppaea Sabina and that she coveted the *horti*, once owned by L. Licinius Lucullus, which Asiaticus was then adorning with exceptional lavishness (*Ann.* 11.1.1). She convinced her husband that Asiaticus aspired to the principate; Claudius dispatched the commander of the guard Rufrius Crispinus, who found Asiaticus at Baiae and returned with him in chains to Rome. As has been seen (cf. Catalogue I above, no. 7, Clodia) *Baiae* may mean "an estate at Baiae"; it is in any case likely that Valerius Asiaticus, wealthy (cf. Cass Dio 60.27.2–3) and endowed with a penchant for the luxurious and magnificent, owned a villa at the most fashionable of Roman coastal resorts. He was the first man from Narbonensis to attain the consulship (in 35, under Tiberius: see Syme, *Tacitus*, 455–456; cf. *PIR* V 25); and his career and tastes well illustrate the tendency among some successful provincials to adopt the ways—and properties—of the Roman *nobiles* (cf. esp. Syme, *Tacitus*, 602).

44. P. Vedius Pollio Pausilypon 15 B.C.

Cass. Dio 54.23.5: τοιοῦτος οὖν δή τις ὁ Πωλίων ὢν ἐτελεύτησεν ἄλλοις τε πολλοῖς πολλὰ καὶ τῷ Ἀυγούστῳ τοῦ τε κλήρου συχνὸν μέρος καὶ τὸν Παυσίλυπον, τὸ χωρίον μεταξὺ τῆς τε Νέας πόλεως καὶ τῶν Ποντεόλων ὄν, καταλιπών, τῷ τε δήμῳ περικαλλὲς ἔργον οἰκοδομηθῆναι κελεύσας. Cf. Sen. *De Ira* 3.40.2; *De Clem.* 1.18.2; Pliny *NH* 9.167.

According to Dio, P. Vedius Pollio, an *eques* of libertine parentage, willed to Augustus at his death in 15 B.C. the villa named Pausilypon on the promontory southwest of Neapolis (cf. Pliny *NH* 9.167: *Pausilypum villa est Campaniae haut procul Neapoli*; Cass. Dio 54.23.5: τὸ χωρίον τὸ μεταξὺ τῆς τε Νέας πόλεως καὶ τῶν Πουτεόλων ὄν). To Dio (54.23.1–6), Seneca, and the Elder Pliny (all of whom preserve accounts of the scandal of his fishponds), Vedius Pollio was memorable for the luxury and the cruelty of his ways; Seneca and Pliny completely ignore, and Dio expressly denies, the significance of his contributions as an agent in Augustan government, particularly in Asia (on which see *CIL* III, 7124; *PIR* V 213; and above all Syme, *JRS* 51 [1961] 23–30). He may have come from Beneventum, where he constructed a *Caesareum* in honor of his benefactor and where one of his freedmen had his monument (*CIL* IX, 1556 [*ILS* 109]; *CIL* IX, 1703; Syme, *JRS* 51 [1961], 30). For the epigraphical evidence conclusively establishing the villa's subsequent ownership by the emperors, see above, Chapter 4, pp. 111–112. The remains at the site include a theater, an odeon, nymphaeum, *sacrarium*, and an elevated villa; the most complete discussion remains that of Günther (*Pausilypon*, 29–76).

45. P. Vergilius Maro   Neapolis   *ca.* 37 B.C.

Virg. *G.* 4.563–564: *Illo Vergilium me tempore dulcis alebat* / *Parthenope, studiis florentem ignobilis oti; Vita Vergilii* 13: *Possedit prope centiens sestertium ex liberalitatibus amicorum habuitque domum Romae Esquiliis iuxta hortos Maecenatianos, quamquam secessu Campaniae Siciliaeque plurimum uteretur*. Cf. *Catalepton* 8.1–6: *Villula, quae Sironis eras, et pauper agelle,* / *verum illi domino tu quoque divitiae,* / *me tibi, et hos una mecum, quos semper amavi,* / *si quid de patria tristius audiero,* / *commendo, in primisque patrem. Tu nunc eris illi,* / *Mantua quod fuerat, quodque Cremona prius.*

Servius states unequivocally that the young Virgil had studied with Siro (*ad Ecl.* 6.13: *vult exequi sectam Epicuream quam didicerant tam Vergilius quam Varus docente Sirone*; cf. *Catalepton* 5.9: *magni petentes docta dicta Sironis*). Siro's Italian base was Neapolis: a papyrus fragment from Herculaneum (quoted above, Chapter 3, n. 95) decisively corroborates the more circumstantial statements of Cicero (*Fin.* 2.119; *Acad.* 2.106; *Fam.* 6.11.2; cf. T. Frank, *Vergil*, 48, cited above, Chapter 3, n. 93) and Servius; this point should at last be regarded as settled (for further references, cf. K. Büchner, *RE* 8 A [1955], 1044). The evidence for Virgil's association with Neapolis thus spans the length of his mature life. There he first studied with Siro, there composed the *Georgics* during the thirties (*G.* 4.563–564, cited above), there began the *Aeneid* (Prisc. 10.43: *Caesar ad Vergilium: Excucurristi a Neapoli*; cf. Cichorius, *Röm. Stud.*, 269–271; Büchner, *RE* 8 A [1955] 1059), and there, finally, he was buried (*Vita Verg.* 36: *Ossa eius Neapolim translata sunt tumuloque condita qui est via Puteolana intra lapidem secundum*). That Virgil owned a house or villa in Neapolis is implied by *Vita Verg.* 13; and if *Catalepton* 8 is genuinely Virgilian (cf. Westendorp Boerma, ed. *Catalepton* I [Assen, Holland 1949], 153–155), he acquired the *villula* of Siro. He seems also to have owned property at nearby Nola: on which see Maiuri, "Virgilio e Nola" *Quaderni di Studi Romani* 4 (1939); and cf. Aul. Gell. 6.20.1; Servius *ad Aen.* 7.740. His *monimentum* at Neapolis was revered by Silius Italicus: see on no. 12 above; for a recent discussion of its location see Maiuri, *Campi Flegrèi*, 9–13).

46. M. Vipsanius Agrippa (*cos.* III, 27 B.C.)   near Pompeii   12 B.C.

CIL IV, 6499: Νεικασίου Ἀγρ[ίππου] [ac]toris; CIL IV, 6893: *Caesaris Augusti femina mater erat*; *Not. d. Sc.* (1922), 478: *Pupil[li] Agrip[pae] Tub[erone] [et] Fabio co[n]s[ulibus]*: 11 B.C. Ibid., 460: *Ti. Claudius Eutychus Caesaris l[ibertus]*. Cf. CIL X, 924 (*ILS*, 6381). Cass. Dio 54.28.2: . . . ἐκπλαγέντων δὲ τῶν Παννονίων πρὸς τὴν ἔφοδον αὐτοῦ καὶ μηδὲν ἔτι νεωτερισάντων ἐπανῆλθε, καὶ ἐν Καμπανίᾳ γενόμενος ἐνόσησε.

Between the years 1903 and 1905, E. Santini excavated in the contrada Rota (commune di Boscotrecase) a now famous villa; it had been set elegantly into the slopes of the hillside northwest of Pompeii, and commanded a stunning view of the gulf of Naples to the south. In 1906 the property was reburied by the flow of lava from an eruption of Mt. Vesuvius; the record of the original finds and the ground plan published by Della Corte in *Not. d. Sc.* (1922), 459–469, have remained the basis for all subsequent discussions. Two seals of *Ti. Claudius Eutychus Caesaris l[ibertus]* were found on a cupboard of the villa; Della Corte (*Not. d. Sc.* [1922], 460) argued that this person was the original owner. Rostovtzeff analysed this and other evidence and did not concur. Drawing attention to inscriptions on amphorae of Greek names of slaves or freedmen of an Agrippa (CIL IV, 6499, with Mau's note *ad loc.*), to a graffito on a column in the peristyle (CIL IV, 6893), and to a tile stamped *Pupil[lus] Agrip[pa]* and with the names of the consuls of 11 B.C., Rostovtzeff acutely concluded that the villa was the property of Agrippa Postumus (on *Pupillus* [= *pupus*, "the child"] cf. CIL VI, 18548), the last son of M. Vipsanius Agrippa and Julia; he reasoned further that after the death of

Agrippa Postumus in 14, the villa passed into the possession of the imperial house; the two seals of Ti. Claudius Eutychus reflect this later stage of the villa's history, and its management by an imperial freedman (Rostovtzeff, *SEHRE*², 552–553, no. 31). Rostovtzeff's conclusions, promptly accepted by Della Corte (see *CeA*³, 415) have been followed also by other scholars, and most recently by Blanckenhagen (P. H. v. Blanckenhagen and C. Alexander, *The Paintings from Boscotrecase, MDAI, Rom. Abt.*, supp. 6 [Heidelberg 1962], 9–11; *q.v.* also for additional bibliography); this matter is now beyond dispute. But who built the villa? Rostovtzeff tentatively suggested M. Vipsanius Agrippa, noting that the wall decorations support a date during the period of transition between Second and Third Styles (Rostovtzeff, *SEHRE*², 553); Blanckenhagen states unequivocally that the construction of the villa was begun by Agrippa between 21 and 16 B.C.; the Third Style came into fashion about 15 B.C. (Blanckenhagen, *The Paintings from Boscotrecase*, 11). M. Vipsanius Agrippa must indeed have built this villa: testimony of Dio, which has gone unnoticed in the otherwise excellent discussions of the property by Rostovtzeff, Della Corte, and Blanckenhagen, is decisive. Dio (54.28.2) states that Agrippa returned from Pannonia and was in Campania when he died in late March, 12 B.C.; moreover, it appears from Dio's language that Campania was no way station on Agrippa's route back from Pannonia, but rather his chosen location after his return. The most natural interpretation of this passage is that Agrippa owned estates somewhere in Campania; Gardthausen so conjectured long ago (V. Gardthausen, *Augustus und Seine Zeit* I, 860; rejected, without arguments, by M. Reinhold, *Marcus Agrippa—A Biography* [New York 1933], 125, n. 10), before the publication of the materials found at Boscotrecase. Agrippa will have died in his handsome *villa suburbana* in Boscotrecase near Pompeii. Augustus was the chief beneficiary from his friend Agrippa's vast estate (Cass. Dio 54.29.5), but the villa passed to the son, born posthumously in 12 B.C. Suetonius notices (*Aug.* 66.4) that the practice of Augustus, whenever close friends named him as a beneficiary, was invariably to transmit to the friends' children his share of the estate, and to hold the property in trust if the children were under age.

47. Memmius Vitrasius Orfitus Honorius (*praef. urb.*   Bauli   375
II, 357–359)

Symmachus *Ep.* 1.1.5.
Discussed above, no. 42 (Symmachus).

SELECT BIBLIOGRAPHY

The following list consists chiefly of the books and articles which have been cited frequently in the foregoing pages. A few titles of works mentioned only once or twice have been included if concerned specifically with the Bay of Naples; but most of the items which are only rarely cited appear instead in the notes and Catalogues with full bibliographical details. Articles in standard works of reference (e.g., *RE* and *CAH*) have been omitted, as have editions and collections of ancient evidence, both literary and epigraphical: it has been assumed that these are familiar to readers. Also omitted here are the important notices of archaeological discoveries published regularly in *Not. d. Sc.*; when directly relevant to the present inquiry they too have been cited above in the appropriate place.

Annecchino, R., "Il Puteolanum di Cicerone," *Camp. Rom.* I, 19–43.
——— *Storia di Pozzuoli* (Pozzuoli 1960).
Austin, R. G., *Commentary on Cicero's* Pro Caelio, 3rd ed. (Oxford 1960).
Badian, E., "Caepio and Norbanus," *Historia* 6 (1957), 318–346.
——— *Foreign Clientelae* (Oxford 1958).
——— Review of Taylor, *Voting Districts of the Roman Republic*, *JRS* 52 (1962), 200–210.
Balsdon, J. P. V. D., *The Emperor Gaius* (Oxford 1934).
——— "*Auctoritas, Dignitas, Otium*," *CQ* N.S. 10 (1960), 43–50.
Beloch, K. J., *Campanien: Geschichte und Topographie des antiken Neapel und seiner Umgebung*, 2nd ed. (Breslau 1890).
Bernert, E., "Otium," *Würzburger Jahrbücher für die Altertumswissenschaft* 4 (1949–1950), 89–99.
Bicknell, P. J., "Agrippina's villa at Bauli," *CR* N.S. 13 (1963), 261–262.
Blake, M. E., *Ancient Roman Construction in Italy from the Prehistoric Period to Augustus* (Washington 1947).
——— *Roman Construction in Italy from Tiberius through the Flavians* (Washington 1959).
Bloch, H., "L. Calpurnius Piso Caesoninus in Samothrace and Herculaneum," *AJA* 44 (1940), 485–493.

Bloch, H., Review of Nisbet, *Commentary on Cicero's* In Pisonem, *Gnomon* 37 (1965), 558–562.

Boëthius, A., *The Golden House of Nero* (Ann Arbor 1960).

Bowersock, G. W., *Augustus and the Greek World* (Oxford 1965).

Breglia, L., "Avanzi di una villa romana a Torre del Greco," *Camp. Rom.* I, 91–98.

Broughton, T. R. S., *The Magistrates of the Roman Republic* (New York, 1951–1952), 2 vols.

Brunt, P. A., "The 'Fiscus' and its Development," *JRS* 56 (1966), 75–91.

Carney, T. F., "The Flight and Exile of Marius," *Greece and Rome* N.S. 8 (1961), 98–121.

——— *A Biography of C. Marius* (Netherlands 1962).

Causa, V., "Segnalazioni epigrafiche nell'agro campano," *RAAN* N.S. 38 (1963), 19–22.

Chianese, G., "Ruderi di villa romana a Napoli in contrada S. Rocco di Capodimonte," *Camp. Rom.* I, 81–87.

Cichorius, C., *Römische Studien* (Berlin 1922).

Crova, B., "Le terme romane nella Campania," *Atti del VIII Convegno Nazionale di Storia dell'Architettura* (Rome 1956), 271–288.

D'Arms, J. H., "Roman Campania: Two Passages from Cicero's Correspondence," *AJP* 88 (1967), 195–202.

——— "Canidia and Campania," *Philologus* 111 (1967), 141–145.

De Franciscis, A., *Il Ritratto Romano a Pompei* (Naples 1951).

——— "Le recenti scoperte in S. Chiara e la topografia di Napoli romana," *Archeologia Classica* 6 (1954), 277–283.

——— "Chi era C. Claudio Pollione Frugiano?" *Mélanges d'Archéologie et d'Histoire offerts à André Piganiol*, vol. 1 (Paris 1966), 229–232.

——— "Underwater Discoveries around the Bay of Naples," *Archaeology* 20 (1967), 209–216.

Degrassi, A., *Scritti Vari di Antichità*, vol. 1 (Rome 1962).

Della Corte, M., "Sui rapporti d'affezione fra la casa Giulio-Claudia e la Campania," *Atti del IV Cong. Naz. di Studi Romani*, vol. 2 (Rome 1938), 297–302.

——— *Case ed Abitanti di Pompei*, 3rd ed., ed. P. Soprano (Naples 1965).

Della Valle, G., "*Platonopolis*," *RAAN* N.S. 19 (1938–1939), 237–263.

——— "La villa sillana ed augustea *Pausilypon*," *Camp. Rom.* I, 207–267.

De Martino, F., "Le istituzioni di Napoli greco-romana," *PdP* fasc. 25–27 (1952), 333–343.

Dennison, W., "Some New Inscriptions from Puteoli, Baiae, Misenum, and Cumae," *AJA* 2 (1898), 373–398.

Di Capua, F., "Contributi all'epigrafia e alla storia della antica Stabia," *RAAN* N.S. 19 (1938–1939), 83–124.

Drumann, W., and Groebe, P., *Geschichte Roms*, 2nd ed. (Leipzig 1899–1929), 2 vols.

Dubois, C., *Pouzzoles Antique*. Bibliothèque des Écoles Françaises d'Athènes et de Rome, fasc. 98 (Paris 1907).

Dudley, D. R., "Blossius of Cumae," *JRS* 31 (1941), 94–99.

Étienne, R., *La vie quotidienne à Pompéi* (Paris 1966).

Fitzhardinge, L. F., "Naval Epitaphs from Misenum in the Nicholson Museum, Sydney," *JRS* 41 (1951), 17–21.

Frank, T., *An Economic Survey of Ancient Rome*, vol. 1 (Baltimore 1933), vol. 5 (Baltimore 1940).

Frederiksen, M. W., "Republican Capua: a Social and Economic Study," *PBSR* N.S. 14 (1959), 80–130.

Friedländer, L., *Sittengeschichte Roms*, 9th ed., vol. 1 (Leipzig 1919).

Gabba, E., "Ricerche sull' esercito professionale romano da Mario ad Augusto," *Athenaeum* N.S. 29 (1951), 171–272.

Geer, R. M., "The Greek Games at Naples," *TAPA* 66 (1935), 208–221.

Gigante, M., "La cultura letteraria a Pompei," *Pompeiana, Raccolta di stud per il secondo centenario degli scavi di Pompei* (Naples 1950), 111–143.

Gordon, M. L., "The *Ordo* of Pompeii," *JRS* 17 (1927), 168–183.

Grimal, P., *Jardins Romains*, Bibliothèque des Écoles Françaises d'Athènes et de Rome, fasc. 155 (Paris 1943).

——— *Le Siècle des Scipions* (Paris 1953).

Günther, R. T., *Pausilypon, the Imperial Villa near Naples* (Oxford 1913).

Hahn, G., *Der Villenbesitz der römischen Grossen in Italien zur Zeit der Republik*, unpublished dissertation (Bonn 1920).

Hatzfeld, J., "Les Italiens résidant a Délos," *BCH* 36 (1912), 5–218.

——— *Les Trafiquants italiens dans l'orient hellénique* (Paris 1919).

Hirschfeld, O., "Der Grundbesitz der römischen Kaiser in den ersten drei Jahrhunderten," *Klio* 2 (1902), 45–72; 284–315 (reprinted in *Kleine Schriften* [1913], 516–575).

How, W. W., and Clark, A. C., *Cicero, Select Letters* (Oxford 1925–1926), 2 vols.

Jacono, L., "Note di archeologia marittima," *Neapolis* 1 (1913), 353–371.

——— "Solarium di una villa romana nell'isola di Ponza," *Not. d. Sc.* (1926), 219–232.

Jacono, L., "*Piscinae in litore constructae*," *Not. d. Sc.* (1924), 333–340.

———— "Un porto duomillenario," *Atti del III Cong. Naz. di Studi Romani*, vol. 1 (Rome 1934), 318–324.

———— "Una singolare piscina marittima in Ponza," *Camp. Rom.* I, 145–162.

Johannowsky, W., "Contributi all topografia della Campania antica," *RAAN* N.S. 27 (1952), 83–146.

Kroll, W., "Die Kultur der Ciceronischen Zeit," *Das Erbe der Alten* 22 (Leipzig 1933), 1–155.

Lehmann, P. W., *Roman Wall Paintings from Boscoreale* (Cambridge Mass. 1953).

Lepore, E., "Per la storia economico-sociale di Neapolis," *PdP* fasc. 25–27 (1952), 300–332.

———— "Neapolis città dell'impero romano," in *Storia di Napoli*, vol. 1, *Società Editrice Storia di Napoli* (Naples 1967), 289–333.

MacDonald, W. L., *The Architecture of the Roman Empire*, vol. 1 (New Haven 1965).

Mahaffy, J. P., *The Greek World under Roman Sway* (London 1890).

Maiuri, A., "Il palazzo di Tiberio detto 'villa Jovis' a Capri," *Atti del III Cong. Naz. di Studi Romani*, vol. 1 (Rome 1934), 156–171.

———— "La villa augustea di 'Palazzo a Mare' a Capri," *Camp. Rom.* I, 115–141.

———— "Virgilio e Nola," *Quaderni di Studi Romani* 4 (1939).

———— "Note di topografia campana," *Atti della Reale Accademia d'Italia, Rendiconti*, 7th ser., vol. 2 (Rome 1941), 249–260.

———— Review of Mingazzini-Pfister, *Surrentum*, *PdP* 1 (1946), 391–394.

———— "La Specola Misenate," *RAAN* N.S. 24/25 (1949/1950), 259–285.

———— *Passeggiate Campane* (Florence 1950).

———— *Saggi di Varia Antichità* (Venice 1954).

———— "Le vicende dei monumenti antichi della costa amalfitana e sorrentina al luce delle recenti alluvioni," *RAAN* N.S. 29 (1954), 87–98.

———— *Capri* (Itinerari dei musei e monumenti d'Italia, no. 93), Rome 1958.

———— *Vita d'Archeologo* (Naples 1959).

———— "Note di topografia pompeiana," *RAAN* N.S. 34 (1959), 73–79.

———— *Ercolano* (Itinerari dei musei e monumenti d'Italia, no. 53), 6th ed. (Rome 1962).

———— *I Campi Flegrèi* (Itinerari dei musei e monumenti d'Italia, no. 32), 4th ed. (Rome 1963).

———— *Pompei* (Itinerari dei musei e monumenti d'Italia, no. 3), 12th ed. (Rome 1965).

Mau, A., and Kelsey, F. W. (translator), *Pompeii, Its Life and Art* (New York 1899).

Meiggs, R., *Roman Ostia* (Oxford 1960).

Millar, F., "The Fiscus in the First Two Centuries," *JRS* 53 (1963), 29–42.

—— *A Study of Cassius Dio* (Oxford 1964).

Mingazzini, P. and Pfister, F., *Surrentum* (*Forma Italiae, Regio* I, vol. 2), Florence 1946.

Moretti, L., *Iscrizioni Agonistiche Greche* (Rome 1953).

Münzer F., *Römische Adelsparteien und Adelsfamilien* (Stuttgart 1920).

Mustilli, D., "Iscrizione di M. Cornelio Frontone rinvenuta a Sorrento," *Epigraphica* 2 (1940), 214–216.

—— "La villa pseudourbana ercolanese," *RAAN* N.S. 31 (1956), 77–97.

Napoli, M., *Napoli Greco-Romana* (Naples 1959).

—— "Statua ritratto di Virio Audenzio Emiliano consolare della Campania," *Bollettino d'Arte* 44 (1959), 107–113.

Nisbet, R. G. M., *Commentary on Cicero's* in Pisonem (Oxford 1961).

Nissen, H., *Italische Landeskunde*, vol. 2, pt. 2 (Berlin, 1902).

Onorato, G. O., "La data del terremoto di Pompei, 5 febbraio 62 d. Cr," *Rendiconti dell'Accademia dei Lincei, classe sci. mor.*, 8th ser., 4 (1949), 644–661.

—— *Iscrizioni Pompeiane* (Florence 1957).

D'Orsi, L., *Come ritrovai l'antica Stabia*, 2nd ed. (Milan 1962).

—— *Gli scavi archeologici di Stabia*, 2nd ed. (Milan 1965).

Paget, R. F., "The 'Great Antrum' at Baiae: a Preliminary Report," *PBSR* N.S. 22 (1967), 102–112.

—— "The Ancient Ports of Cumae," *JRS* 58 (1968), 152–159.

Peterson, R. M., *The Cults of Campania*, Papers and Monographs of the American Academy in Rome, no. 1 (Rome 1919).

Picard, C., "Pouzzoles et le paysage portuaire," *Latomus* 18 (1959), 23–51.

Pugliese Carratelli, G., "Napoli antica," *PdP* fasc. 25–27 (1952), 243–268.

Robert, L., "Pantomimen in griechischen Orient," *Hermes* 65 (1930), 106–122.

—— *Études Anatoliennes* (Paris 1937).

Rogers, R. S., "The Roman Emperors as Heirs and Legatees," *TAPA* 78 (1947), 140–158.

Rose, K. F. C., "Time and Place in the *Satyricon*," *TAPA* 93 (1962), 402–409.

Rostagni, A., "La cultura letteraria di Napoli antica," *PdP* fasc. 25–27 (1952), 344–357.

Rostovtzeff, M., "Pompeianische Landschaften und römische Villen," *Jahrbuch des Kaiserlich Deutschen Instituts* 19 (1904), 103–126.

—— "Die hellenistisch-römische Architekturlandschaft," *Röm. Mitt.* 26 (1911), 1–160.

—— *The Social and Economic History of the Roman Empire*, 2nd ed., edited by P. M. Fraser (Oxford 1957), 2 vols.

Salinas, R., "Le cupole nell'architettura della Campania," *Atti del VIII Convegno Nazionale di Storia dell'Architettura* (Rome 1956), 289–291.

Sartori, F., *Problemi di Storia Costituzionale Italiota* (Rome 1953).

Schmidt, O. E., "Ciceros Villen," *Neue Jahrbücher für das klassische Altertum* (1899), 328–355; 466–497.

Scott, K., "Notes on the Destruction of Two Roman Villas," *AJP* 60 (1939), 459–462.

Shackleton Bailey, D. R., *Cicero's Letters to Atticus*, vols. 1–2 (Cambridge 1965), vols. 3–4 (Cambridge 1968); vols. 5–6 (Cambridge 1967). (= Cambridge Classical Texts and Commentaries, no. 3).

Sgobbo, I., "Terme flegree e origine delle terme romane," *Atti del I Cong. Naz. di Studi Romani* (Rome 1928), 186–194.

Sherwin-White, A. N., *The Letters of Pliny. A Historical and Social Commentary* (Oxford 1966).

Starr, C. G., *The Roman Imperial Navy*, 2nd ed. (Cambridge Eng. 1960).

Swoboda, K. M., *Römische und Römanische Paläste*, 2nd ed. (Vienna 1924).

Syme, R., "The Colony of Cornelius Fuscus: an Episode in the 'Bellum Neronis,'" *AJP* 58 (1937), 7–18.

—— *The Roman Revolution* (Oxford 1939).

—— *Tacitus* (Oxford 1958), 2 vols.

—— "Who was Vedius Pollio?" *JRS* 51 (1961), 23–30.

—— "The Bogus Names in the *Historia Augusta*," *Antiquitas* (4te Reihe), Beiträge zur *Historia-Augusta* Forschung 4 (Bonn 1966), 257–272.

Tanzer, H. H., *The Villas of Pliny the Younger* (New York 1924).

Taylor, L. R., *The Voting Districts of the Roman Republic*, Papers and Monographs of the American Academy in Rome, no. 20 (Rome 1960).

Tyrrell, R. Y. and Purser, L. C., *The Correspondence of Cicero*, vol. 1 (3rd ed., Dublin, 1904) vols. 2–6 (2nd ed., Dublin 1906–1933) vol. 7 (index, Dublin 1901).

Van Buren, A. W., "The Text of Two Sources for Campanian Topography," *AJP* 51 (1930), 378–381.

—— "Pompeii-Nero-Poppaea," in *Studies Presented to D. M. Robinson*, vol. 2 (St. Louis 1953), 970–974.

Vollmer, F., *P. Papinii Statii Silvarum Libri* (Leipzig 1898).

INDEX

Emperors, members of the imperial house, and authors are listed under their conventional English names. All other Romans are registered according to *gentilicia*. The index covers material discussed in the text, the footnotes, and the catalogues; but names of modern scholars have been omitted except when mentioned in the text.